CSI:

CRIME SCENE INVESTIGATION™

INTERN AT YOUR OWN RISK

WRITTEN BY SEKOU HAMILTON

ART BY STEVEN CUMMINGS

 **TOKYOPOP®**

HAMBURG // LONDON // LOS ANGELES // TOKYO

CSI: Crime Scene Investigation™
Intern at Your Own Risk
Writer: Sekou Hamilton
Artists: Steven & Megumi Cummings

Lettering - Lucas Rivera
Cover Colors - rem
Cover Design - Al-Insan Lashley

Editor - Lillian Diaz-Przybyl
Print Production Manager - Lucas Rivera
Managing Editor - Vy Nguyen
Senior Designer - Louis Csontos
Art Director - Al-Insan Lashley
Director of Sales and Manufacturing - Allyson De Simone
Associate Publisher - Marco F. Pavia
President and C.O.O. - John Parker
C.E.O. and Chief Creative Officer - Stu Levy

"CSI: CRIME SCENE INVESTIGATION" produced by CBS Productions, a business unit of CBS Broadcasting Inc. in association with Jerry Bruckheimer Television. Executive Producers: Jerry Bruckheimer, Carol Mendelsohn, Anthony E. Zuiker, Ann Donahue, Naren Shankar, Cynthia Chvatal, William Petersen, Jonathan Littman • Series Created By: Anthony E. Zuiker

A 🔲TOKYOPOP® Manga

TOKYOPOP and 🔲 are trademarks or registered trademarks of TOKYOPOP Inc.

TOKYOPOP Inc.
5900 Wilshire Blvd. Suite 2000
Los Angeles, CA 90036

E-mail: info@TOKYOPOP.com
Come visit us online at www.TOKYOPOP.com

ISBN: 978-1-4278-1550-7

First TOKYOPOP printing: September 2009
10 9 8 7 6 5 4 3 2 1
Printed in the USA

TABLE OF CONTENTS

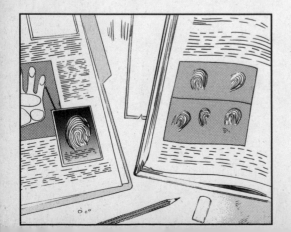

PROLOGUE

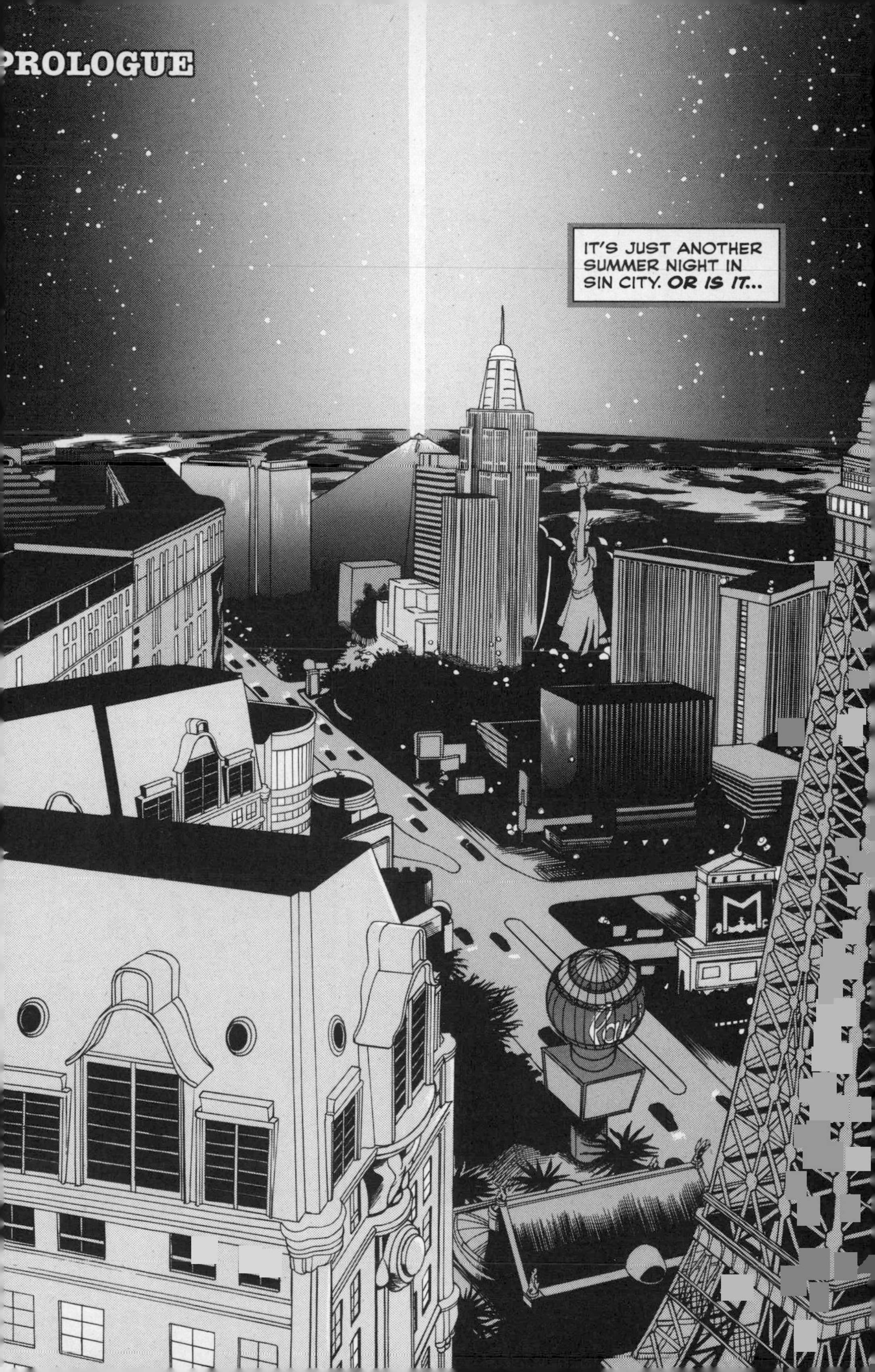
IT'S JUST ANOTHER SUMMER NIGHT IN SIN CITY. *OR IS IT...*

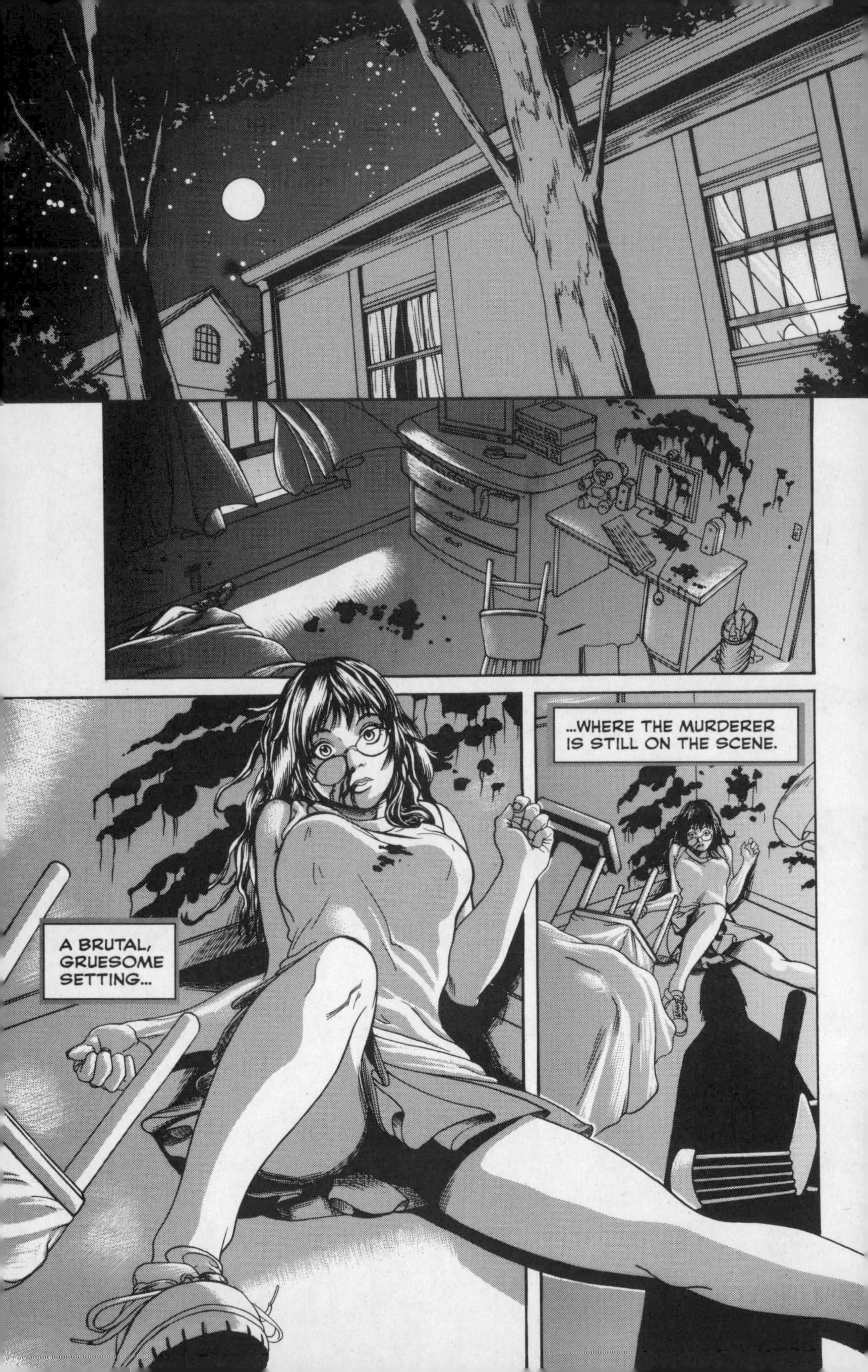
A BRUTAL, GRUESOME SETTING...
...WHERE THE MURDERER IS STILL ON THE SCENE.

FULL SERVICE KILLER...

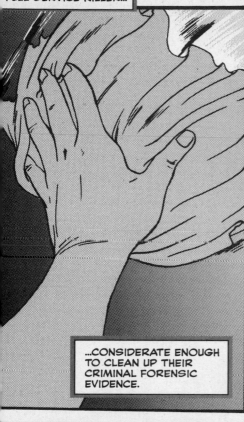

BUT THE KILLER IS INADVERTENTLY LEAVING THEIR OWN *PERSONAL FORENSIC EVIDENCE.*

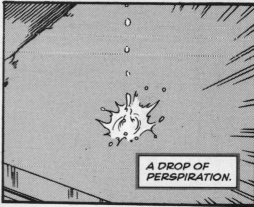

...CONSIDERATE ENOUGH TO CLEAN UP THEIR CRIMINAL FORENSIC EVIDENCE.

A DROP OF *PERSPIRATION.*

SPITTLE FROM A SNEEZE.

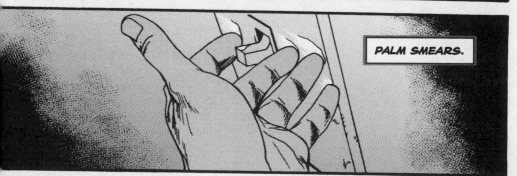

PALM SMEARS.

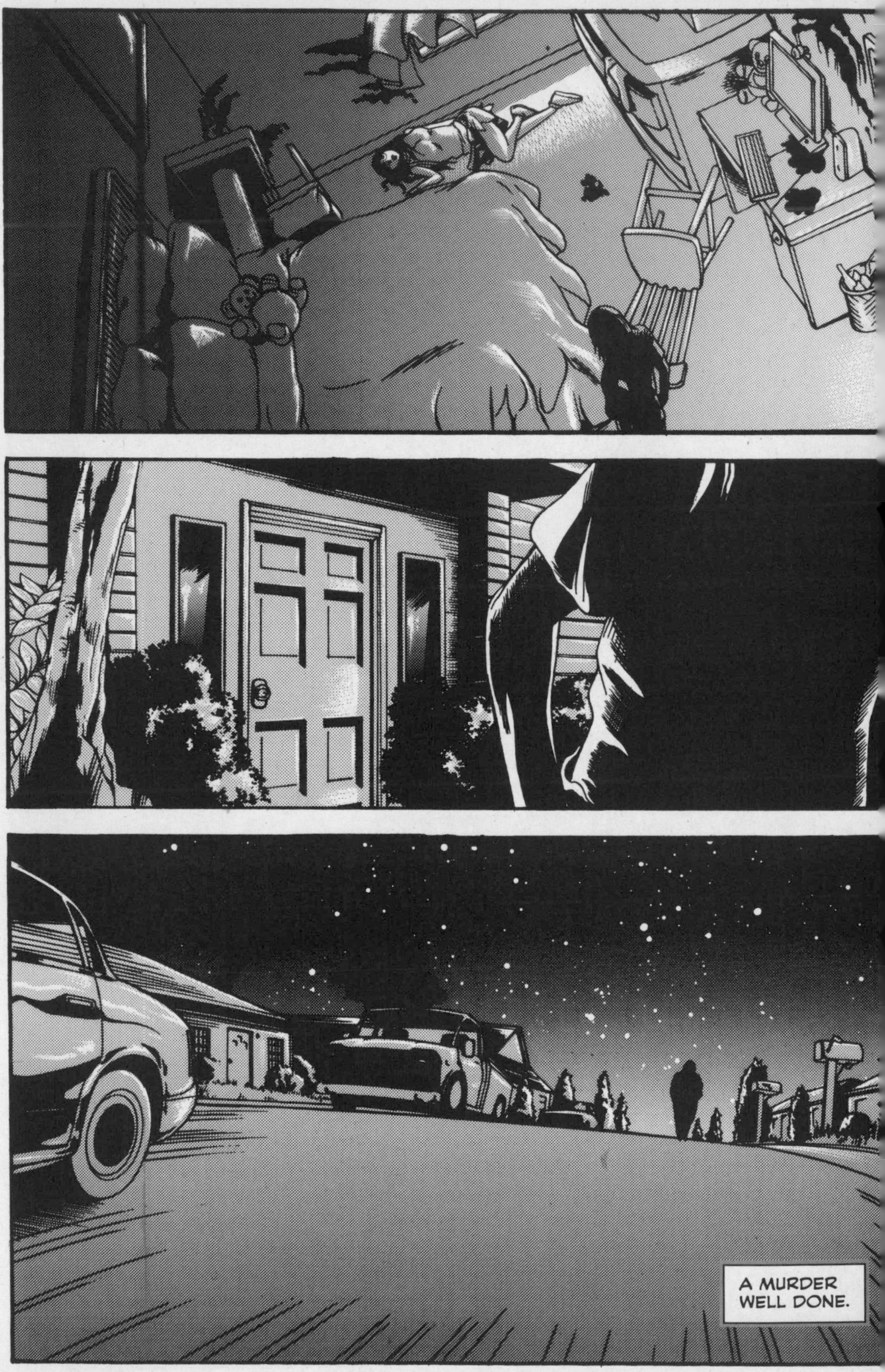
A MURDER
WELL DONE.

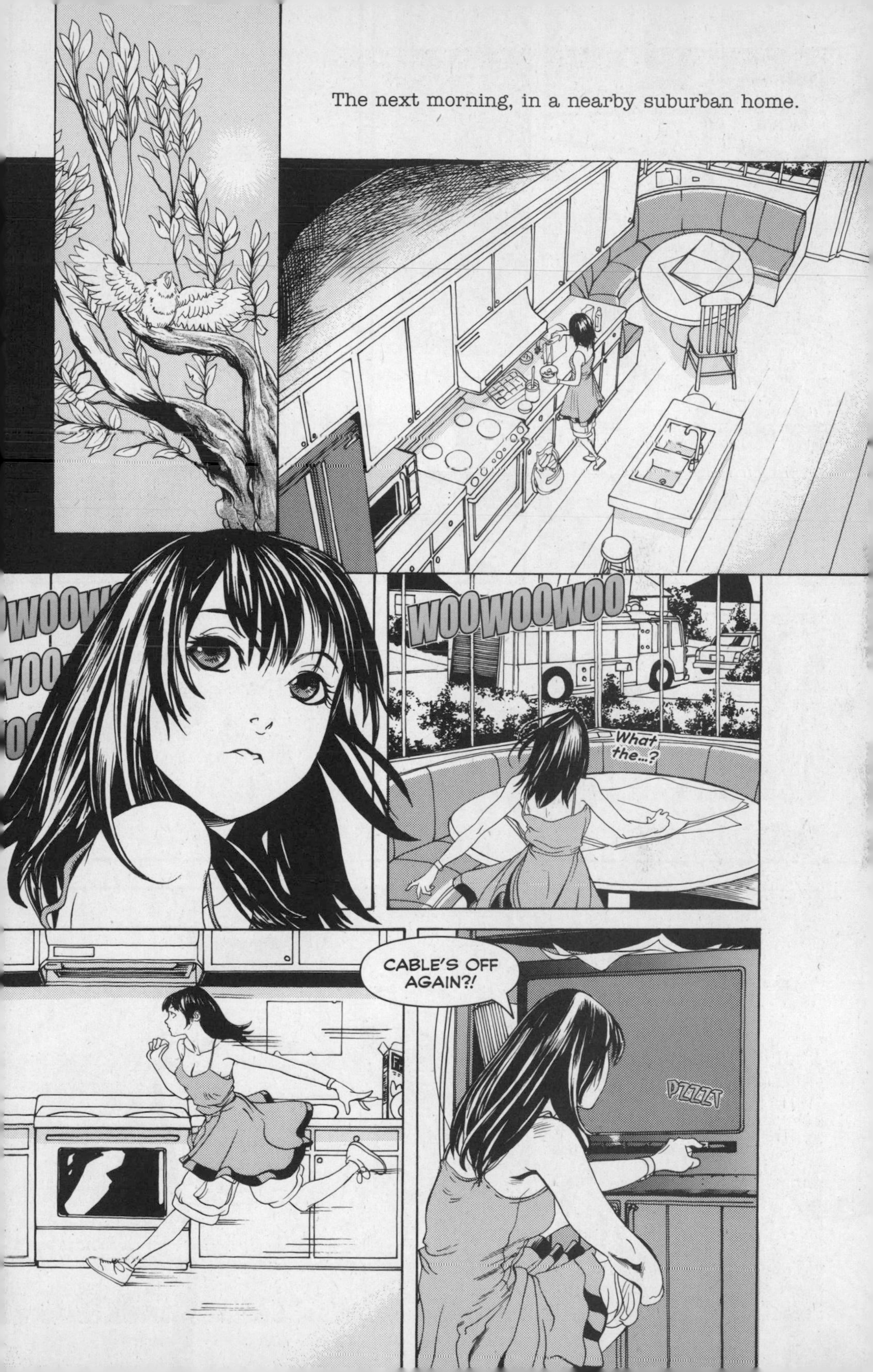

The next morning, in a nearby suburban home.
WOOWOOWOO
What the...?
CABLE'S OFF AGAIN?!
PZZZT

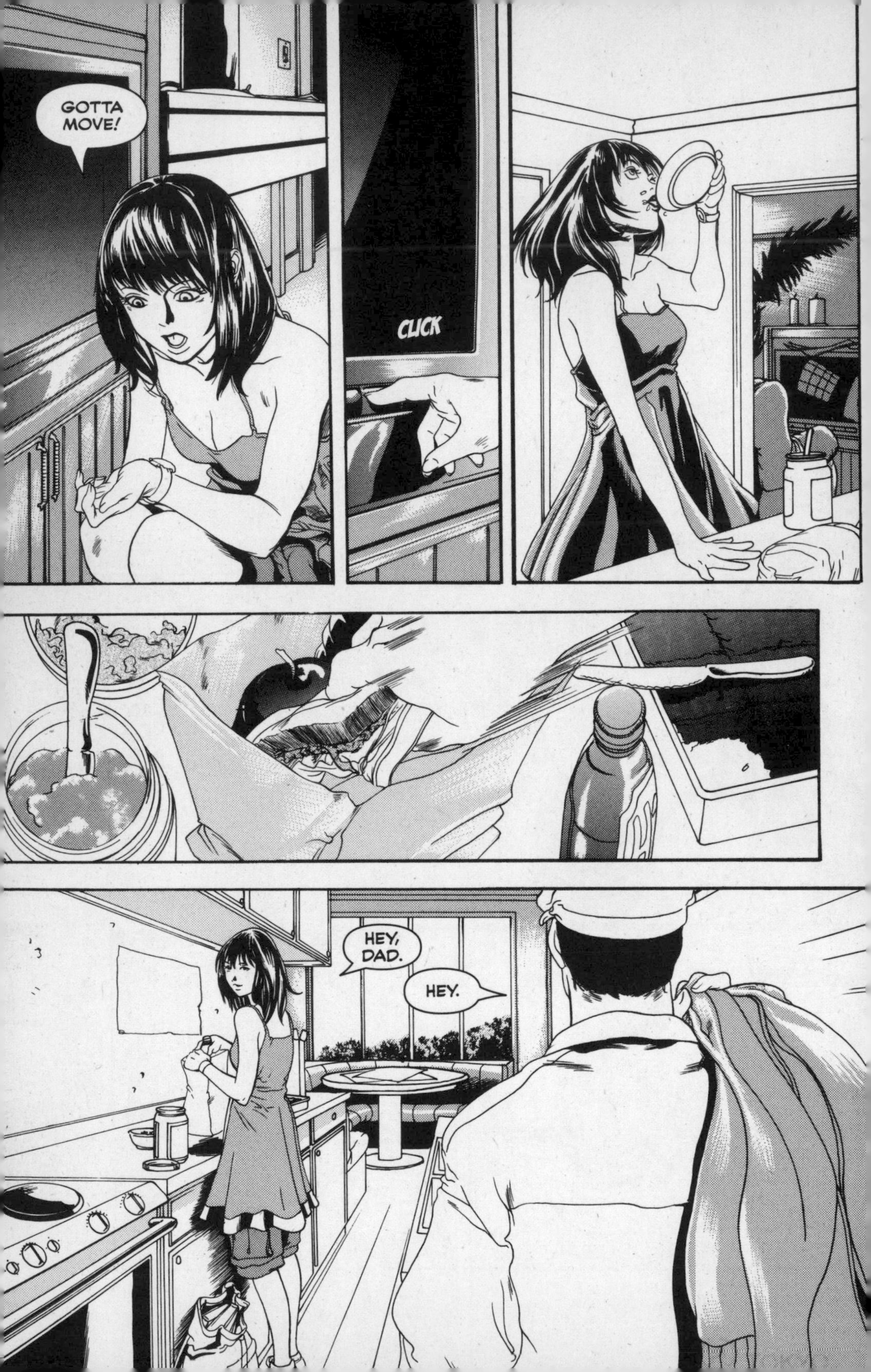
GOTTA MOVE!
CLICK
HEY, DAD.
HEY.

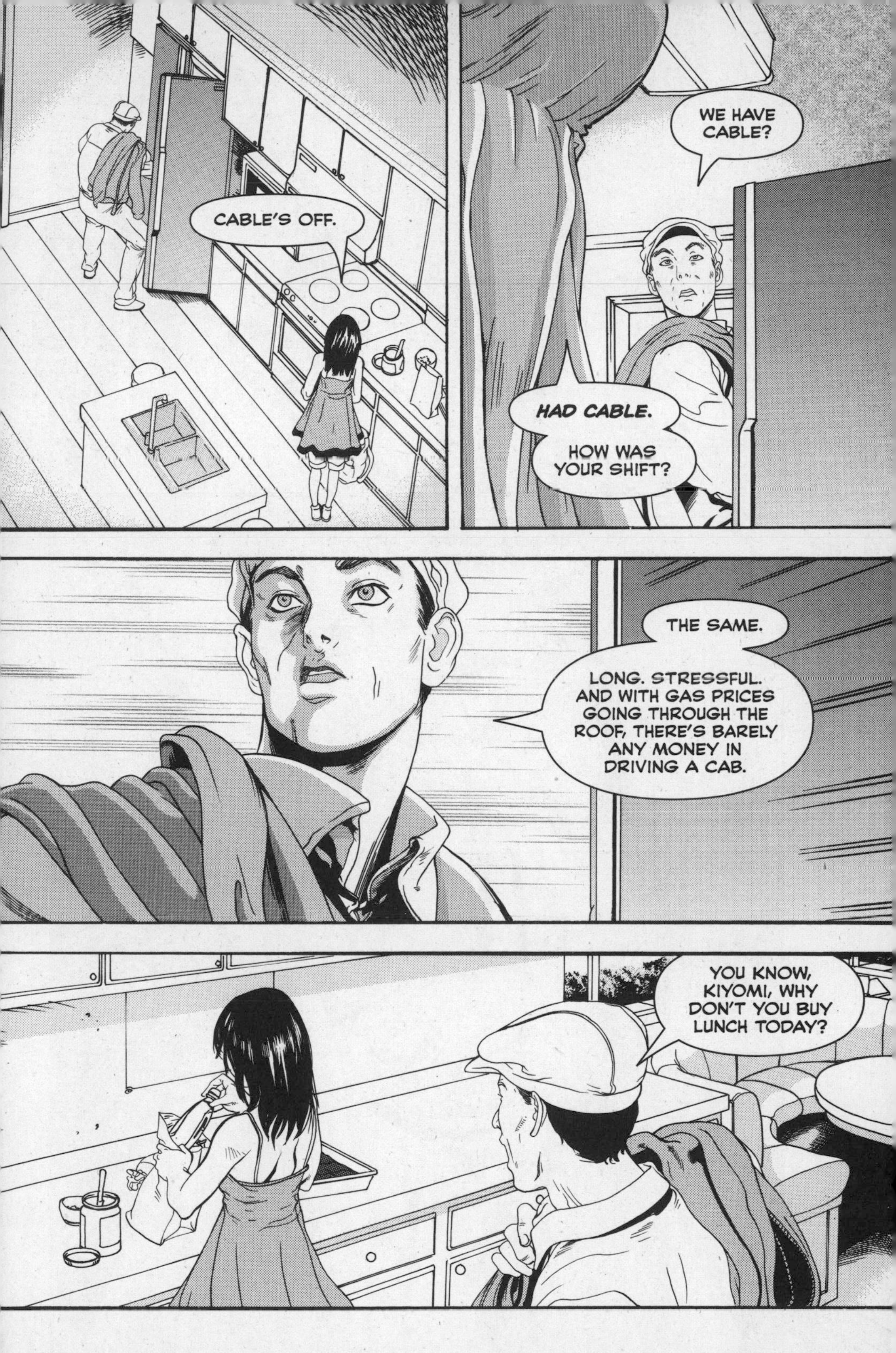
CABLE'S OFF.
WE HAVE CABLE?
HAD CABLE.
HOW WAS YOUR SHIFT?
THE SAME.
LONG. STRESSFUL. AND WITH GAS PRICES GOING THROUGH THE ROOF, THERE'S BARELY ANY MONEY IN DRIVING A CAB.
YOU KNOW, KIYOMI, WHY DON'T YOU BUY LUNCH TODAY?

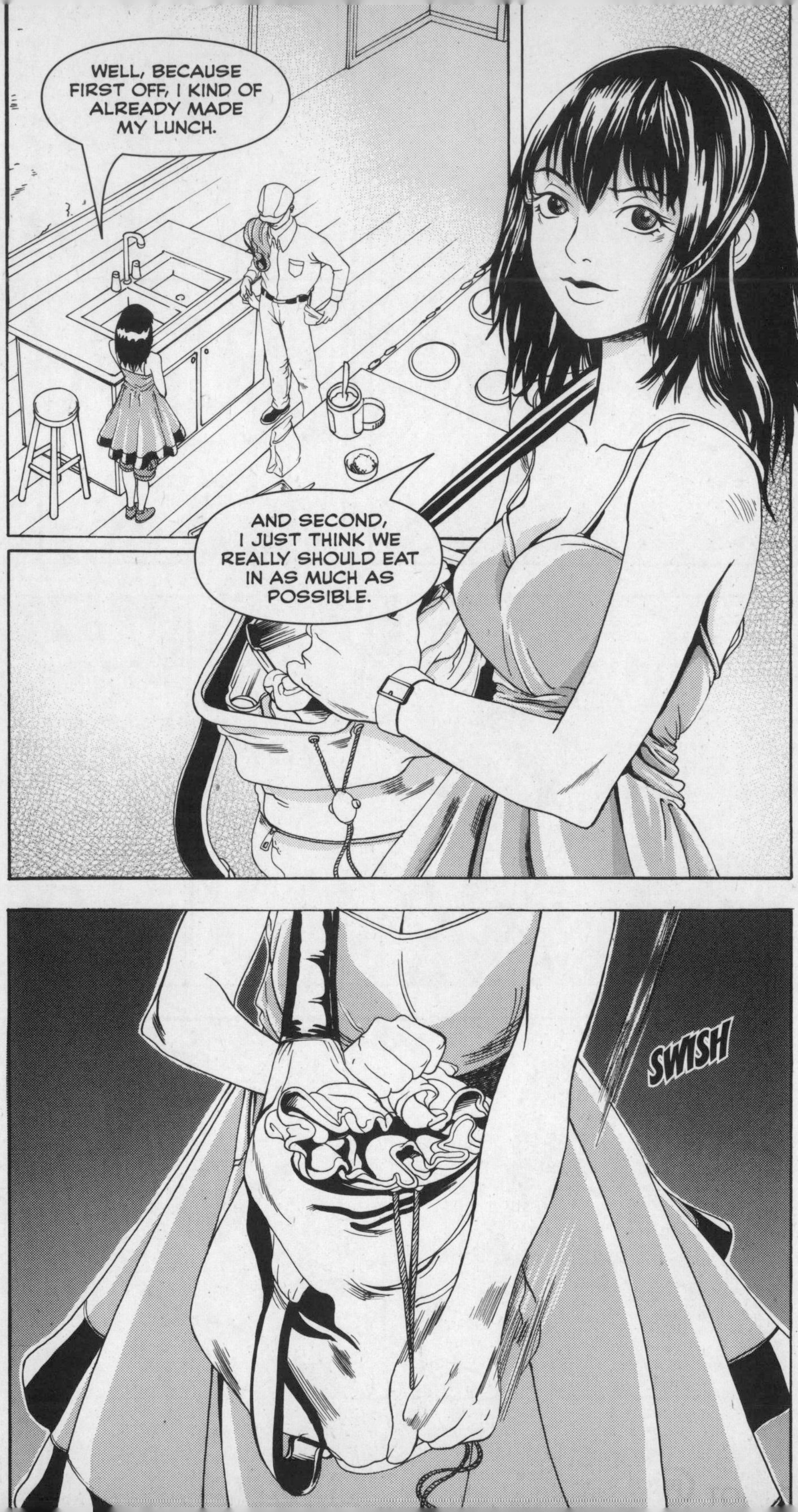
WELL, BECAUSE FIRST OFF, I KIND OF ALREADY MADE MY LUNCH.
AND SECOND, I JUST THINK WE REALLY SHOULD EAT IN AS MUCH AS POSSIBLE.
SWISH

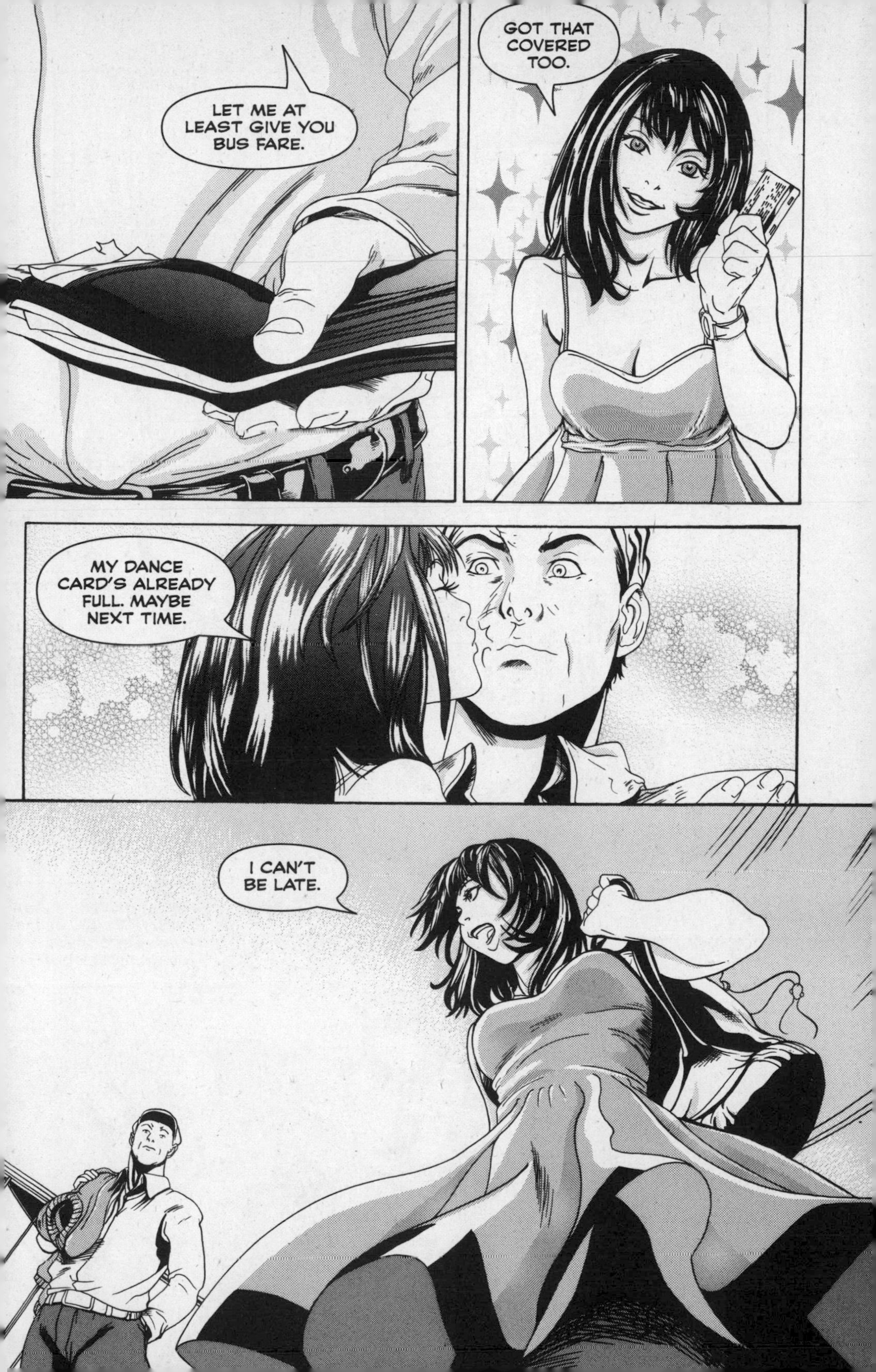
LET ME AT LEAST GIVE YOU BUS FARE.
GOT THAT COVERED TOO.
MY DANCE CARD'S ALREADY FULL. MAYBE NEXT TIME.
I CAN'T BE LATE.

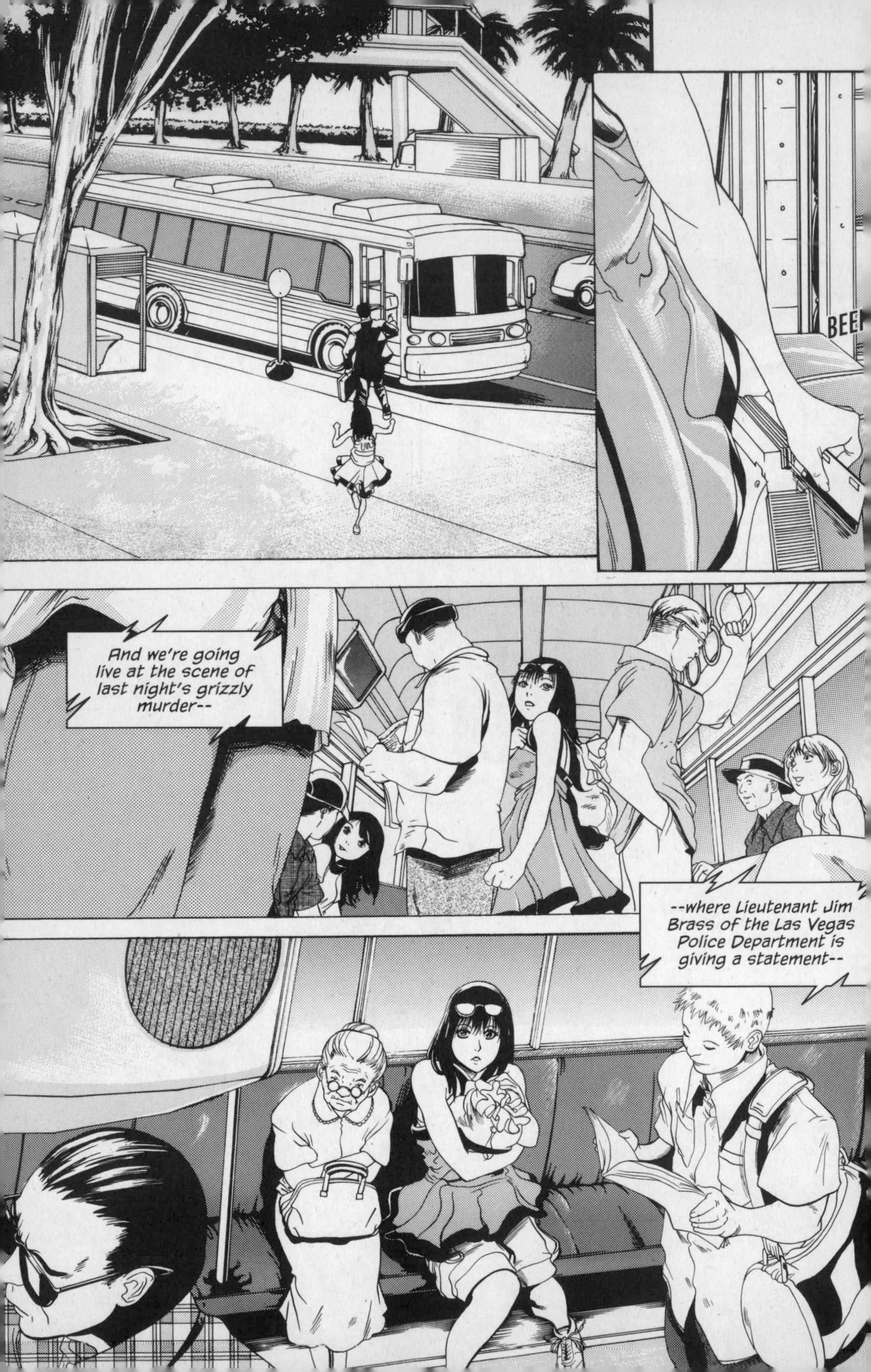
BEE
And we're going live at the scene of last night's grizzly murder--
--where Lieutenant Jim Brass of the Las Vegas Police Department is giving a statement--

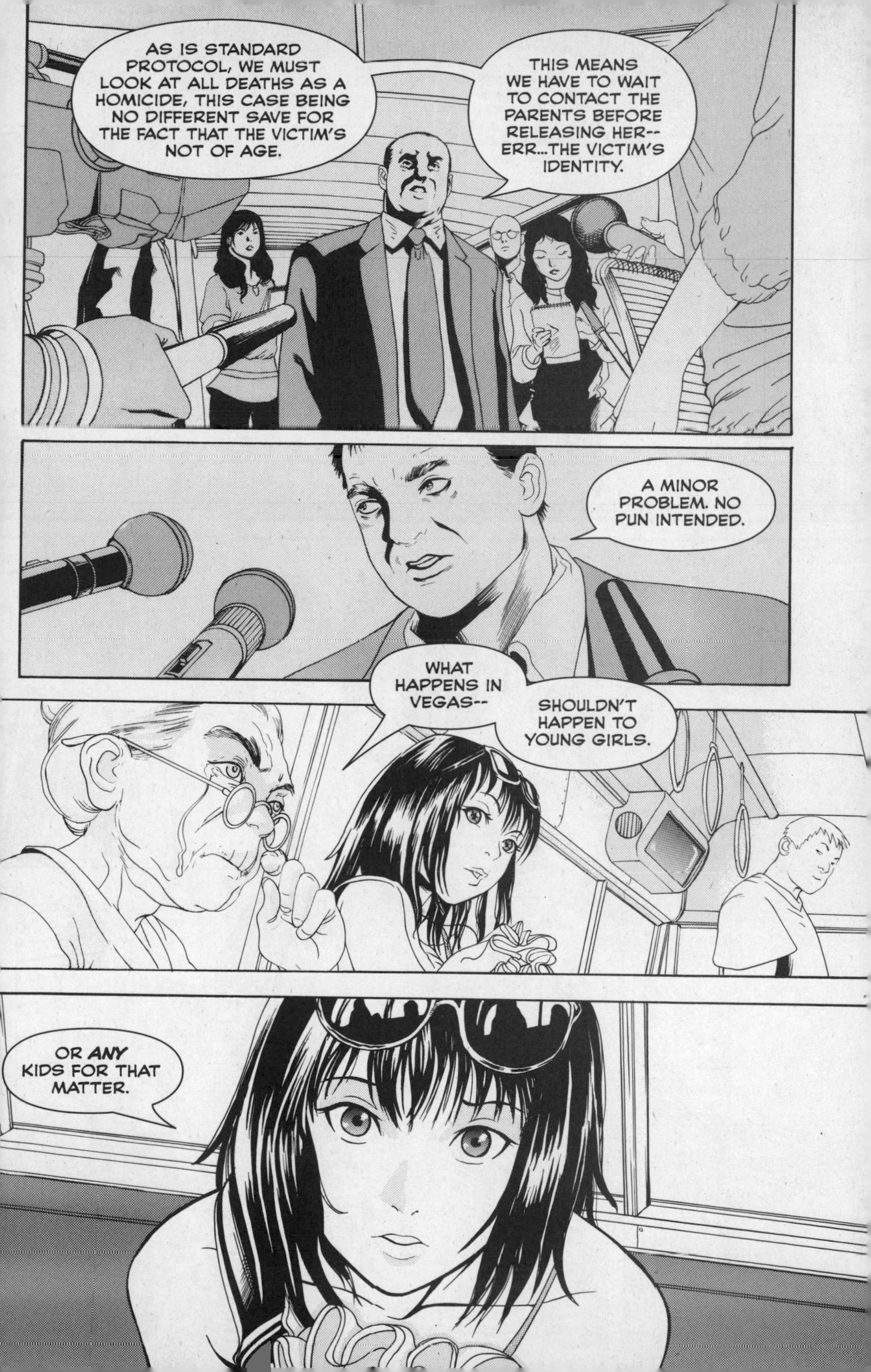
AS IS STANDARD PROTOCOL, WE MUST LOOK AT ALL DEATHS AS A HOMICIDE, THIS CASE BEING NO DIFFERENT SAVE FOR THE FACT THAT THE VICTIM'S NOT OF AGE.
THIS MEANS WE HAVE TO WAIT TO CONTACT THE PARENTS BEFORE RELEASING HER--ERR...THE VICTIM'S IDENTITY.
A MINOR PROBLEM. NO PUN INTENDED.
WHAT HAPPENS IN VEGAS--
SHOULDN'T HAPPEN TO YOUNG GIRLS.
OR *ANY* KIDS FOR THAT MATTER.

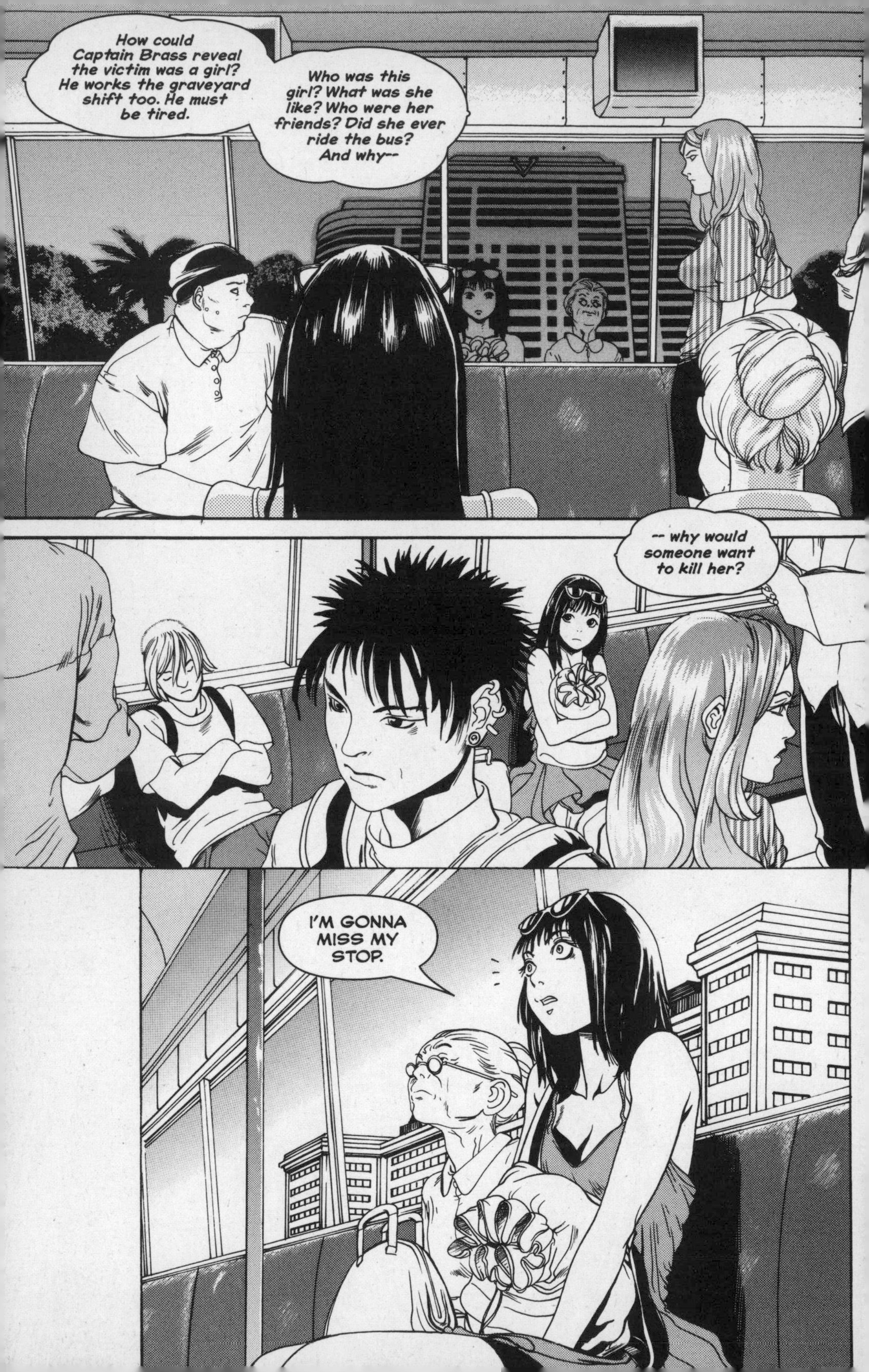
How could Captain Brass reveal the victim was a girl? He works the graveyard shift too. He must be tired.
Who was this girl? What was she like? Who were her friends? Did she ever ride the bus? And why--
-- why would someone want to kill her?
I'M GONNA MISS MY STOP.

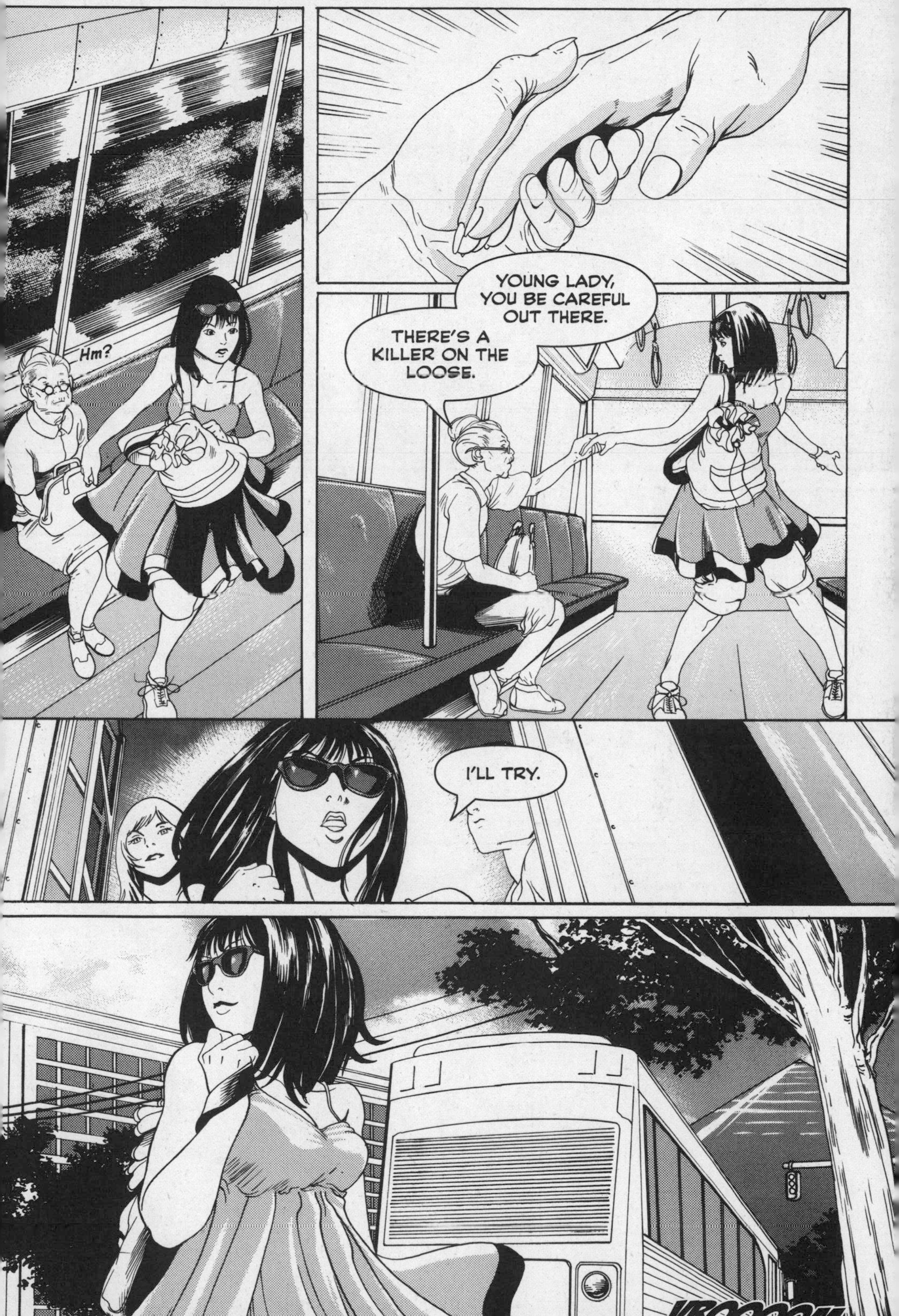
Hm?
YOUNG LADY, YOU BE CAREFUL OUT THERE.
THERE'S A KILLER ON THE LOOSE.
I'LL TRY.
VROOOOM

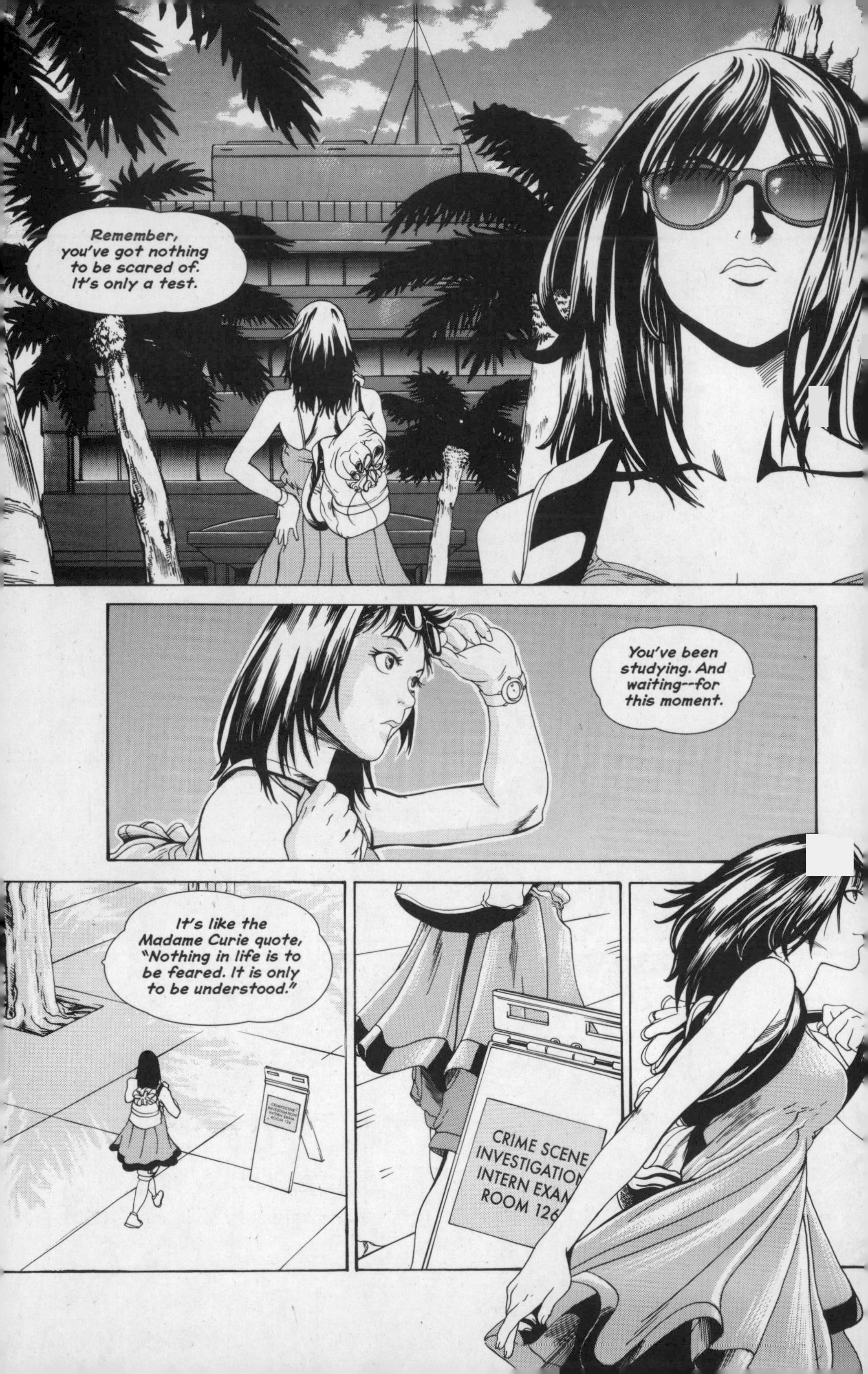
Remember, you've got nothing to be scared of. It's only a test.
You've been studying. And waiting--for this moment.
It's like the Madame Curie quote, "Nothing in life is to be feared. It is only to be understood."
CRIME SCENE INVESTIGATION INTERN EXAM ROOM 126

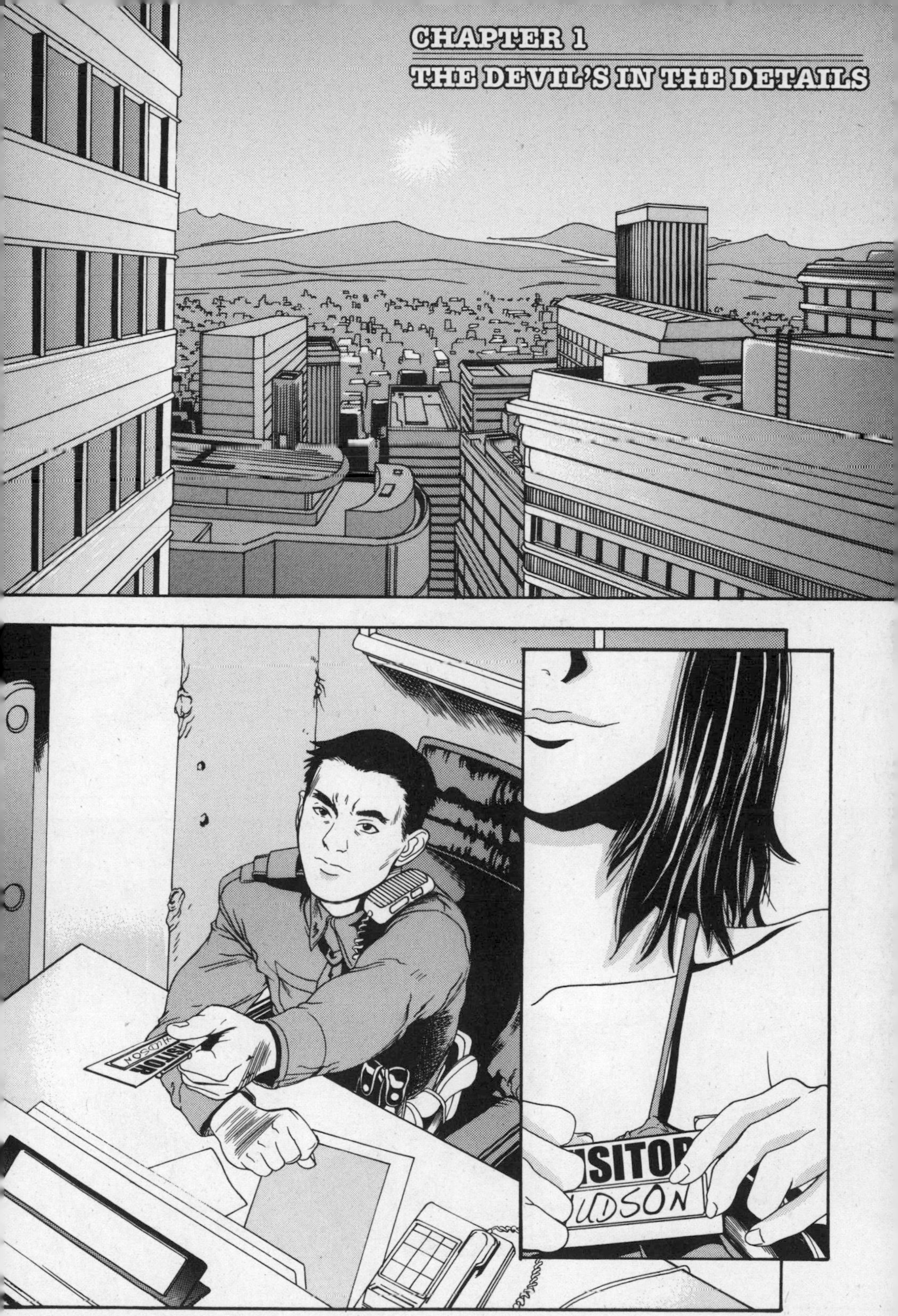
CHAPTER 1
THE DEVIL'S IN THE DETAILS

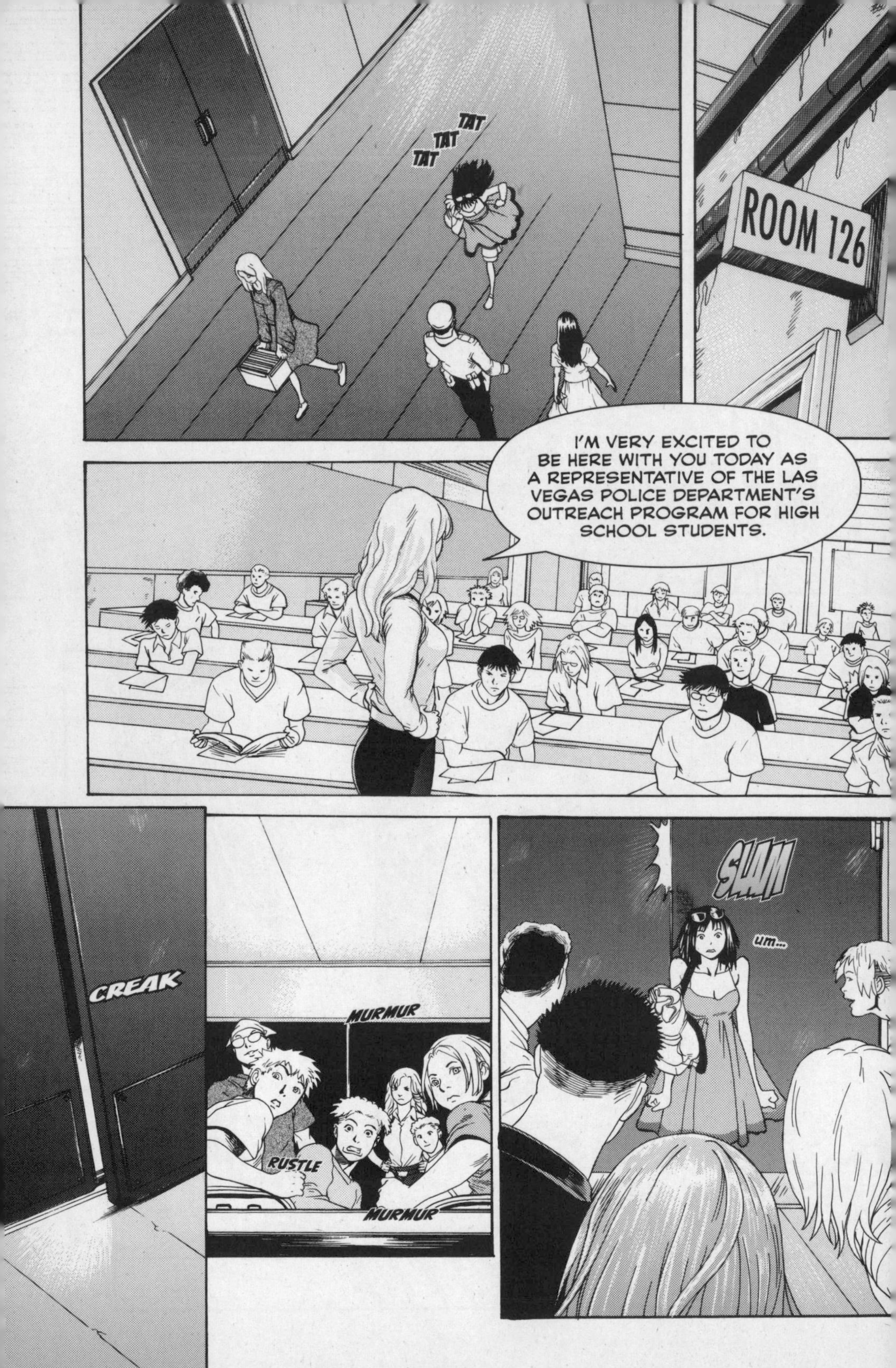
TAT
TAT
TAT
ROOM 126
I'M VERY EXCITED TO BE HERE WITH YOU TODAY AS A REPRESENTATIVE OF THE LAS VEGAS POLICE DEPARTMENT'S OUTREACH PROGRAM FOR HIGH SCHOOL STUDENTS.
CREAK
MURMUR
RUSTLE
MURMUR
SLAM
um...

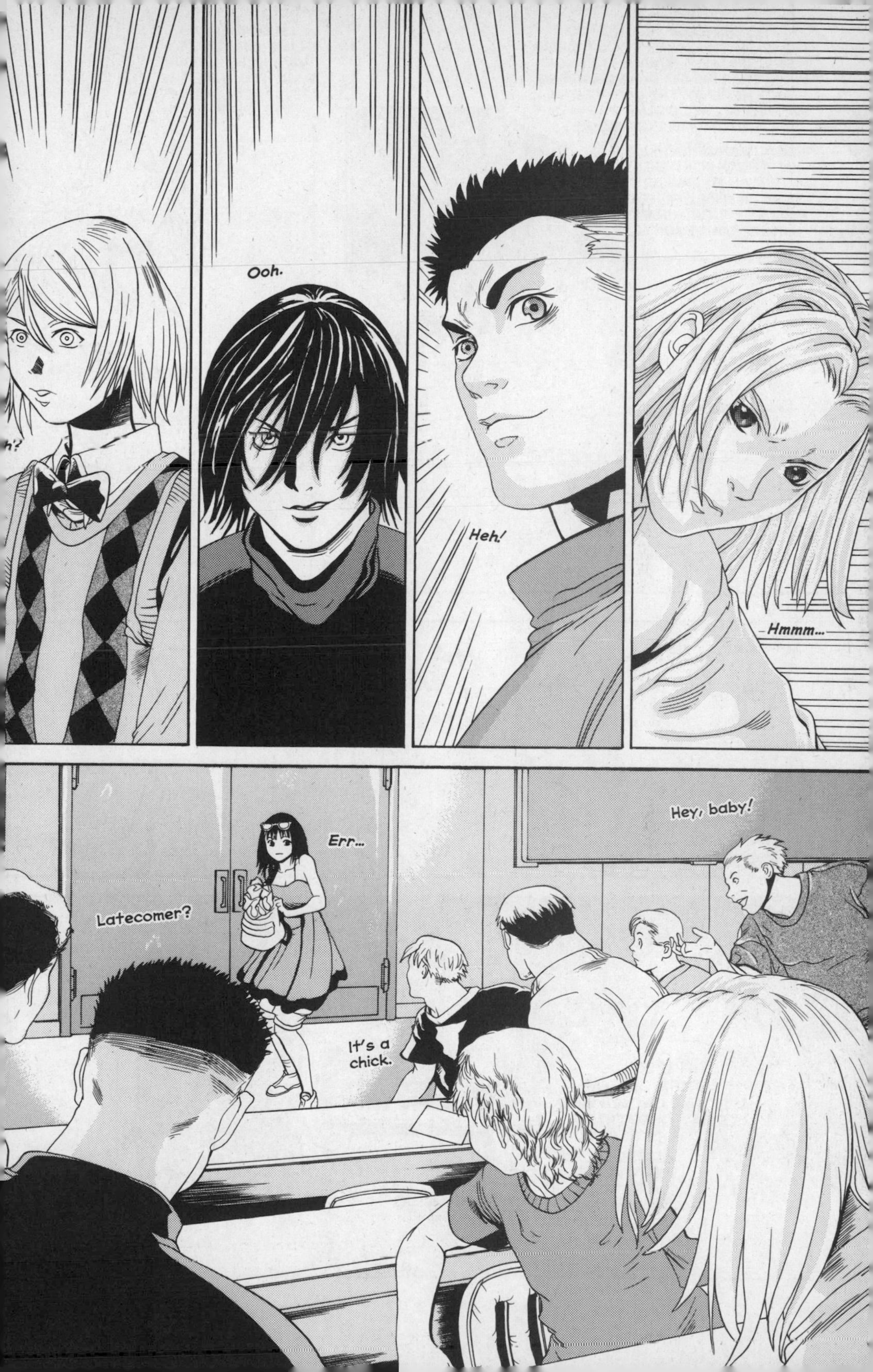
Hmmm...
Heh!
Ooh.
Hey, baby!
Err...
Latecomer?
It's a chick.

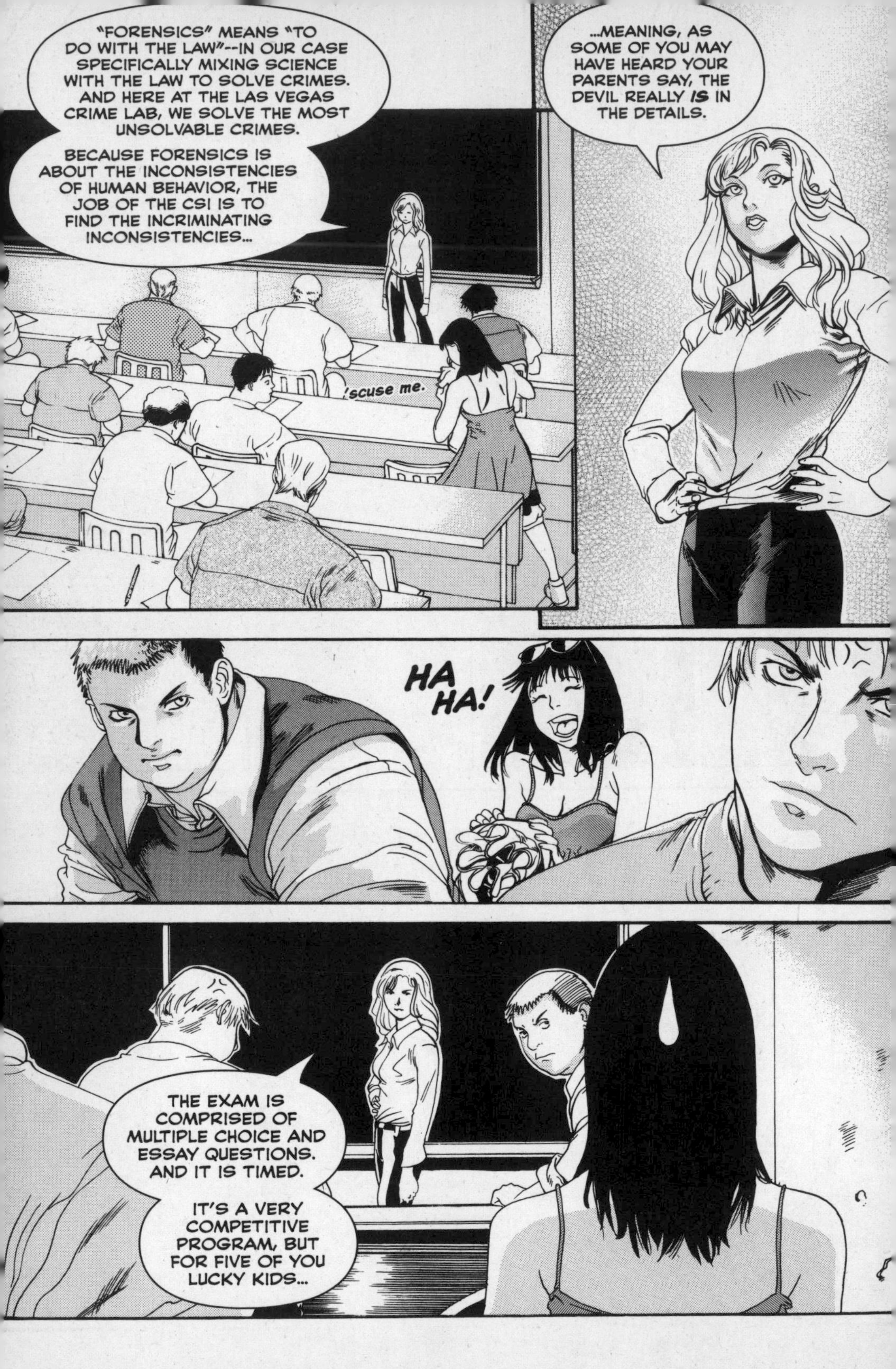
"FORENSICS" MEANS "TO DO WITH THE LAW"--IN OUR CASE SPECIFICALLY MIXING SCIENCE WITH THE LAW TO SOLVE CRIMES. AND HERE AT THE LAS VEGAS CRIME LAB, WE SOLVE THE MOST UNSOLVABLE CRIMES.
BECAUSE FORENSICS IS ABOUT THE INCONSISTENCIES OF HUMAN BEHAVIOR, THE JOB OF THE CSI IS TO FIND THE INCRIMINATING INCONSISTENCIES...
'scuse me.
...MEANING, AS SOME OF YOU MAY HAVE HEARD YOUR PARENTS SAY, THE DEVIL REALLY IS IN THE DETAILS.
HA HA!
THE EXAM IS COMPRISED OF MULTIPLE CHOICE AND ESSAY QUESTIONS. AND IT IS TIMED.
IT'S A VERY COMPETITIVE PROGRAM, BUT FOR FIVE OF YOU LUCKY KIDS...

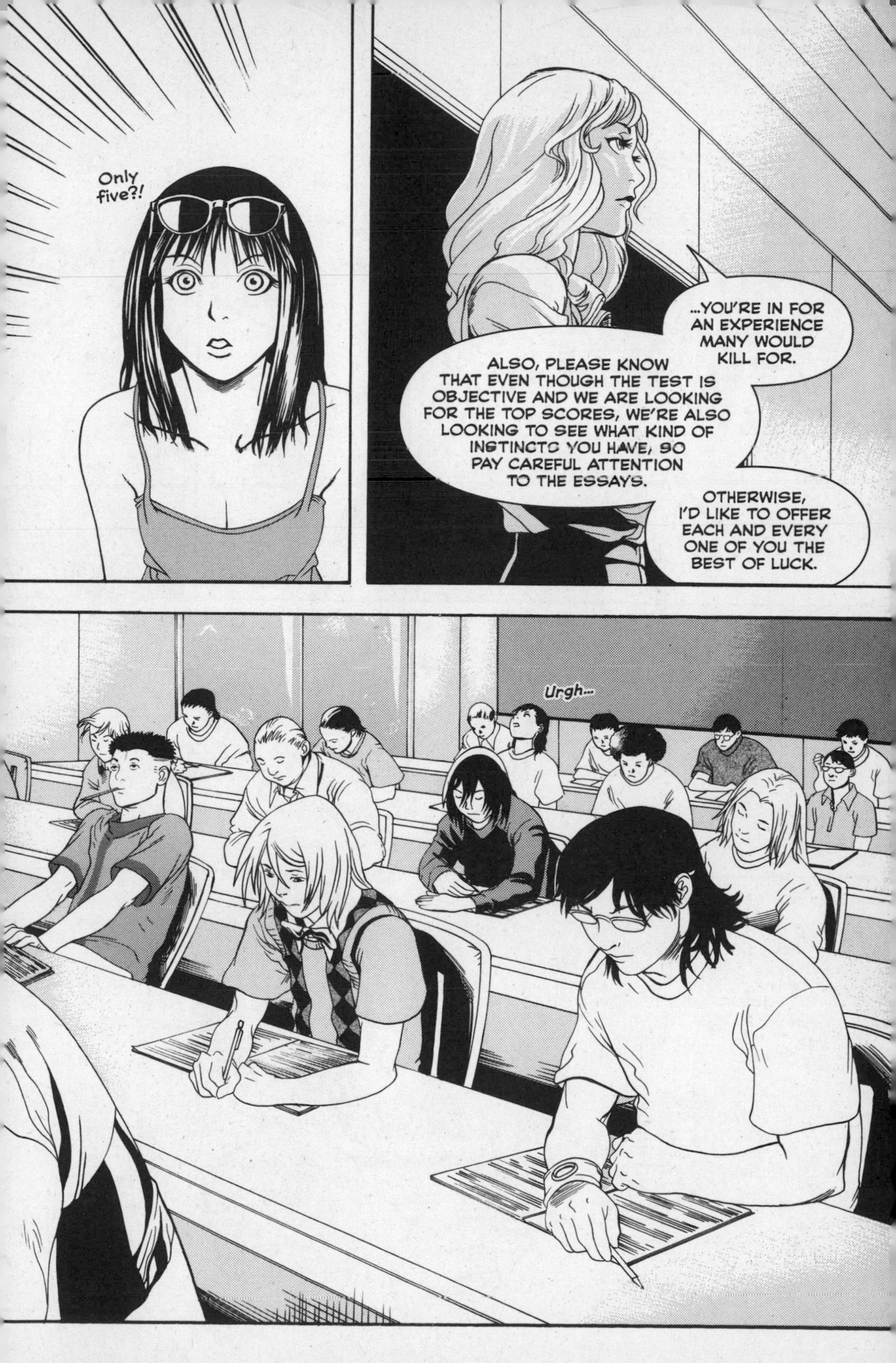
Only five?!
...YOU'RE IN FOR AN EXPERIENCE MANY WOULD KILL FOR.
ALSO, PLEASE KNOW THAT EVEN THOUGH THE TEST IS OBJECTIVE AND WE ARE LOOKING FOR THE TOP SCORES, WE'RE ALSO LOOKING TO SEE WHAT KIND OF INSTINCTS YOU HAVE, SO PAY CAREFUL ATTENTION TO THE ESSAYS.
OTHERWISE, I'D LIKE TO OFFER EACH AND EVERY ONE OF YOU THE BEST OF LUCK.
Urgh...

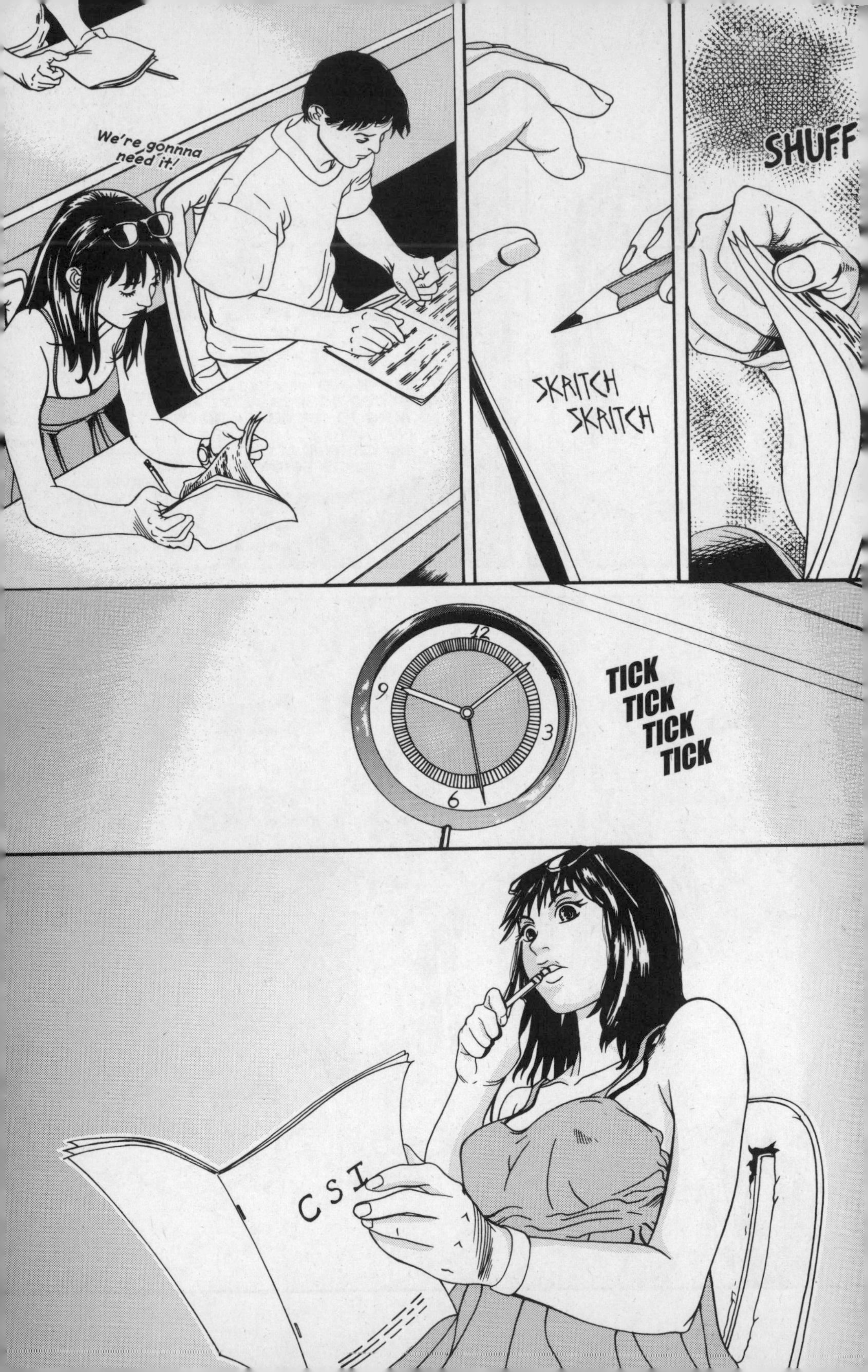
We're gonnna need it!
SKRITCH
SKRITCH
SHUFF
TICK
TICK
TICK
TICK
CSI

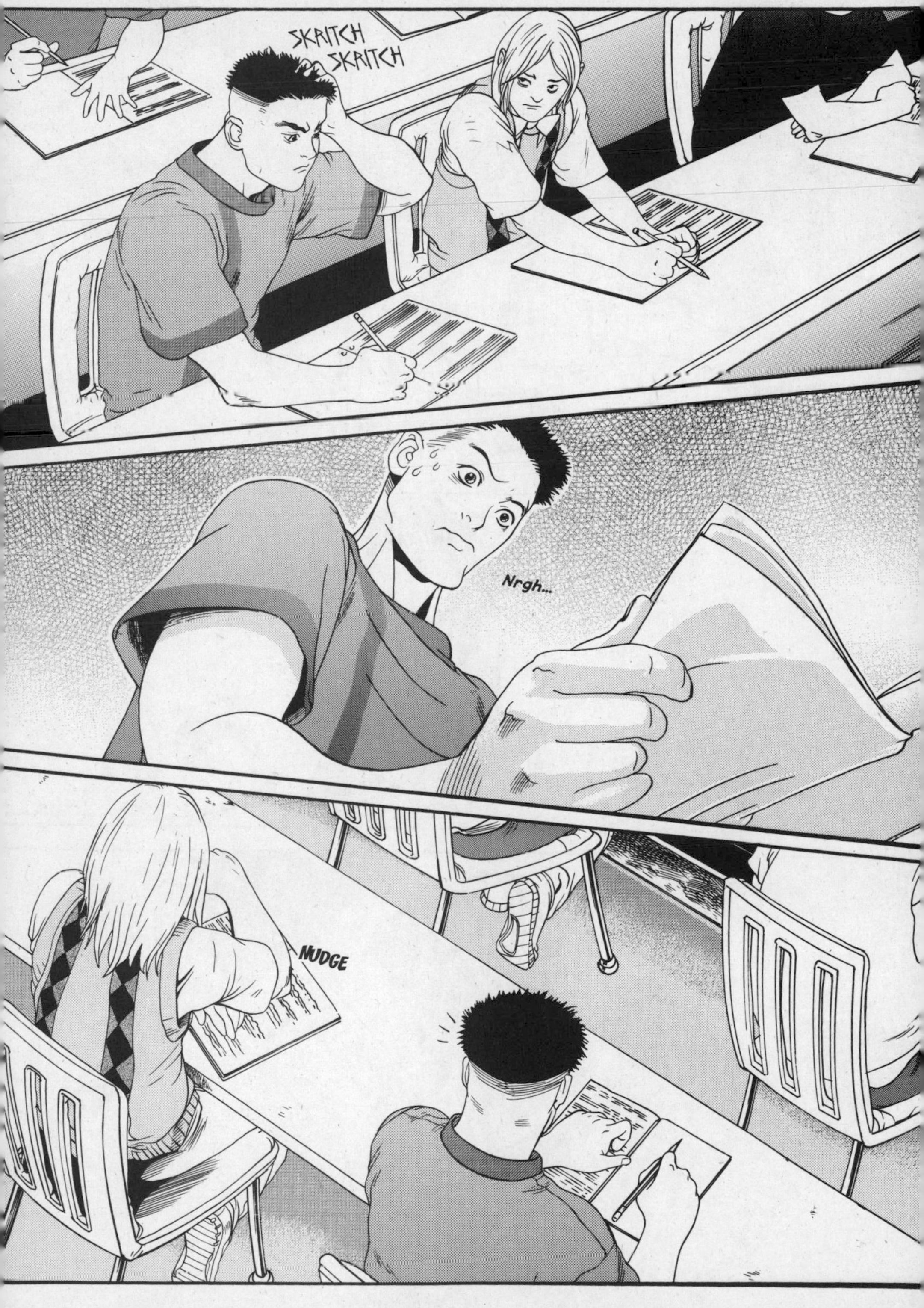
SKRITCH
SKRITCH
Nrgh...
NUDGE

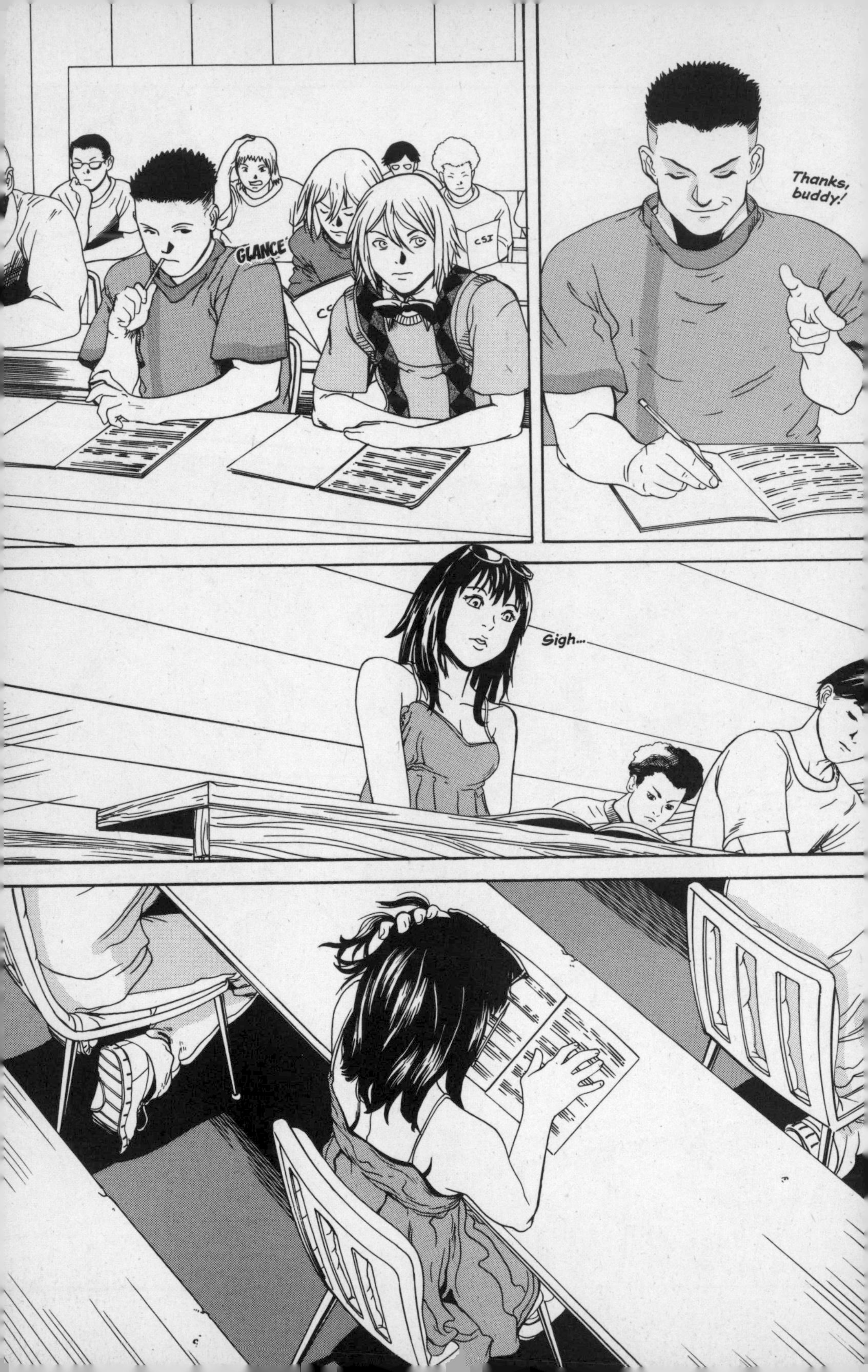

Thanks, buddy!
GLANCE
CSI
Sigh...

1.) BASED ON THE RESULTS OF THE BLOOD TYPE ANALYSIS, CAN YOU EXCLUDE ANY OF THE SUSPECTS AS HAVING LEFT THE BLOOD STAIN FOUND AT THE CRIME SCENE?

2.) BASED ON THE RESULTS OF THE BLOOD TYPE ANALYSIS, WHICH SUSPECT(S) COULD HAVE LEFT THE BLOOD STAIN AT THE CRIME SCENE?

3.) IF YOU WERE ALLOWED TO PERFORM ADDITIONAL TESTS USING THIS BLOOD STAIN FROM THE CRIME SCENE, WHAT WOULD YOU RECOMMEND?

4.) DESCRIBE HOW TO ANALYZE BOTH PHYSICAL AND MATERIAL EVIDENCE WHEN INVESTIGATING A CRIME SCENE.

5.) PROTECTING THE EVIDENCE--DESCRIBE HOW TO MAINTAIN A PRISTINE CRIME SCENE THAT IS FREE OF CONTAMINATION.

7.) TAL INTE

8.) IDEN CLUSION AT A CRI

9.) TYPES OF MATERIAL EV

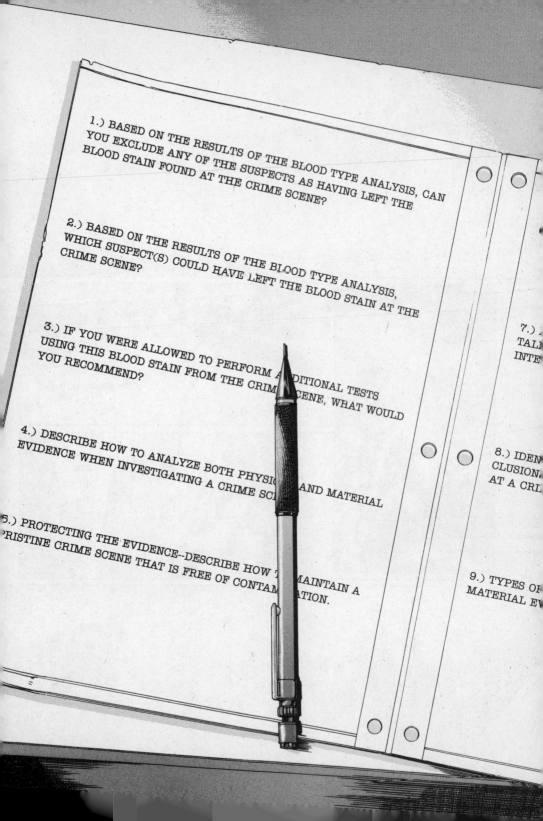

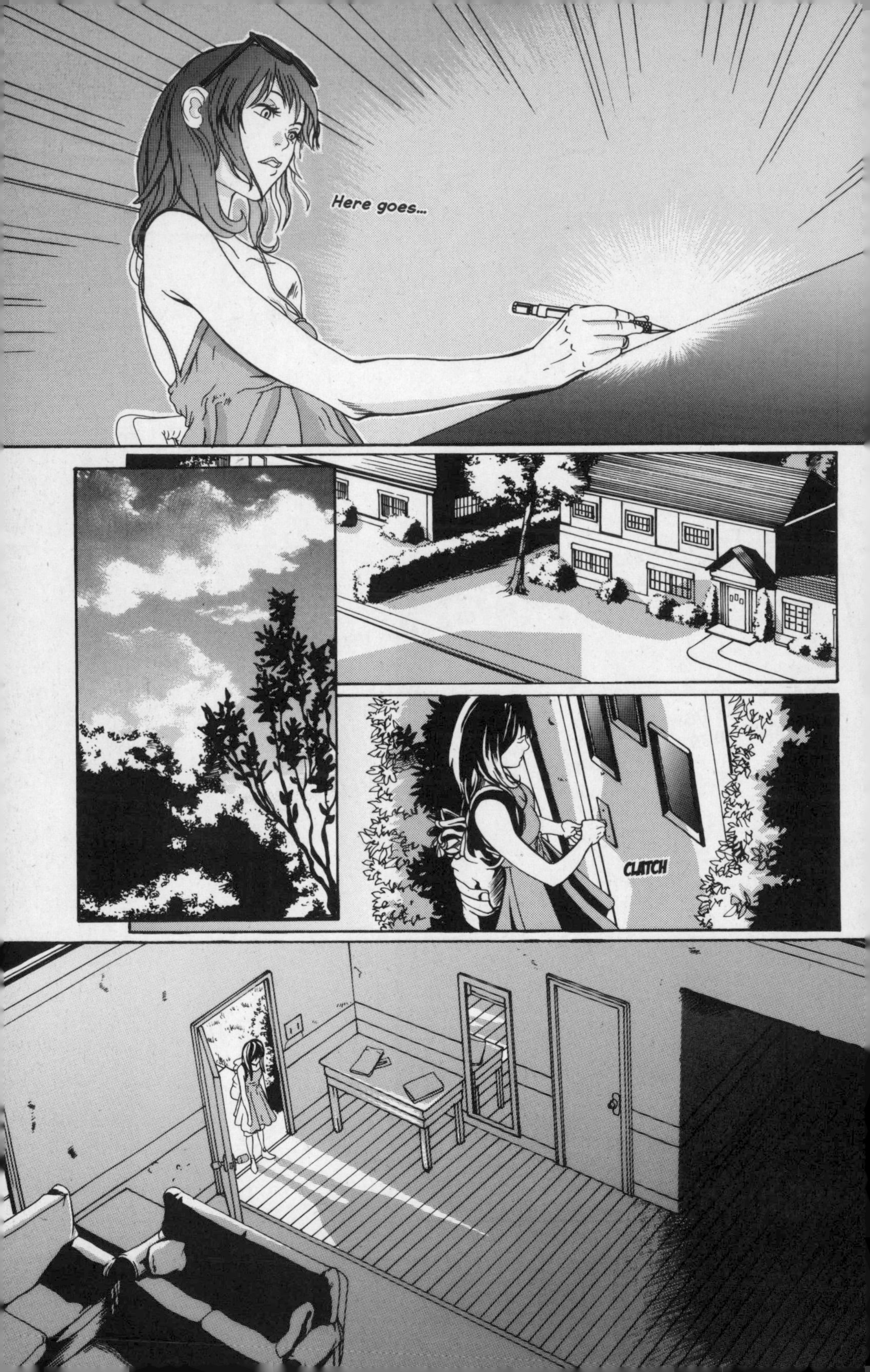
Here goes...
CLATCH

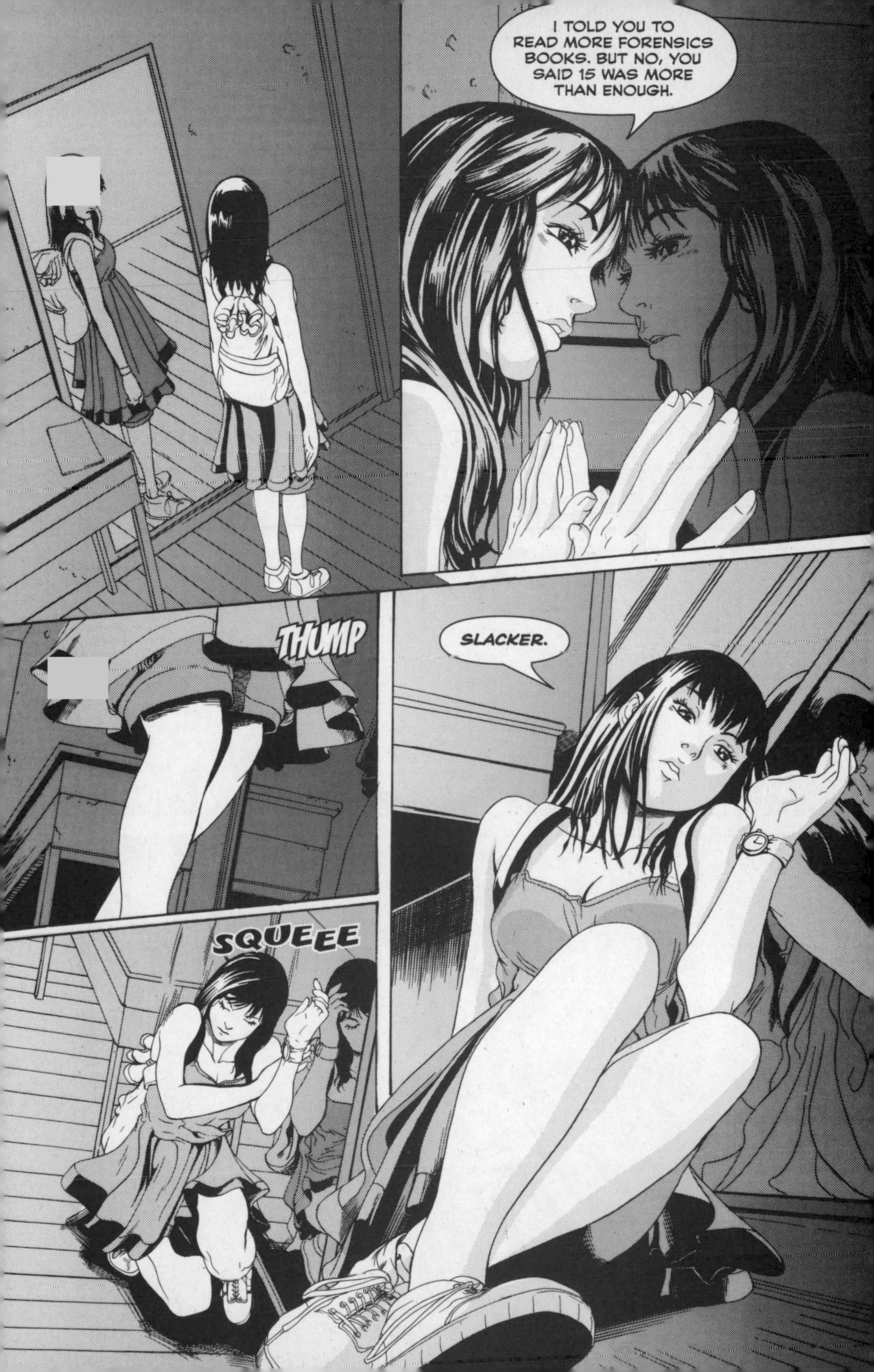
I TOLD YOU TO READ MORE FORENSICS BOOKS. BUT NO, YOU SAID 15 WAS MORE THAN ENOUGH.
THUMP
SLACKER.
SQUEEE

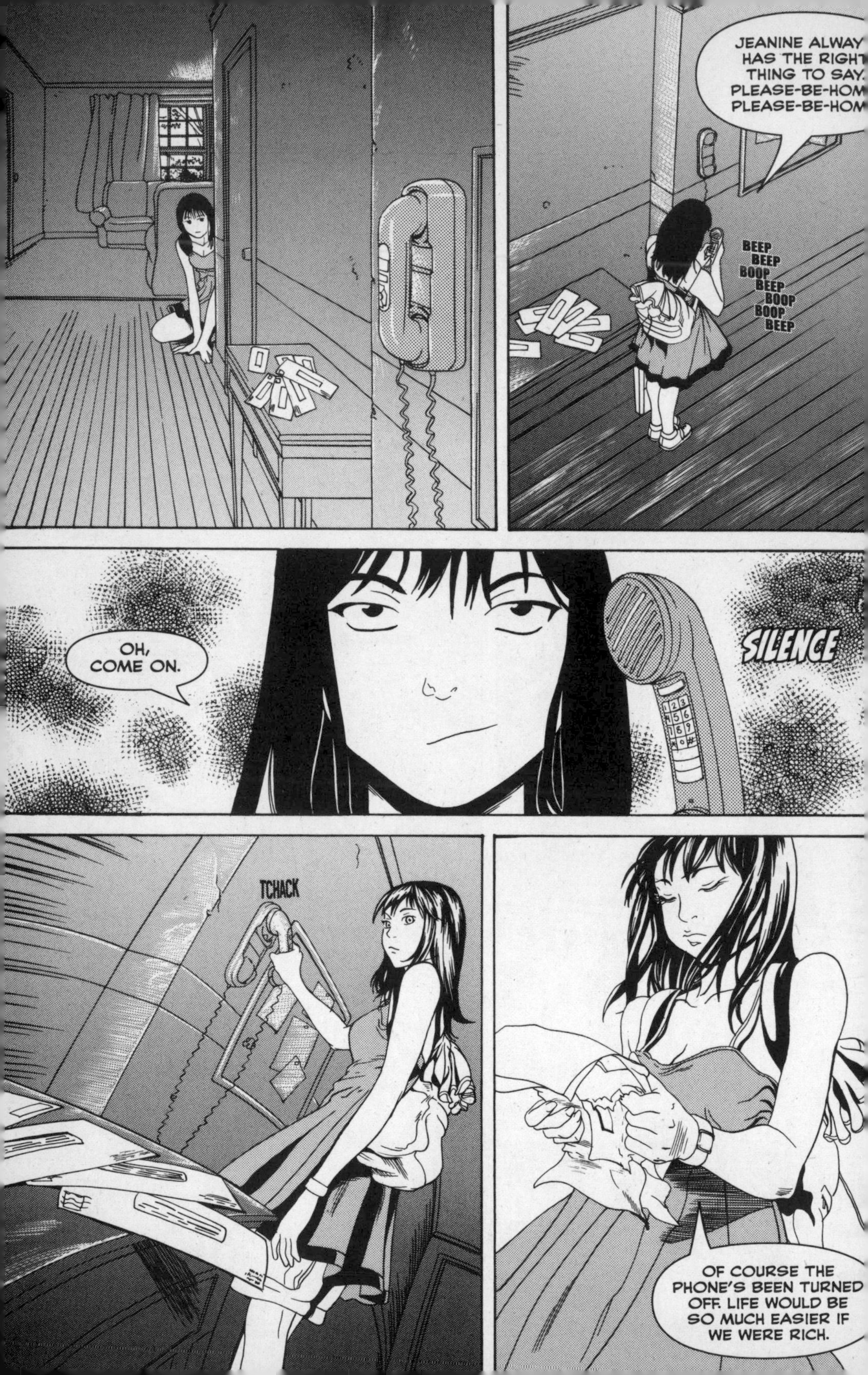
JEANINE ALWAY
HAS THE RIGHT
THING TO SAY.
PLEASE-BE-HOM
PLEASE-BE-HOM
BEEP
BEEP
BOOP
BEEP
BOOP
BOOP
BEEP
OH, COME ON.
SILENCE
TCHACK
OF COURSE THE PHONE'S BEEN TURNED OFF. LIFE WOULD BE SO MUCH EASIER IF WE WERE RICH.

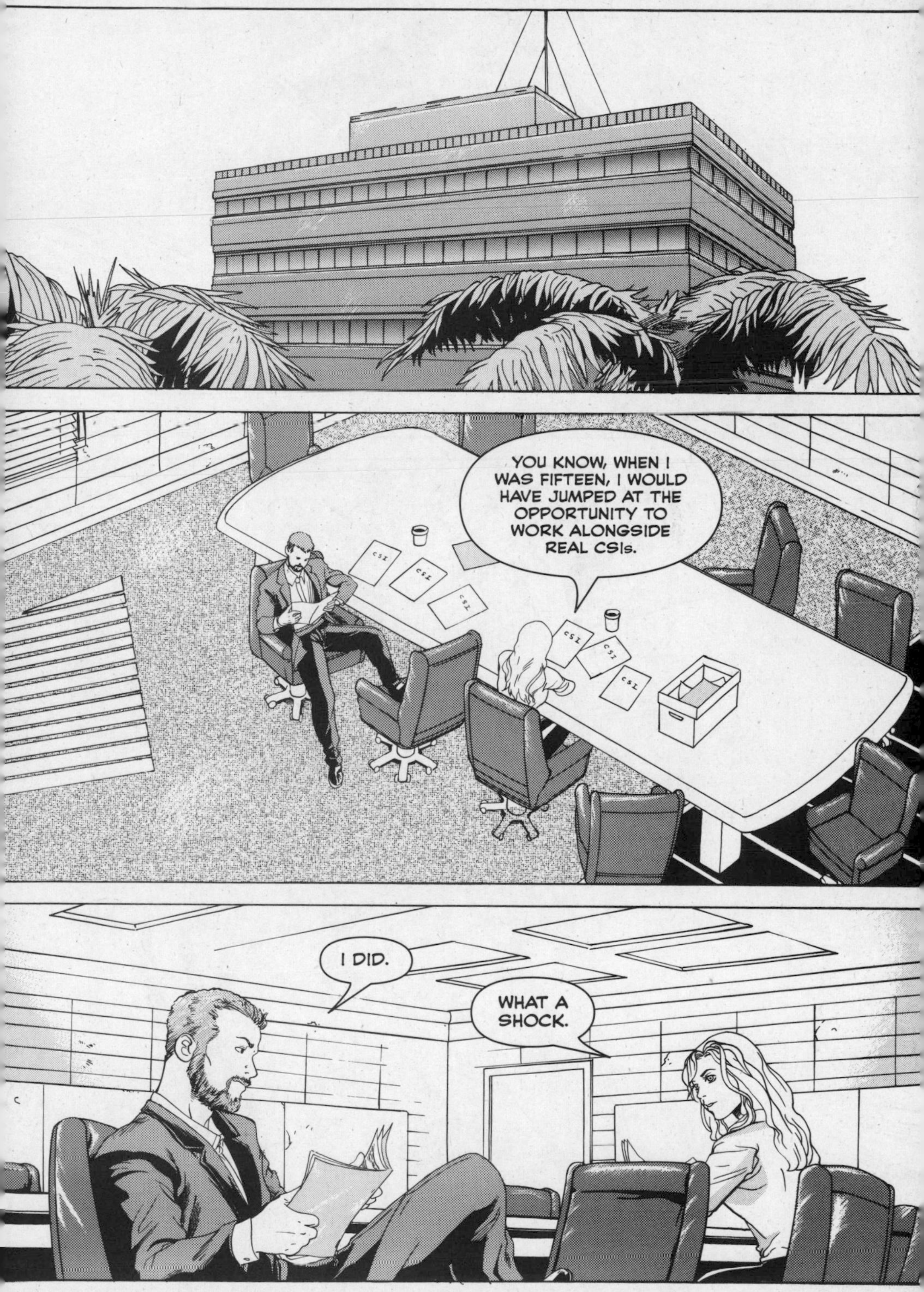
YOU KNOW, WHEN I WAS FIFTEEN, I WOULD HAVE JUMPED AT THE OPPORTUNITY TO WORK ALONGSIDE REAL CSIs.
CSI
I DID.
WHAT A SHOCK.

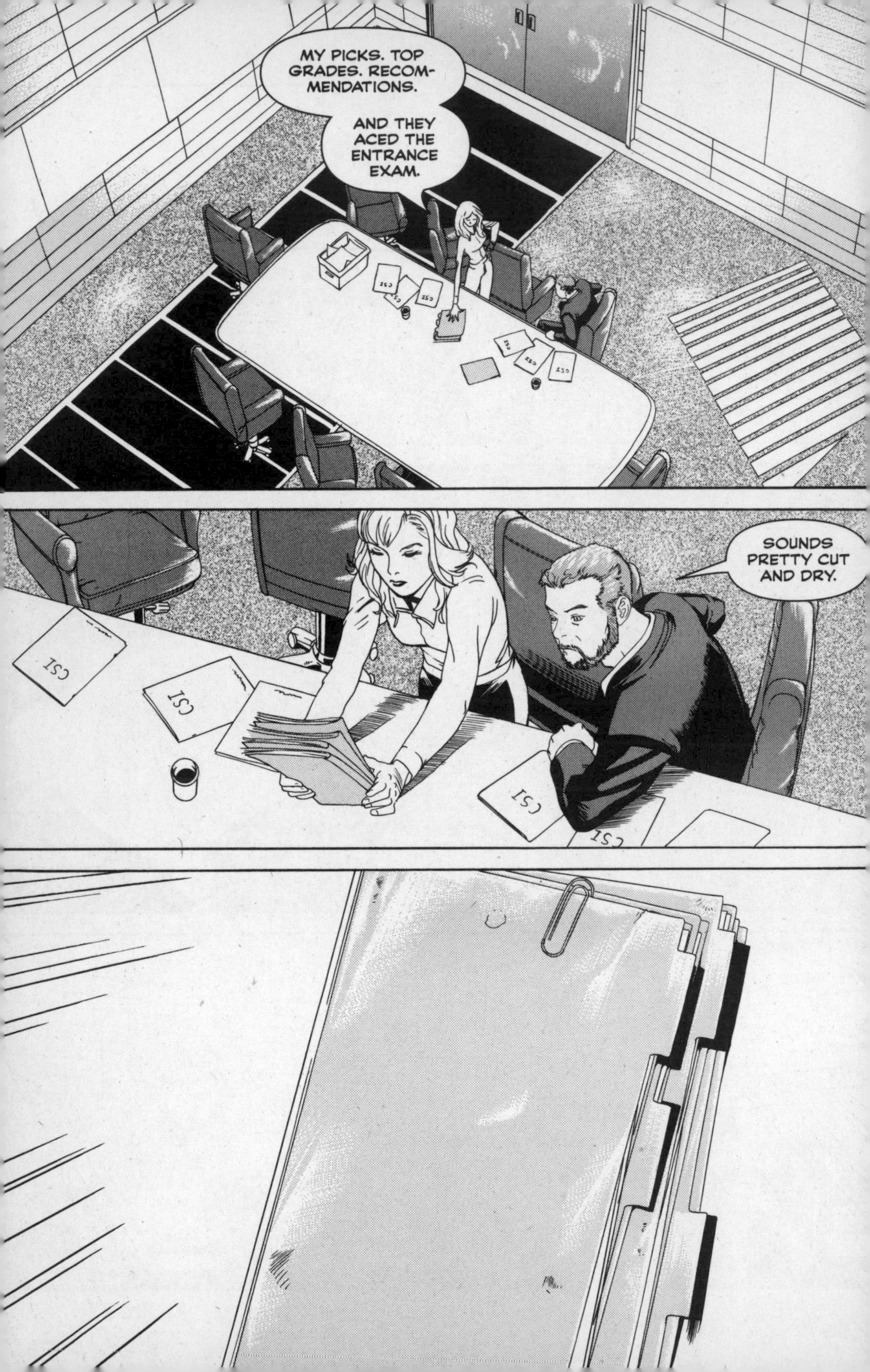

MY PICKS. TOP GRADES. RECOMMENDATIONS.
AND THEY ACED THE ENTRANCE EXAM.
SOUNDS PRETTY CUT AND DRY.

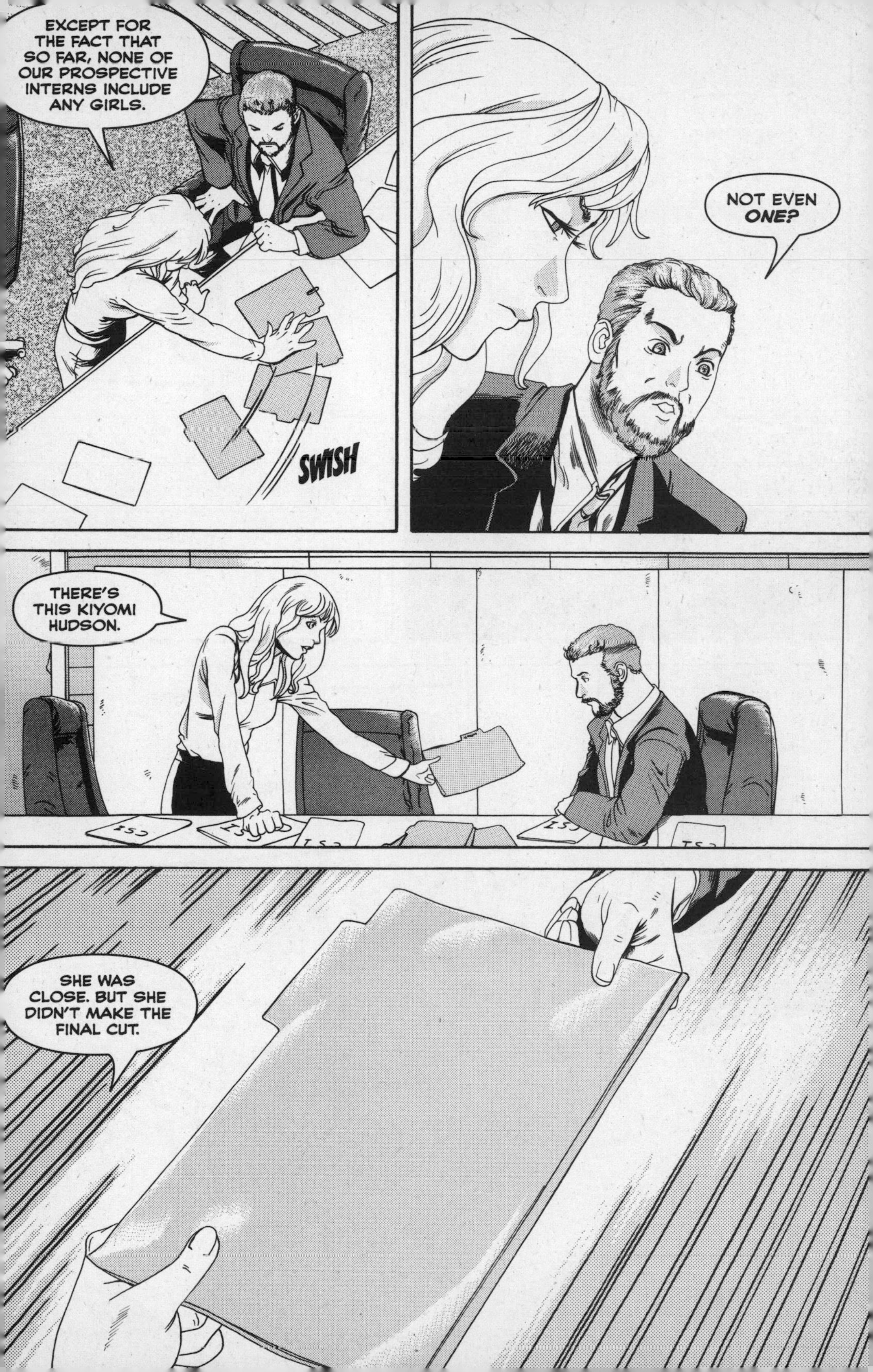
EXCEPT FOR THE FACT THAT SO FAR, NONE OF OUR PROSPECTIVE INTERNS INCLUDE ANY GIRLS.
SWISH
NOT EVEN ONE?
THERE'S THIS KIYOMI HUDSON.
SHE WAS CLOSE. BUT SHE DIDN'T MAKE THE FINAL CUT.

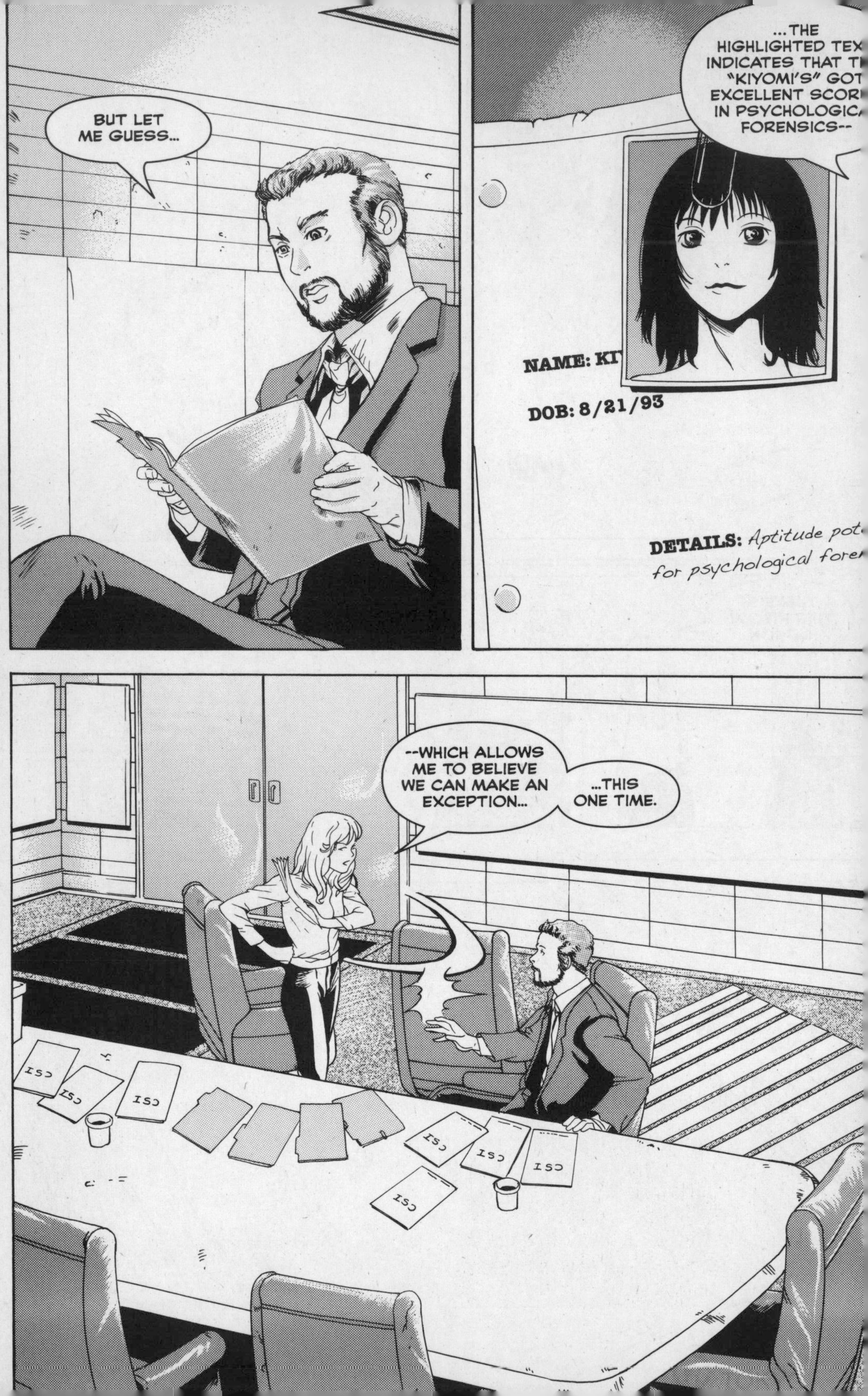
BUT LET ME GUESS...
...THE HIGHLIGHTED TEX INDICATES THAT T "KIYOMI'S" GOT EXCELLENT SCOR IN PSYCHOLOGIC FORENSICS--
NAME: KI
DOB: 8/21/93
DETAILS: Aptitude pot for psychological fore
--WHICH ALLOWS ME TO BELIEVE WE CAN MAKE AN EXCEPTION...
...THIS ONE TIME.
CSI
CSI
CSI
CSI
CSI
CSI
CSI

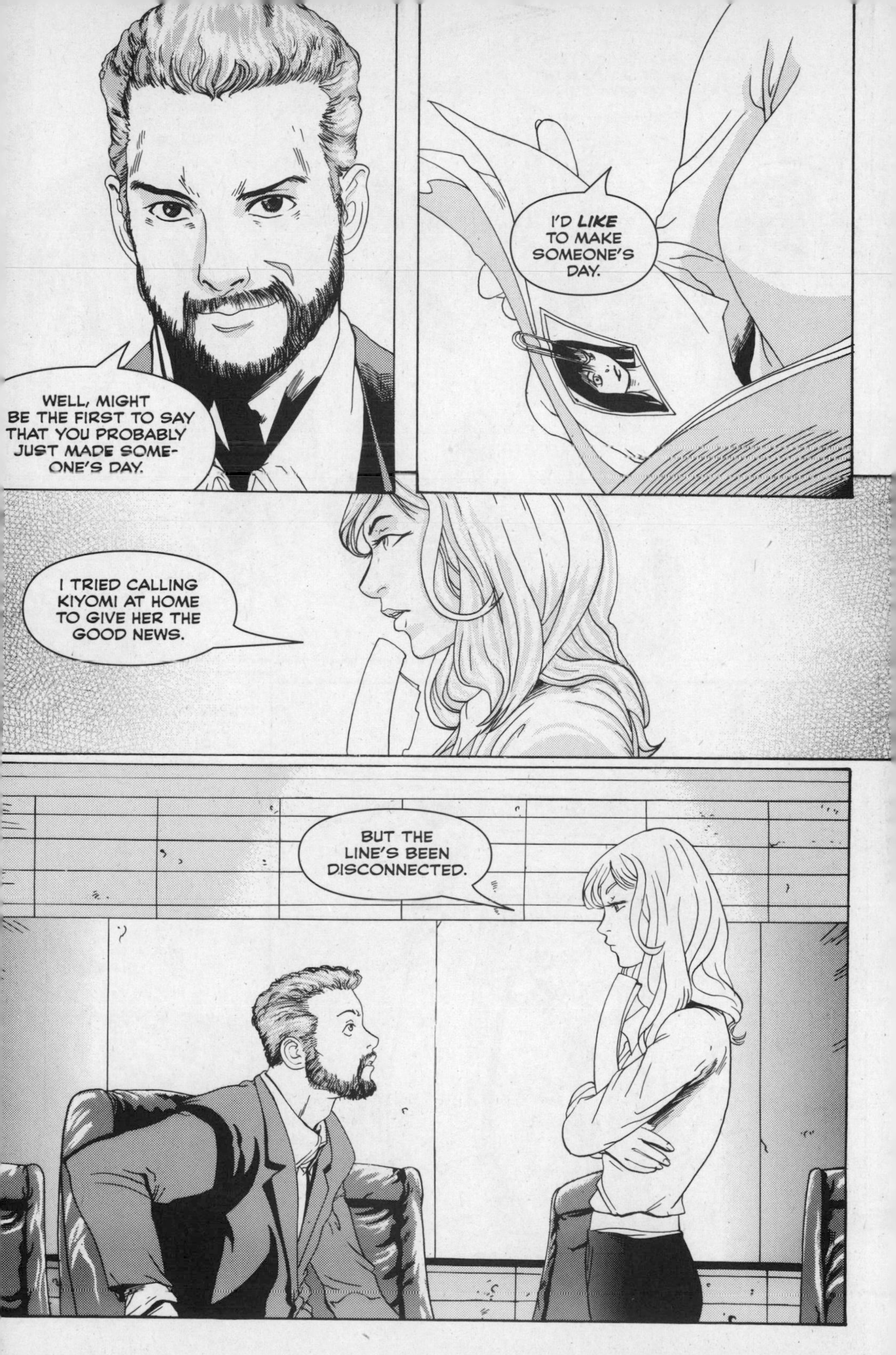
WELL, MIGHT BE THE FIRST TO SAY THAT YOU PROBABLY JUST MADE SOME-ONE'S DAY.
I'D LIKE TO MAKE SOMEONE'S DAY.
I TRIED CALLING KIYOMI AT HOME TO GIVE HER THE GOOD NEWS.
BUT THE LINE'S BEEN DISCONNECTED.

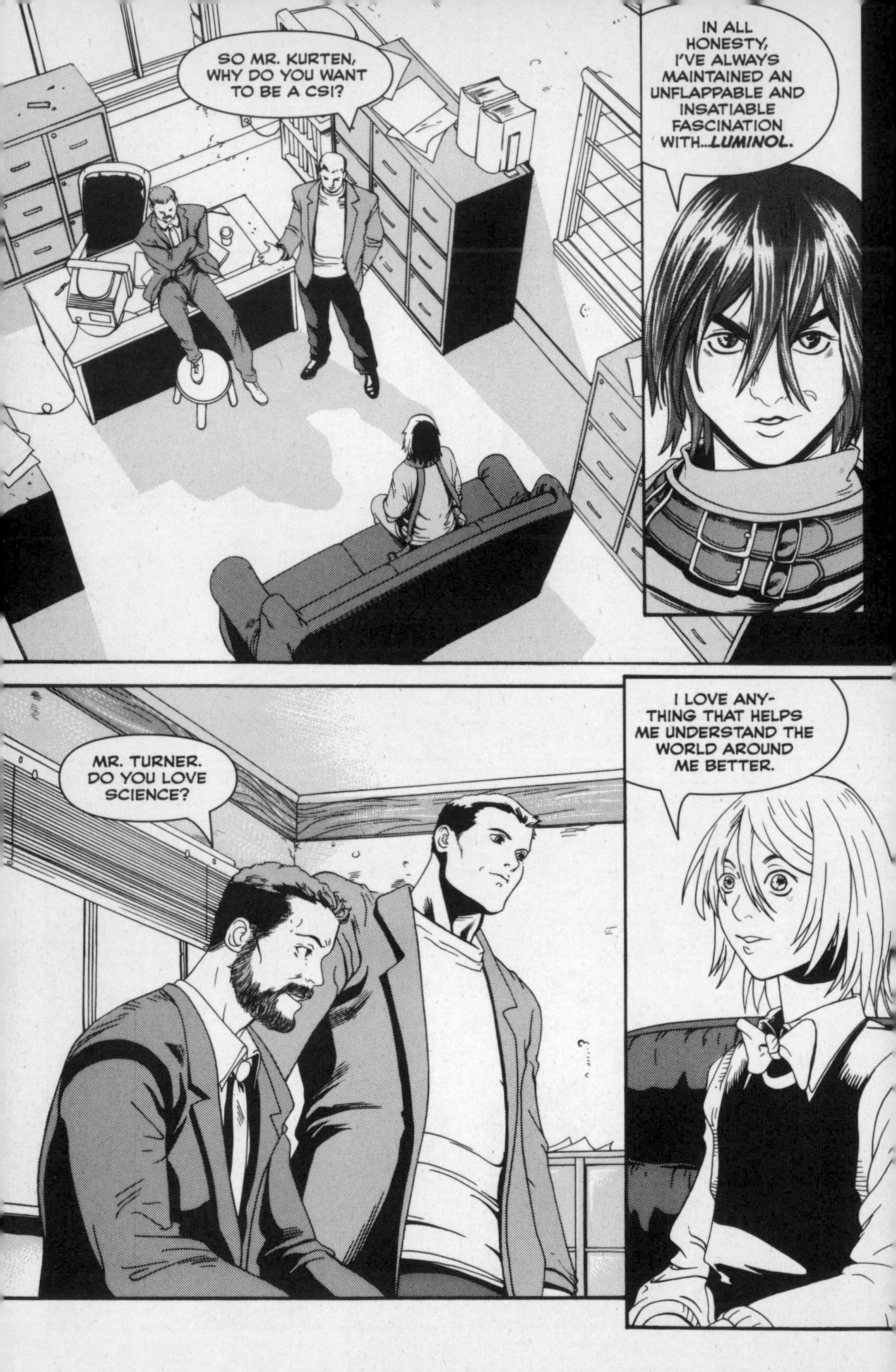
SO MR. KURTEN, WHY DO YOU WANT TO BE A CSI?
IN ALL HONESTY, I'VE ALWAYS MAINTAINED AN UNFLAPPABLE AND INSATIABLE FASCINATION WITH...*LUMINOL.*
MR. TURNER. DO YOU LOVE SCIENCE?
I LOVE ANY-THING THAT HELPS ME UNDERSTAND THE WORLD AROUND ME BETTER.

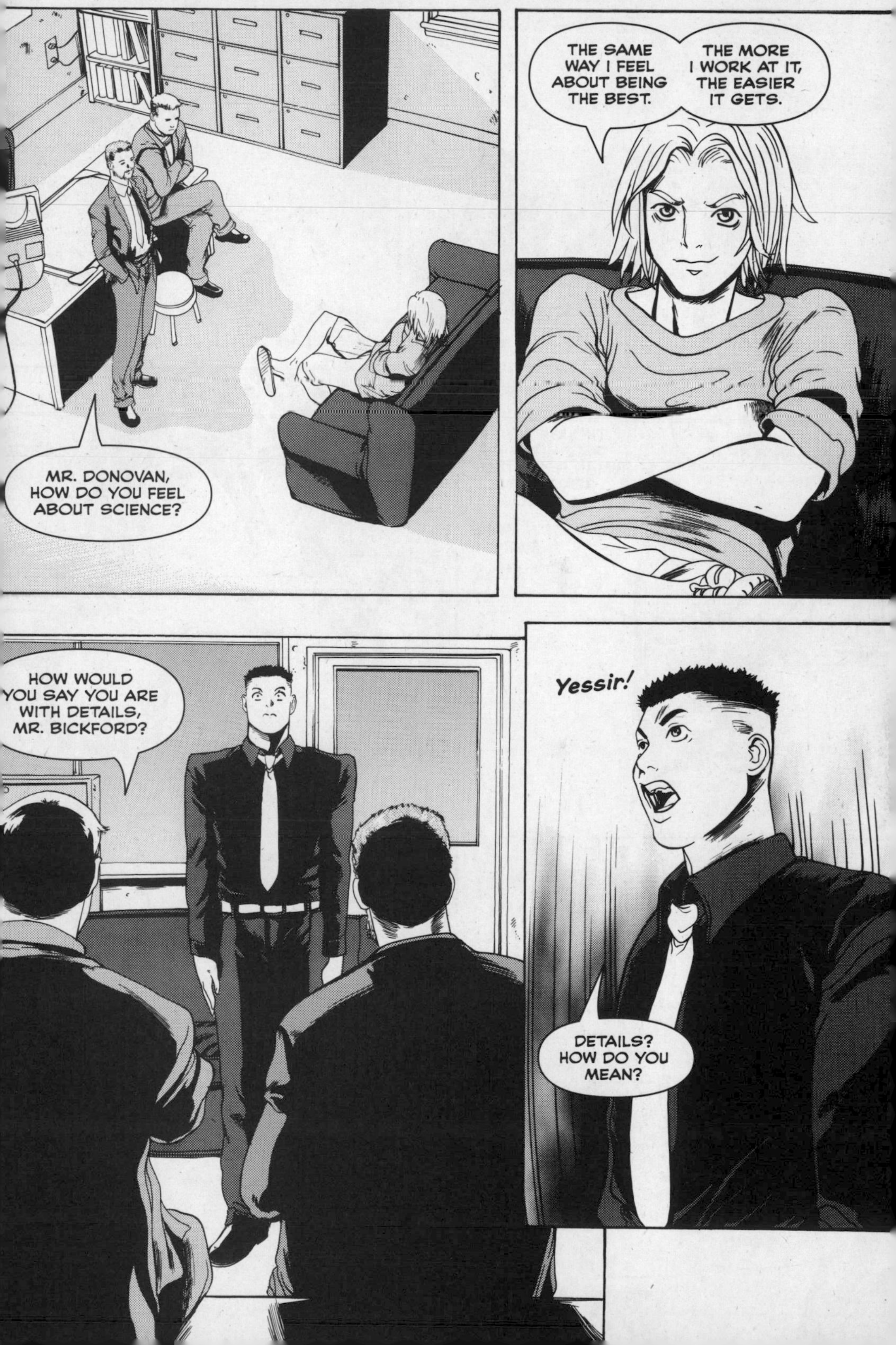
MR. DONOVAN, HOW DO YOU FEEL ABOUT SCIENCE?
THE SAME WAY I FEEL ABOUT BEING THE BEST.
THE MORE I WORK AT IT, THE EASIER IT GETS.
HOW WOULD YOU SAY YOU ARE WITH DETAILS, MR. BICKFORD?
Yessir!
DETAILS? HOW DO YOU MEAN?

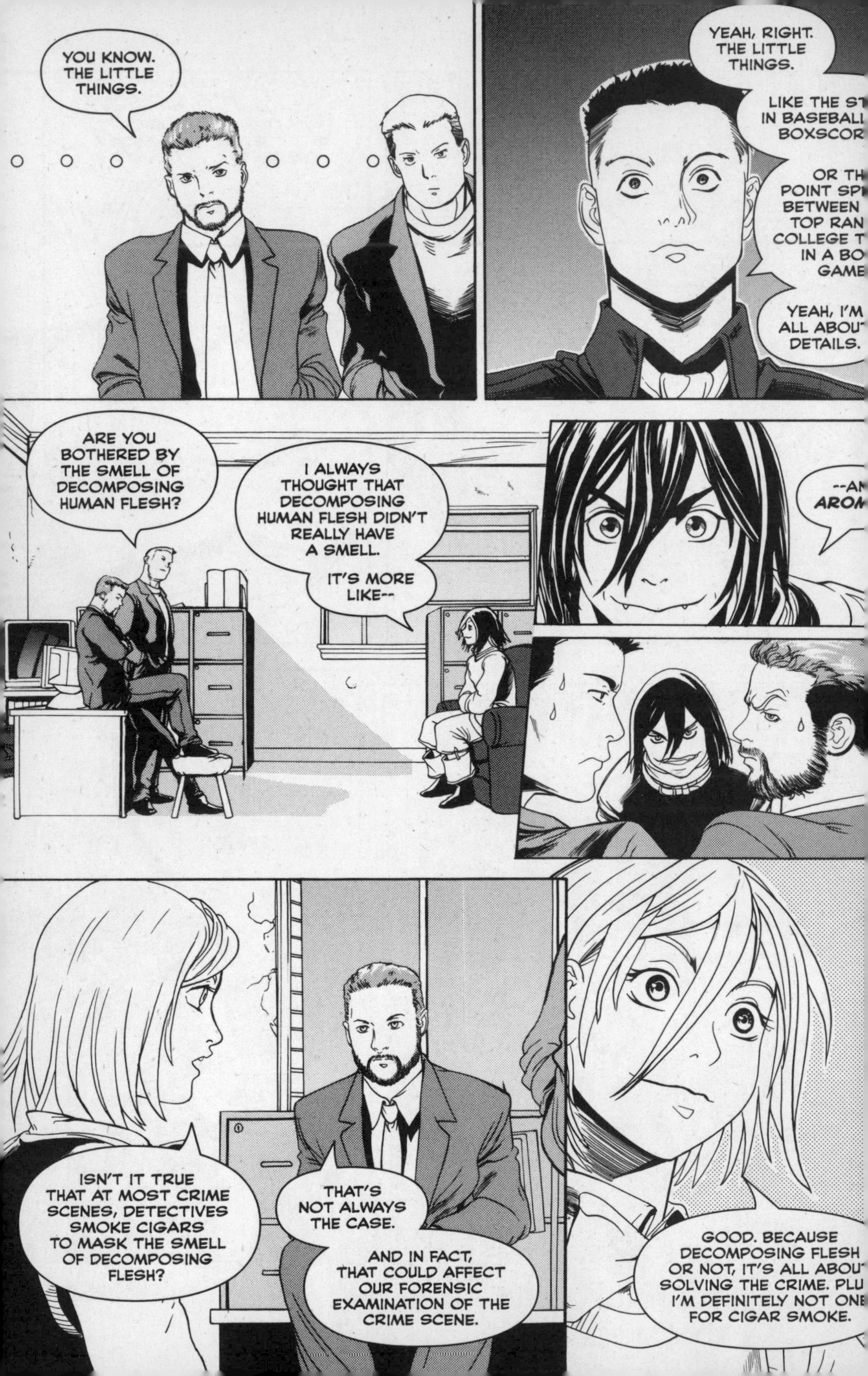

YOU KNOW. THE LITTLE THINGS.
YEAH, RIGHT. THE LITTLE THINGS.
LIKE THE ST IN BASEBALL BOXSCOR
OR TH POINT SP BETWEEN TOP RAN COLLEGE T IN A BO GAME
YEAH, I'M ALL ABOU DETAILS.
ARE YOU BOTHERED BY THE SMELL OF DECOMPOSING HUMAN FLESH?
I ALWAYS THOUGHT THAT DECOMPOSING HUMAN FLESH DIDN'T REALLY HAVE A SMELL.
IT'S MORE LIKE--
--A AROM
ISN'T IT TRUE THAT AT MOST CRIME SCENES, DETECTIVES SMOKE CIGARS TO MASK THE SMELL OF DECOMPOSING FLESH?
THAT'S NOT ALWAYS THE CASE.
AND IN FACT, THAT COULD AFFECT OUR FORENSIC EXAMINATION OF THE CRIME SCENE.
GOOD. BECAUSE DECOMPOSING FLESH OR NOT, IT'S ALL ABOU SOLVING THE CRIME. PLU I'M DEFINITELY NOT ONE FOR CIGAR SMOKE.

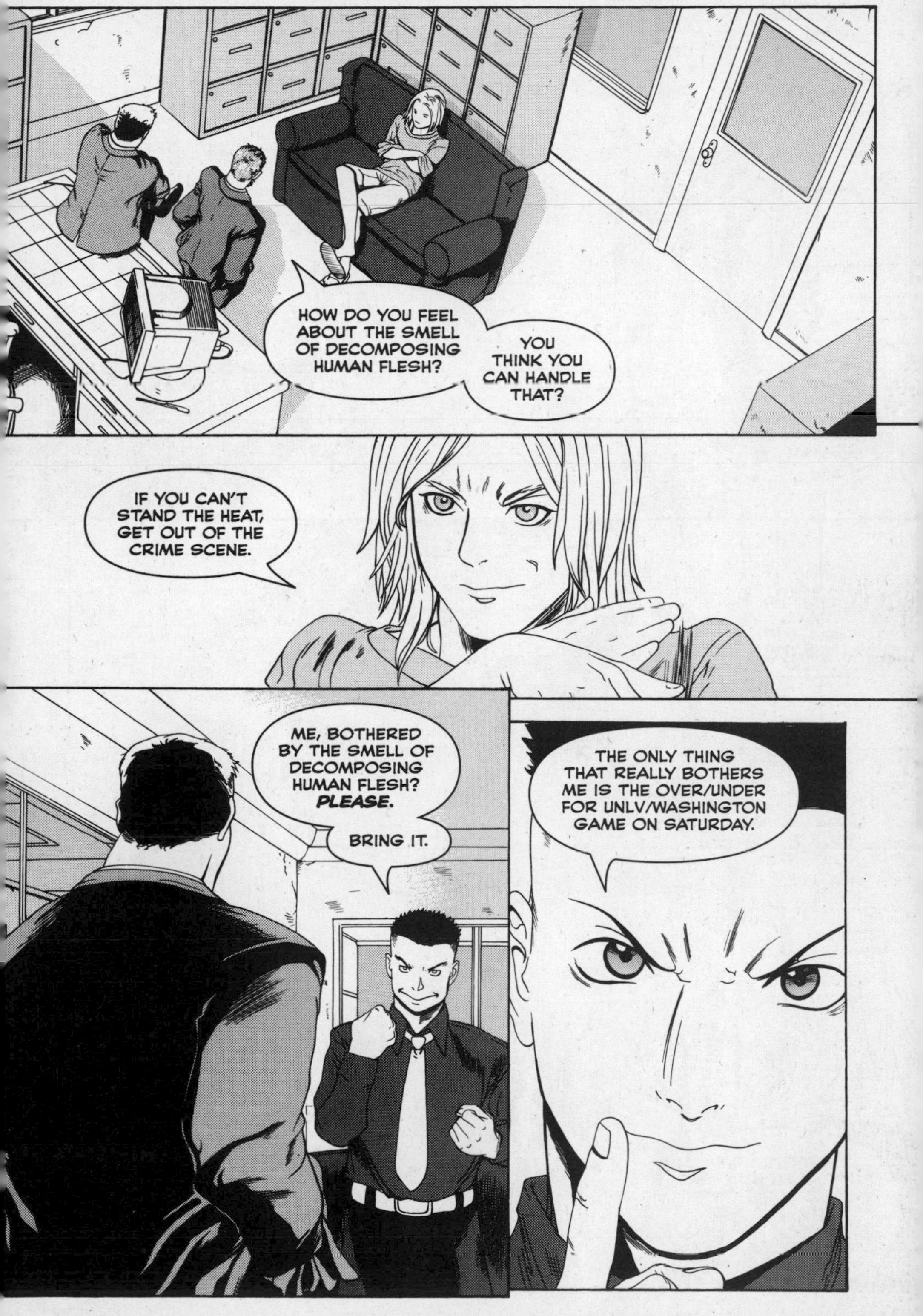
HOW DO YOU FEEL ABOUT THE SMELL OF DECOMPOSING HUMAN FLESH?
YOU THINK YOU CAN HANDLE THAT?
IF YOU CAN'T STAND THE HEAT, GET OUT OF THE CRIME SCENE.
ME, BOTHERED BY THE SMELL OF DECOMPOSING HUMAN FLESH? *PLEASE.*
BRING IT.
THE ONLY THING THAT REALLY BOTHERS ME IS THE OVER/UNDER FOR UNLV/WASHINGTON GAME ON SATURDAY.

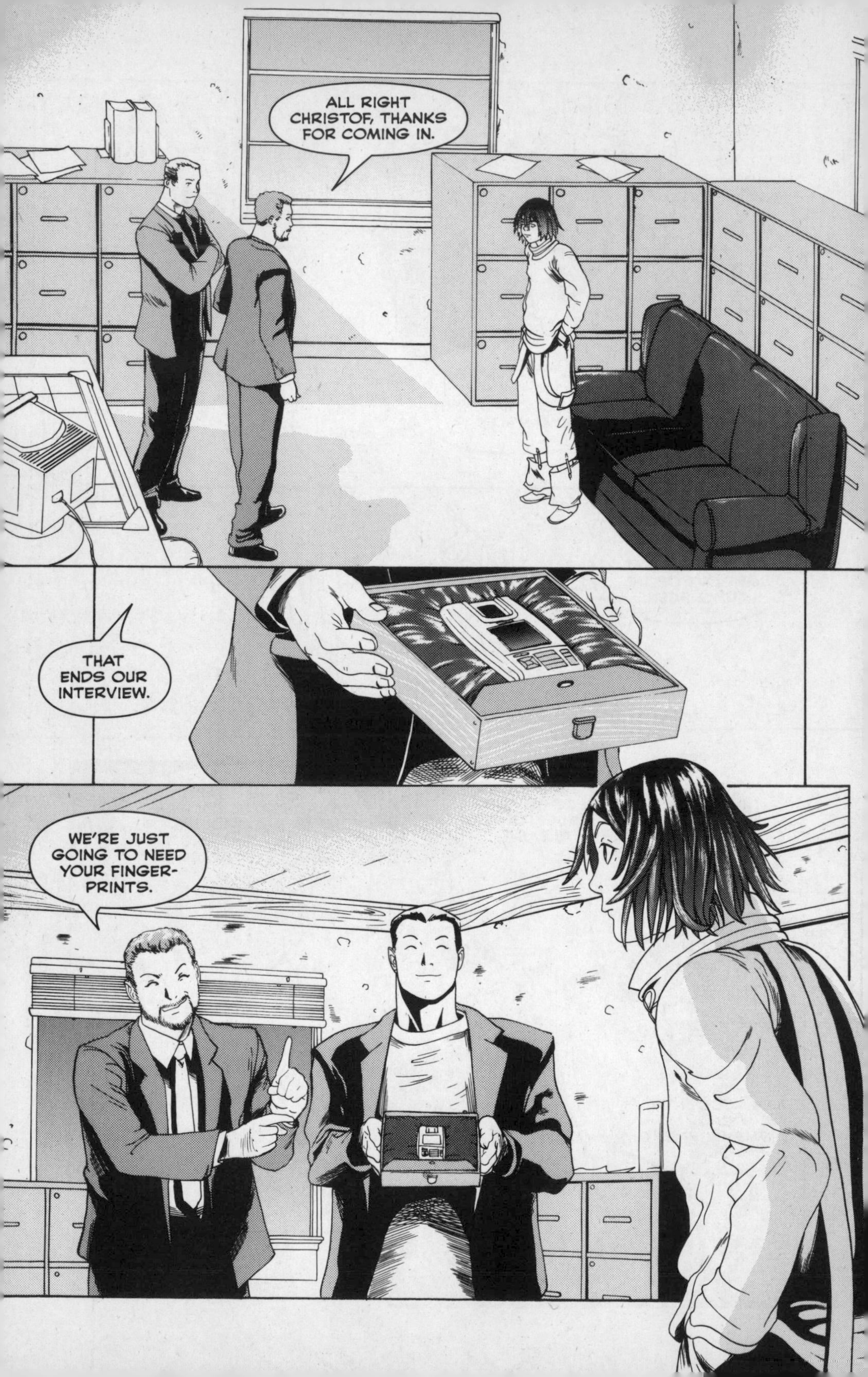
ALL RIGHT CHRISTOF, THANKS FOR COMING IN.
THAT ENDS OUR INTERVIEW.
WE'RE JUST GOING TO NEED YOUR FINGER-PRINTS.

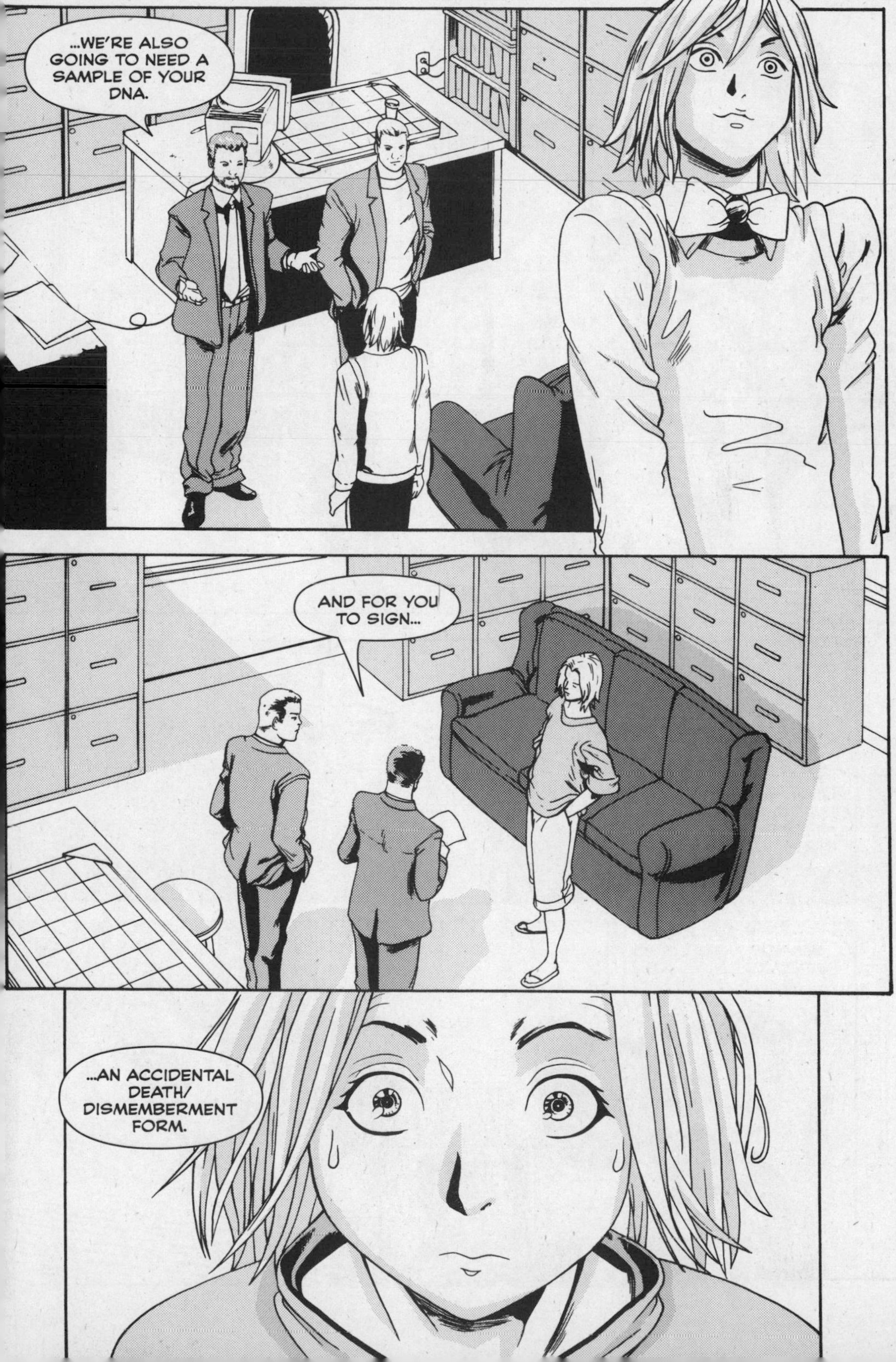
...WE'RE ALSO GOING TO NEED A SAMPLE OF YOUR DNA.
AND FOR YOU TO SIGN...
...AN ACCIDENTAL DEATH/ DISMEMBERMENT FORM.

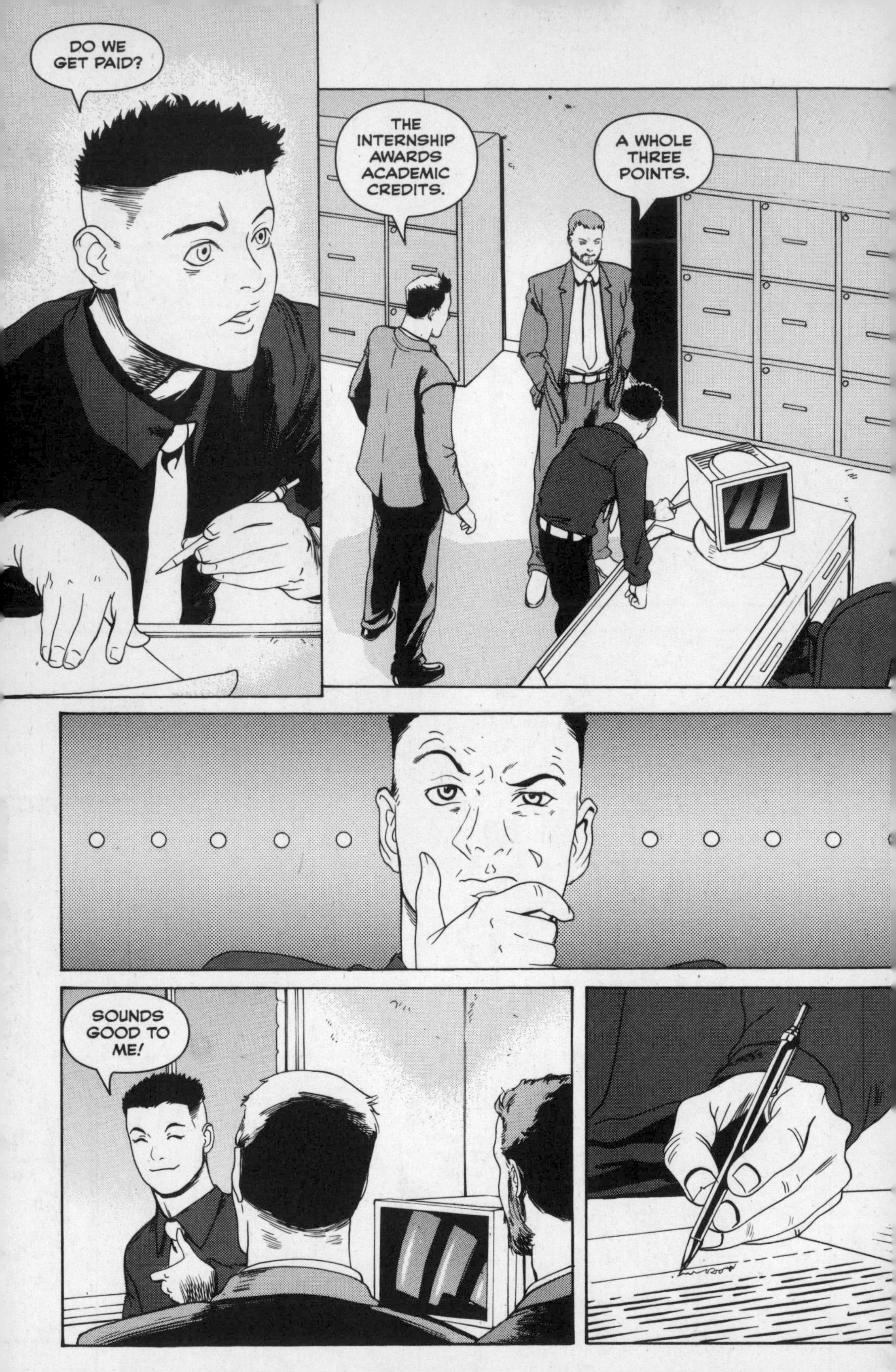
DO WE GET PAID?
THE INTERNSHIP AWARDS ACADEMIC CREDITS.
A WHOLE THREE POINTS.
SOUNDS GOOD TO ME!

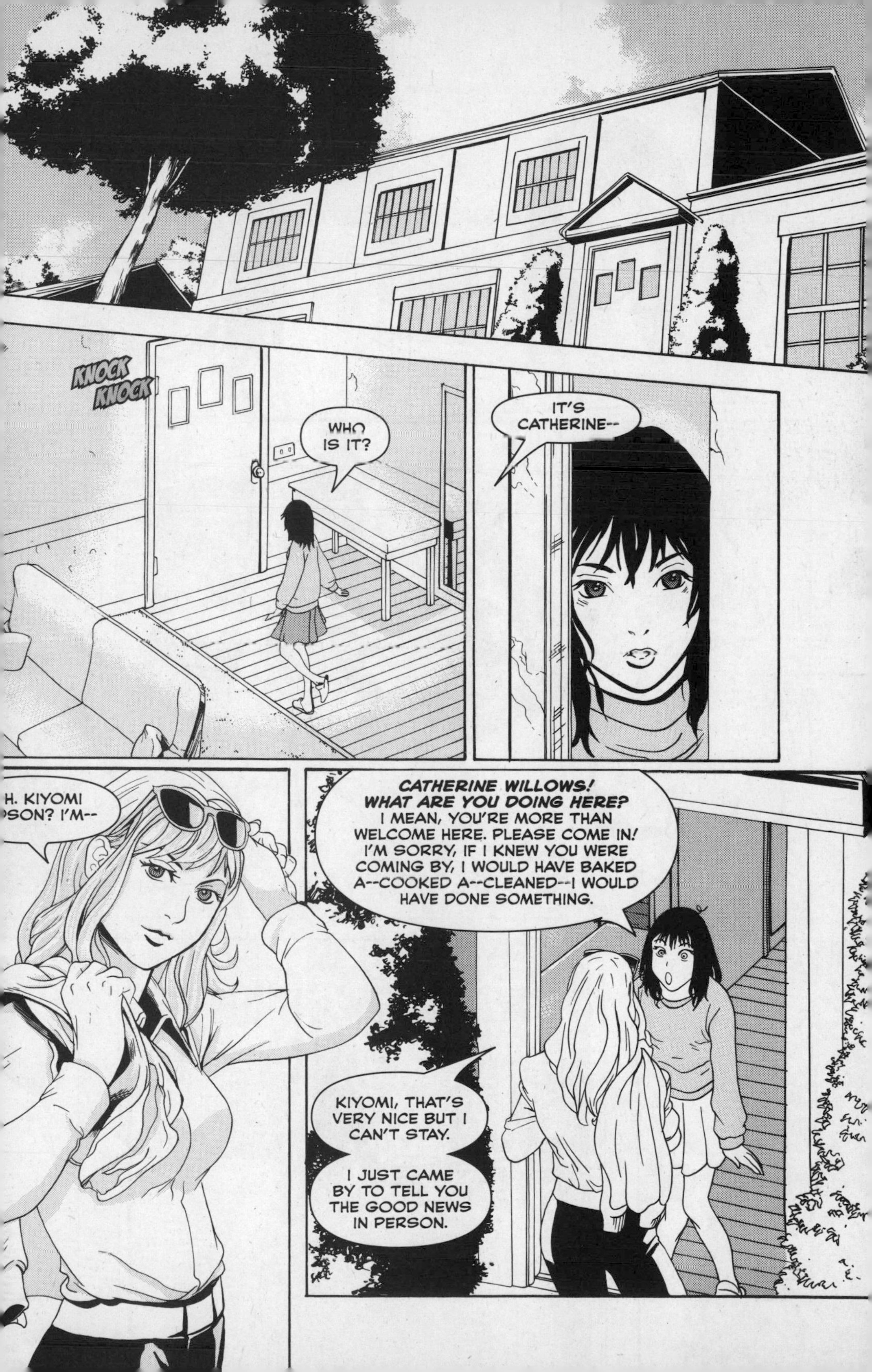

KNOCK KNOCK
WHO IS IT?
IT'S CATHERINE--
H. KIYOMI PSON? I'M--
CATHERINE WILLOWS! WHAT ARE YOU DOING HERE? I MEAN, YOU'RE MORE THAN WELCOME HERE. PLEASE COME IN! I'M SORRY, IF I KNEW YOU WERE COMING BY, I WOULD HAVE BAKED A--COOKED A--CLEANED--I WOULD HAVE DONE SOMETHING.
KIYOMI, THAT'S VERY NICE BUT I CAN'T STAY.
I JUST CAME BY TO TELL YOU THE GOOD NEWS IN PERSON.

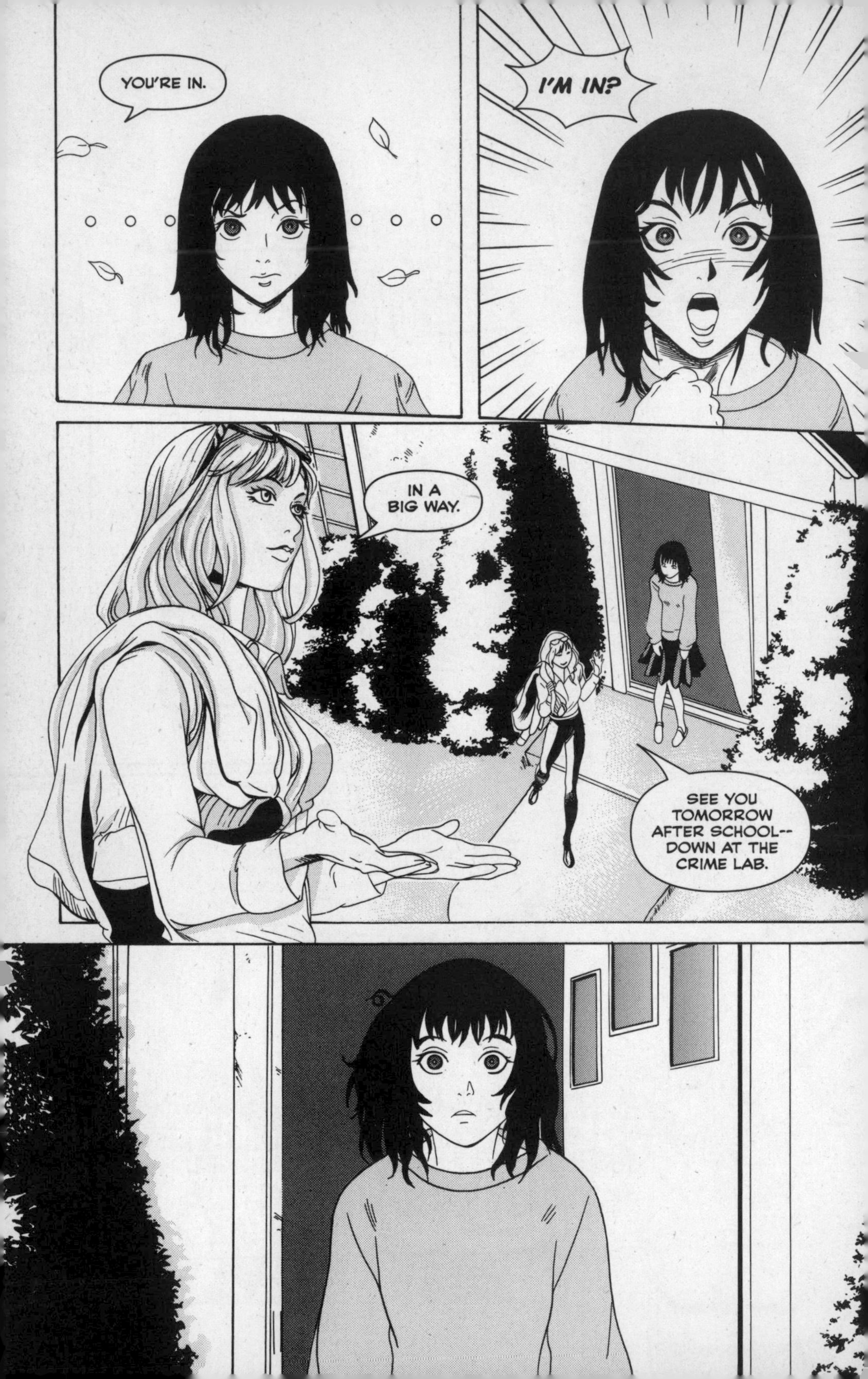
YOU'RE IN.
I'M IN?
IN A BIG WAY.
SEE YOU TOMORROW AFTER SCHOOL-- DOWN AT THE CRIME LAB.

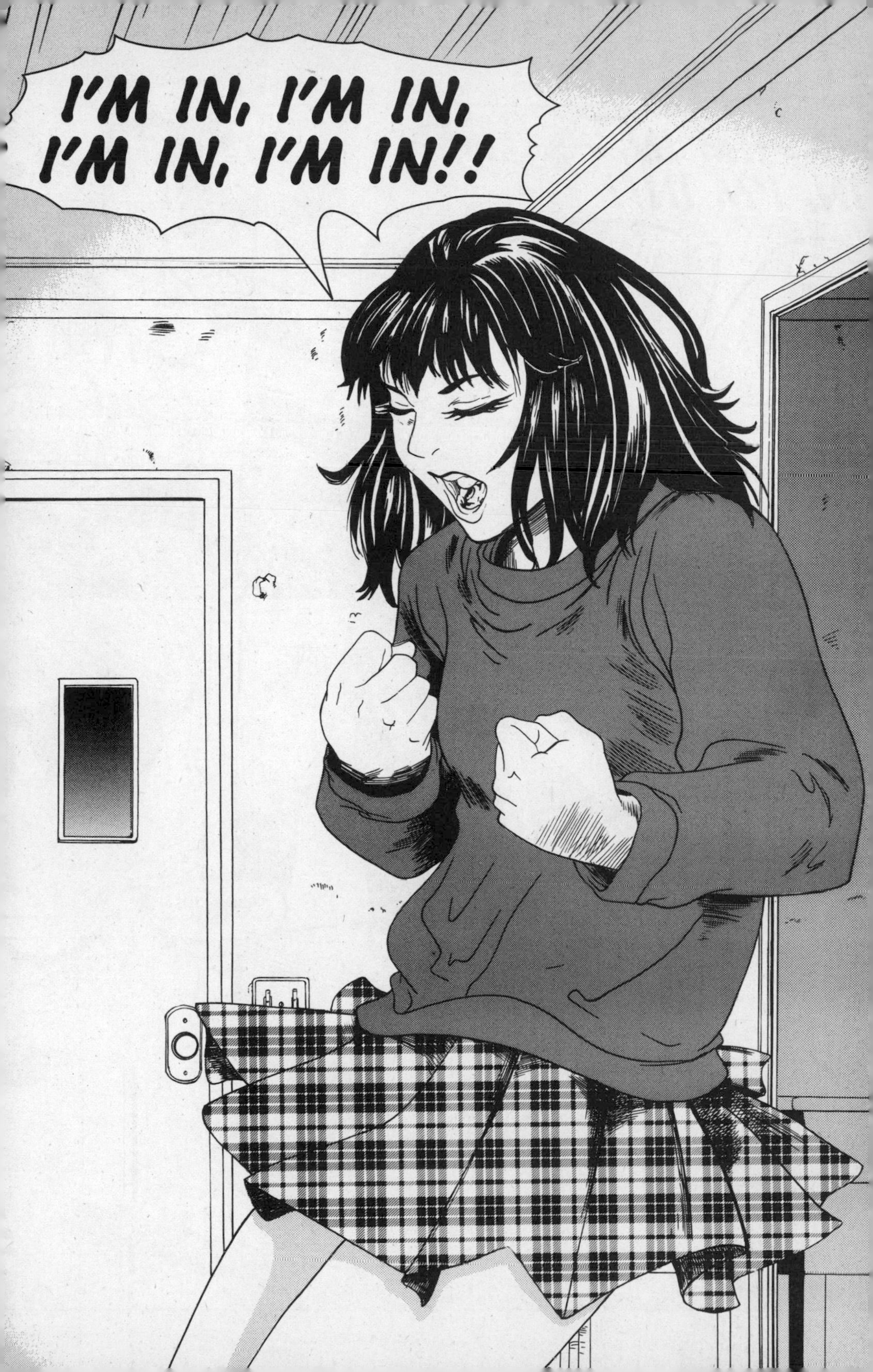
I'M IN, I'M IN, I'M IN, I'M IN!!

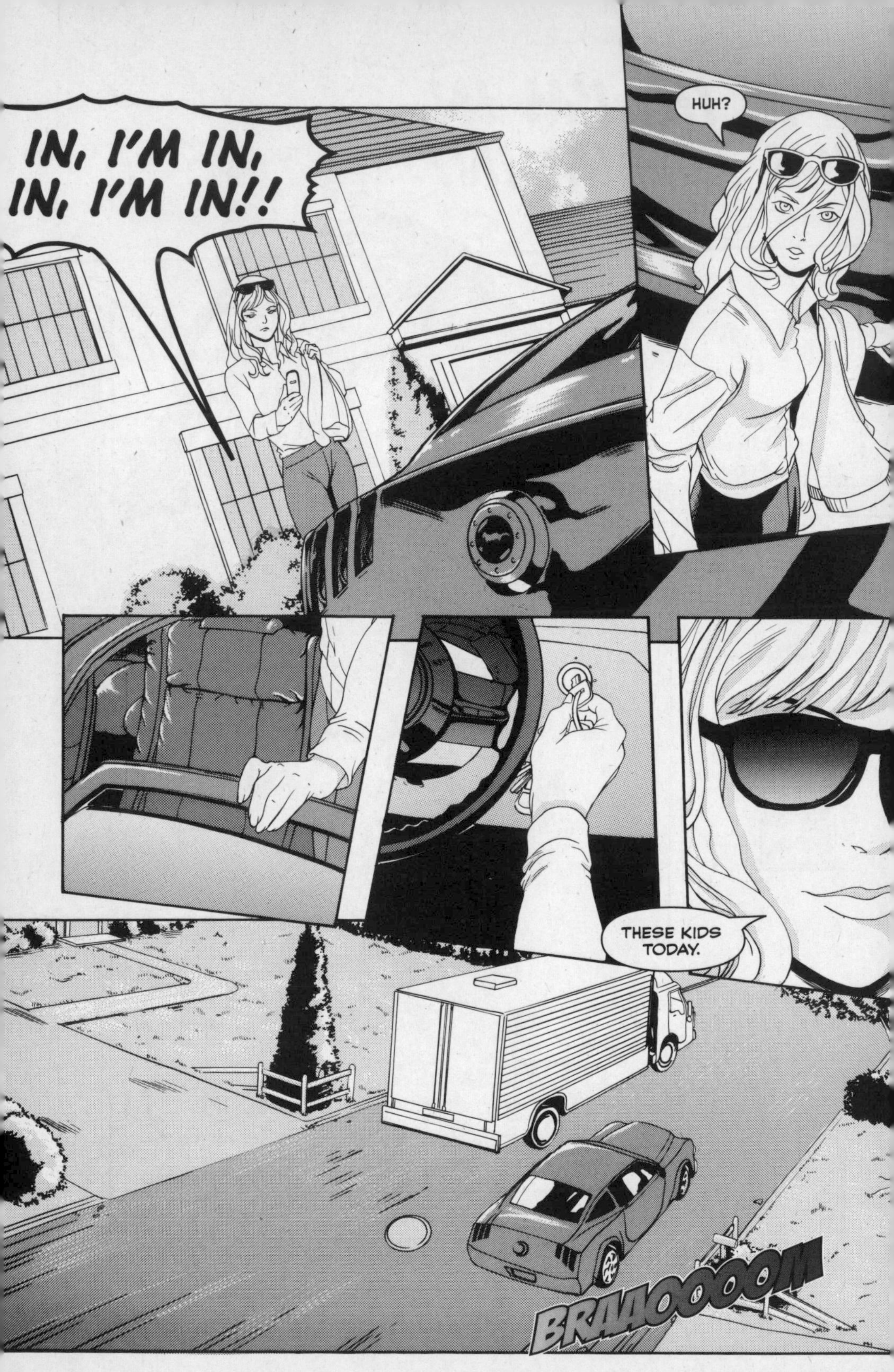
IN, I'M IN,
IN, I'M IN!!
HUH?
THESE KIDS TODAY.
BRAAOOOOM

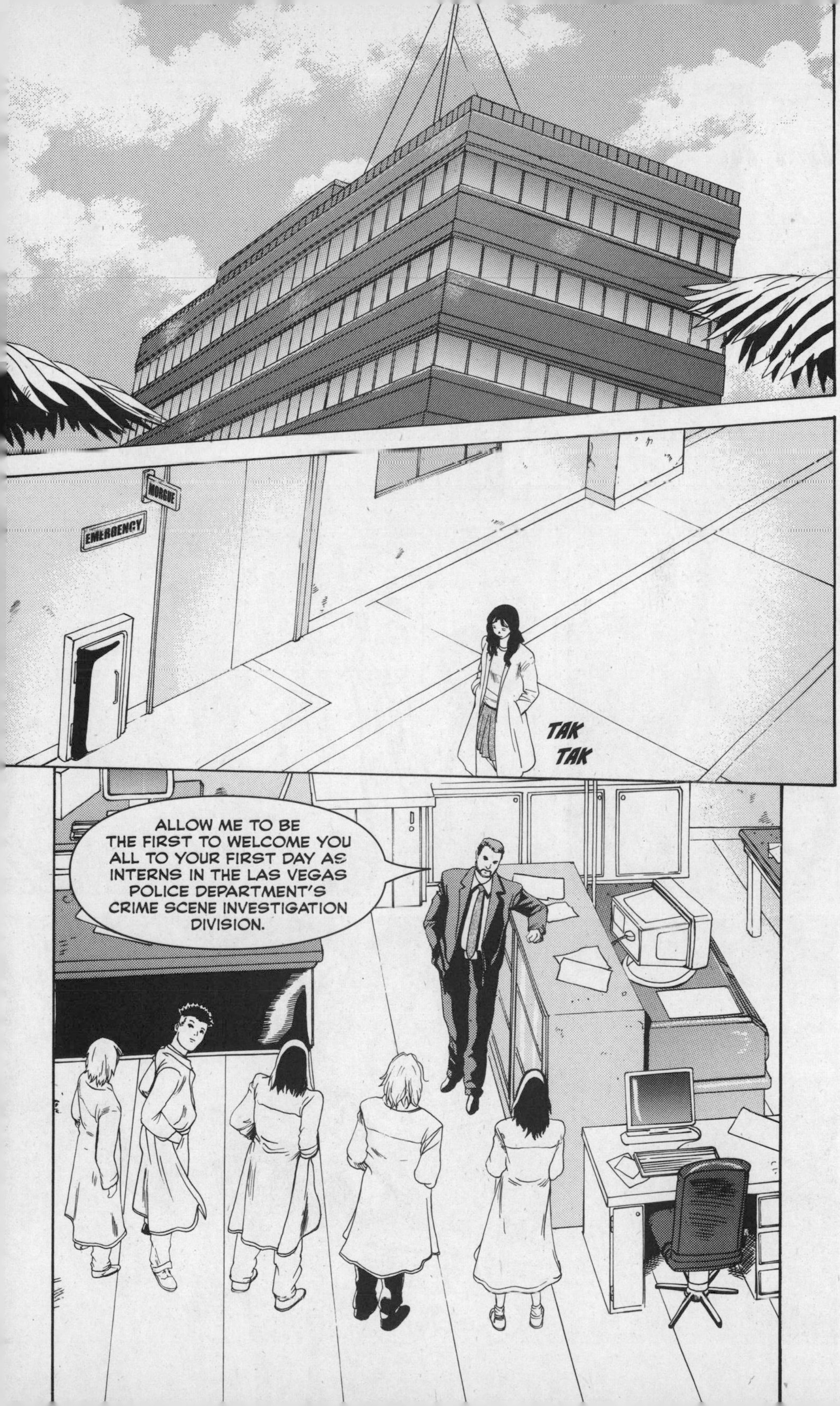

MORGUE
EMERGENCY
TAK TAK
ALLOW ME TO BE THE FIRST TO WELCOME YOU ALL TO YOUR FIRST DAY AS INTERNS IN THE LAS VEGAS POLICE DEPARTMENT'S CRIME SCENE INVESTIGATION DIVISION.

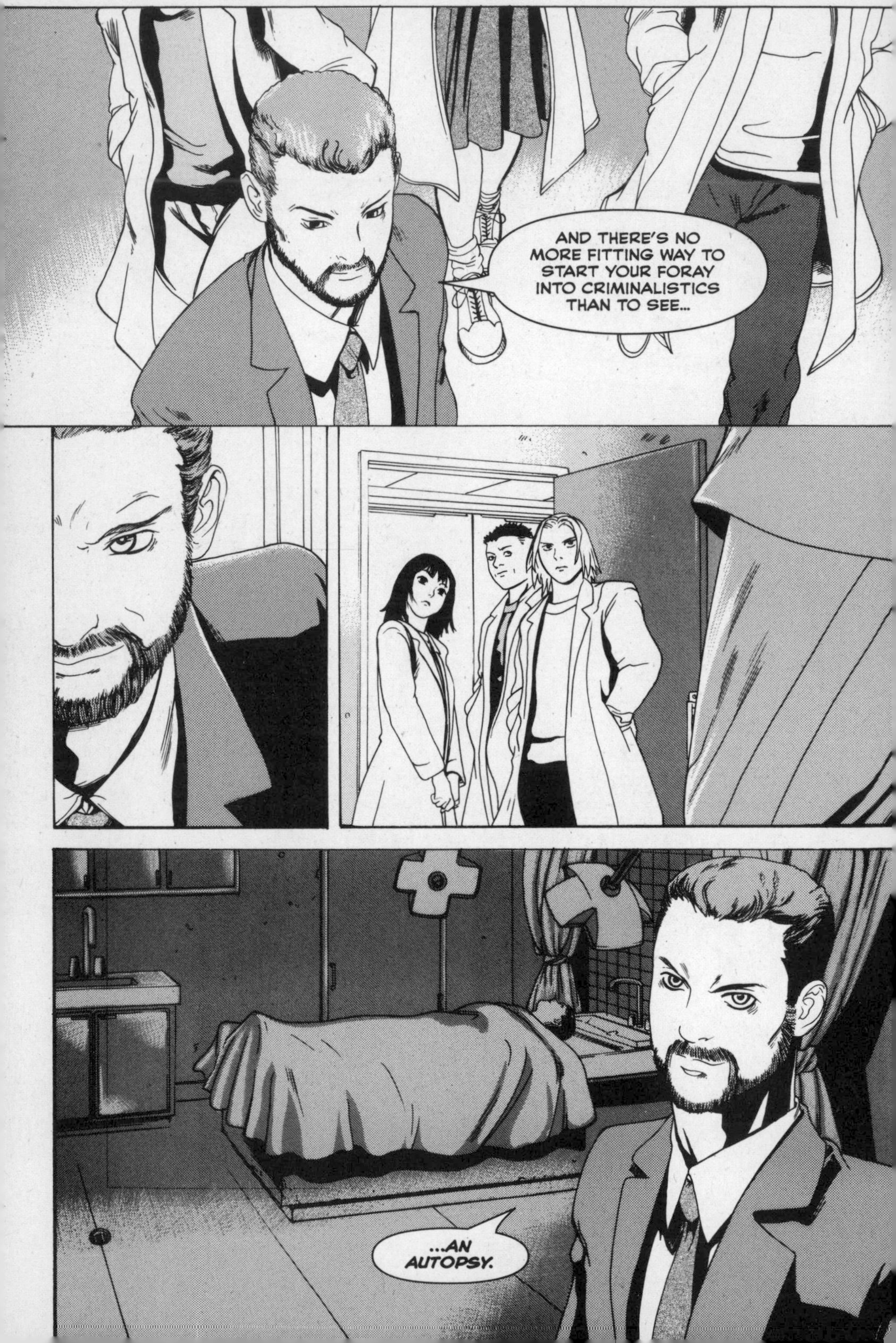
AND THERE'S NO MORE FITTING WAY TO START YOUR FORAY INTO CRIMINALISTICS THAN TO SEE...
...AN AUTOPSY.

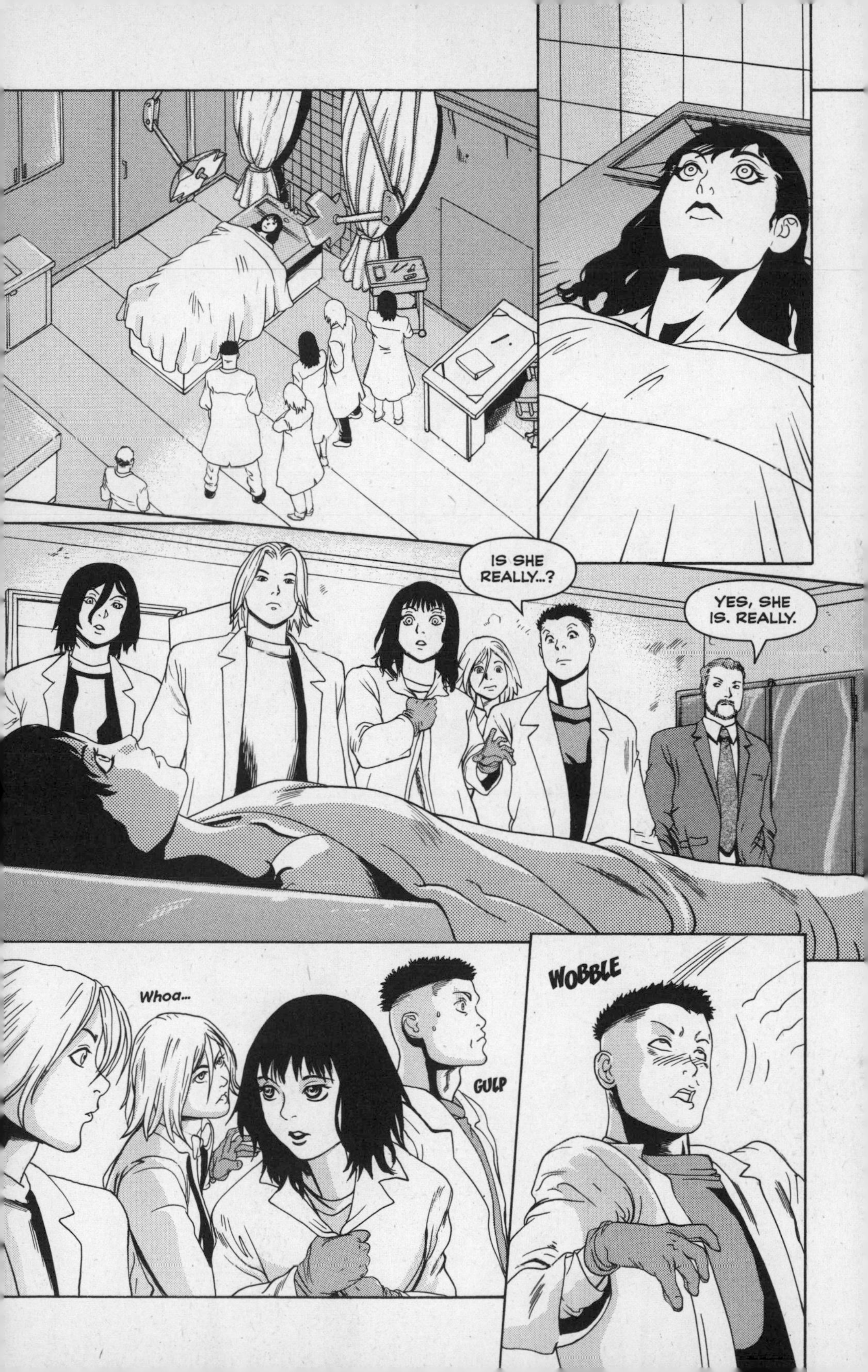
IS SHE REALLY...?
YES, SHE IS. REALLY.
Whoa...
GULP
WOBBLE

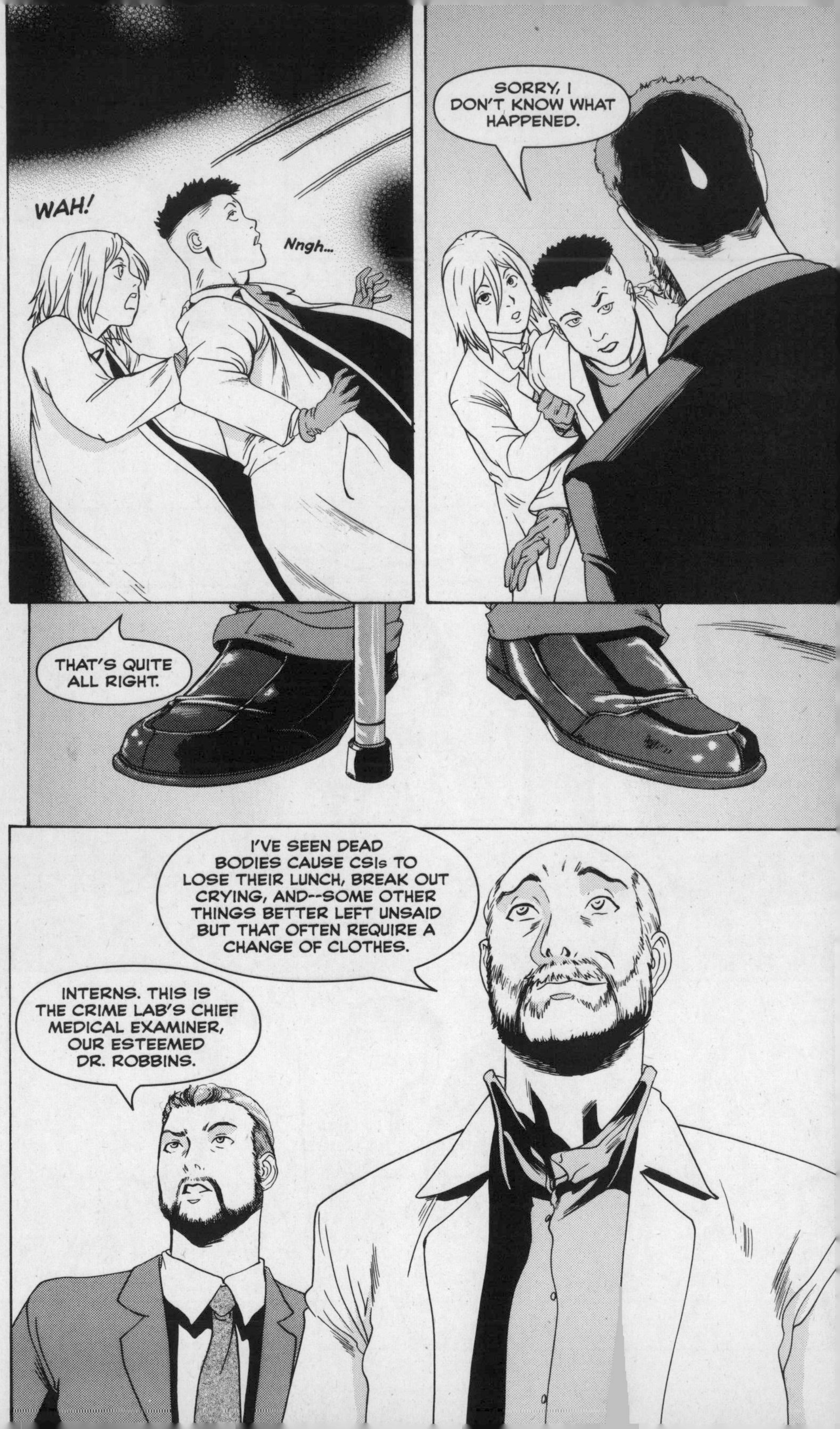
WAH!
Nngh...
SORRY, I DON'T KNOW WHAT HAPPENED.
THAT'S QUITE ALL RIGHT.
INTERNS. THIS IS THE CRIME LAB'S CHIEF MEDICAL EXAMINER, OUR ESTEEMED DR. ROBBINS.
I'VE SEEN DEAD BODIES CAUSE CSIs TO LOSE THEIR LUNCH, BREAK OUT CRYING, AND--SOME OTHER THINGS BETTER LEFT UNSAID BUT THAT OFTEN REQUIRE A CHANGE OF CLOTHES.

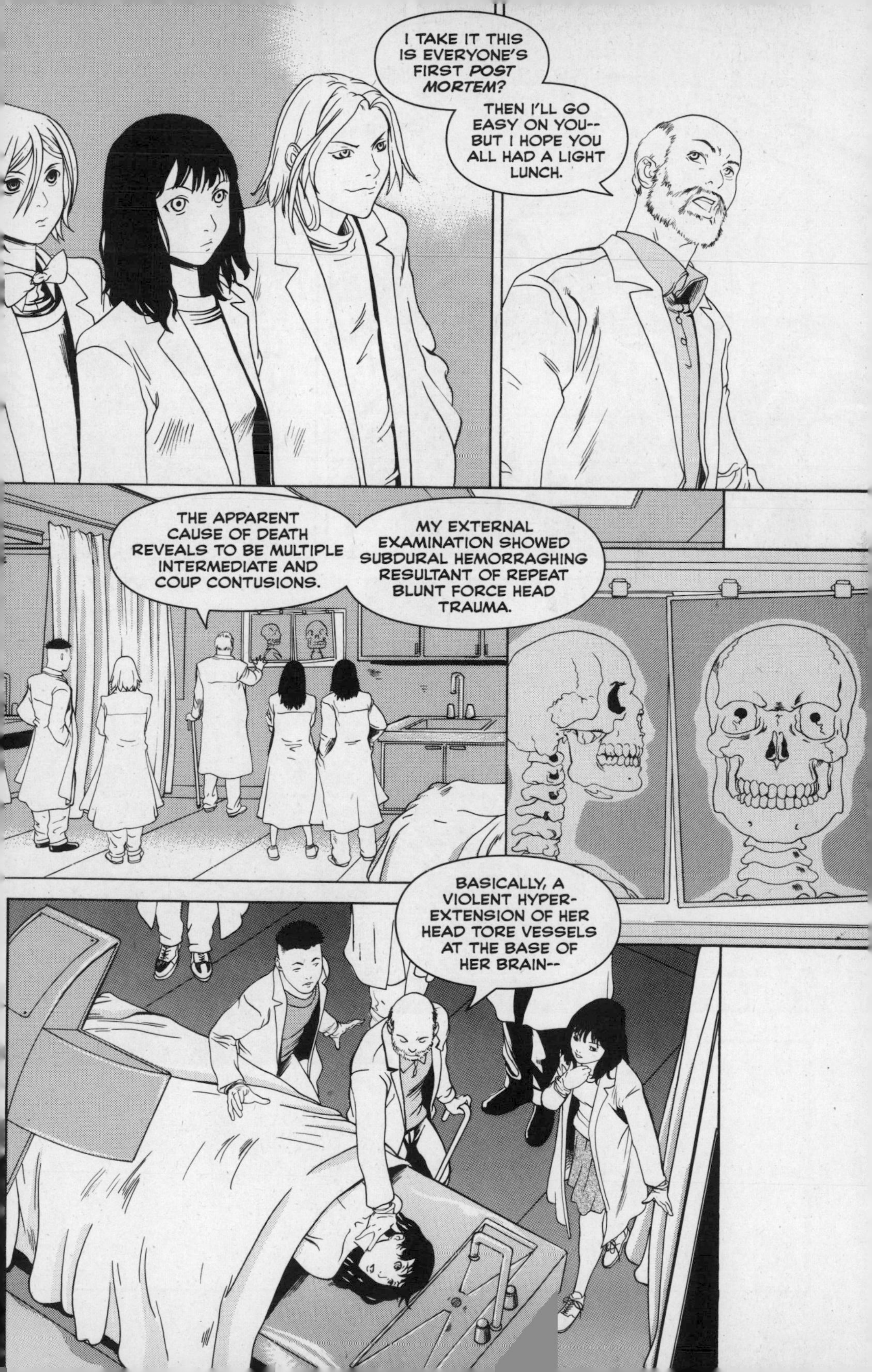
I TAKE IT THIS IS EVERYONE'S FIRST *POST MORTEM*?
THEN I'LL GO EASY ON YOU-- BUT I HOPE YOU ALL HAD A LIGHT LUNCH.
THE APPARENT CAUSE OF DEATH REVEALS TO BE MULTIPLE INTERMEDIATE AND COUP CONTUSIONS.
MY EXTERNAL EXAMINATION SHOWED SUBDURAL HEMORRAGHING RESULTANT OF REPEAT BLUNT FORCE HEAD TRAUMA.
BASICALLY, A VIOLENT HYPER-EXTENSION OF HER HEAD TORE VESSELS AT THE BASE OF HER BRAIN--

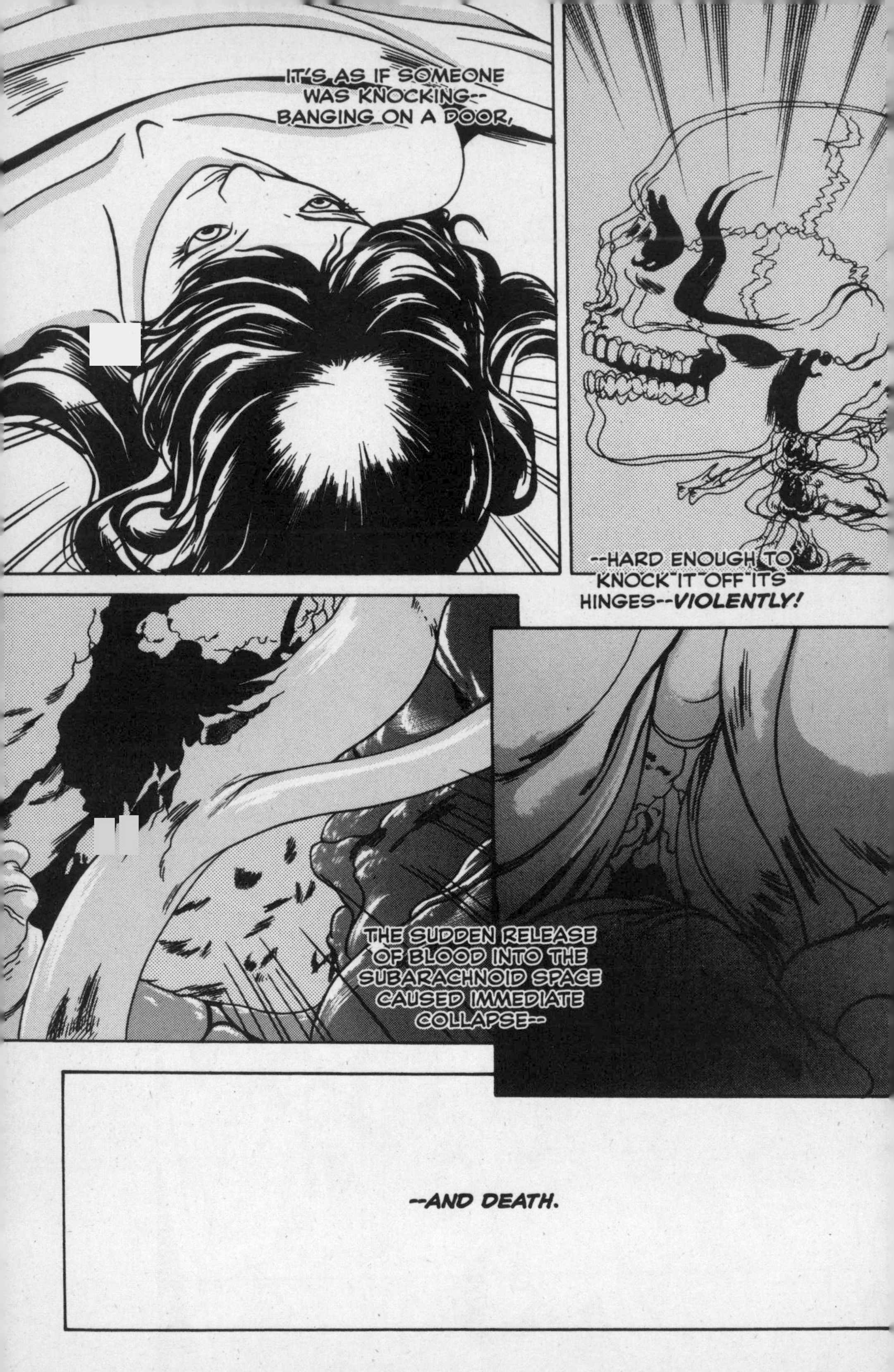
IT'S AS IF SOMEONE WAS KNOCKING-- BANGING ON A DOOR,
--HARD ENOUGH TO KNOCK IT OFF ITS HINGES--VIOLENTLY!
THE SUDDEN RELEASE OF BLOOD INTO THE SUBARACHNOID SPACE CAUSED IMMEDIATE COLLAPSE--
--AND DEATH.

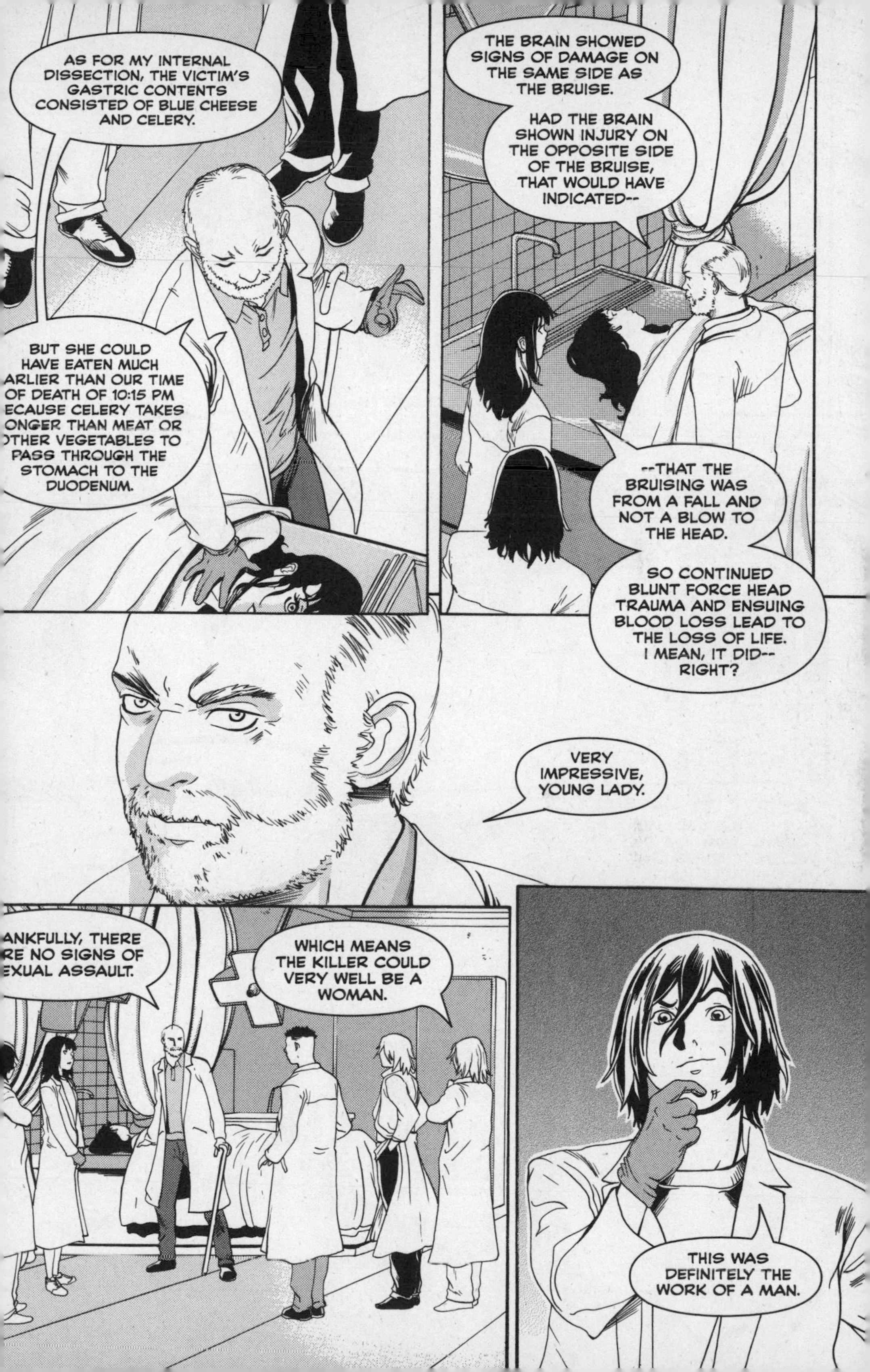
AS FOR MY INTERNAL DISSECTION, THE VICTIM'S GASTRIC CONTENTS CONSISTED OF BLUE CHEESE AND CELERY.
BUT SHE COULD HAVE EATEN MUCH ARLIER THAN OUR TIME OF DEATH OF 10:15 PM ECAUSE CELERY TAKES ONGER THAN MEAT OR OTHER VEGETABLES TO PASS THROUGH THE STOMACH TO THE DUODENUM.
THE BRAIN SHOWED SIGNS OF DAMAGE ON THE SAME SIDE AS THE BRUISE.
HAD THE BRAIN SHOWN INJURY ON THE OPPOSITE SIDE OF THE BRUISE, THAT WOULD HAVE INDICATED--
--THAT THE BRUISING WAS FROM A FALL AND NOT A BLOW TO THE HEAD.
SO CONTINUED BLUNT FORCE HEAD TRAUMA AND ENSUING BLOOD LOSS LEAD TO THE LOSS OF LIFE. I MEAN, IT DID-- RIGHT?
VERY IMPRESSIVE, YOUNG LADY.
ANKFULLY, THERE RE NO SIGNS OF EXUAL ASSAULT.
WHICH MEANS THE KILLER COULD VERY WELL BE A WOMAN.
THIS WAS DEFINITELY THE WORK OF A MAN.

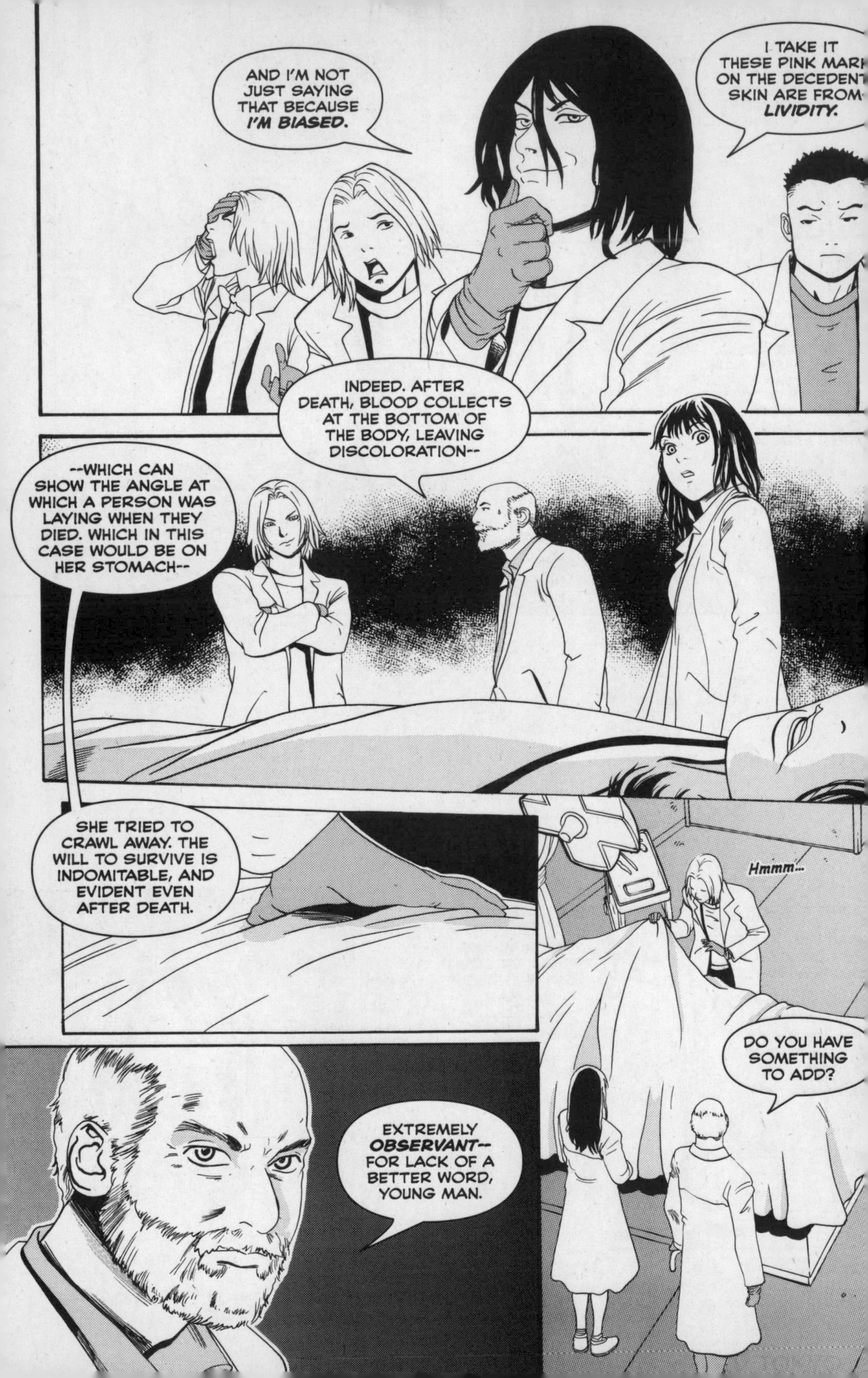
AND I'M NOT JUST SAYING THAT BECAUSE *I'M BIASED.*
I TAKE IT THESE PINK MARK ON THE DECEDENT SKIN ARE FROM *LIVIDITY.*
INDEED. AFTER DEATH, BLOOD COLLECTS AT THE BOTTOM OF THE BODY, LEAVING DISCOLORATION--
--WHICH CAN SHOW THE ANGLE AT WHICH A PERSON WAS LAYING WHEN THEY DIED. WHICH IN THIS CASE WOULD BE ON HER STOMACH--
SHE TRIED TO CRAWL AWAY. THE WILL TO SURVIVE IS INDOMITABLE, AND EVIDENT EVEN AFTER DEATH.
Hmmm...
DO YOU HAVE SOMETHING TO ADD?
EXTREMELY *OBSERVANT*-- FOR LACK OF A BETTER WORD, YOUNG MAN.

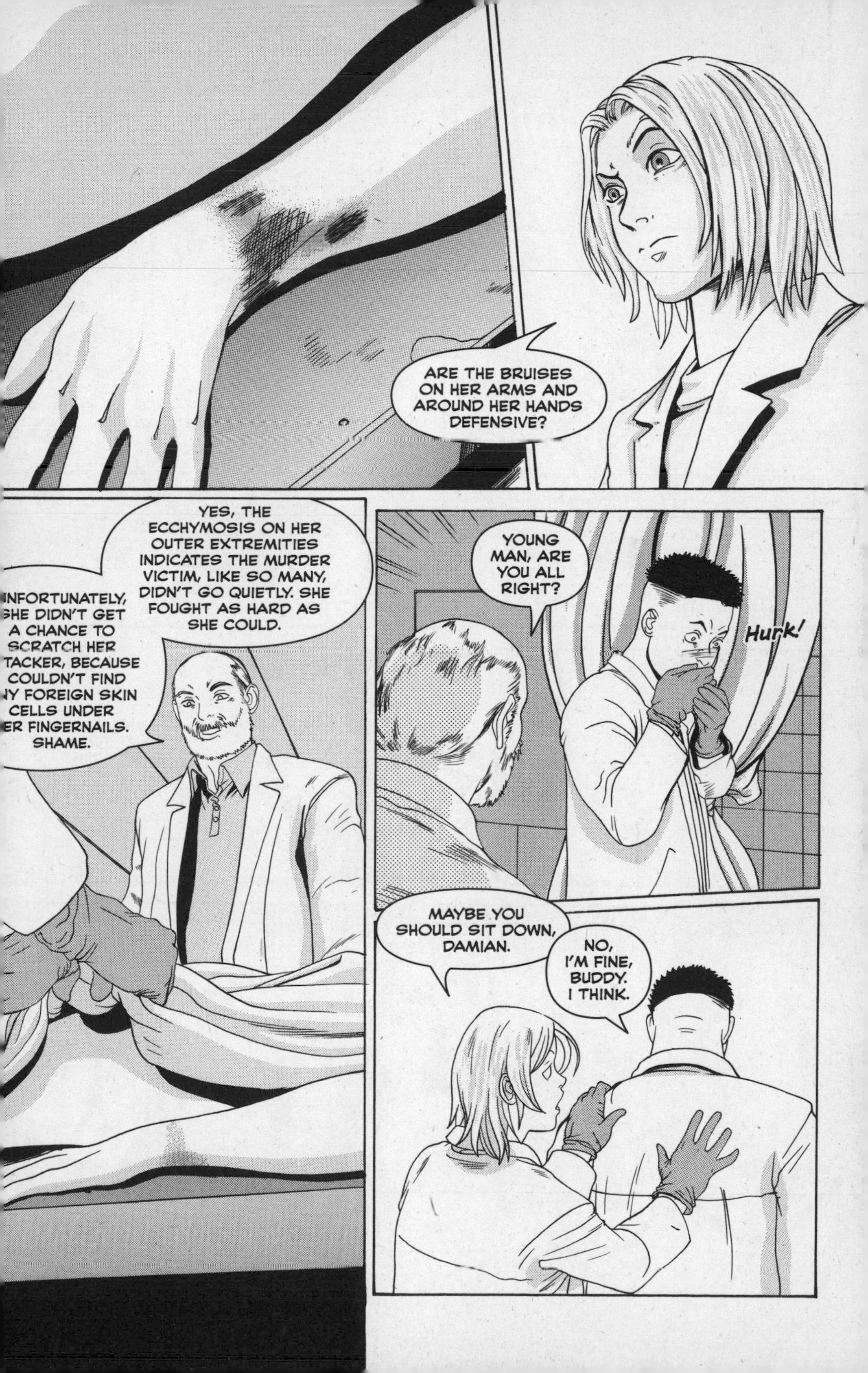

ARE THE BRUISES ON HER ARMS AND AROUND HER HANDS DEFENSIVE?
YES, THE ECCHYMOSIS ON HER OUTER EXTREMITIES INDICATES THE MURDER VICTIM, LIKE SO MANY, DIDN'T GO QUIETLY. SHE FOUGHT AS HARD AS SHE COULD.
NFORTUNATELY, HE DIDN'T GET A CHANCE TO SCRATCH HER TACKER, BECAUSE COULDN'T FIND NY FOREIGN SKIN CELLS UNDER ER FINGERNAILS. SHAME.
YOUNG MAN, ARE YOU ALL RIGHT?
Hurk!
MAYBE YOU SHOULD SIT DOWN, DAMIAN.
NO, I'M FINE, BUDDY. I THINK.

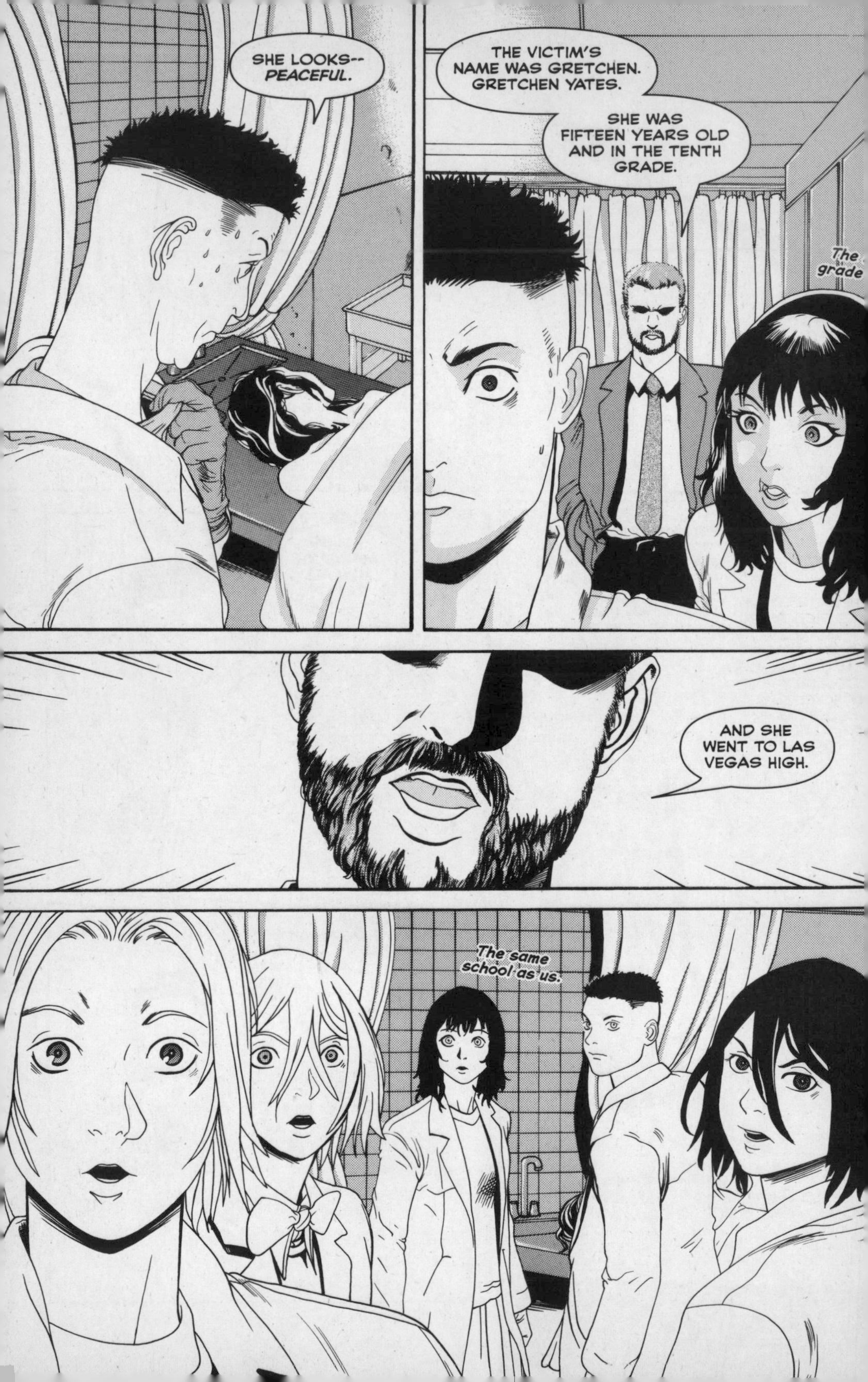
SHE LOOKS-- PEACEFUL.
THE VICTIM'S NAME WAS GRETCHEN. GRETCHEN YATES.
SHE WAS FIFTEEN YEARS OLD AND IN THE TENTH GRADE.
AND SHE WENT TO LAS VEGAS HIGH.
The same school as us.

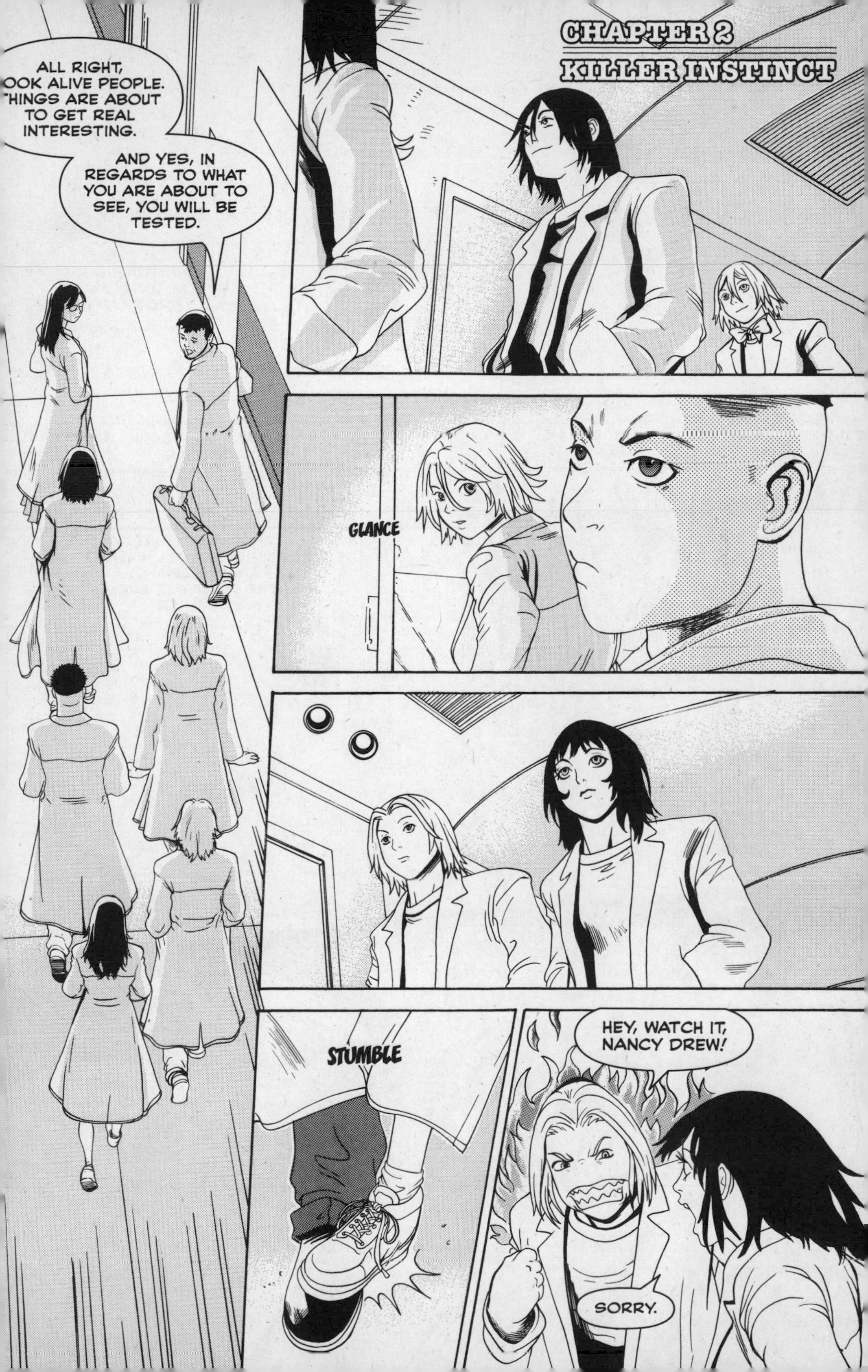
CHAPTER 2
KILLER INSTINCT
ALL RIGHT, LOOK ALIVE PEOPLE. THINGS ARE ABOUT TO GET REAL INTERESTING.
AND YES, IN REGARDS TO WHAT YOU ARE ABOUT TO SEE, YOU WILL BE TESTED.
GLANCE
STUMBLE
HEY, WATCH IT, NANCY DREW!
SORRY.

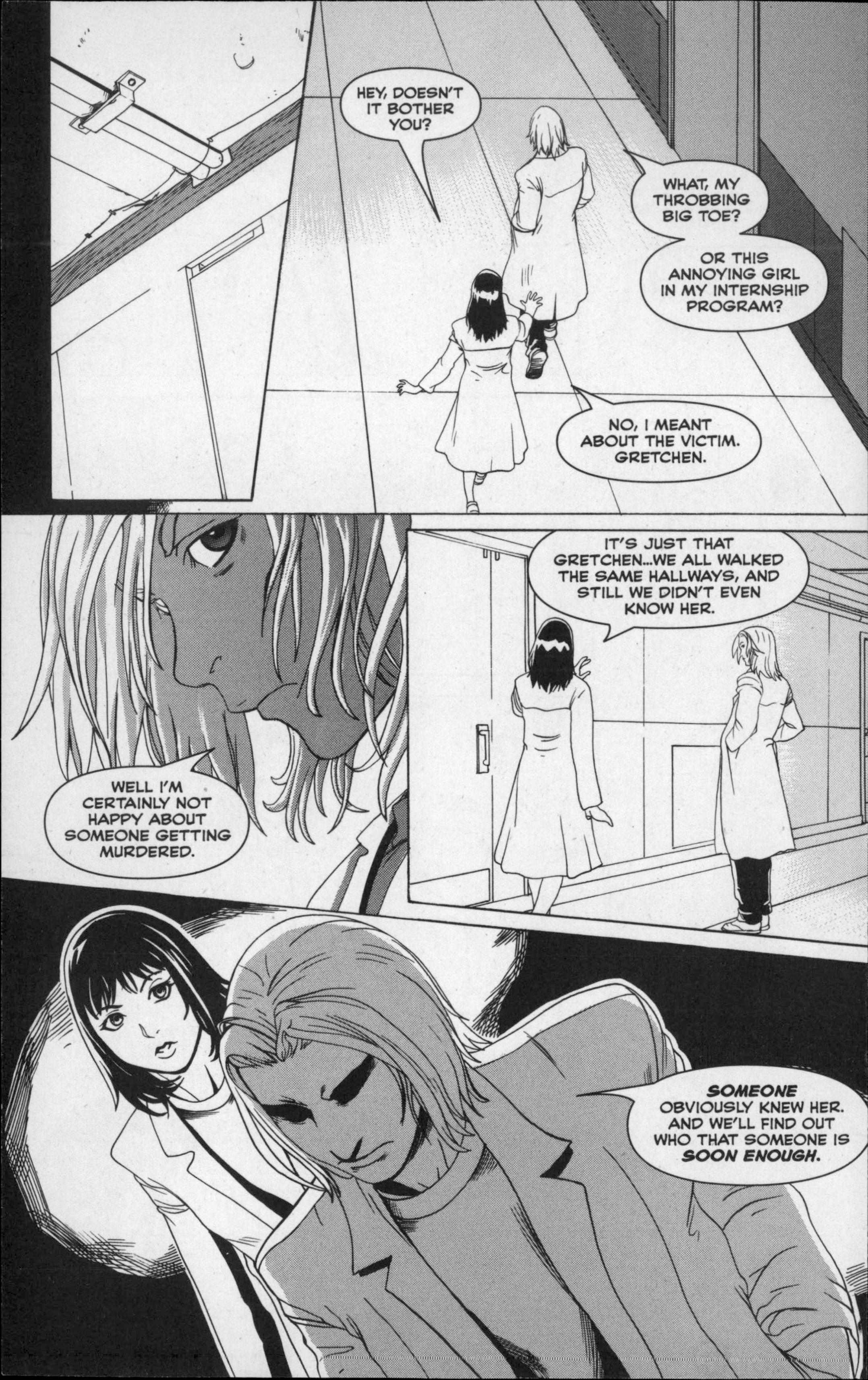
HEY, DOESN'T IT BOTHER YOU?
WHAT, MY THROBBING BIG TOE?
OR THIS ANNOYING GIRL IN MY INTERNSHIP PROGRAM?
NO, I MEANT ABOUT THE VICTIM. GRETCHEN.
WELL I'M CERTAINLY NOT HAPPY ABOUT SOMEONE GETTING MURDERED.
IT'S JUST THAT GRETCHEN...WE ALL WALKED THE SAME HALLWAYS, AND STILL WE DIDN'T EVEN KNOW HER.
SOMEONE OBVIOUSLY KNEW HER. AND WE'LL FIND OUT WHO THAT SOMEONE IS SOON ENOUGH.

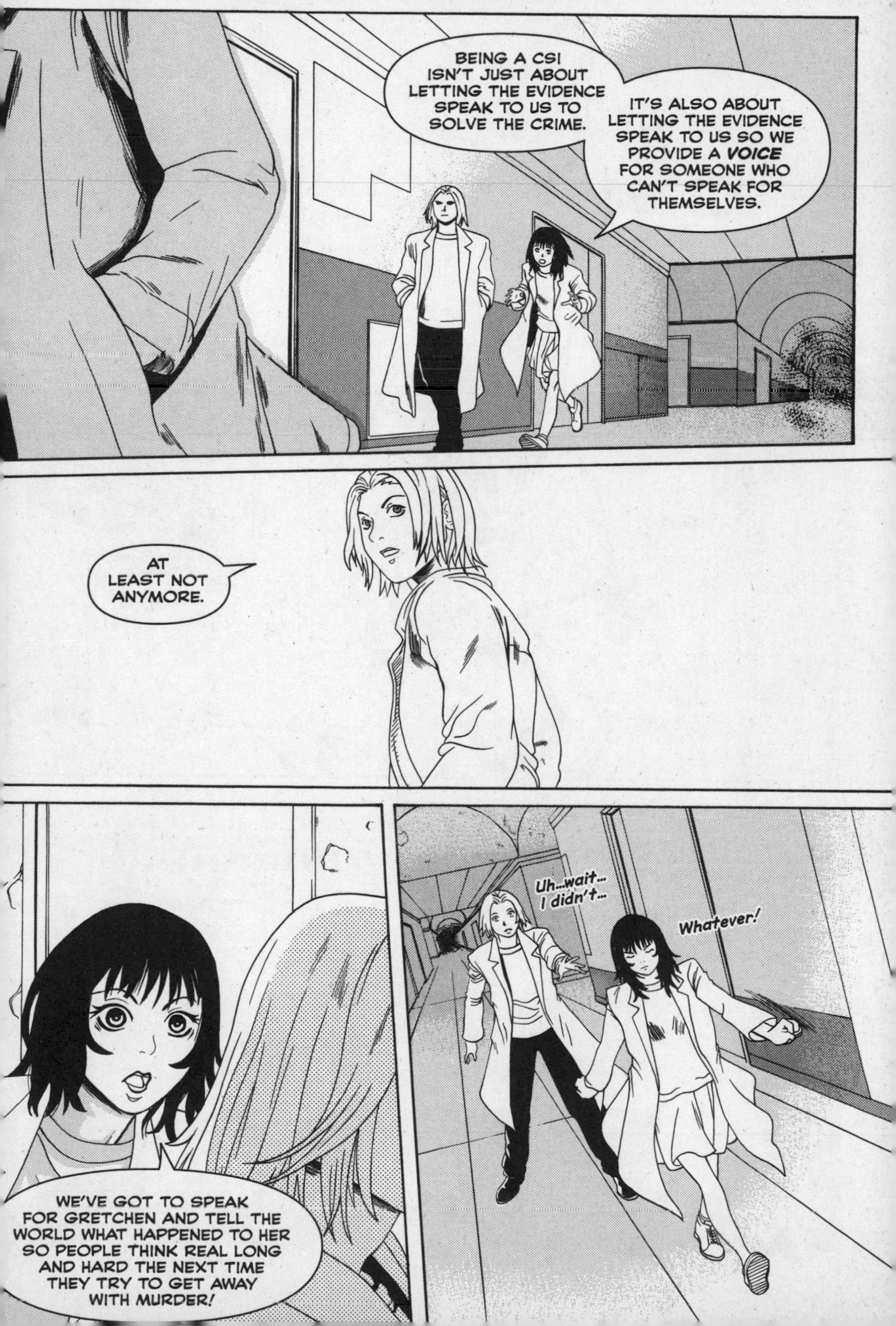
BEING A CSI ISN'T JUST ABOUT LETTING THE EVIDENCE SPEAK TO US TO SOLVE THE CRIME.
IT'S ALSO ABOUT LETTING THE EVIDENCE SPEAK TO US SO WE PROVIDE A *VOICE* FOR SOMEONE WHO CAN'T SPEAK FOR THEMSELVES.
AT LEAST NOT ANYMORE.
WE'VE GOT TO SPEAK FOR GRETCHEN AND TELL THE WORLD WHAT HAPPENED TO HER SO PEOPLE THINK REAL LONG AND HARD THE NEXT TIME THEY TRY TO GET AWAY WITH MURDER!
Uh...wait... I didn't...
Whatever!

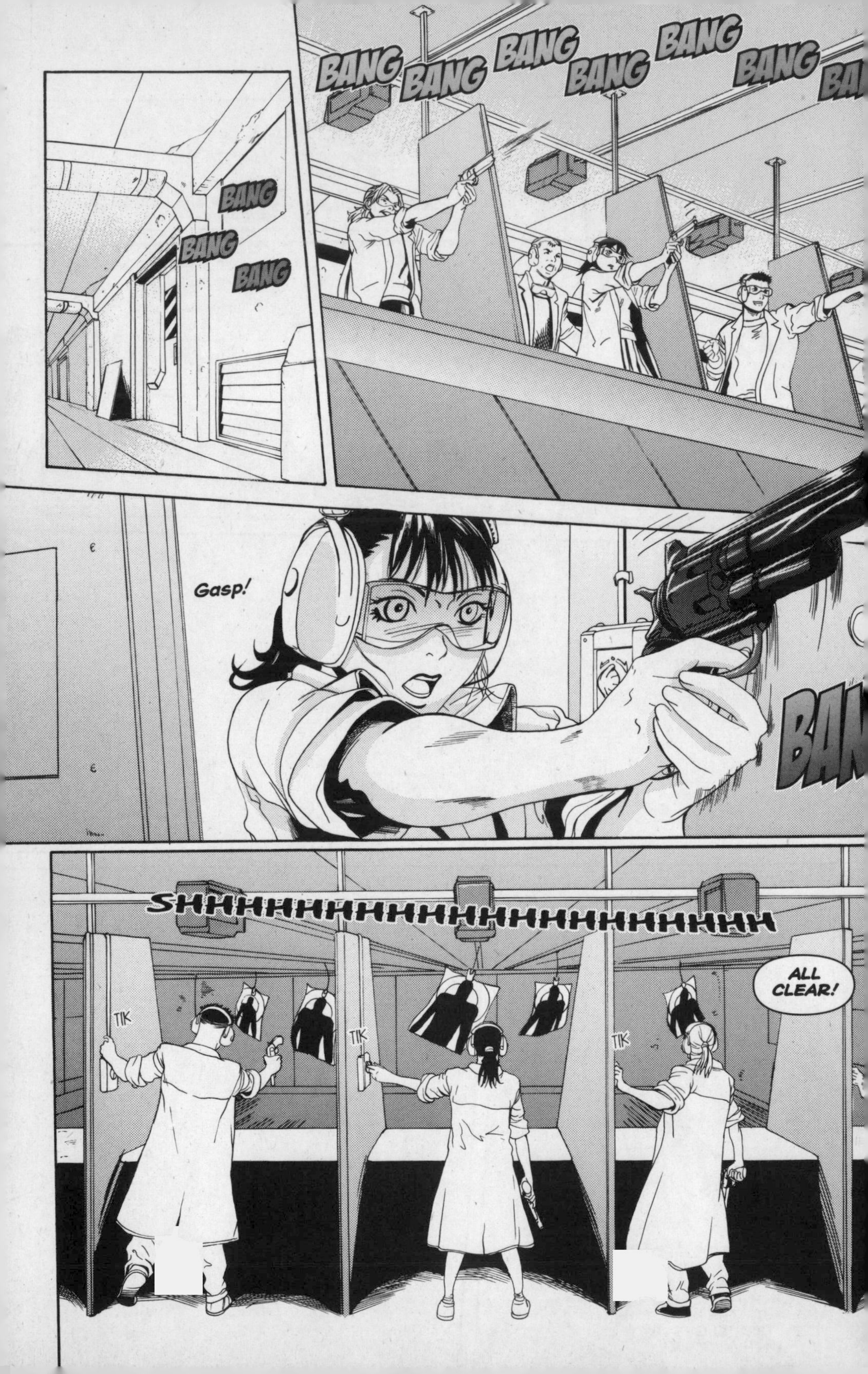
BANG
BANG
BANG
BANG
BANG
BANG
BANG
BANG
BANG
Gasp!
SHHHHHHHHHHHHHHHHHHHHHHHH
TIK
TIK
TIK
ALL CLEAR!

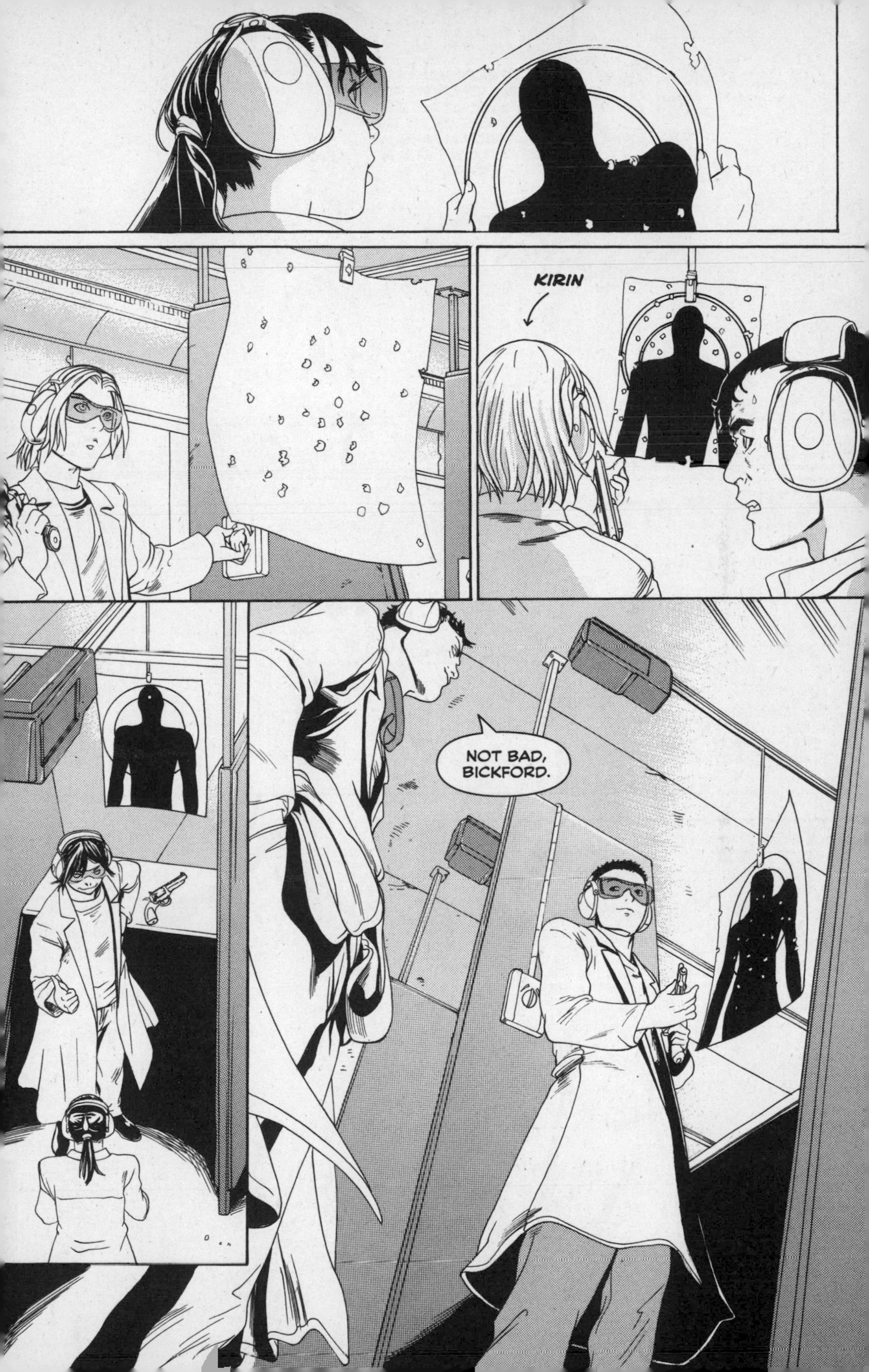
KIRIN
NOT BAD, BICKFORD.

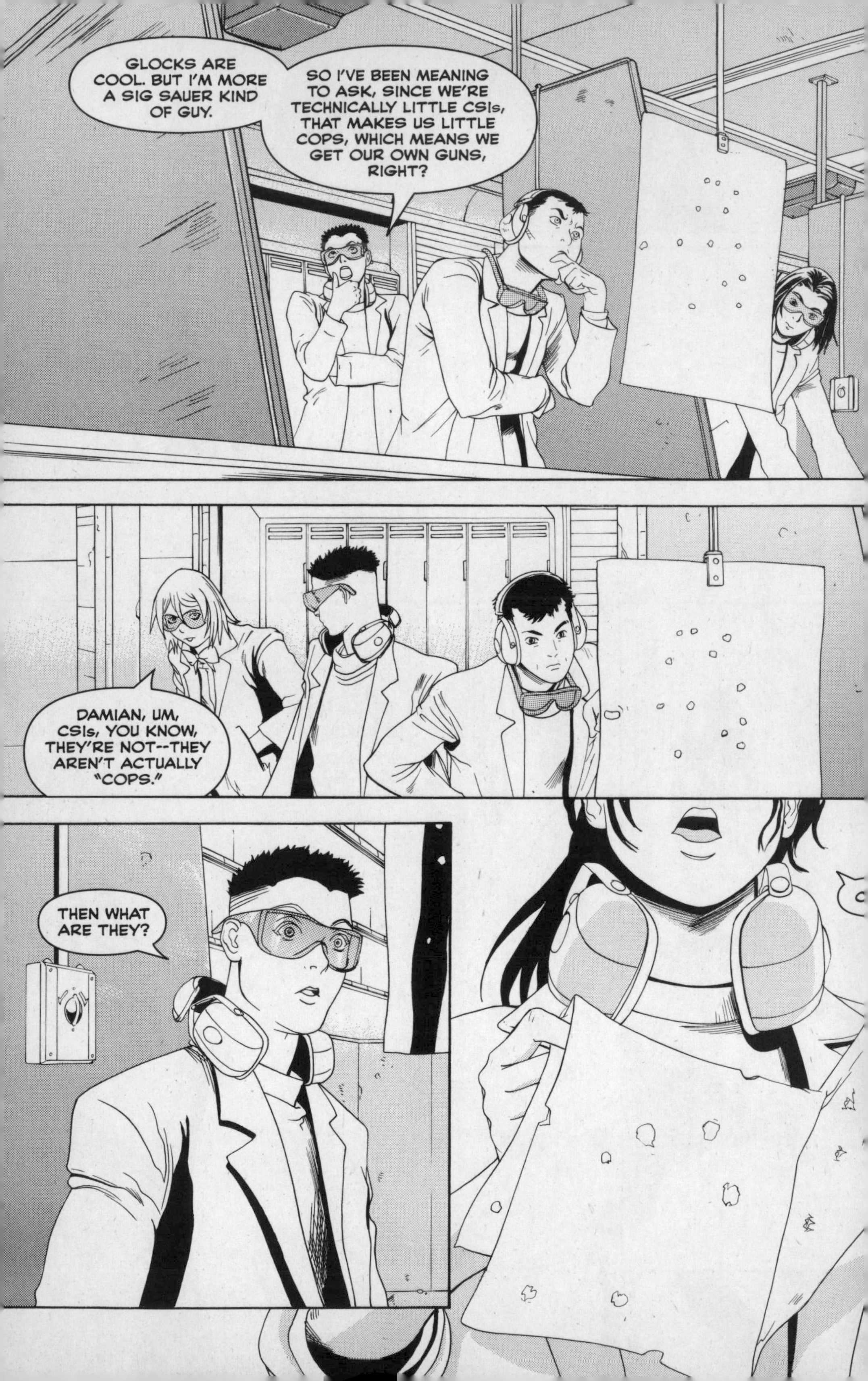
GLOCKS ARE COOL. BUT I'M MORE A SIG SAUER KIND OF GUY.
SO I'VE BEEN MEANING TO ASK, SINCE WE'RE TECHNICALLY LITTLE CSIs, THAT MAKES US LITTLE COPS, WHICH MEANS WE GET OUR OWN GUNS, RIGHT?
DAMIAN, UM, CSIs, YOU KNOW, THEY'RE NOT--THEY AREN'T ACTUALLY "COPS."
THEN WHAT ARE THEY?

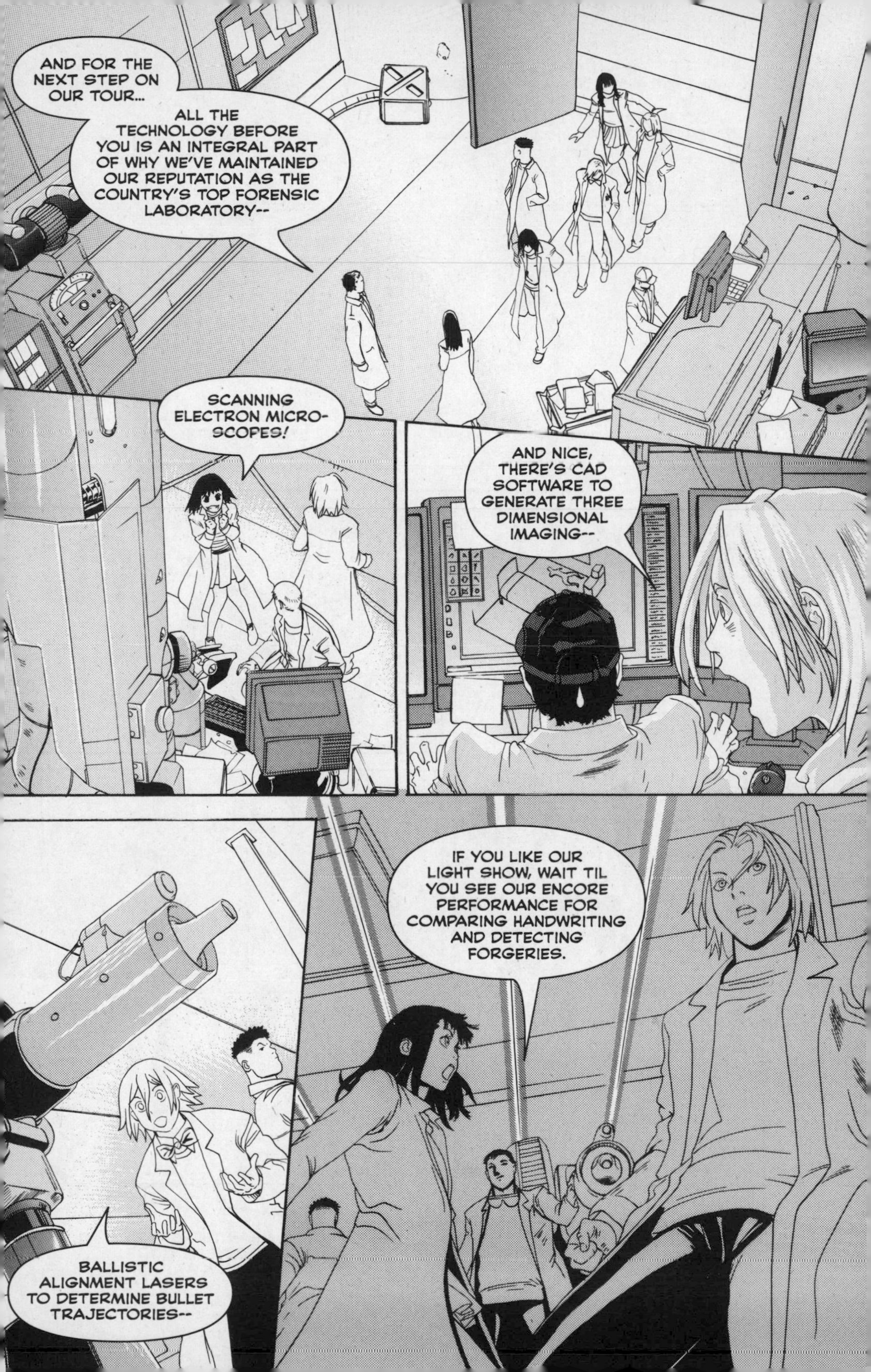
AND FOR THE NEXT STEP ON OUR TOUR...
ALL THE TECHNOLOGY BEFORE YOU IS AN INTEGRAL PART OF WHY WE'VE MAINTAINED OUR REPUTATION AS THE COUNTRY'S TOP FORENSIC LABORATORY--
SCANNING ELECTRON MICRO-SCOPES!
AND NICE, THERE'S CAD SOFTWARE TO GENERATE THREE DIMENSIONAL IMAGING--
BALLISTIC ALIGNMENT LASERS TO DETERMINE BULLET TRAJECTORIES--
IF YOU LIKE OUR LIGHT SHOW, WAIT TIL YOU SEE OUR ENCORE PERFORMANCE FOR COMPARING HANDWRITING AND DETECTING FORGERIES.

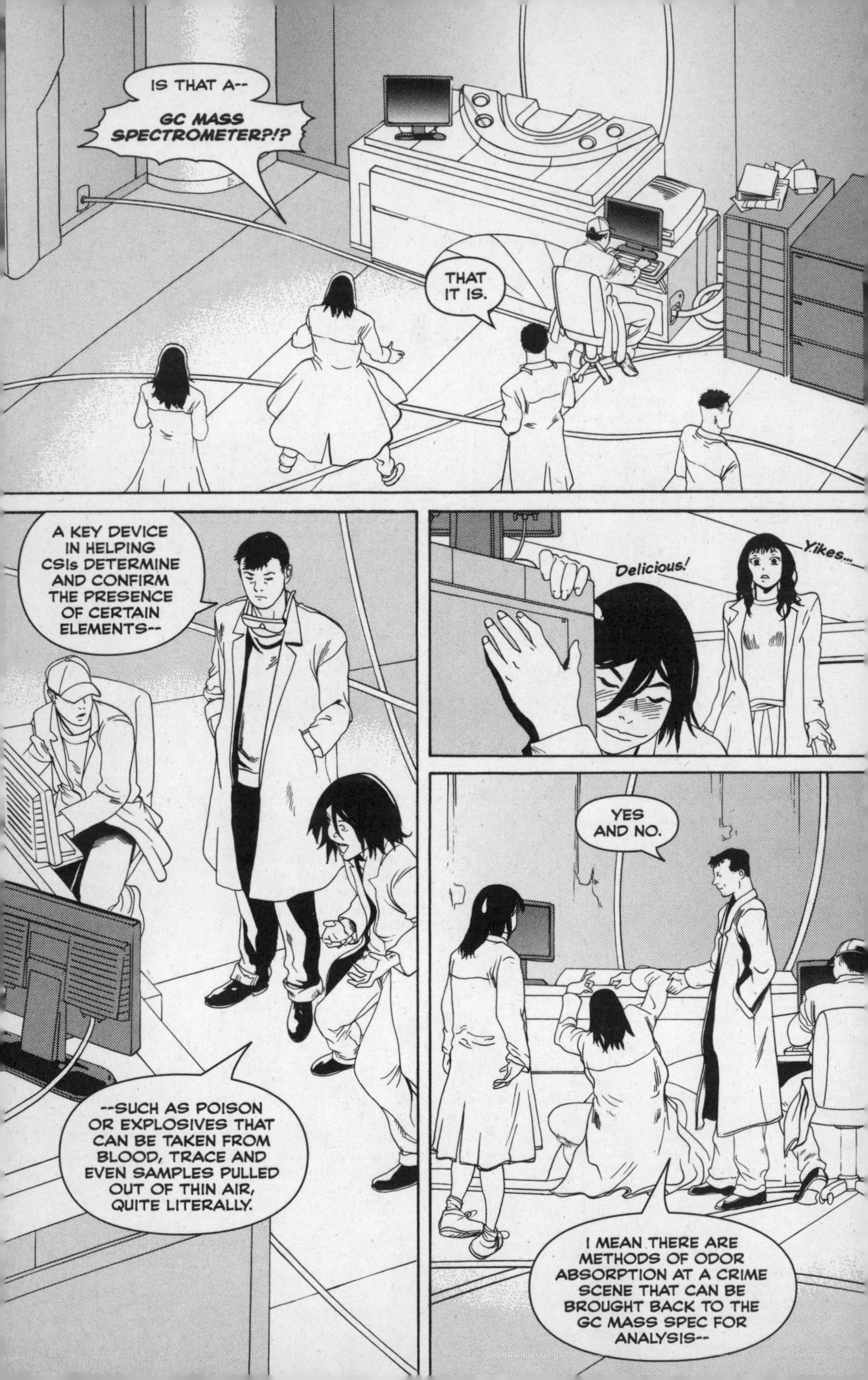

IS THAT A--
GC MASS SPECTROMETER?!?
THAT IT IS.
A KEY DEVICE IN HELPING CSIs DETERMINE AND CONFIRM THE PRESENCE OF CERTAIN ELEMENTS--
--SUCH AS POISON OR EXPLOSIVES THAT CAN BE TAKEN FROM BLOOD, TRACE AND EVEN SAMPLES PULLED OUT OF THIN AIR, QUITE LITERALLY.
Delicious!
Yikes...
YES AND NO.
I MEAN THERE ARE METHODS OF ODOR ABSORPTION AT A CRIME SCENE THAT CAN BE BROUGHT BACK TO THE GC MASS SPEC FOR ANALYSIS--

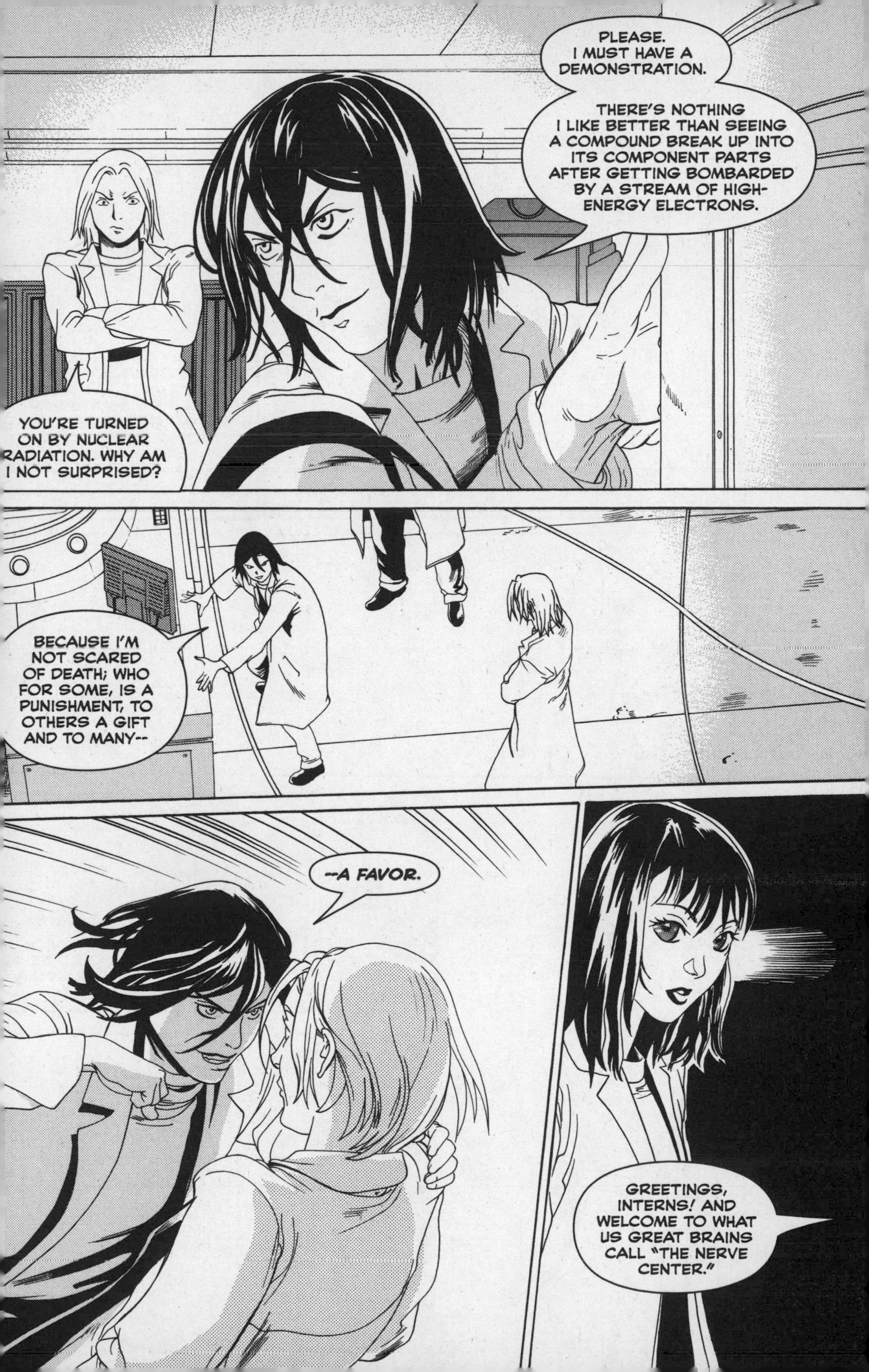
PLEASE. I MUST HAVE A DEMONSTRATION.
THERE'S NOTHING I LIKE BETTER THAN SEEING A COMPOUND BREAK UP INTO ITS COMPONENT PARTS AFTER GETTING BOMBARDED BY A STREAM OF HIGH-ENERGY ELECTRONS.
YOU'RE TURNED ON BY NUCLEAR RADIATION. WHY AM I NOT SURPRISED?
BECAUSE I'M NOT SCARED OF DEATH; WHO FOR SOME, IS A PUNISHMENT, TO OTHERS A GIFT AND TO MANY--
--A FAVOR.
GREETINGS, INTERNS! AND WELCOME TO WHAT US GREAT BRAINS CALL "THE NERVE CENTER."

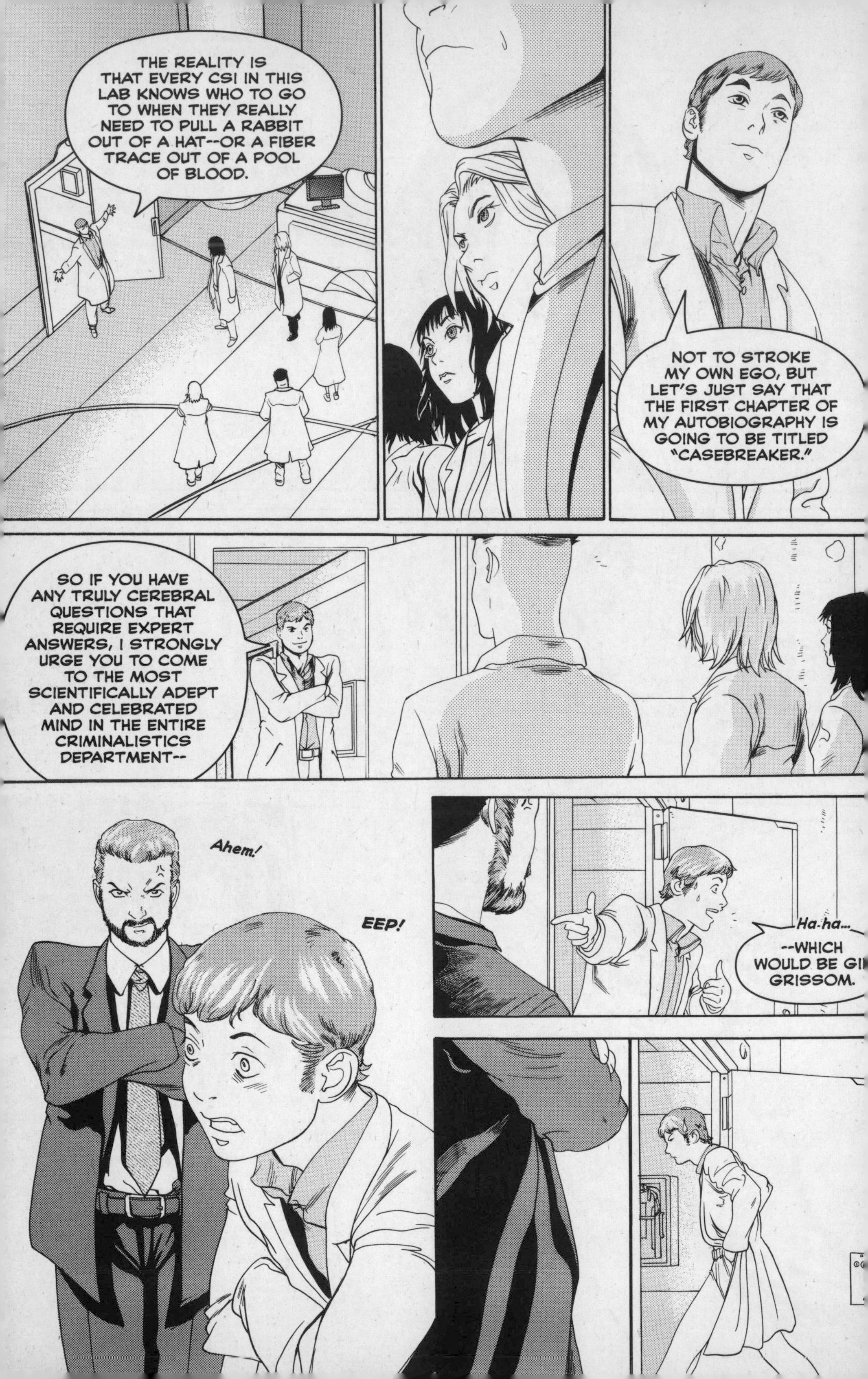
THE REALITY IS THAT EVERY CSI IN THIS LAB KNOWS WHO TO GO TO WHEN THEY REALLY NEED TO PULL A RABBIT OUT OF A HAT--OR A FIBER TRACE OUT OF A POOL OF BLOOD.
NOT TO STROKE MY OWN EGO, BUT LET'S JUST SAY THAT THE FIRST CHAPTER OF MY AUTOBIOGRAPHY IS GOING TO BE TITLED "CASEBREAKER."
SO IF YOU HAVE ANY TRULY CEREBRAL QUESTIONS THAT REQUIRE EXPERT ANSWERS, I STRONGLY URGE YOU TO COME TO THE MOST SCIENTIFICALLY ADEPT AND CELEBRATED MIND IN THE ENTIRE CRIMINALISTICS DEPARTMENT--
Ahem!
EEP!
Ha-ha...
--WHICH WOULD BE GI GRISSOM.

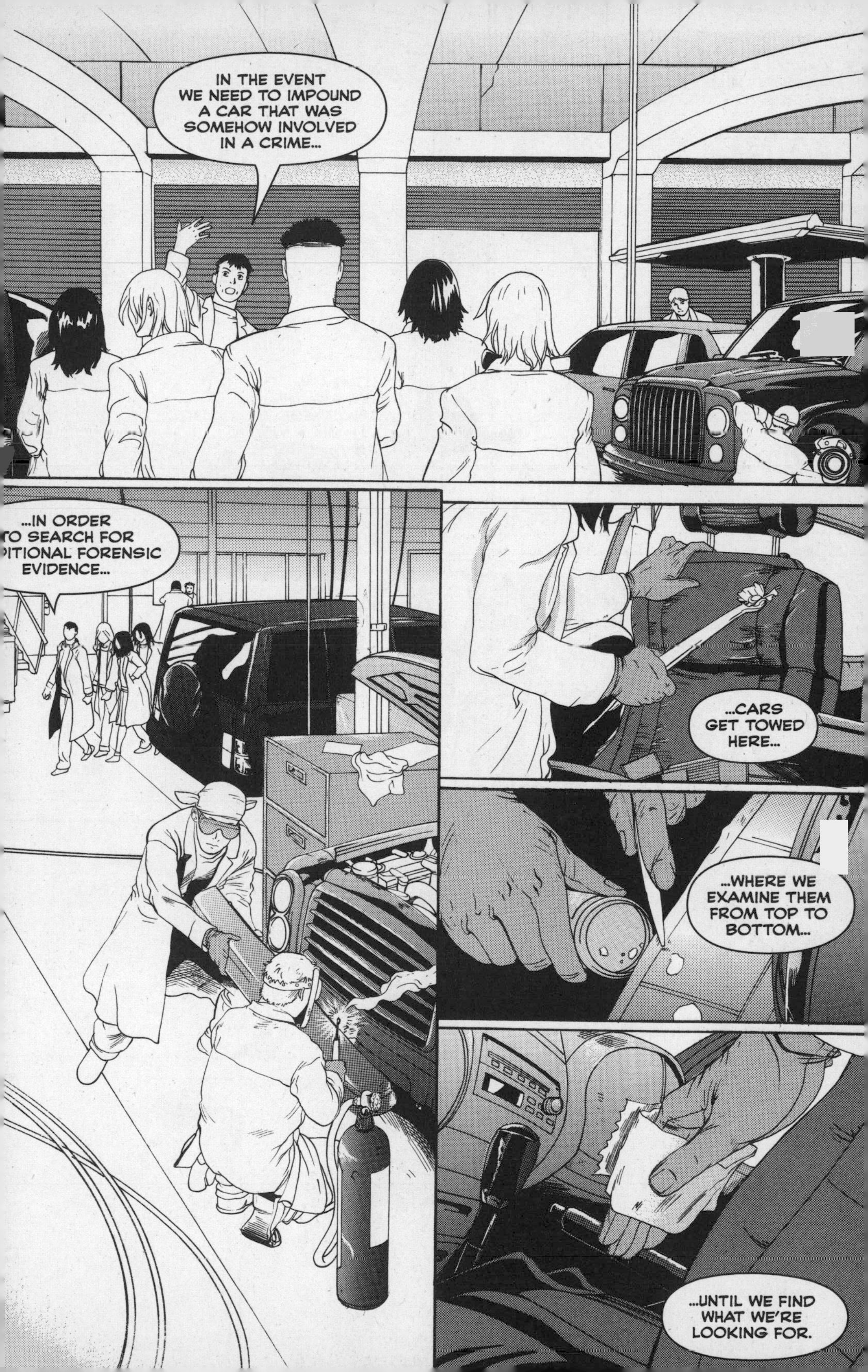
IN THE EVENT WE NEED TO IMPOUND A CAR THAT WAS SOMEHOW INVOLVED IN A CRIME...
...IN ORDER TO SEARCH FOR DITIONAL FORENSIC EVIDENCE...
...CARS GET TOWED HERE...
...WHERE WE EXAMINE THEM FROM TOP TO BOTTOM...
...UNTIL WE FIND WHAT WE'RE LOOKING FOR.

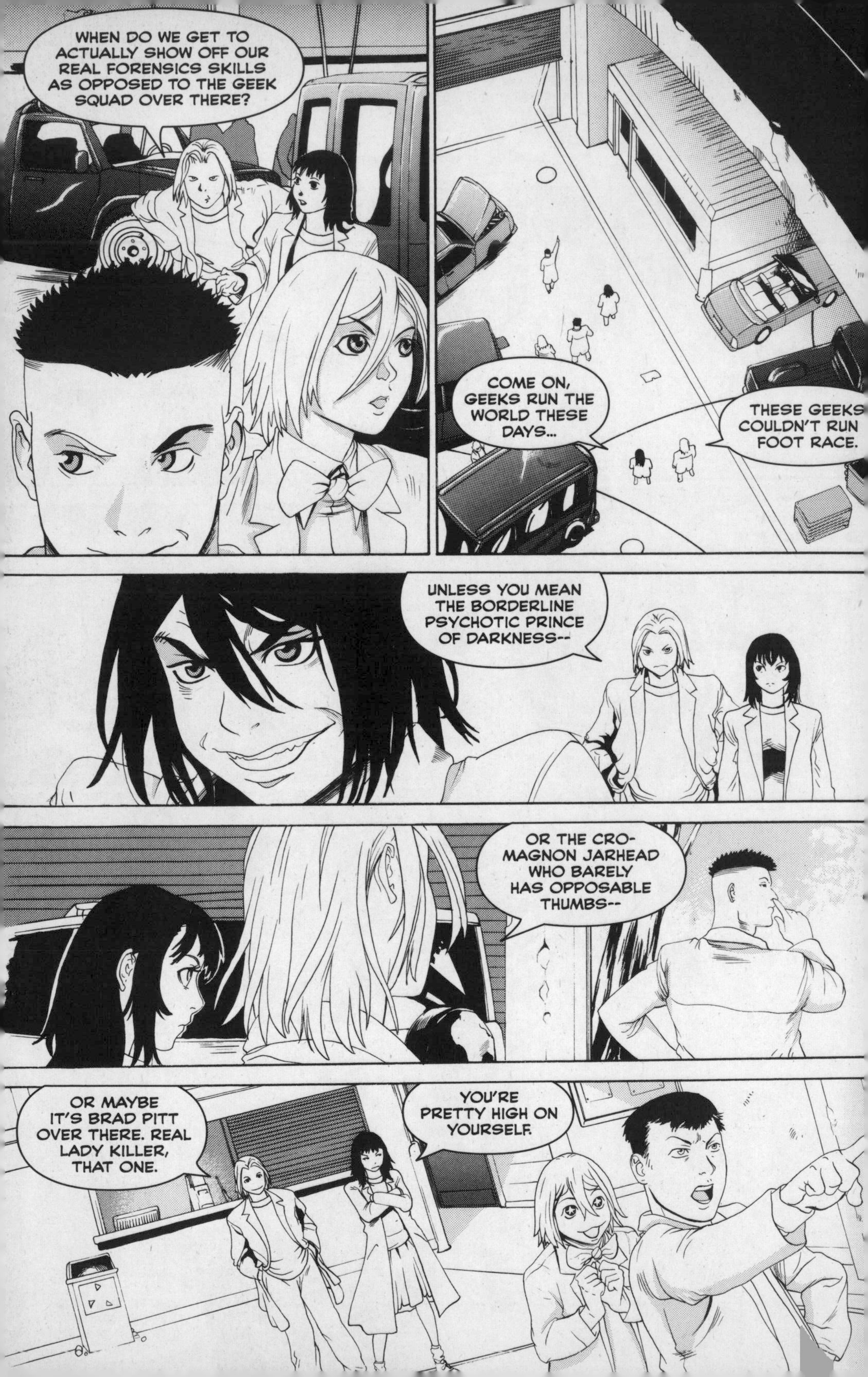
WHEN DO WE GET TO ACTUALLY SHOW OFF OUR REAL FORENSICS SKILLS AS OPPOSED TO THE GEEK SQUAD OVER THERE?
COME ON, GEEKS RUN THE WORLD THESE DAYS...
THESE GEEKS COULDN'T RUN FOOT RACE.
UNLESS YOU MEAN THE BORDERLINE PSYCHOTIC PRINCE OF DARKNESS--
OR THE CRO-MAGNON JARHEAD WHO BARELY HAS OPPOSABLE THUMBS--
OR MAYBE IT'S BRAD PITT OVER THERE. REAL LADY KILLER, THAT ONE.
YOU'RE PRETTY HIGH ON YOURSELF.

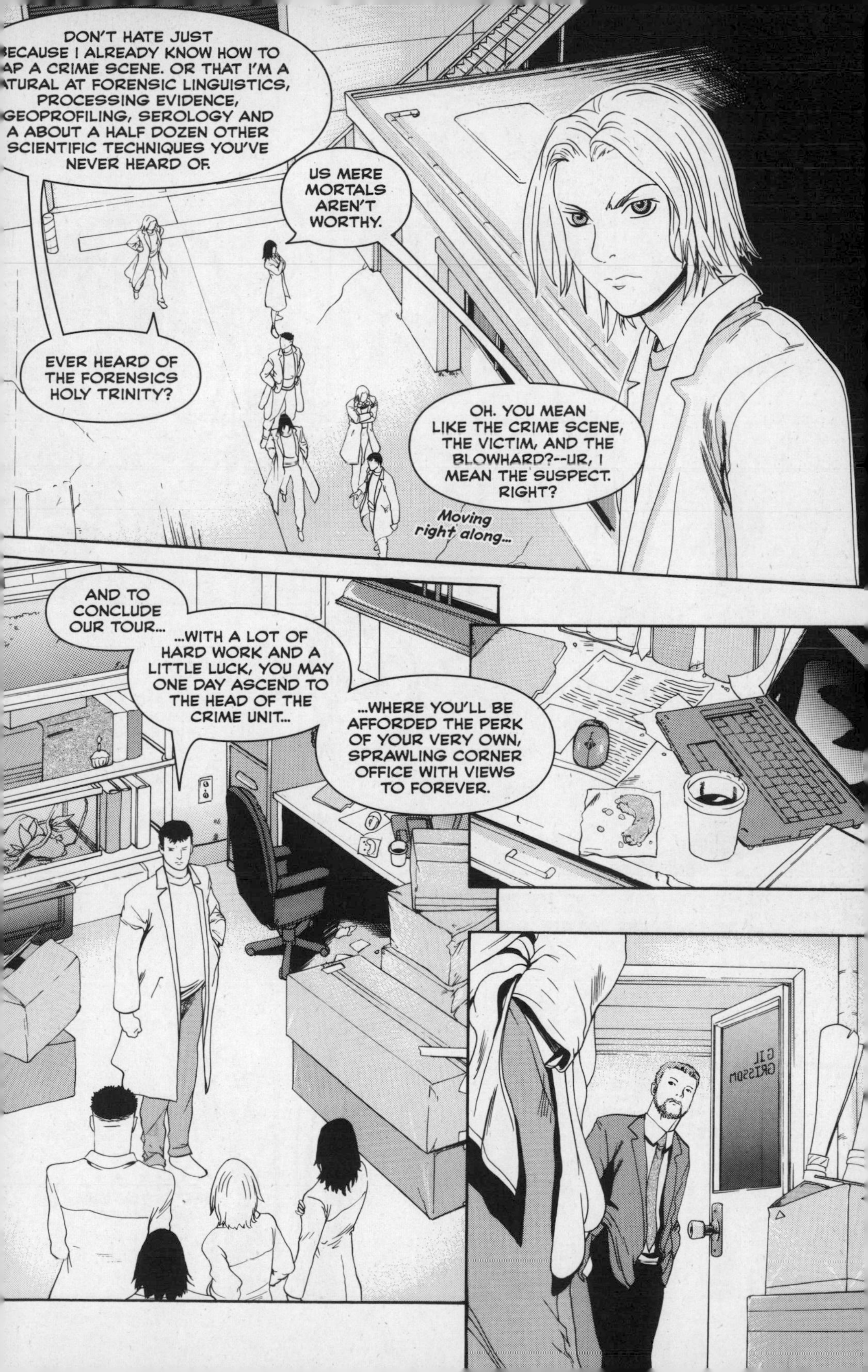
DON'T HATE JUST BECAUSE I ALREADY KNOW HOW TO MAP A CRIME SCENE. OR THAT I'M A NATURAL AT FORENSIC LINGUISTICS, PROCESSING EVIDENCE, GEOPROFILING, SEROLOGY AND A ABOUT A HALF DOZEN OTHER SCIENTIFIC TECHNIQUES YOU'VE NEVER HEARD OF.
US MERE MORTALS AREN'T WORTHY.
EVER HEARD OF THE FORENSICS HOLY TRINITY?
OH. YOU MEAN LIKE THE CRIME SCENE, THE VICTIM, AND THE BLOWHARD?--UR, I MEAN THE SUSPECT. RIGHT?
Moving right along...
AND TO CONCLUDE OUR TOUR...
...WITH A LOT OF HARD WORK AND A LITTLE LUCK, YOU MAY ONE DAY ASCEND TO THE HEAD OF THE CRIME UNIT...
...WHERE YOU'LL BE AFFORDED THE PERK OF YOUR VERY OWN, SPRAWLING CORNER OFFICE WITH VIEWS TO FOREVER.
GIL GRISSOM

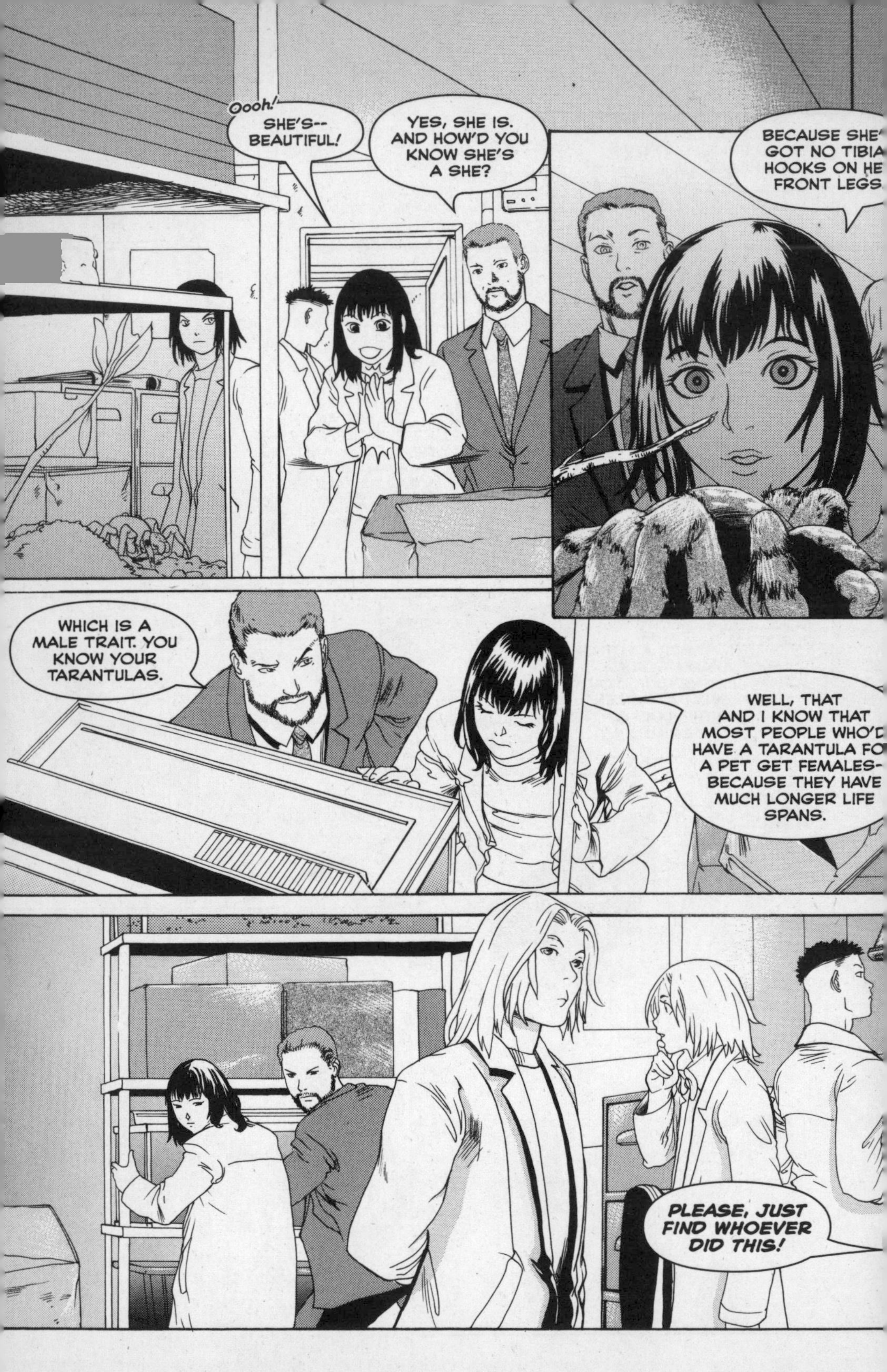
Oooh!
SHE'S-- BEAUTIFUL!
YES, SHE IS. AND HOW'D YOU KNOW SHE'S A SHE?
BECAUSE SHE' GOT NO TIBIA HOOKS ON HE FRONT LEGS.
WHICH IS A MALE TRAIT. YOU KNOW YOUR TARANTULAS.
WELL, THAT AND I KNOW THAT MOST PEOPLE WHO'D HAVE A TARANTULA FO A PET GET FEMALES- BECAUSE THEY HAVE MUCH LONGER LIFE SPANS.
PLEASE, JUST FIND WHOEVER DID THIS!

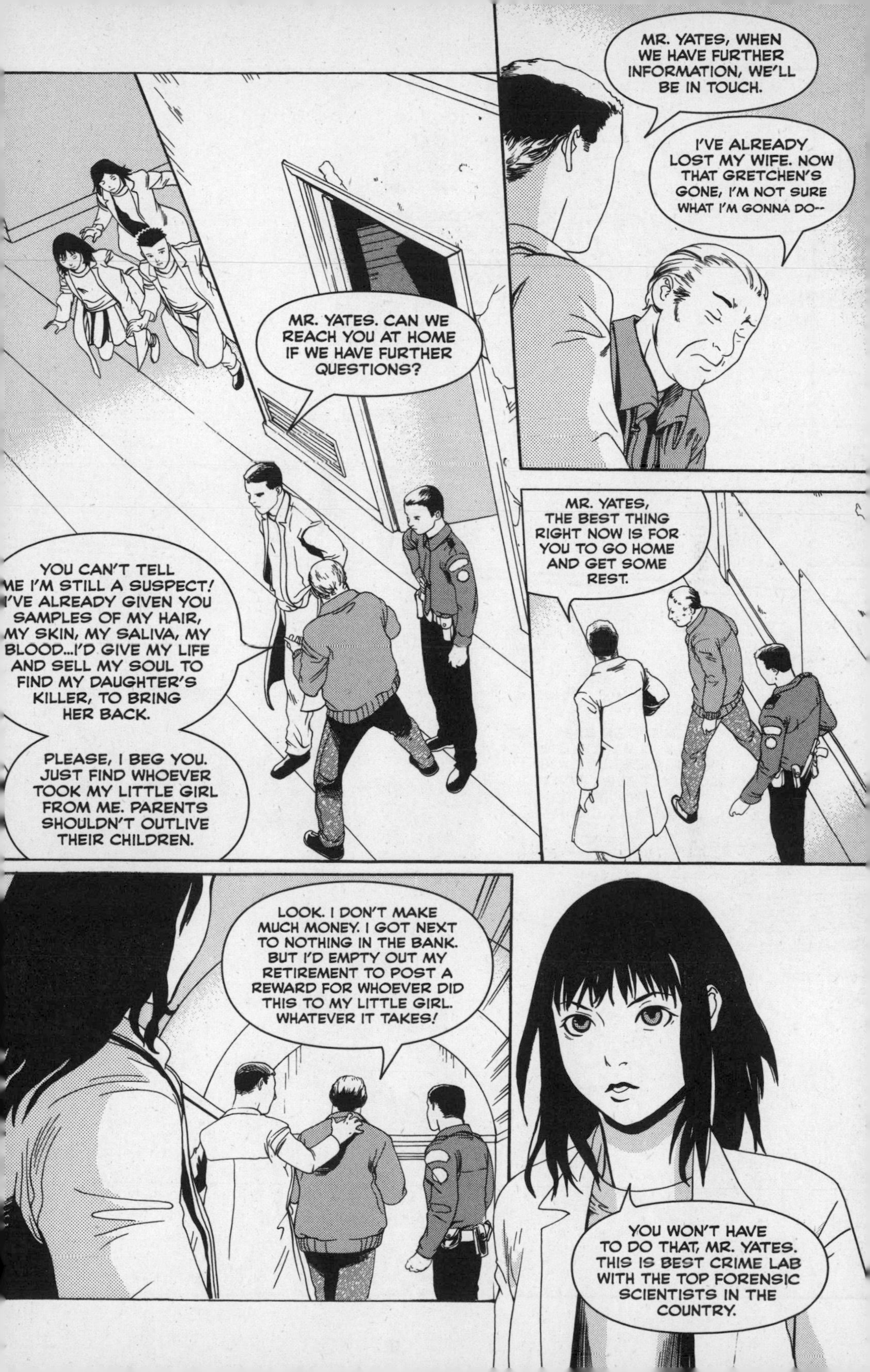
MR. YATES. CAN WE REACH YOU AT HOME IF WE HAVE FURTHER QUESTIONS?
YOU CAN'T TELL ME I'M STILL A SUSPECT! I'VE ALREADY GIVEN YOU SAMPLES OF MY HAIR, MY SKIN, MY SALIVA, MY BLOOD...I'D GIVE MY LIFE AND SELL MY SOUL TO FIND MY DAUGHTER'S KILLER, TO BRING HER BACK.
PLEASE, I BEG YOU. JUST FIND WHOEVER TOOK MY LITTLE GIRL FROM ME. PARENTS SHOULDN'T OUTLIVE THEIR CHILDREN.
MR. YATES, WHEN WE HAVE FURTHER INFORMATION, WE'LL BE IN TOUCH.
I'VE ALREADY LOST MY WIFE. NOW THAT GRETCHEN'S GONE, I'M NOT SURE WHAT I'M GONNA DO--
MR. YATES, THE BEST THING RIGHT NOW IS FOR YOU TO GO HOME AND GET SOME REST.
LOOK. I DON'T MAKE MUCH MONEY. I GOT NEXT TO NOTHING IN THE BANK. BUT I'D EMPTY OUT MY RETIREMENT TO POST A REWARD FOR WHOEVER DID THIS TO MY LITTLE GIRL. WHATEVER IT TAKES!
YOU WON'T HAVE TO DO THAT, MR. YATES. THIS IS BEST CRIME LAB WITH THE TOP FORENSIC SCIENTISTS IN THE COUNTRY.

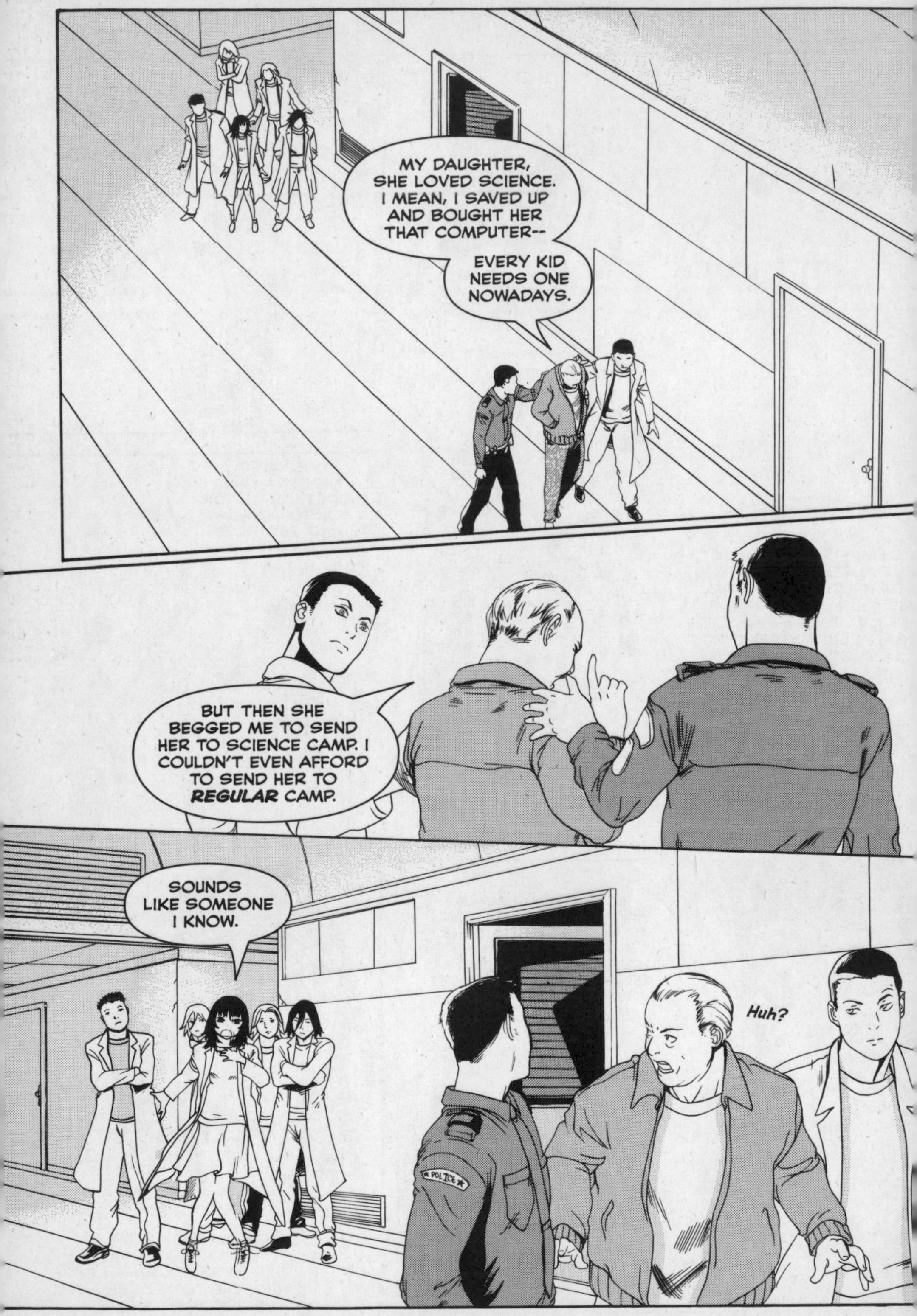
MY DAUGHTER, SHE LOVED SCIENCE. I MEAN, I SAVED UP AND BOUGHT HER THAT COMPUTER--
EVERY KID NEEDS ONE NOWADAYS.
BUT THEN SHE BEGGED ME TO SEND HER TO SCIENCE CAMP. I COULDN'T EVEN AFFORD TO SEND HER TO ***REGULAR*** CAMP.
SOUNDS LIKE SOMEONE I KNOW.
Huh?
POLICE

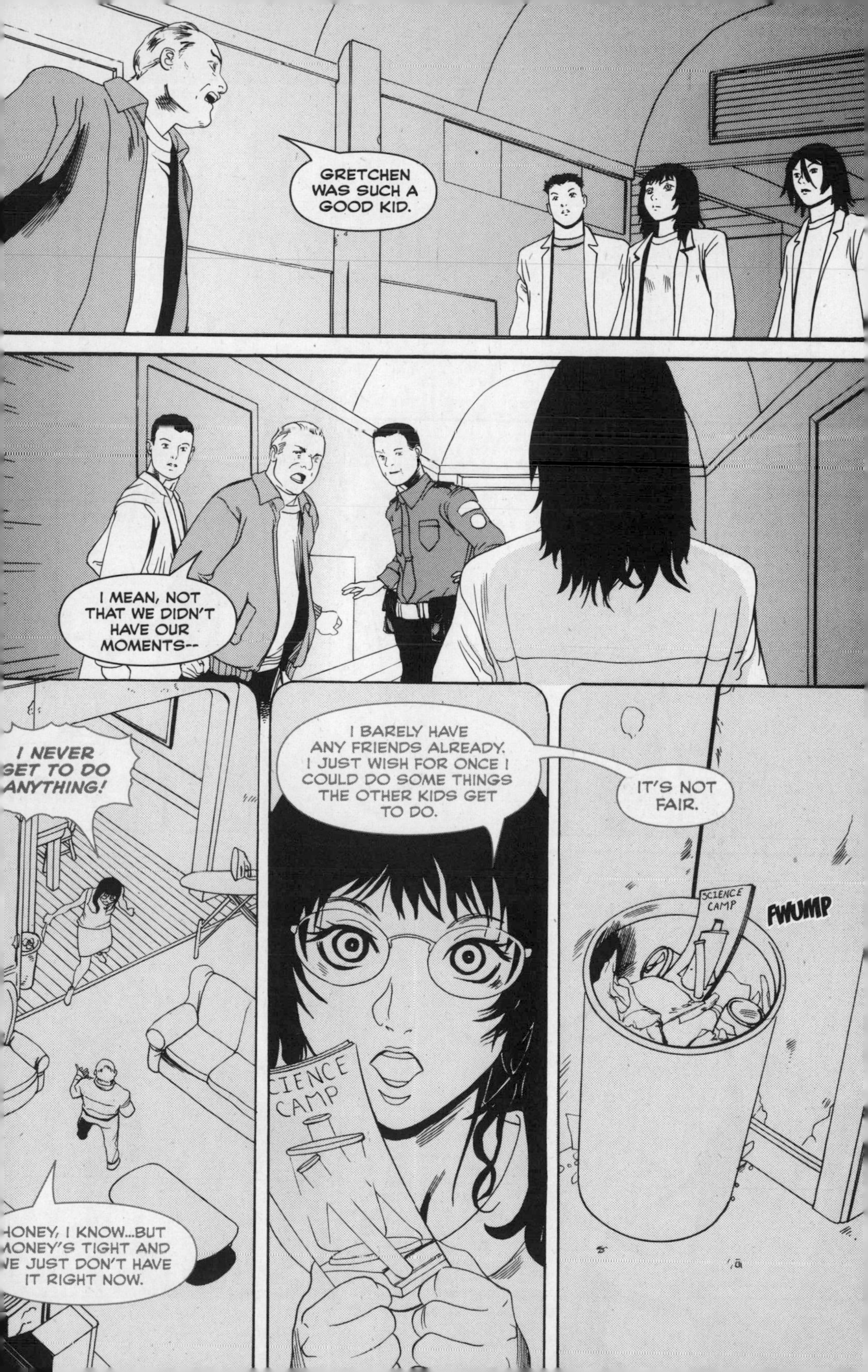
GRETCHEN WAS SUCH A GOOD KID.
I MEAN, NOT THAT WE DIDN'T HAVE OUR MOMENTS--
I NEVER GET TO DO ANYTHING!
HONEY, I KNOW...BUT MONEY'S TIGHT AND WE JUST DON'T HAVE IT RIGHT NOW.
I BARELY HAVE ANY FRIENDS ALREADY. I JUST WISH FOR ONCE I COULD DO SOME THINGS THE OTHER KIDS GET TO DO.
SCIENCE CAMP
IT'S NOT FAIR.
SCIENCE CAMP
FWUMP

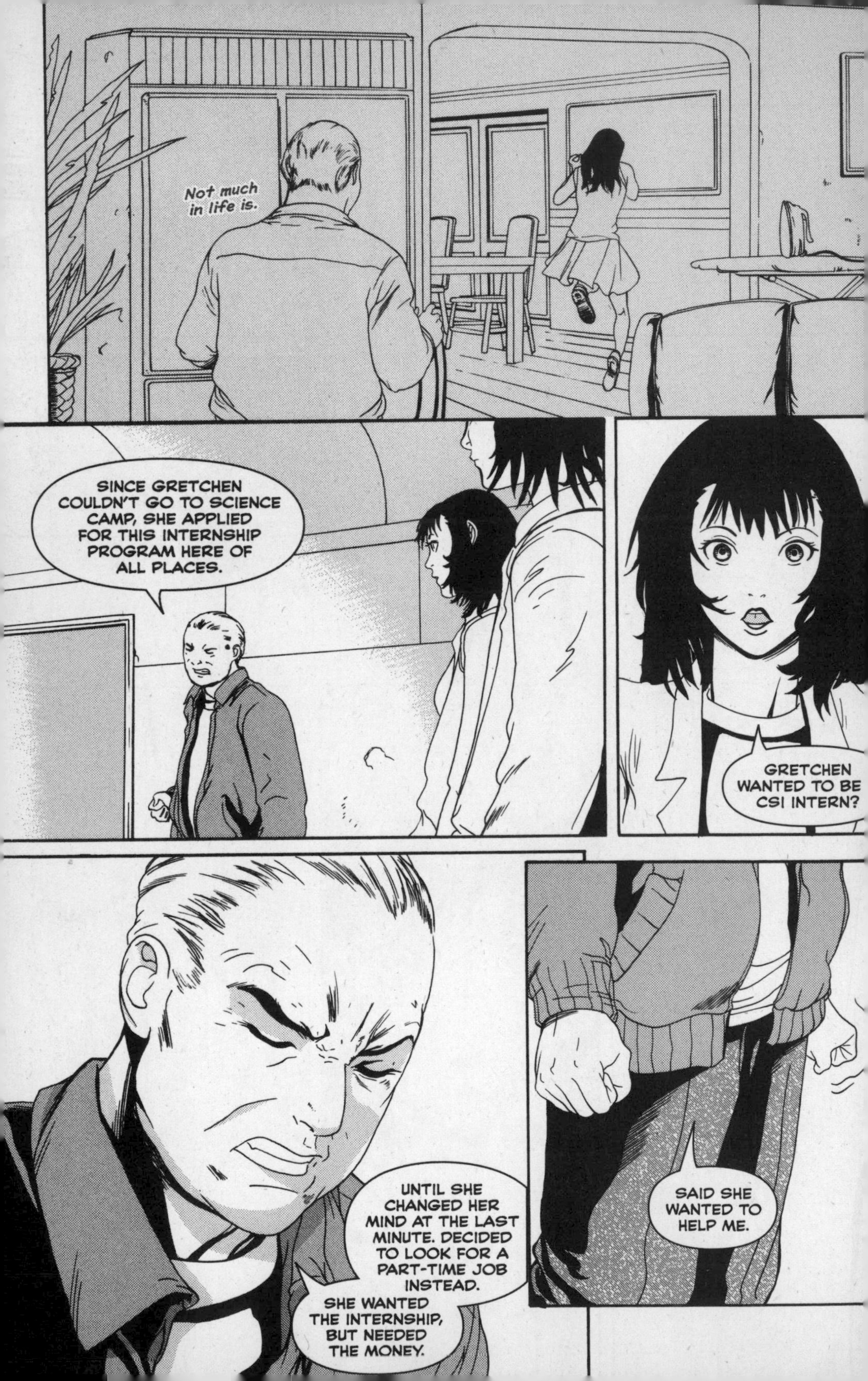
Not much in life is.
SINCE GRETCHEN COULDN'T GO TO SCIENCE CAMP, SHE APPLIED FOR THIS INTERNSHIP PROGRAM HERE OF ALL PLACES.
GRETCHEN WANTED TO BE CSI INTERN?
UNTIL SHE CHANGED HER MIND AT THE LAST MINUTE. DECIDED TO LOOK FOR A PART-TIME JOB INSTEAD.
SHE WANTED THE INTERNSHIP, BUT NEEDED THE MONEY.
SAID SHE WANTED TO HELP ME.

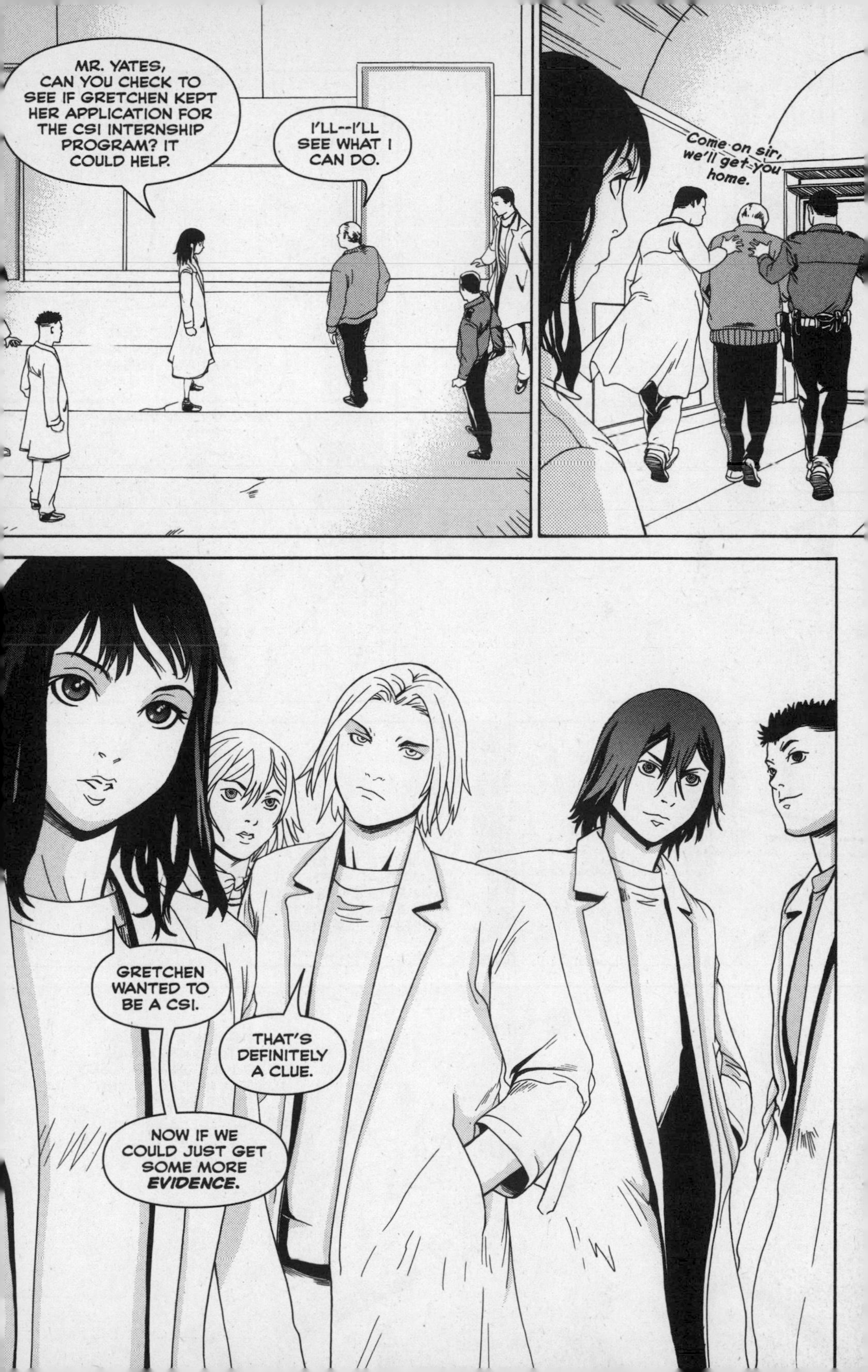
MR. YATES, CAN YOU CHECK TO SEE IF GRETCHEN KEPT HER APPLICATION FOR THE CSI INTERNSHIP PROGRAM? IT COULD HELP.
I'LL--I'LL SEE WHAT I CAN DO.
Come on sir, we'll get you home.
GRETCHEN WANTED TO BE A CSI.
THAT'S DEFINITELY A CLUE.
NOW IF WE COULD JUST GET SOME MORE *EVIDENCE*.

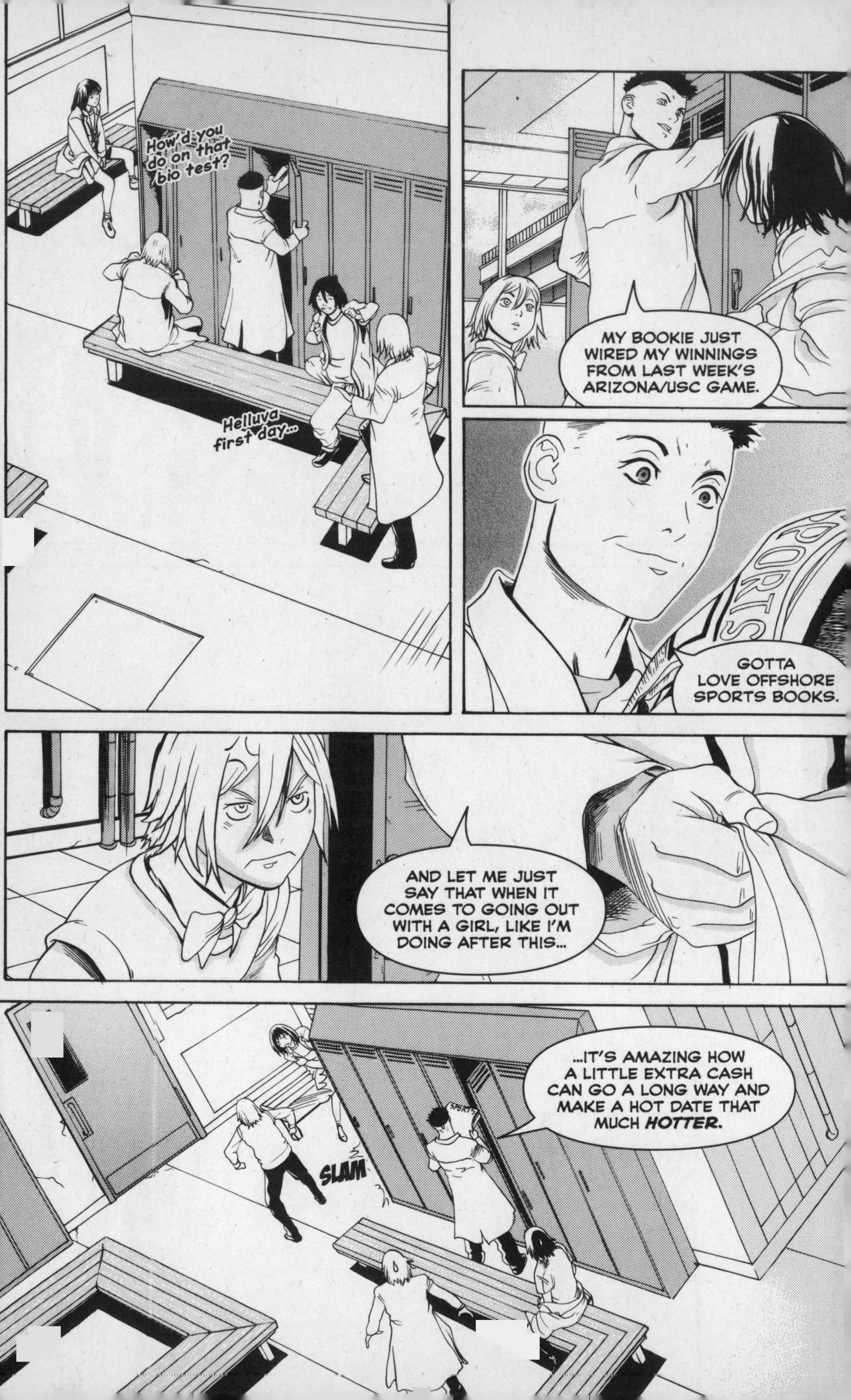
How'd you do on that bio test?
Helluva first day...
MY BOOKIE JUST WIRED MY WINNINGS FROM LAST WEEK'S ARIZONA/USC GAME.
GOTTA LOVE OFFSHORE SPORTS BOOKS.
AND LET ME JUST SAY THAT WHEN IT COMES TO GOING OUT WITH A GIRL, LIKE I'M DOING AFTER THIS...
...IT'S AMAZING HOW A LITTLE EXTRA CASH CAN GO A LONG WAY AND MAKE A HOT DATE THAT MUCH *HOTTER.*
SLAM

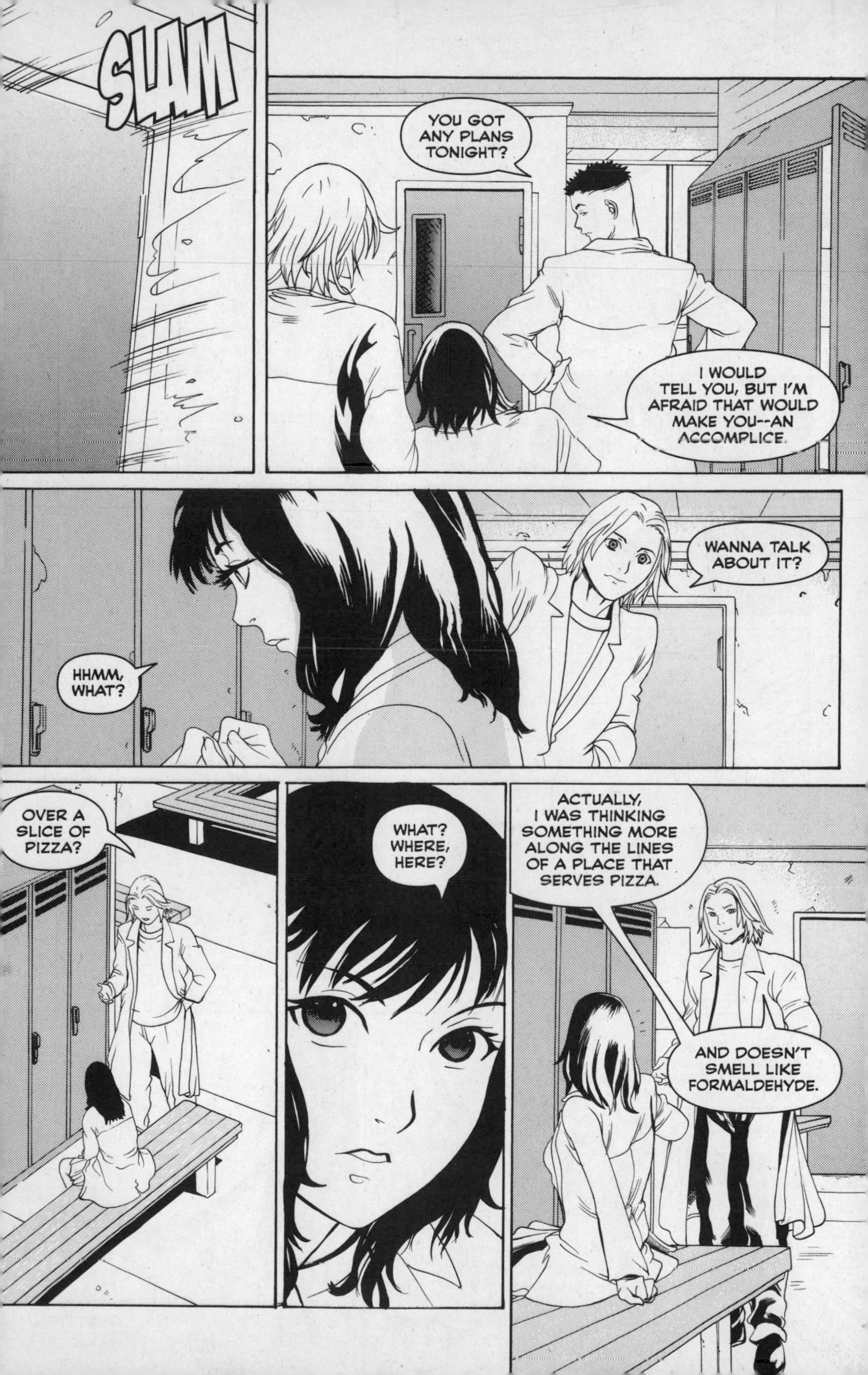
SLAM
YOU GOT ANY PLANS TONIGHT?
I WOULD TELL YOU, BUT I'M AFRAID THAT WOULD MAKE YOU--AN ACCOMPLICE.
WANNA TALK ABOUT IT?
HHMM, WHAT?
OVER A SLICE OF PIZZA?
WHAT? WHERE, HERE?
ACTUALLY, I WAS THINKING SOMETHING MORE ALONG THE LINES OF A PLACE THAT SERVES PIZZA.
AND DOESN'T SMELL LIKE FORMALDEHYDE.

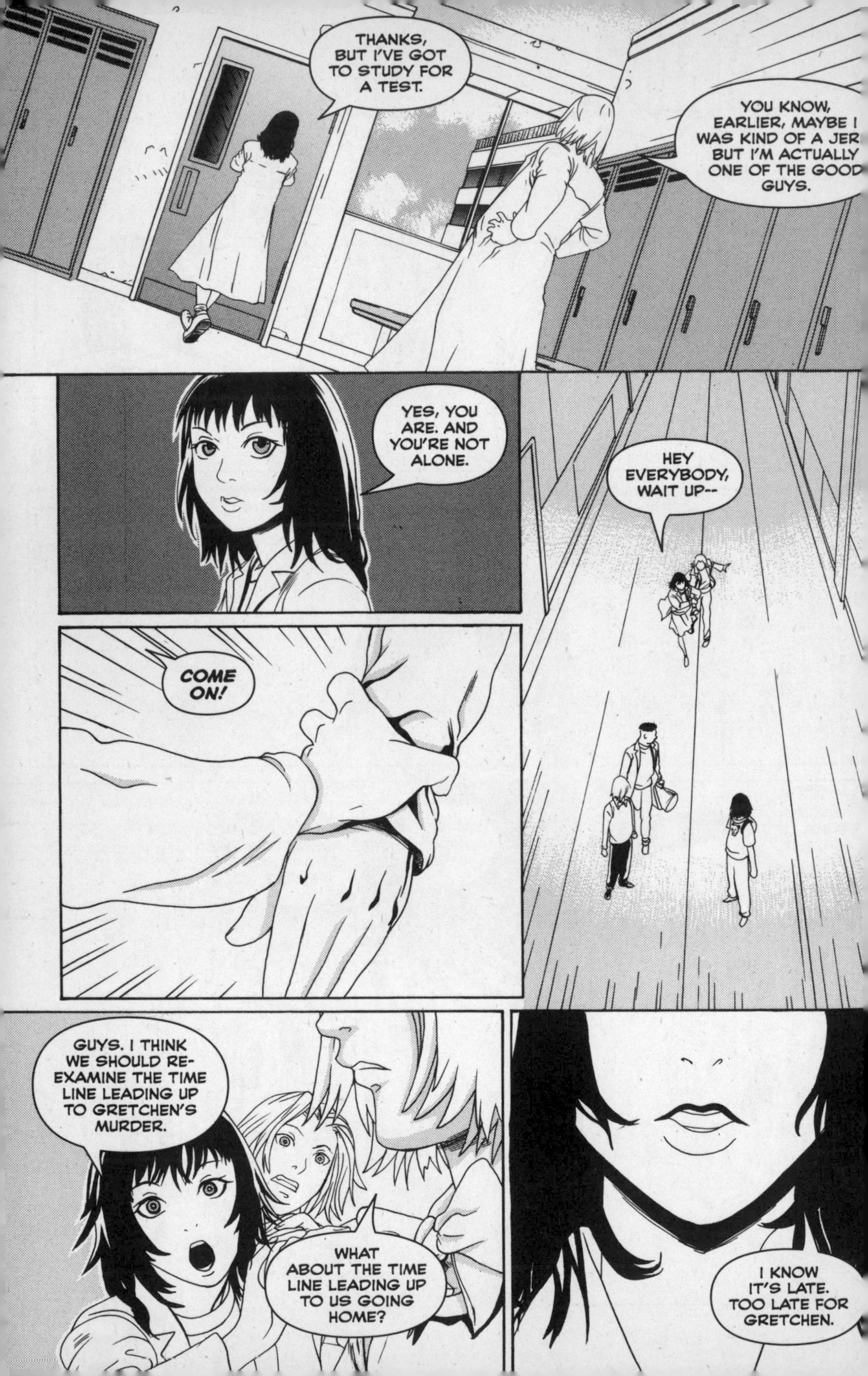
THANKS, BUT I'VE GOT TO STUDY FOR A TEST.
YOU KNOW, EARLIER, MAYBE I WAS KIND OF A JER BUT I'M ACTUALLY ONE OF THE GOOD GUYS.
YES, YOU ARE. AND YOU'RE NOT ALONE.
COME ON!
HEY EVERYBODY, WAIT UP--
GUYS. I THINK WE SHOULD RE-EXAMINE THE TIME LINE LEADING UP TO GRETCHEN'S MURDER.
WHAT ABOUT THE TIME LINE LEADING UP TO US GOING HOME?
I KNOW IT'S LATE. TOO LATE FOR GRETCHEN.

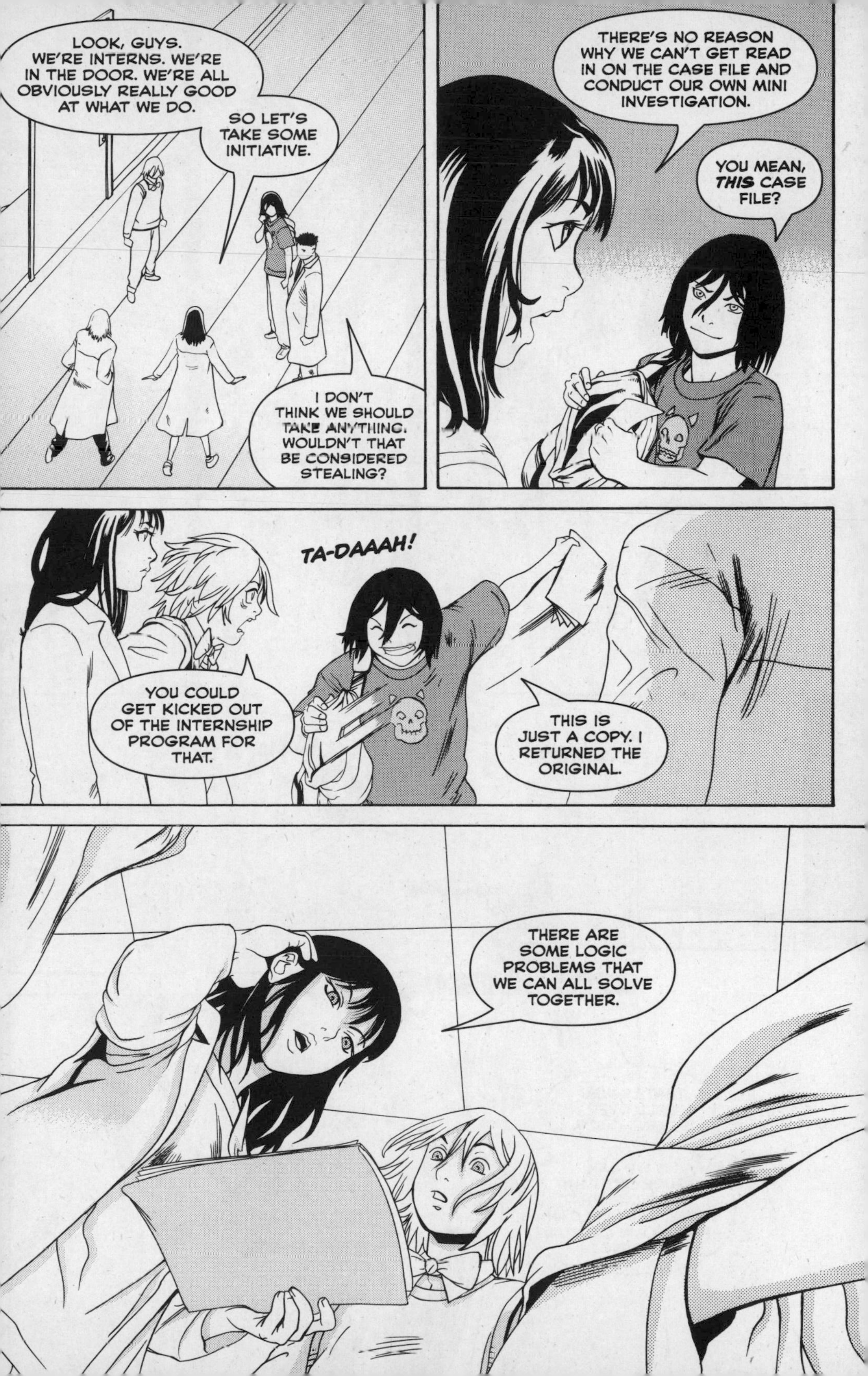
LOOK, GUYS. WE'RE INTERNS. WE'RE IN THE DOOR. WE'RE ALL OBVIOUSLY REALLY GOOD AT WHAT WE DO.
SO LET'S TAKE SOME INITIATIVE.
I DON'T THINK WE SHOULD TAKE ANYTHING. WOULDN'T THAT BE CONSIDERED STEALING?
THERE'S NO REASON WHY WE CAN'T GET READ IN ON THE CASE FILE AND CONDUCT OUR OWN MINI INVESTIGATION.
YOU MEAN, *THIS* CASE FILE?
TA-DAAAH!
YOU COULD GET KICKED OUT OF THE INTERNSHIP PROGRAM FOR THAT.
THIS IS JUST A COPY. I RETURNED THE ORIGINAL.
THERE ARE SOME LOGIC PROBLEMS THAT WE CAN ALL SOLVE TOGETHER.

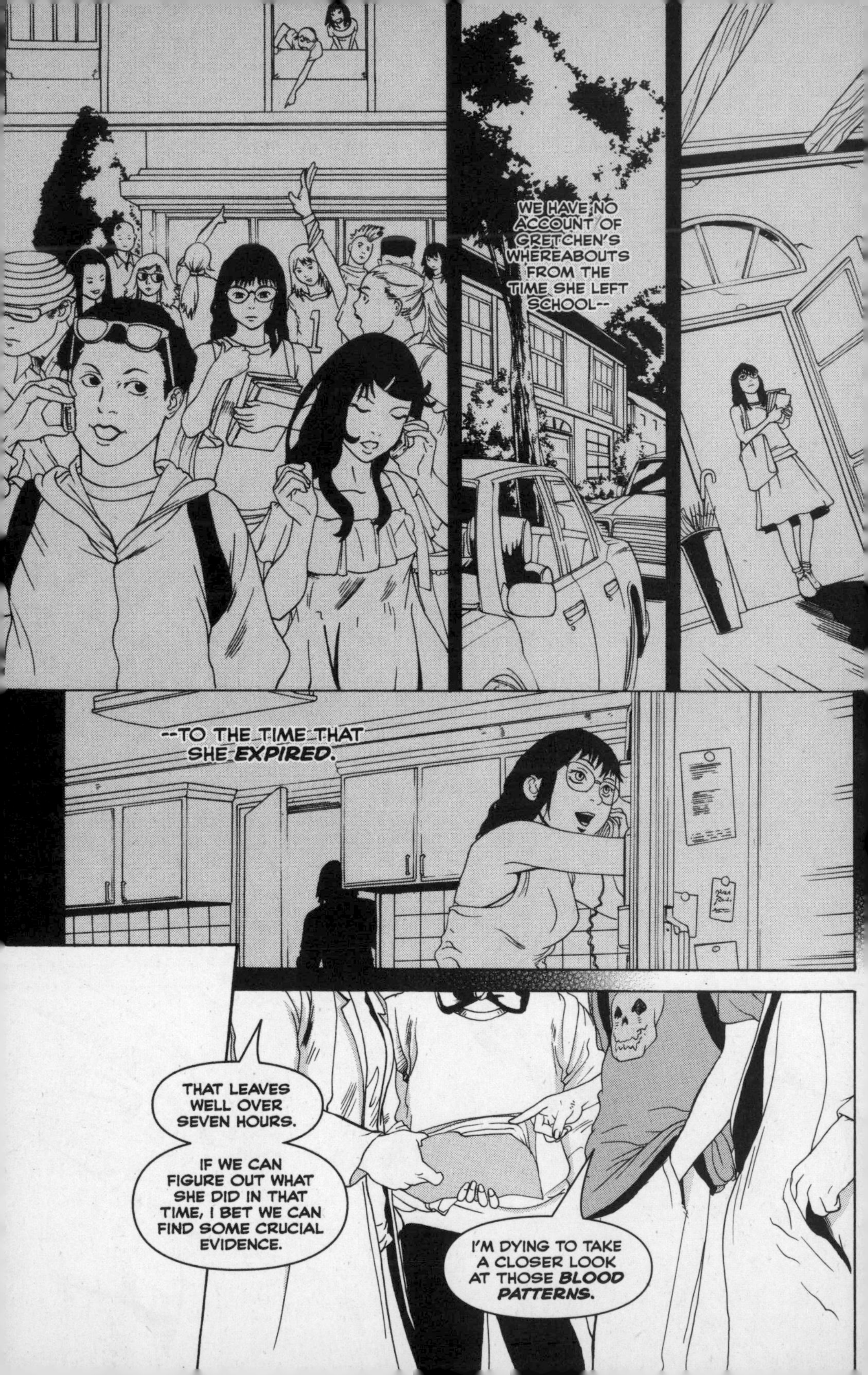
WE HAVE NO ACCOUNT OF GRETCHEN'S WHEREABOUTS FROM THE TIME SHE LEFT SCHOOL--
--TO THE TIME THAT SHE *EXPIRED.*
THAT LEAVES WELL OVER SEVEN HOURS.
IF WE CAN FIGURE OUT WHAT SHE DID IN THAT TIME, I BET WE CAN FIND SOME CRUCIAL EVIDENCE.
I'M DYING TO TAKE A CLOSER LOOK AT THOSE *BLOOD PATTERNS.*

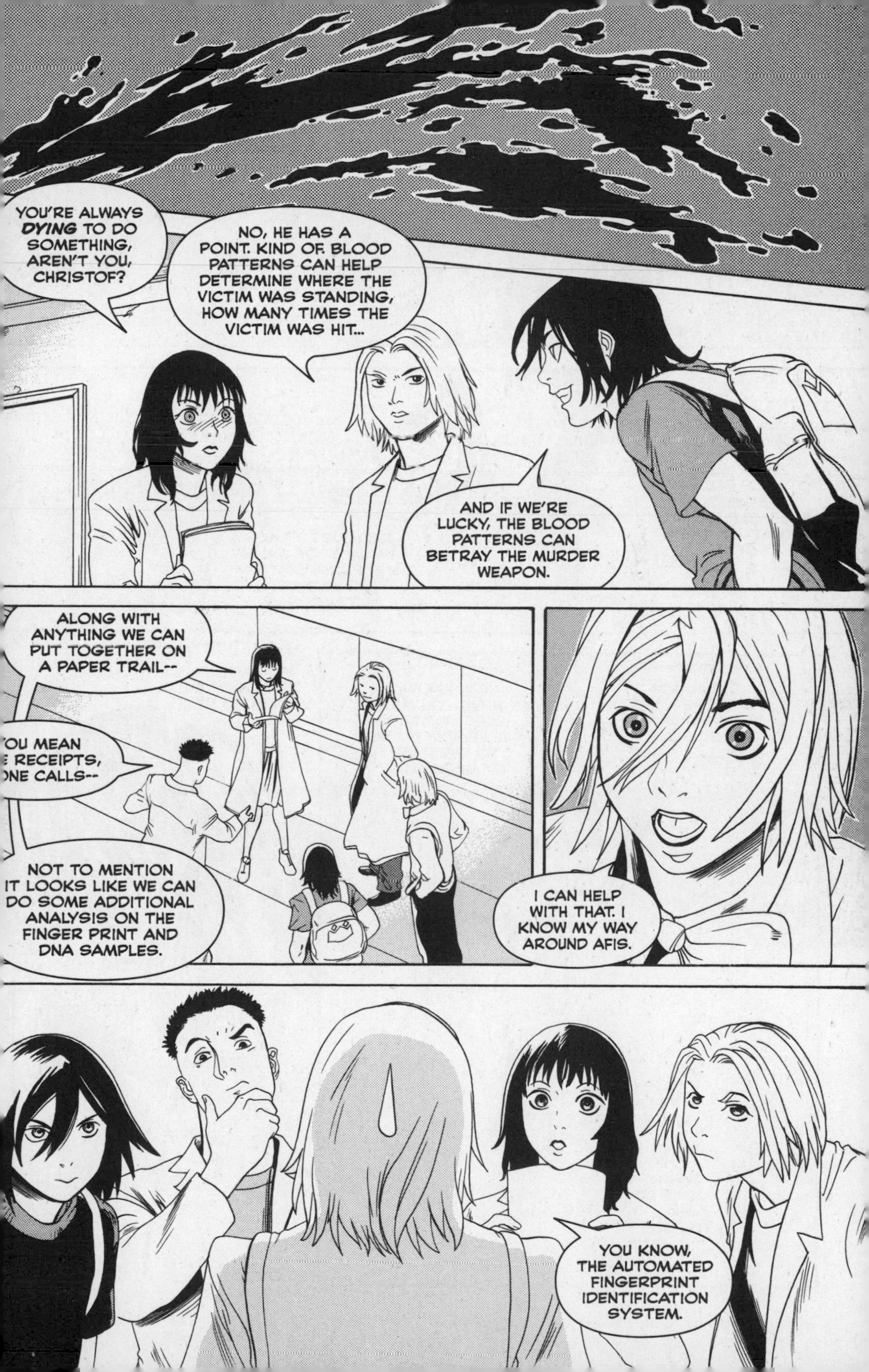
YOU'RE ALWAYS *DYING* TO DO SOMETHING, AREN'T YOU, CHRISTOF?
NO, HE HAS A POINT. KIND OF. BLOOD PATTERNS CAN HELP DETERMINE WHERE THE VICTIM WAS STANDING, HOW MANY TIMES THE VICTIM WAS HIT...
AND IF WE'RE LUCKY, THE BLOOD PATTERNS CAN BETRAY THE MURDER WEAPON.
ALONG WITH ANYTHING WE CAN PUT TOGETHER ON A PAPER TRAIL--
OU MEAN E RECEIPTS, ONE CALLS--
NOT TO MENTION IT LOOKS LIKE WE CAN DO SOME ADDITIONAL ANALYSIS ON THE FINGER PRINT AND DNA SAMPLES.
I CAN HELP WITH THAT. I KNOW MY WAY AROUND AFIS.
YOU KNOW, THE AUTOMATED FINGERPRINT IDENTIFICATION SYSTEM.

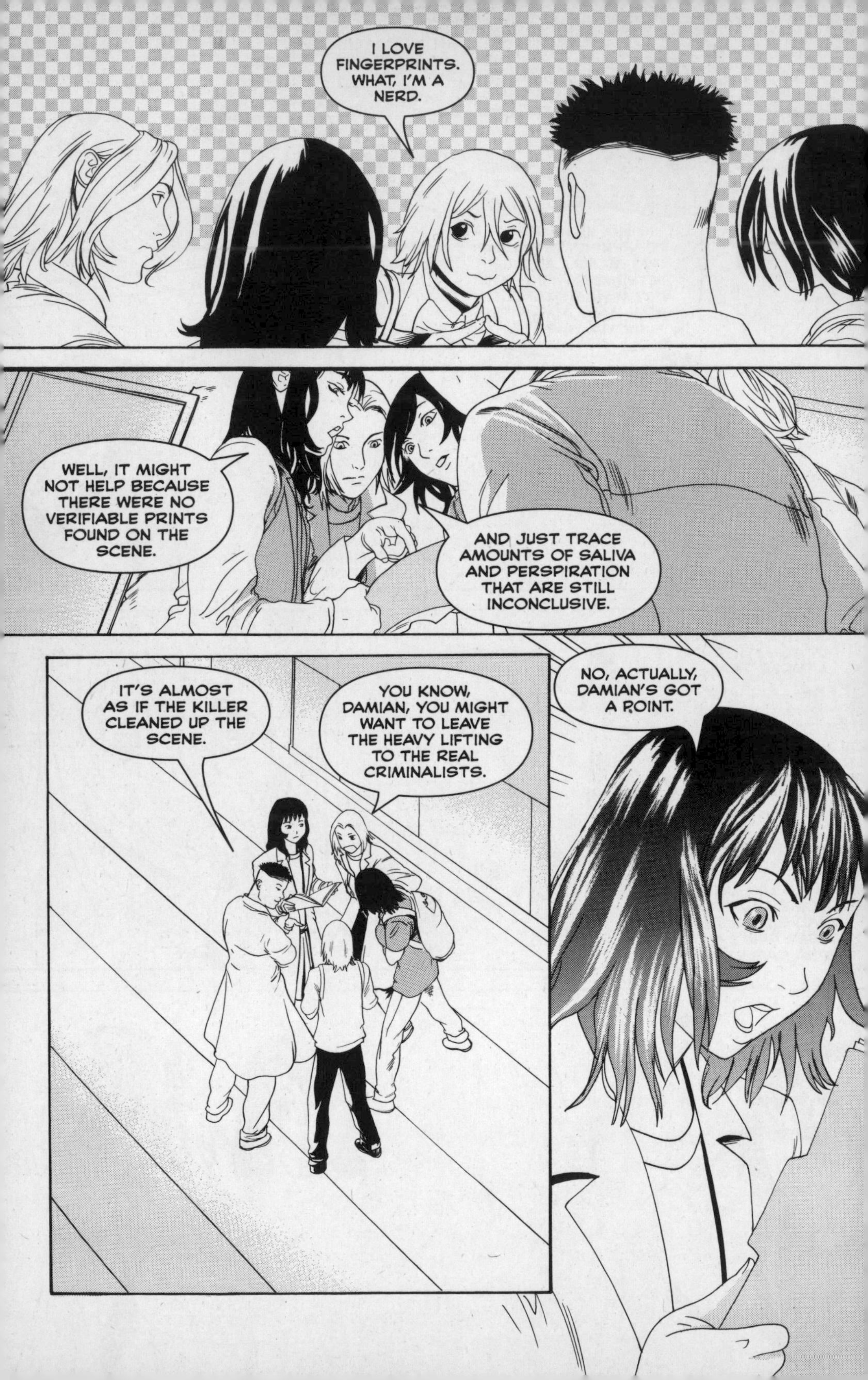
I LOVE FINGERPRINTS. WHAT, I'M A NERD.
WELL, IT MIGHT NOT HELP BECAUSE THERE WERE NO VERIFIABLE PRINTS FOUND ON THE SCENE.
AND JUST TRACE AMOUNTS OF SALIVA AND PERSPIRATION THAT ARE STILL INCONCLUSIVE.
IT'S ALMOST AS IF THE KILLER CLEANED UP THE SCENE.
YOU KNOW, DAMIAN, YOU MIGHT WANT TO LEAVE THE HEAVY LIFTING TO THE REAL CRIMINALISTS.
NO, ACTUALLY, DAMIAN'S GOT A POINT.

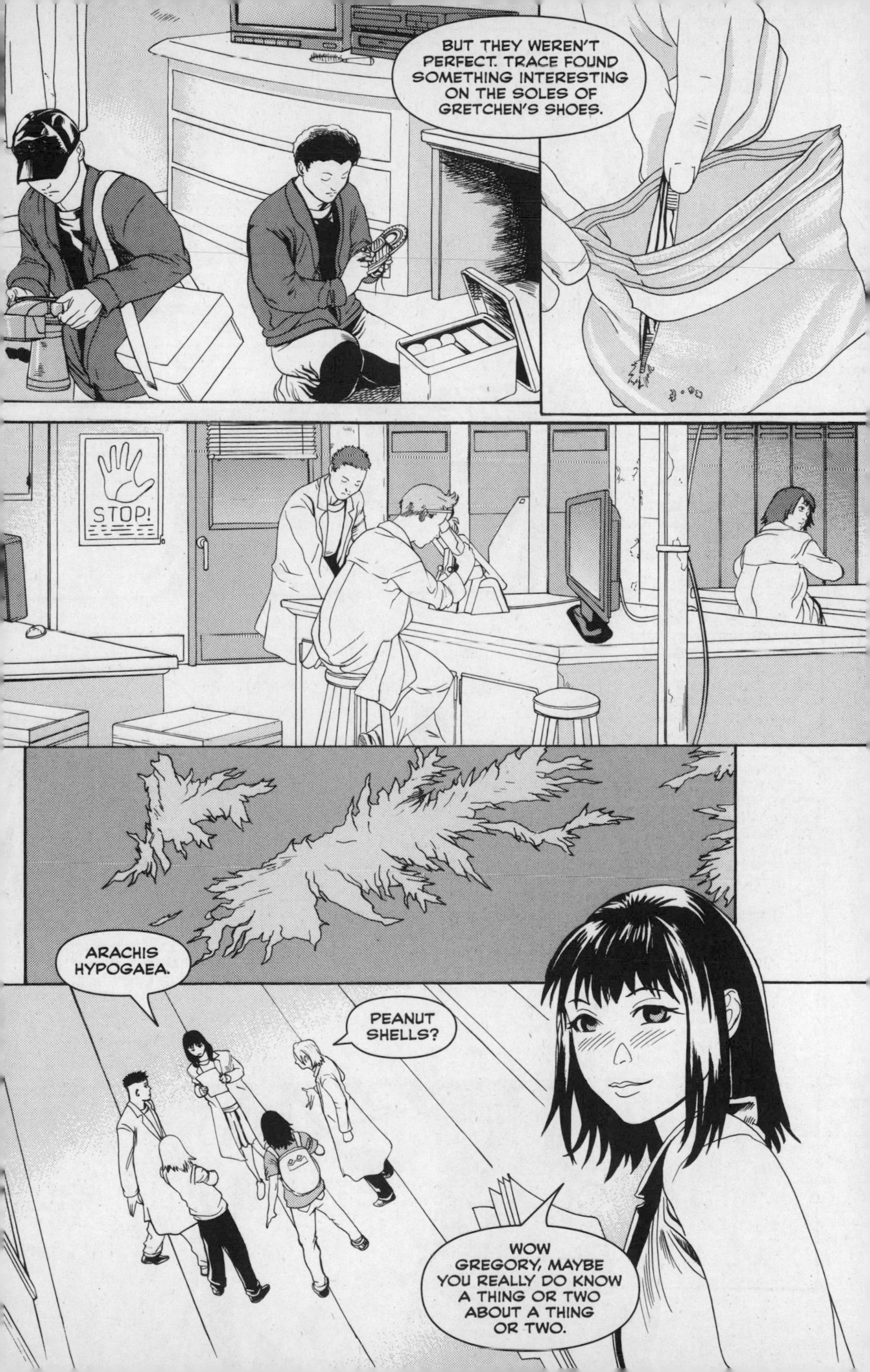
BUT THEY WEREN'T PERFECT. TRACE FOUND SOMETHING INTERESTING ON THE SOLES OF GRETCHEN'S SHOES.
STOP!
ARACHIS HYPOGAEA.
PEANUT SHELLS?
WOW GREGORY, MAYBE YOU REALLY DO KNOW A THING OR TWO ABOUT A THING OR TWO.

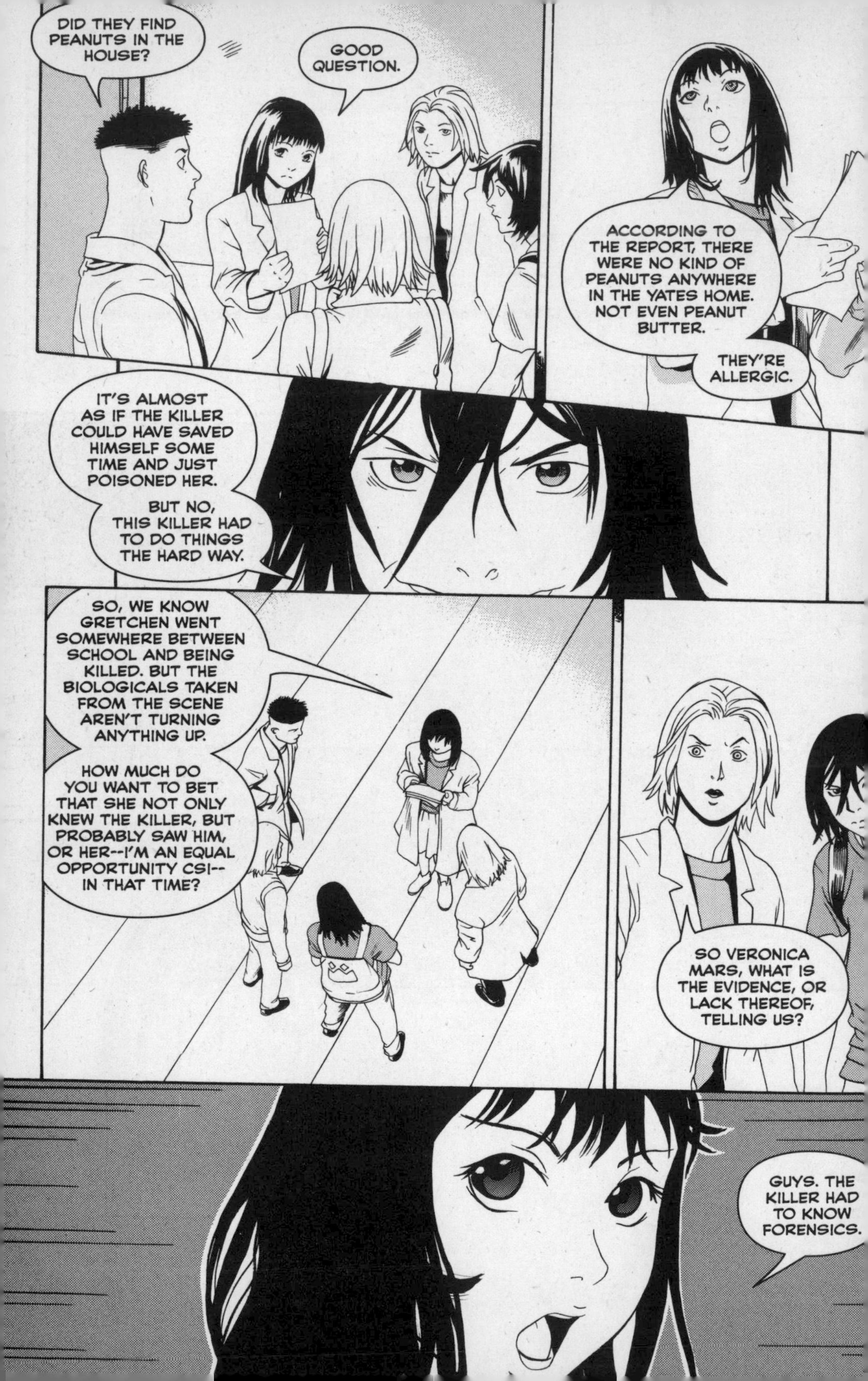
DID THEY FIND PEANUTS IN THE HOUSE?
GOOD QUESTION.
ACCORDING TO THE REPORT, THERE WERE NO KIND OF PEANUTS ANYWHERE IN THE YATES HOME. NOT EVEN PEANUT BUTTER.
THEY'RE ALLERGIC.
IT'S ALMOST AS IF THE KILLER COULD HAVE SAVED HIMSELF SOME TIME AND JUST POISONED HER.
BUT NO, THIS KILLER HAD TO DO THINGS THE HARD WAY.
SO, WE KNOW GRETCHEN WENT SOMEWHERE BETWEEN SCHOOL AND BEING KILLED. BUT THE BIOLOGICALS TAKEN FROM THE SCENE AREN'T TURNING ANYTHING UP.
HOW MUCH DO YOU WANT TO BET THAT SHE NOT ONLY KNEW THE KILLER, BUT PROBABLY SAW HIM, OR HER--I'M AN EQUAL OPPORTUNITY CSI-- IN THAT TIME?
SO VERONICA MARS, WHAT IS THE EVIDENCE, OR LACK THEREOF, TELLING US?
GUYS. THE KILLER HAD TO KNOW FORENSICS.

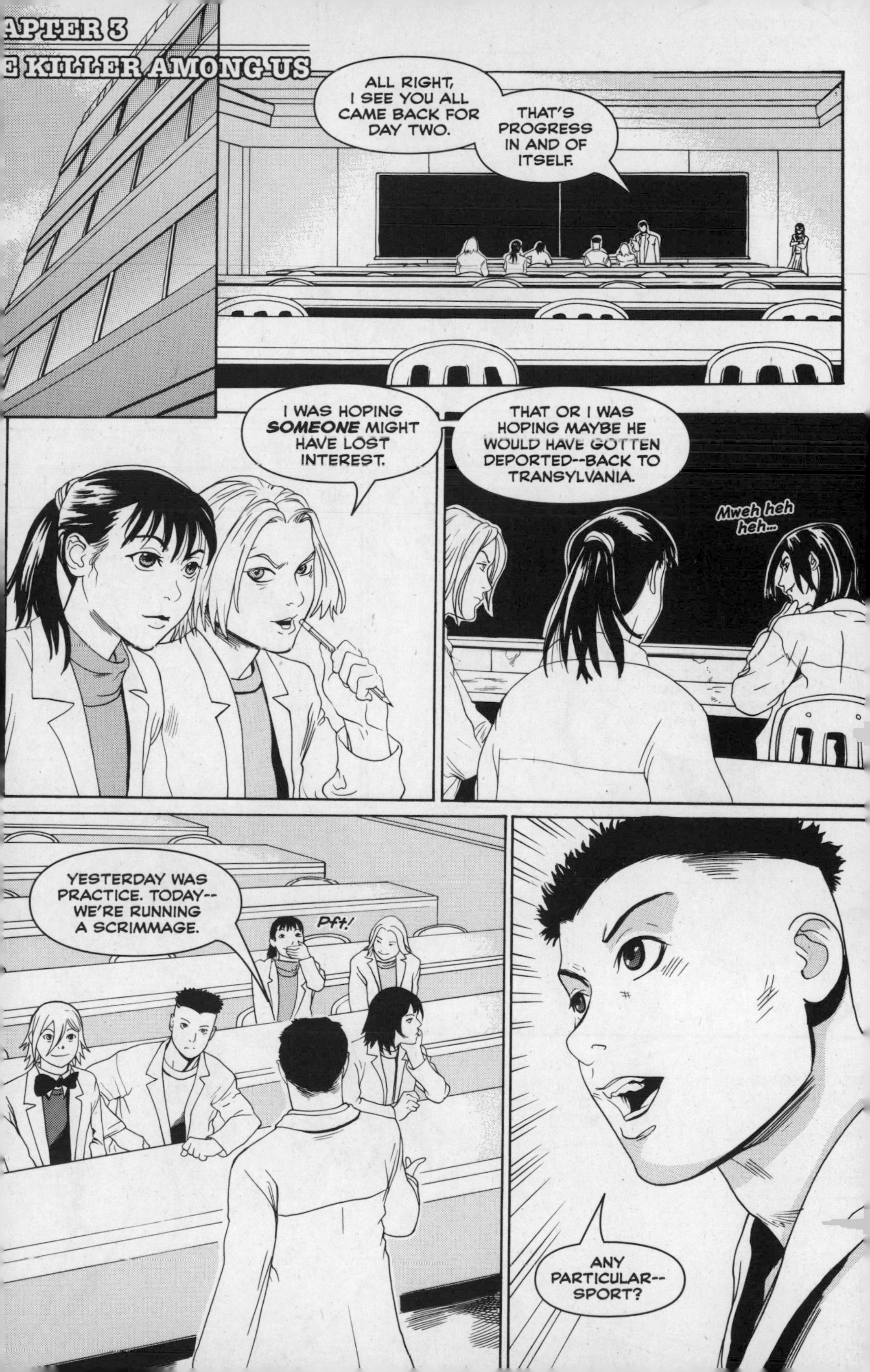
APTER 3
E KILLER AMONG US
ALL RIGHT, I SEE YOU ALL CAME BACK FOR DAY TWO.
THAT'S PROGRESS IN AND OF ITSELF.
I WAS HOPING SOMEONE MIGHT HAVE LOST INTEREST.
THAT OR I WAS HOPING MAYBE HE WOULD HAVE GOTTEN DEPORTED--BACK TO TRANSYLVANIA.
Mweh heh heh...
YESTERDAY WAS PRACTICE. TODAY--WE'RE RUNNING A SCRIMMAGE.
Pft!
ANY PARTICULAR--SPORT?

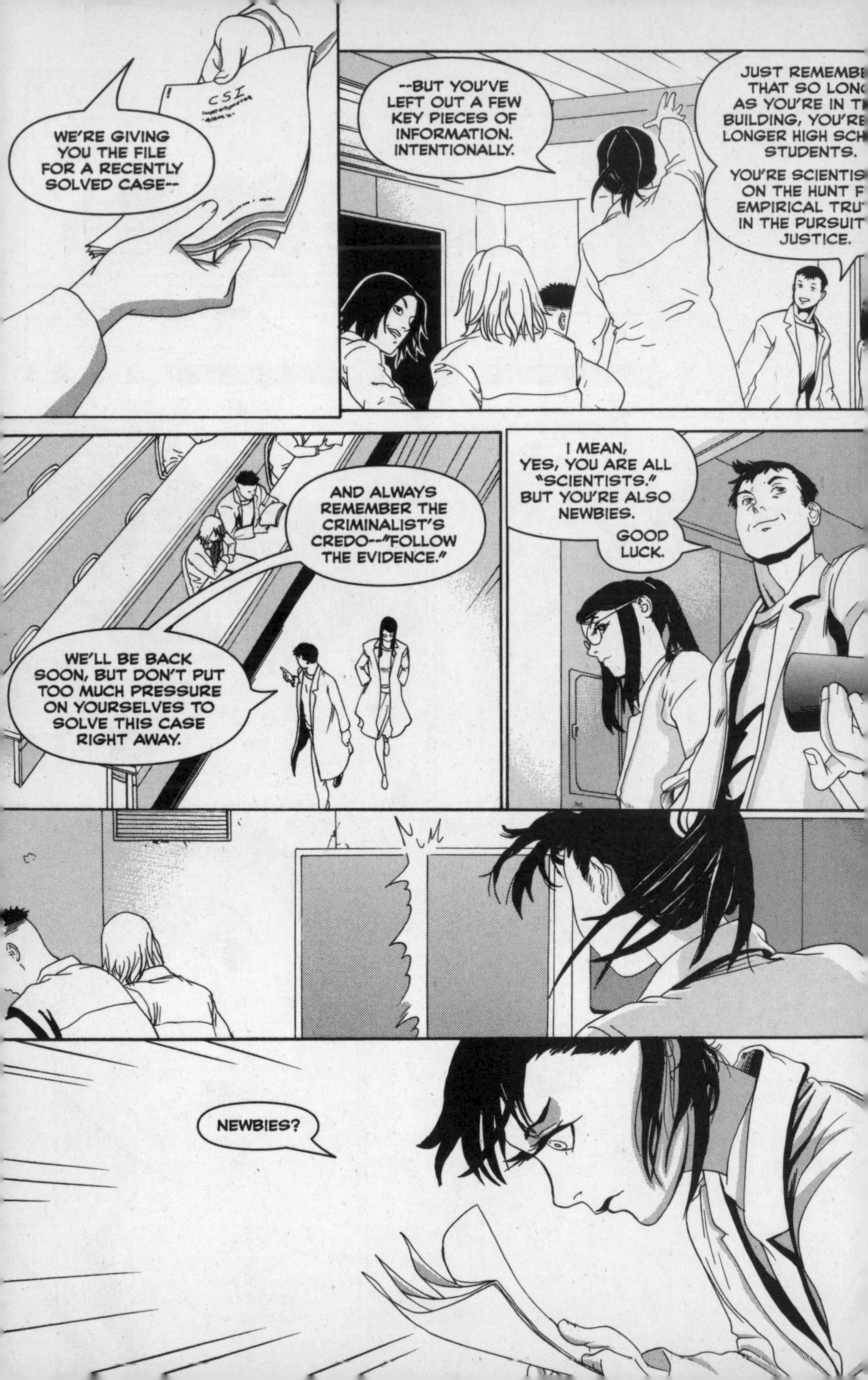

CSI
WE'RE GIVING YOU THE FILE FOR A RECENTLY SOLVED CASE--
--BUT YOU'VE LEFT OUT A FEW KEY PIECES OF INFORMATION. INTENTIONALLY.
JUST REMEMB THAT SO LONG AS YOU'RE IN T BUILDING, YOU'RE LONGER HIGH SCH STUDENTS.
YOU'RE SCIENTIS ON THE HUNT F EMPIRICAL TRU IN THE PURSUIT JUSTICE.
AND ALWAYS REMEMBER THE CRIMINALIST'S CREDO--"FOLLOW THE EVIDENCE."
WE'LL BE BACK SOON, BUT DON'T PUT TOO MUCH PRESSURE ON YOURSELVES TO SOLVE THIS CASE RIGHT AWAY.
I MEAN, YES, YOU ARE ALL "SCIENTISTS." BUT YOU'RE ALSO NEWBIES.
GOOD LUCK.
NEWBIES?

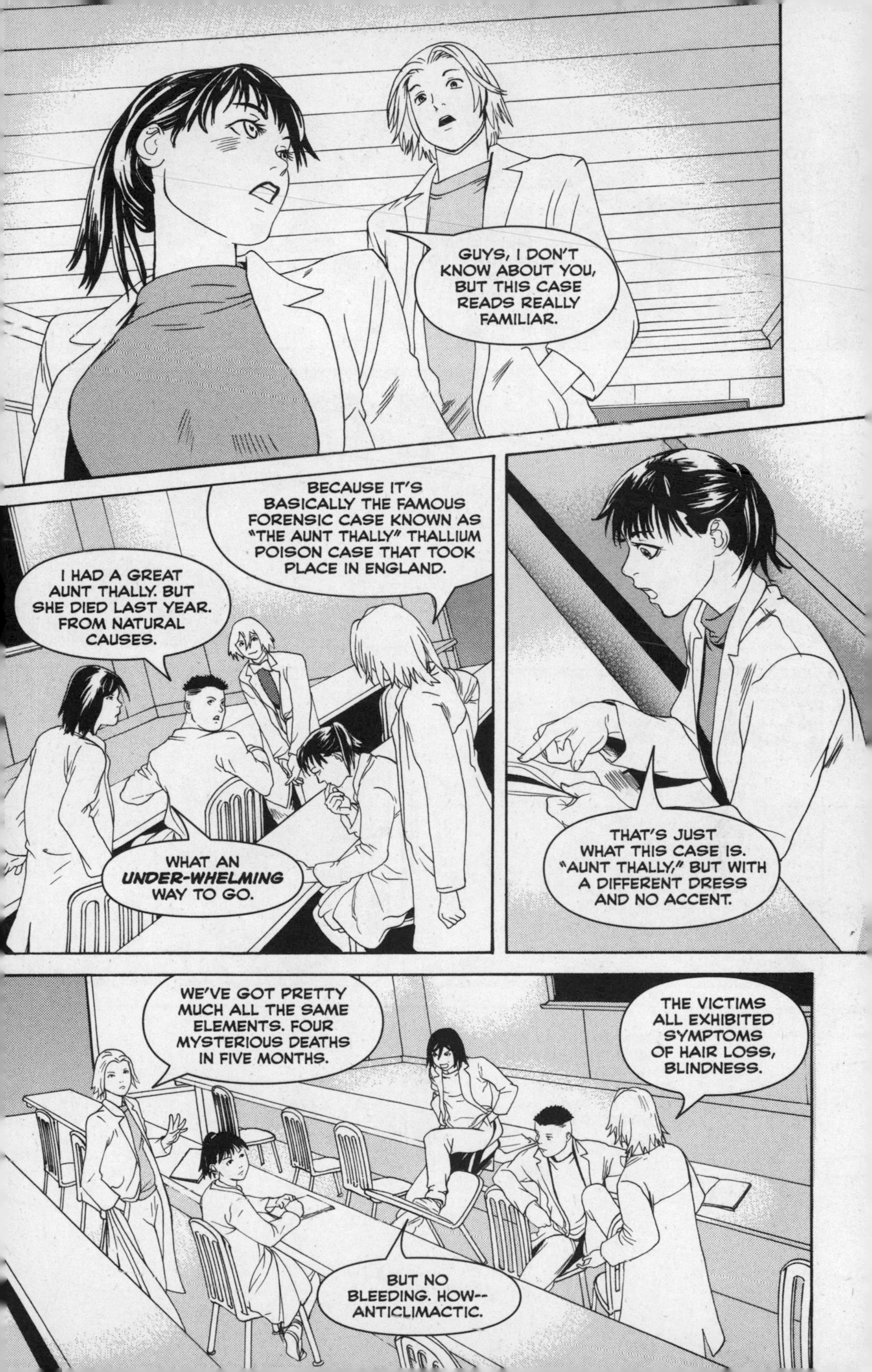
GUYS, I DON'T KNOW ABOUT YOU, BUT THIS CASE READS REALLY FAMILIAR.
BECAUSE IT'S BASICALLY THE FAMOUS FORENSIC CASE KNOWN AS "THE AUNT THALLY" THALLIUM POISON CASE THAT TOOK PLACE IN ENGLAND.
I HAD A GREAT AUNT THALLY. BUT SHE DIED LAST YEAR. FROM NATURAL CAUSES.
WHAT AN UNDER-WHELMING WAY TO GO.
THAT'S JUST WHAT THIS CASE IS. "AUNT THALLY," BUT WITH A DIFFERENT DRESS AND NO ACCENT.
WE'VE GOT PRETTY MUCH ALL THE SAME ELEMENTS. FOUR MYSTERIOUS DEATHS IN FIVE MONTHS.
THE VICTIMS ALL EXHIBITED SYMPTOMS OF HAIR LOSS, BLINDNESS.
BUT NO BLEEDING. HOW--ANTICLIMACTIC.

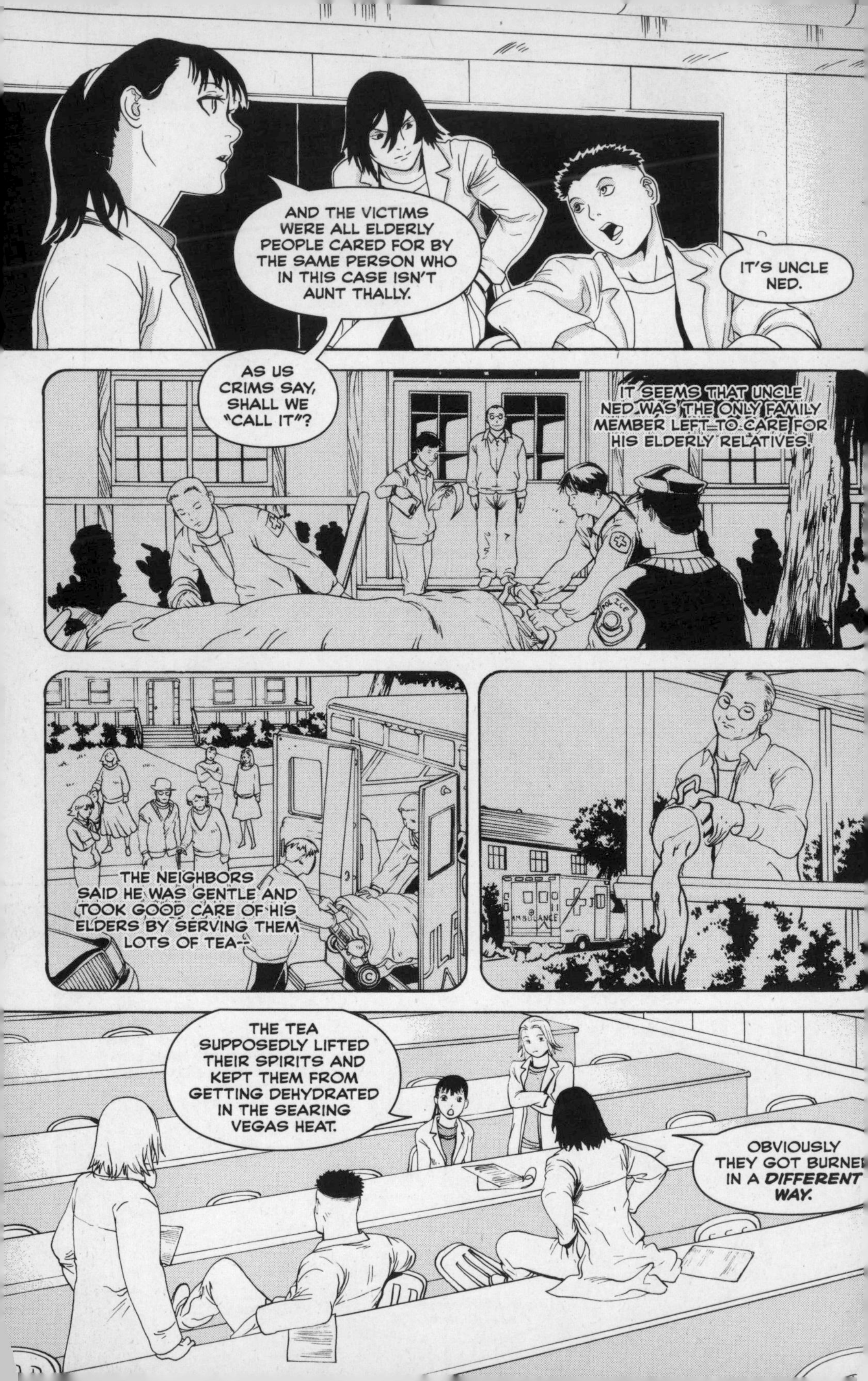
AND THE VICTIMS WERE ALL ELDERLY PEOPLE CARED FOR BY THE SAME PERSON WHO IN THIS CASE ISN'T AUNT THALLY.
IT'S UNCLE NED.
AS US CRIMS SAY, SHALL WE "CALL IT"?
IT SEEMS THAT UNCLE NED WAS THE ONLY FAMILY MEMBER LEFT TO CARE FOR HIS ELDERLY RELATIVES.
POLICE
THE NEIGHBORS SAID HE WAS GENTLE AND TOOK GOOD CARE OF HIS ELDERS BY SERVING THEM LOTS OF TEA--
AMBULANCE
THE TEA SUPPOSEDLY LIFTED THEIR SPIRITS AND KEPT THEM FROM GETTING DEHYDRATED IN THE SEARING VEGAS HEAT.
OBVIOUSLY THEY GOT BURNE IN A *DIFFERENT* WAY.

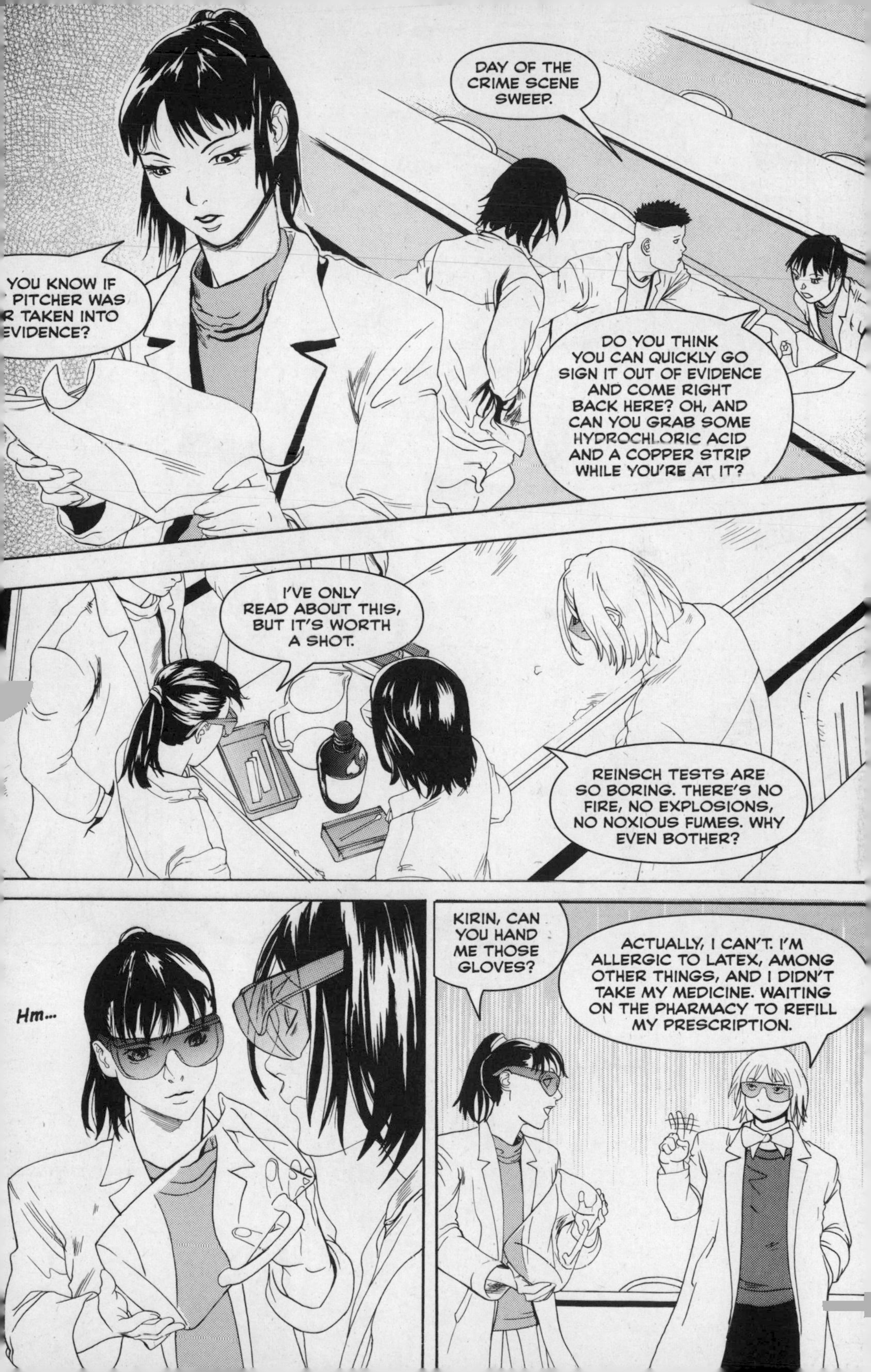

DAY OF THE CRIME SCENE SWEEP.
YOU KNOW IF PITCHER WAS R TAKEN INTO EVIDENCE?
DO YOU THINK YOU CAN QUICKLY GO SIGN IT OUT OF EVIDENCE AND COME RIGHT BACK HERE? OH, AND CAN YOU GRAB SOME HYDROCHLORIC ACID AND A COPPER STRIP WHILE YOU'RE AT IT?
I'VE ONLY READ ABOUT THIS, BUT IT'S WORTH A SHOT.
REINSCH TESTS ARE SO BORING. THERE'S NO FIRE, NO EXPLOSIONS, NO NOXIOUS FUMES. WHY EVEN BOTHER?
Hm...
KIRIN, CAN YOU HAND ME THOSE GLOVES?
ACTUALLY, I CAN'T. I'M ALLERGIC TO LATEX, AMONG OTHER THINGS, AND I DIDN'T TAKE MY MEDICINE. WAITING ON THE PHARMACY TO REFILL MY PRESCRIPTION.

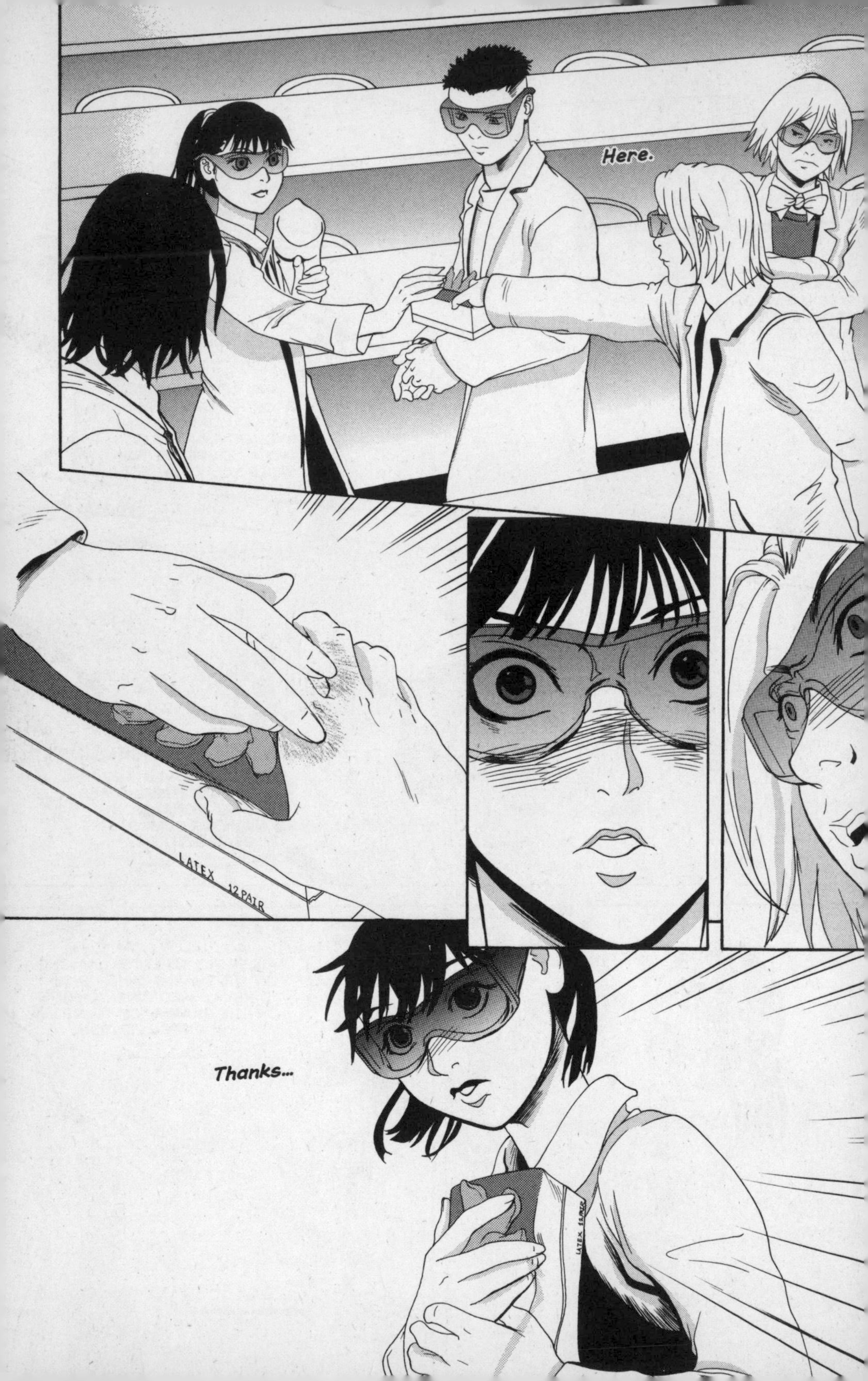
Here.
LATEX 12 PAIR
Thanks...

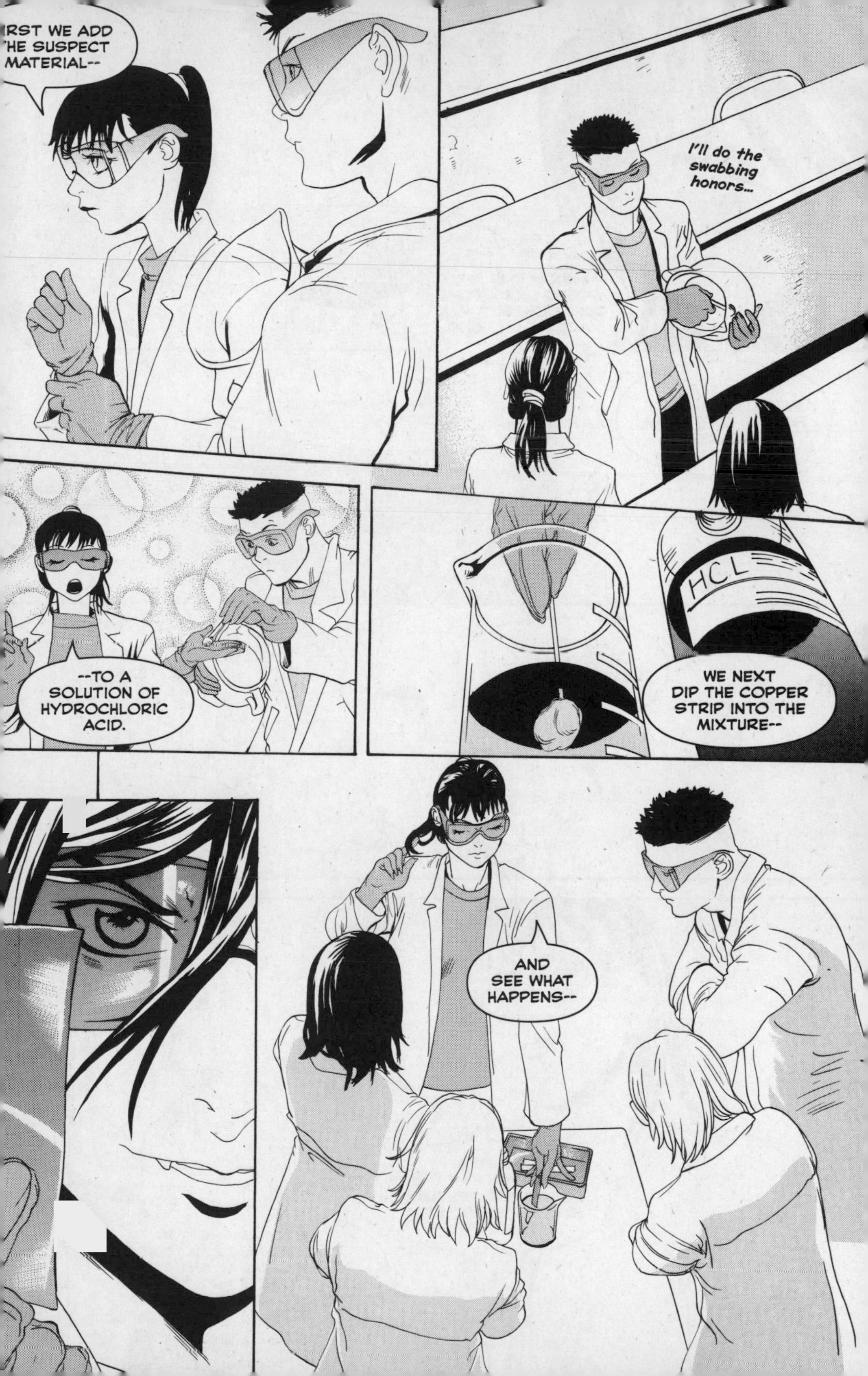

RST WE ADD
HE SUSPECT
MATERIAL--
I'll do the swabbing honors...
--TO A SOLUTION OF HYDROCHLORIC ACID.
HCL
WE NEXT DIP THE COPPER STRIP INTO THE MIXTURE--
AND SEE WHAT HAPPENS--

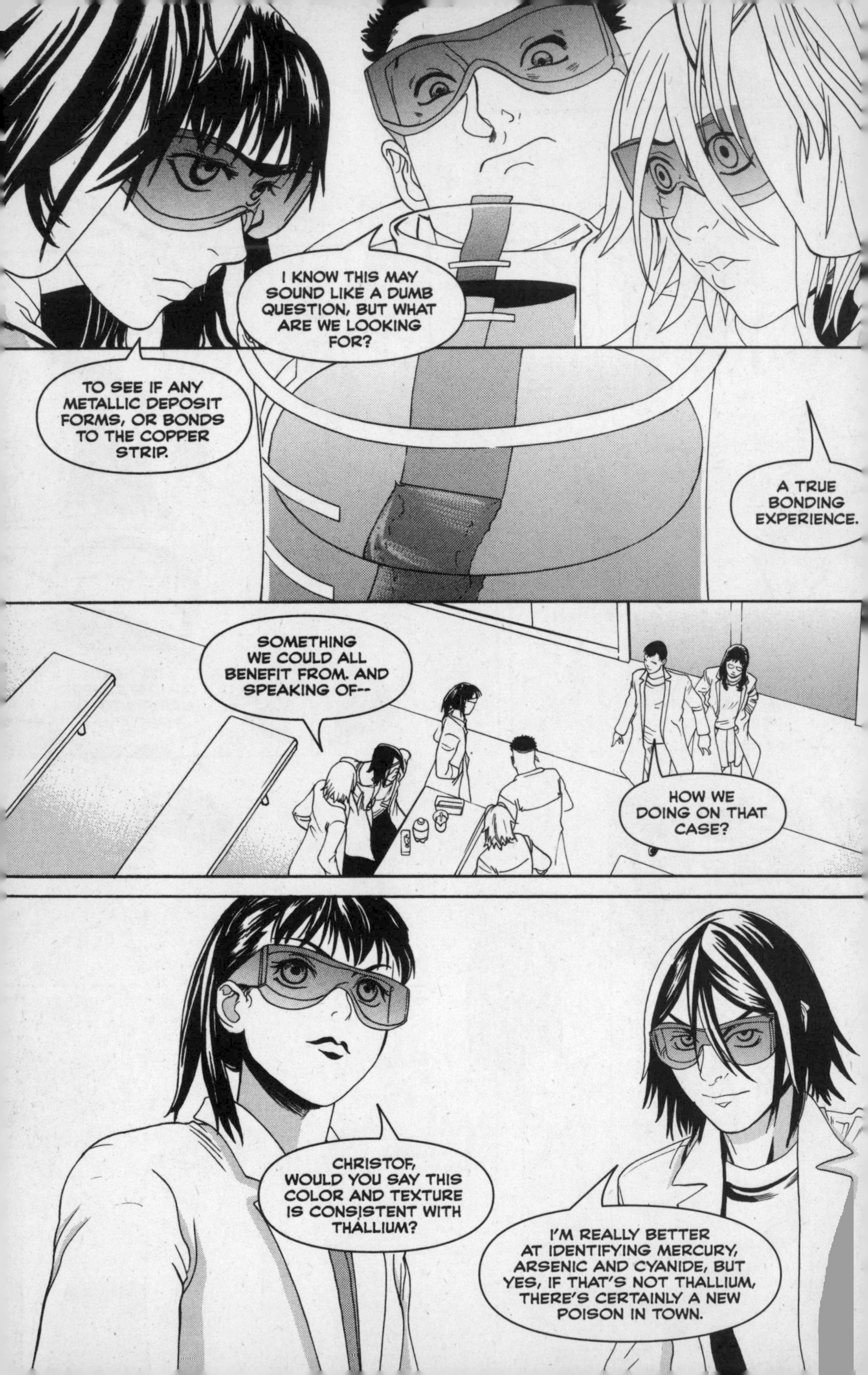
I KNOW THIS MAY SOUND LIKE A DUMB QUESTION, BUT WHAT ARE WE LOOKING FOR?
TO SEE IF ANY METALLIC DEPOSIT FORMS, OR BONDS TO THE COPPER STRIP.
A TRUE BONDING EXPERIENCE.
SOMETHING WE COULD ALL BENEFIT FROM. AND SPEAKING OF--
HOW WE DOING ON THAT CASE?
CHRISTOF, WOULD YOU SAY THIS COLOR AND TEXTURE IS CONSISTENT WITH THALLIUM?
I'M REALLY BETTER AT IDENTIFYING MERCURY, ARSENIC AND CYANIDE, BUT YES, IF THAT'S NOT THALLIUM, THERE'S CERTAINLY A NEW POISON IN TOWN.

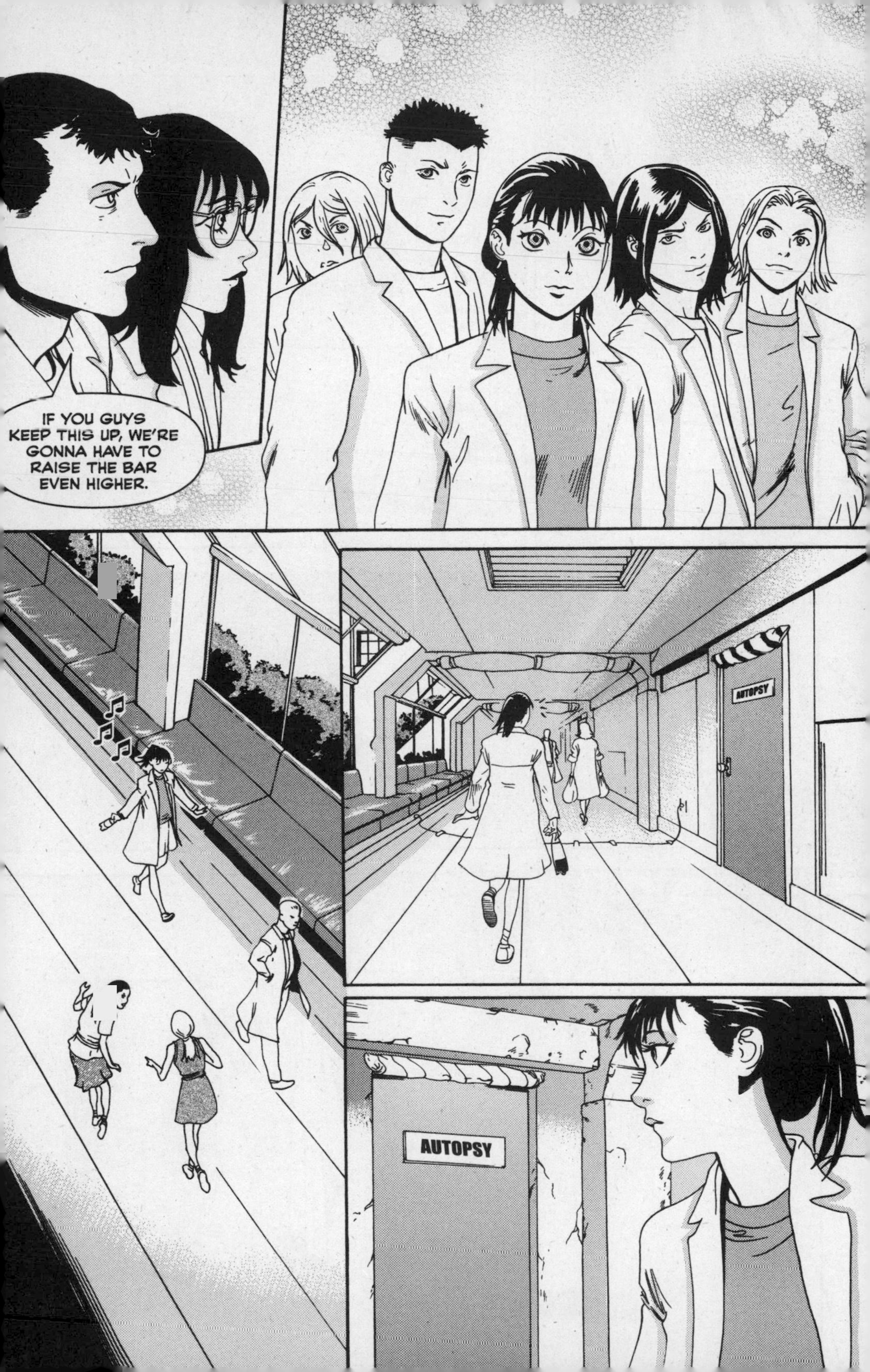
IF YOU GUYS KEEP THIS UP, WE'RE GONNA HAVE TO RAISE THE BAR EVEN HIGHER.
AUTOPSY
AUTOPSY

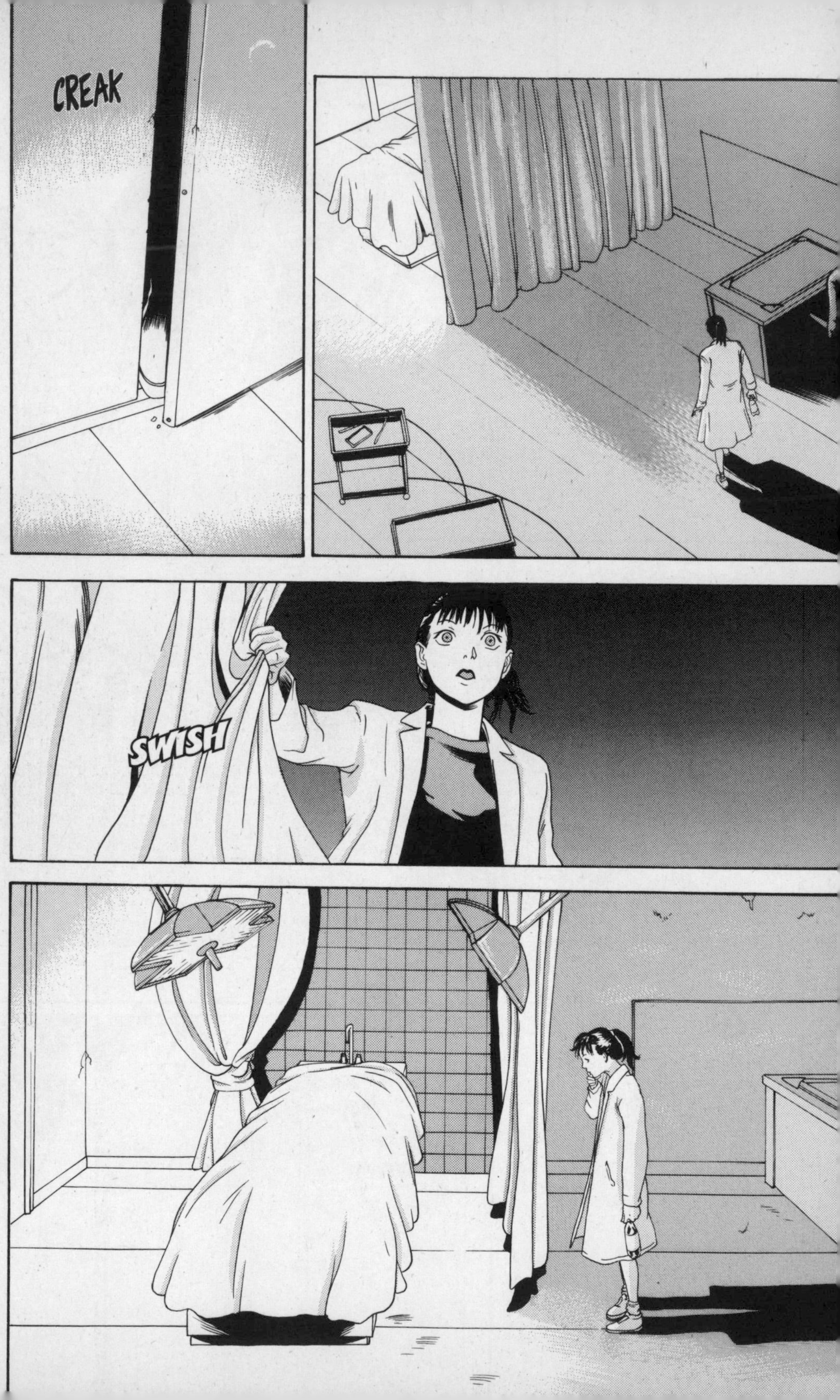
CREAK
SWISH

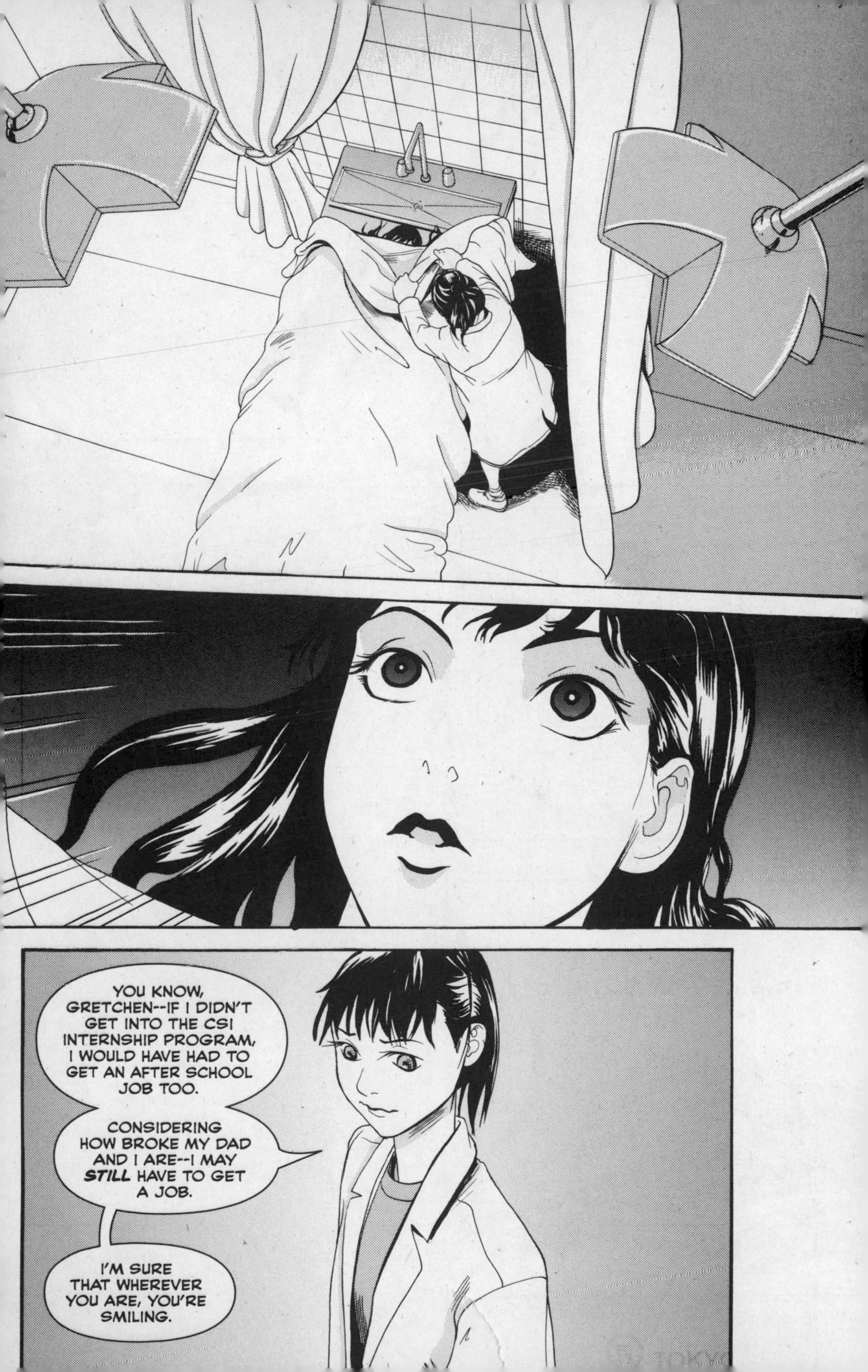
YOU KNOW, GRETCHEN--IF I DIDN'T GET INTO THE CSI INTERNSHIP PROGRAM, I WOULD HAVE HAD TO GET AN AFTER SCHOOL JOB TOO.
CONSIDERING HOW BROKE MY DAD AND I ARE--I MAY *STILL* HAVE TO GET A JOB.
I'M SURE THAT WHEREVER YOU ARE, YOU'RE SMILING.

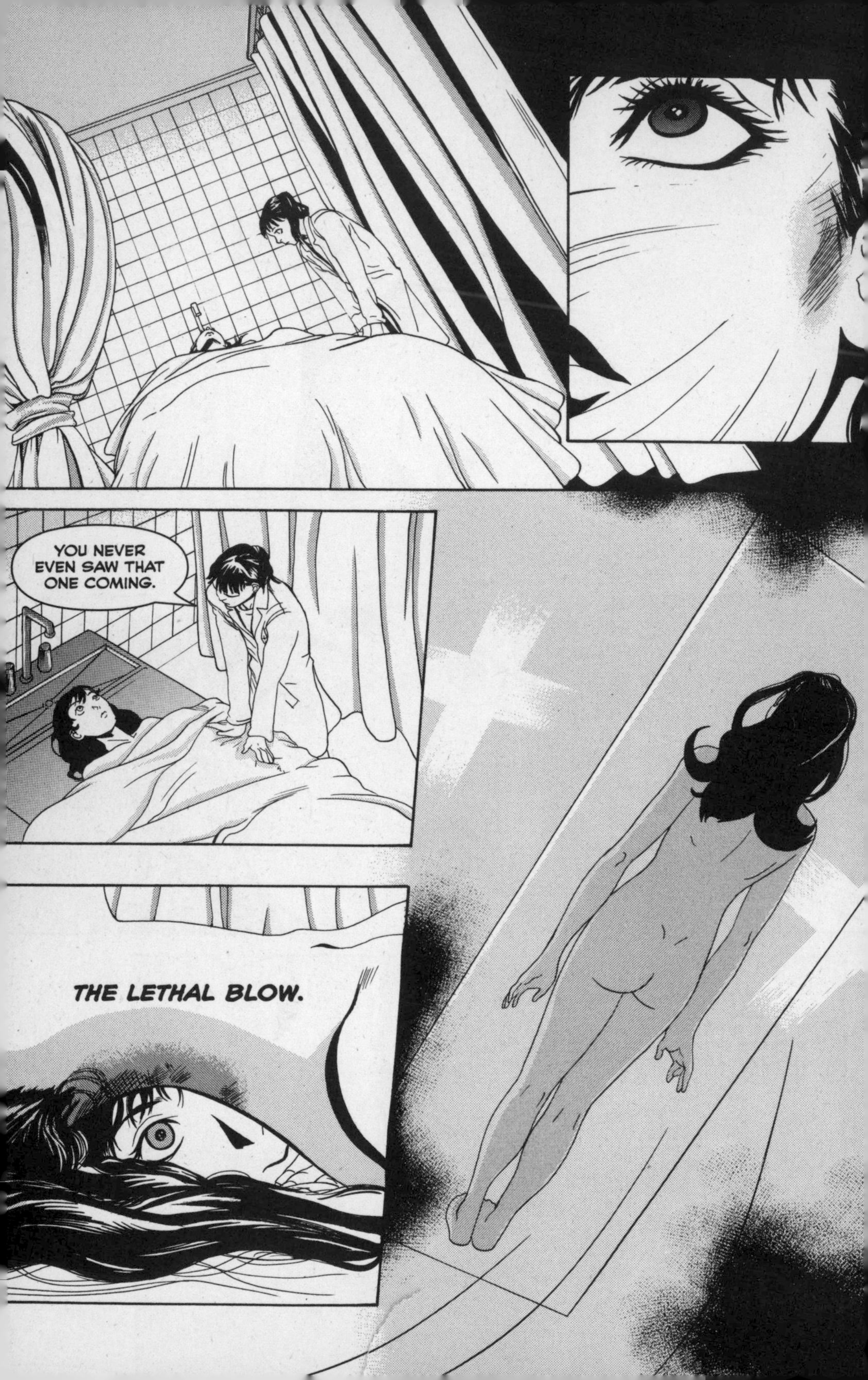
YOU NEVER EVEN SAW THAT ONE COMING.
THE LETHAL BLOW.

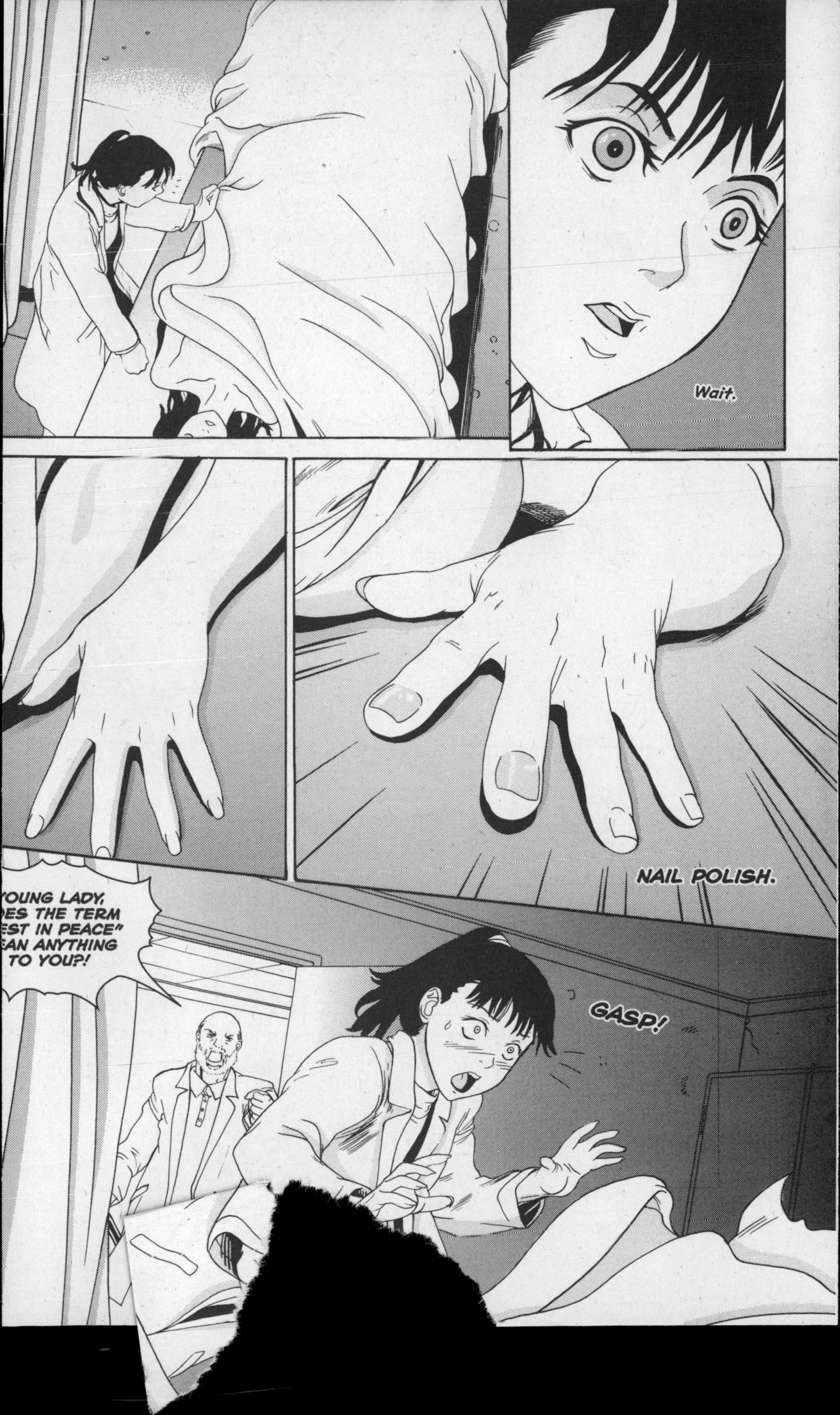
Wait.
NAIL POLISH.
YOUNG LADY, DES THE TERM EST IN PEACE" EAN ANYTHING TO YOU?!
GASP!

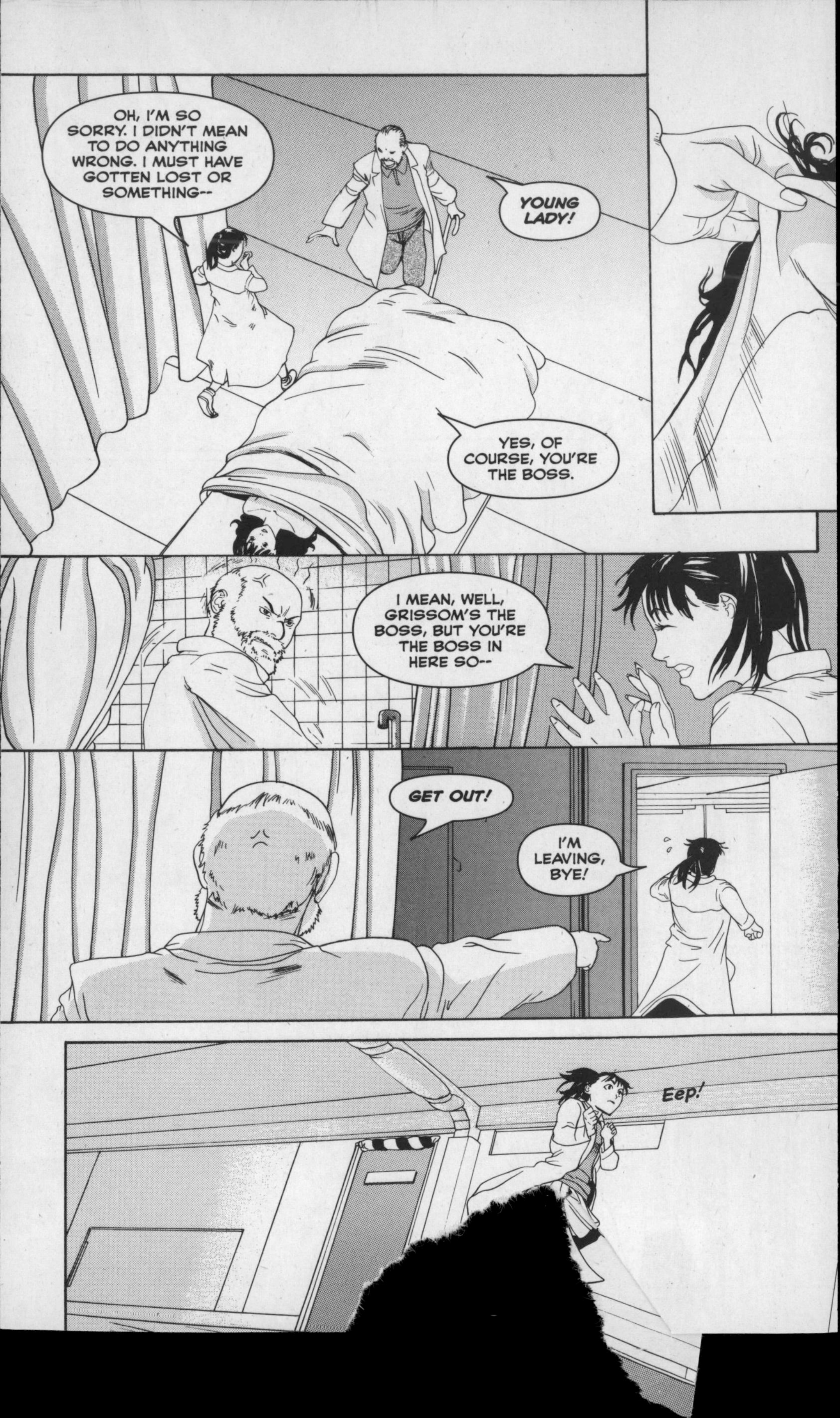
OH, I'M SO SORRY. I DIDN'T MEAN TO DO ANYTHING WRONG. I MUST HAVE GOTTEN LOST OR SOMETHING--
YOUNG LADY!
YES, OF COURSE, YOU'RE THE BOSS.
I MEAN, WELL, GRISSOM'S THE BOSS, BUT YOU'RE THE BOSS IN HERE SO--
GET OUT!
I'M LEAVING, BYE!
Eep!

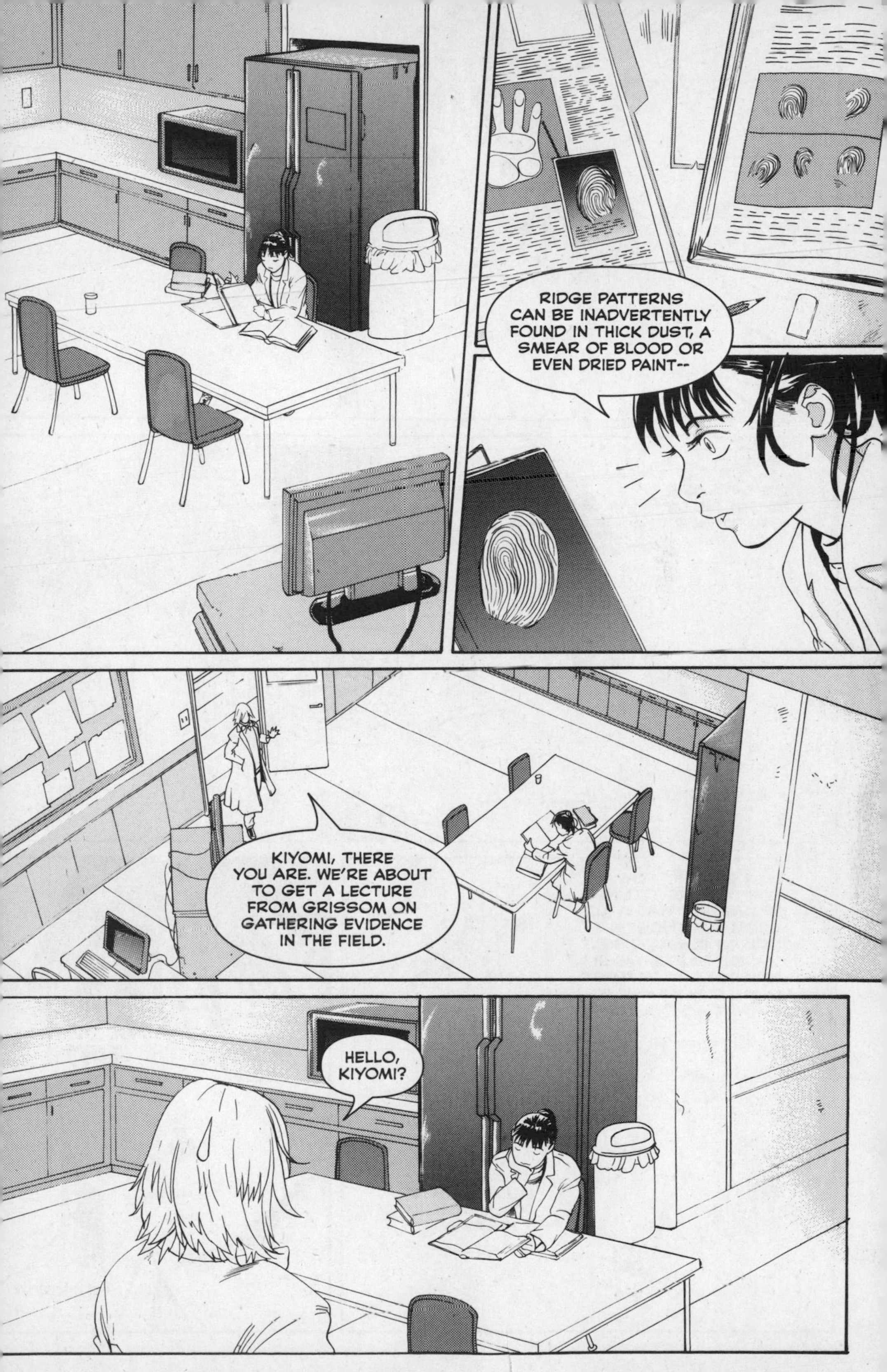
RIDGE PATTERNS CAN BE INADVERTENTLY FOUND IN THICK DUST, A SMEAR OF BLOOD OR EVEN DRIED PAINT--
KIYOMI, THERE YOU ARE. WE'RE ABOUT TO GET A LECTURE FROM GRISSOM ON GATHERING EVIDENCE IN THE FIELD.
HELLO, KIYOMI?

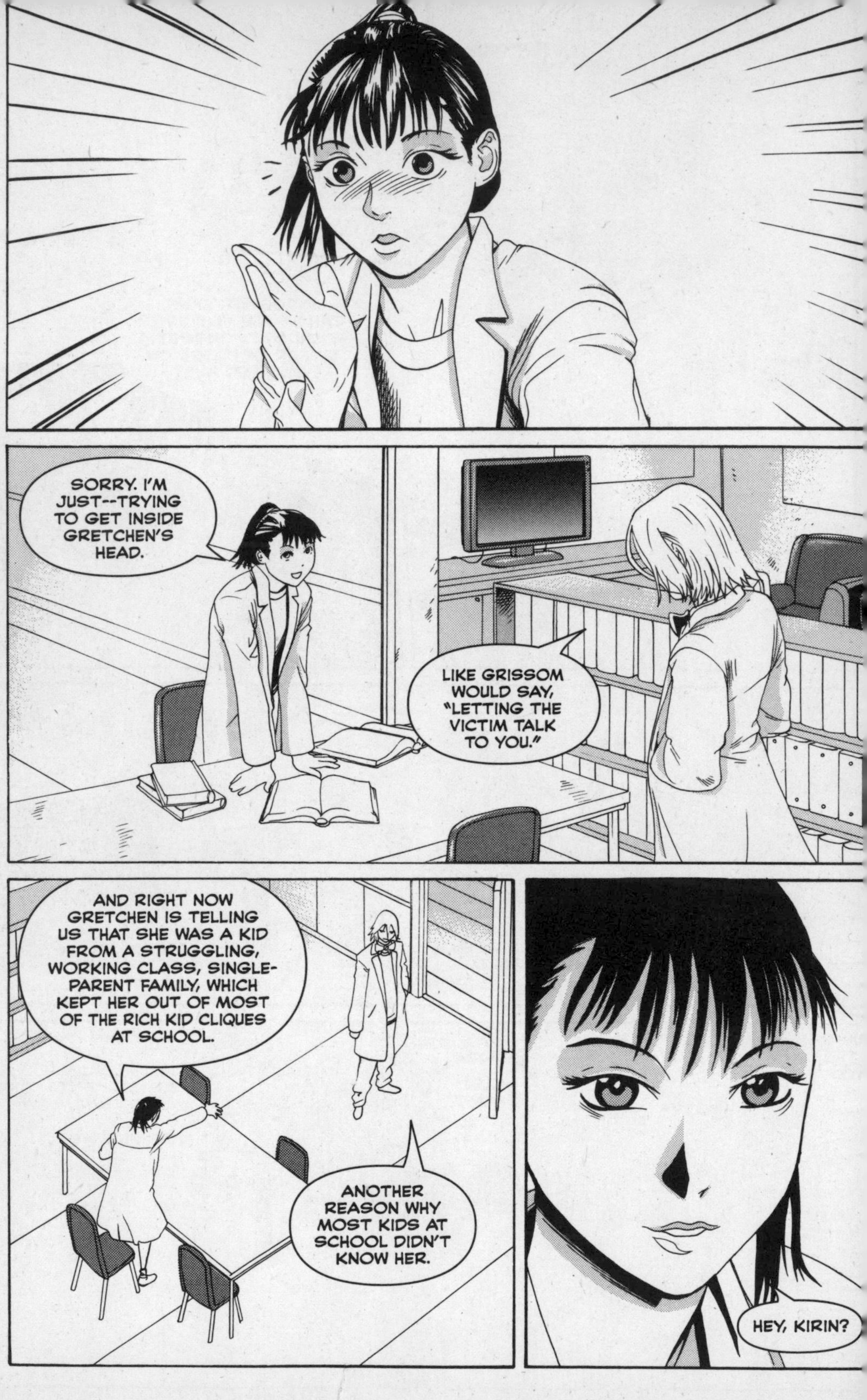
SORRY. I'M JUST--TRYING TO GET INSIDE GRETCHEN'S HEAD.
LIKE GRISSOM WOULD SAY, "LETTING THE VICTIM TALK TO YOU."
AND RIGHT NOW GRETCHEN IS TELLING US THAT SHE WAS A KID FROM A STRUGGLING, WORKING CLASS, SINGLE-PARENT FAMILY, WHICH KEPT HER OUT OF MOST OF THE RICH KID CLIQUES AT SCHOOL.
ANOTHER REASON WHY MOST KIDS AT SCHOOL DIDN'T KNOW HER.
HEY, KIRIN?

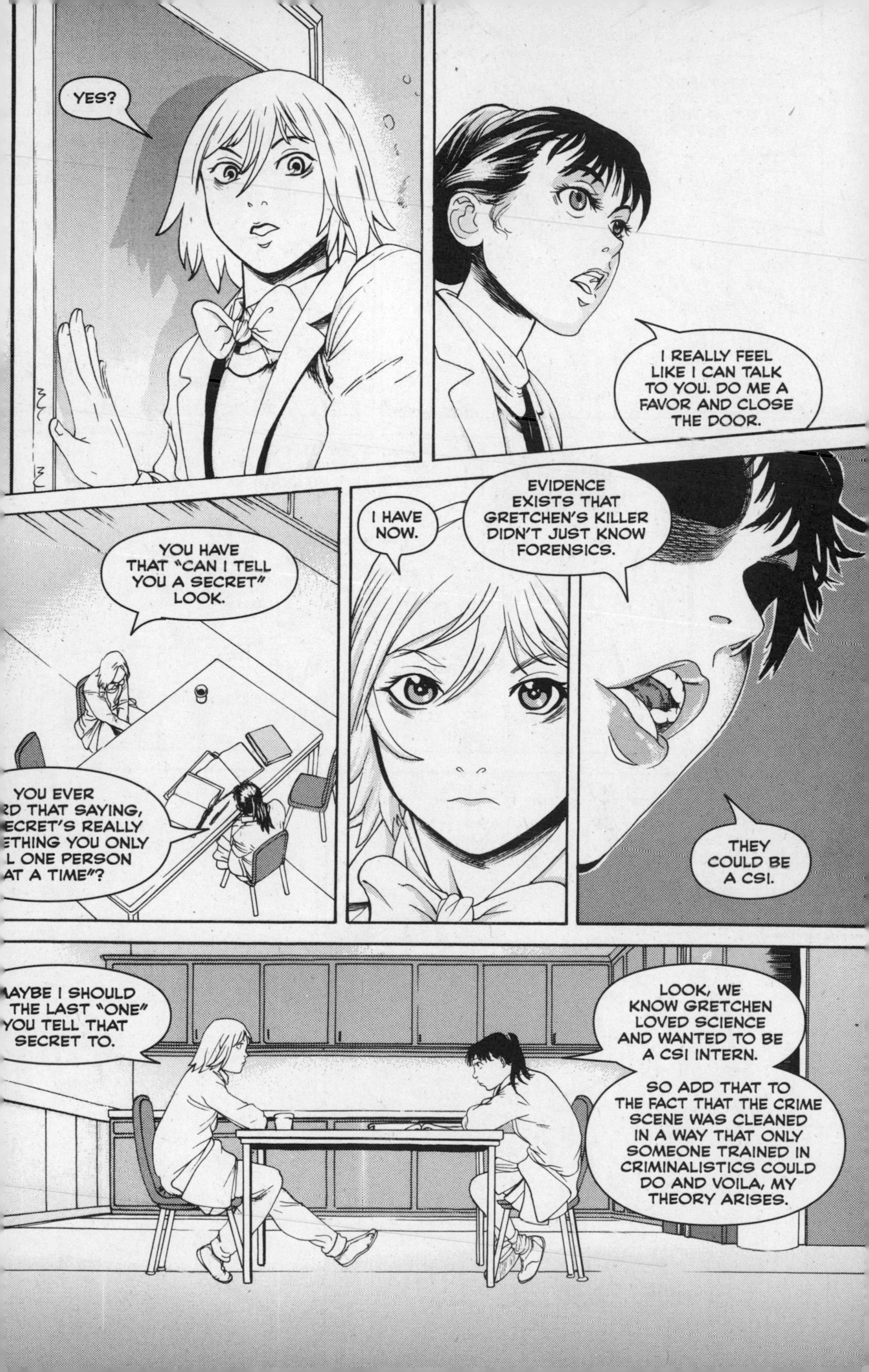
YES?
I REALLY FEEL LIKE I CAN TALK TO YOU. DO ME A FAVOR AND CLOSE THE DOOR.
YOU HAVE THAT "CAN I TELL YOU A SECRET" LOOK.
YOU EVER
RD THAT SAYING,
ECRET'S REALLY
ETHING YOU ONLY
L ONE PERSON
AT A TIME"?
I HAVE NOW.
EVIDENCE EXISTS THAT GRETCHEN'S KILLER DIDN'T JUST KNOW FORENSICS.
THEY COULD BE A CSI.
AYBE I SHOULD
THE LAST "ONE"
YOU TELL THAT
SECRET TO.
LOOK, WE KNOW GRETCHEN LOVED SCIENCE AND WANTED TO BE A CSI INTERN.
SO ADD THAT TO THE FACT THAT THE CRIME SCENE WAS CLEANED IN A WAY THAT ONLY SOMEONE TRAINED IN CRIMINALISTICS COULD DO AND VOILA, MY THEORY ARISES.

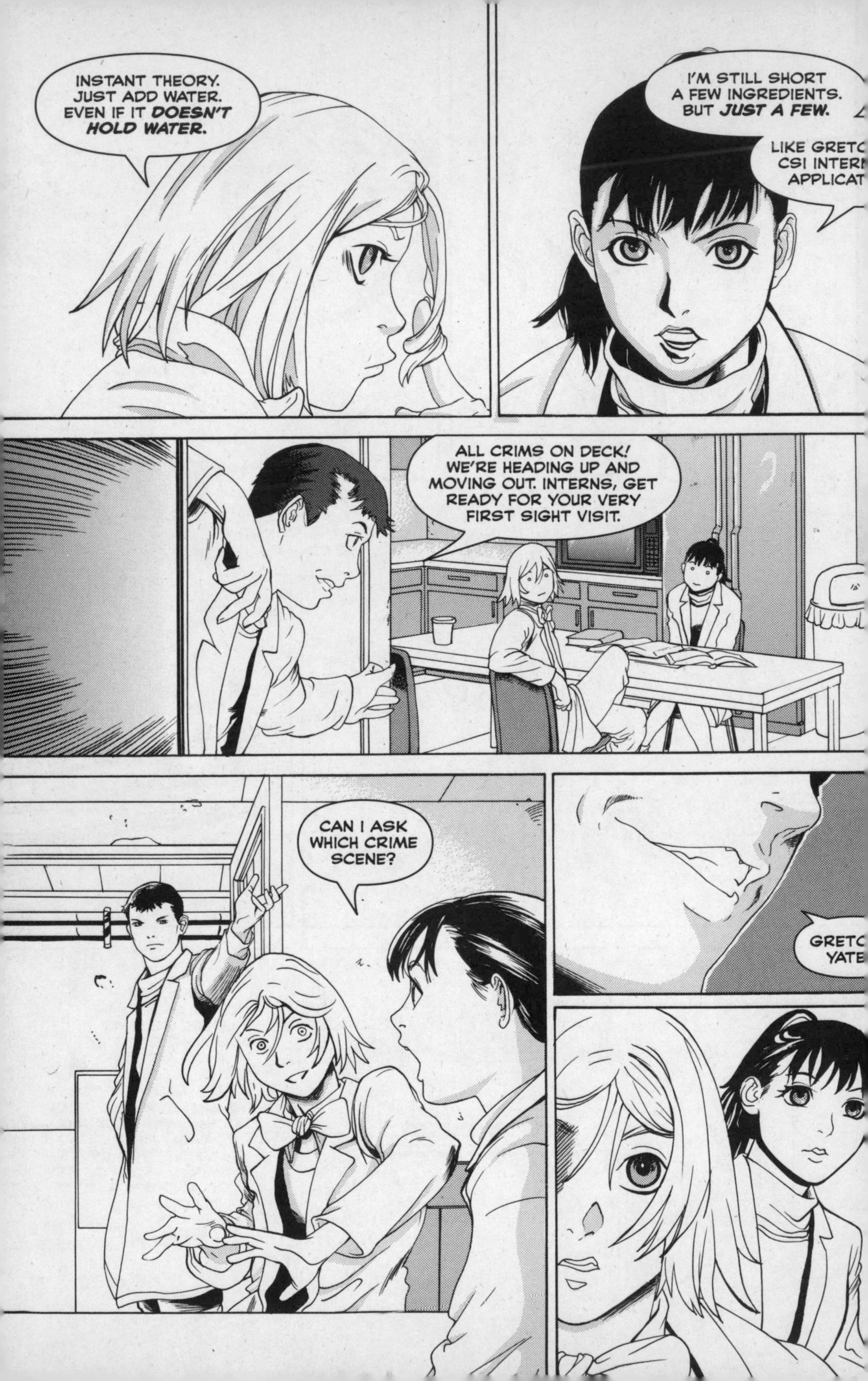
INSTANT THEORY. JUST ADD WATER. EVEN IF IT DOESN'T HOLD WATER.
I'M STILL SHORT A FEW INGREDIENTS. BUT JUST A FEW.
ALL CRIMS ON DECK! WE'RE HEADING UP AND MOVING OUT. INTERNS, GET READY FOR YOUR VERY FIRST SIGHT VISIT.
CAN I ASK WHICH CRIME SCENE?

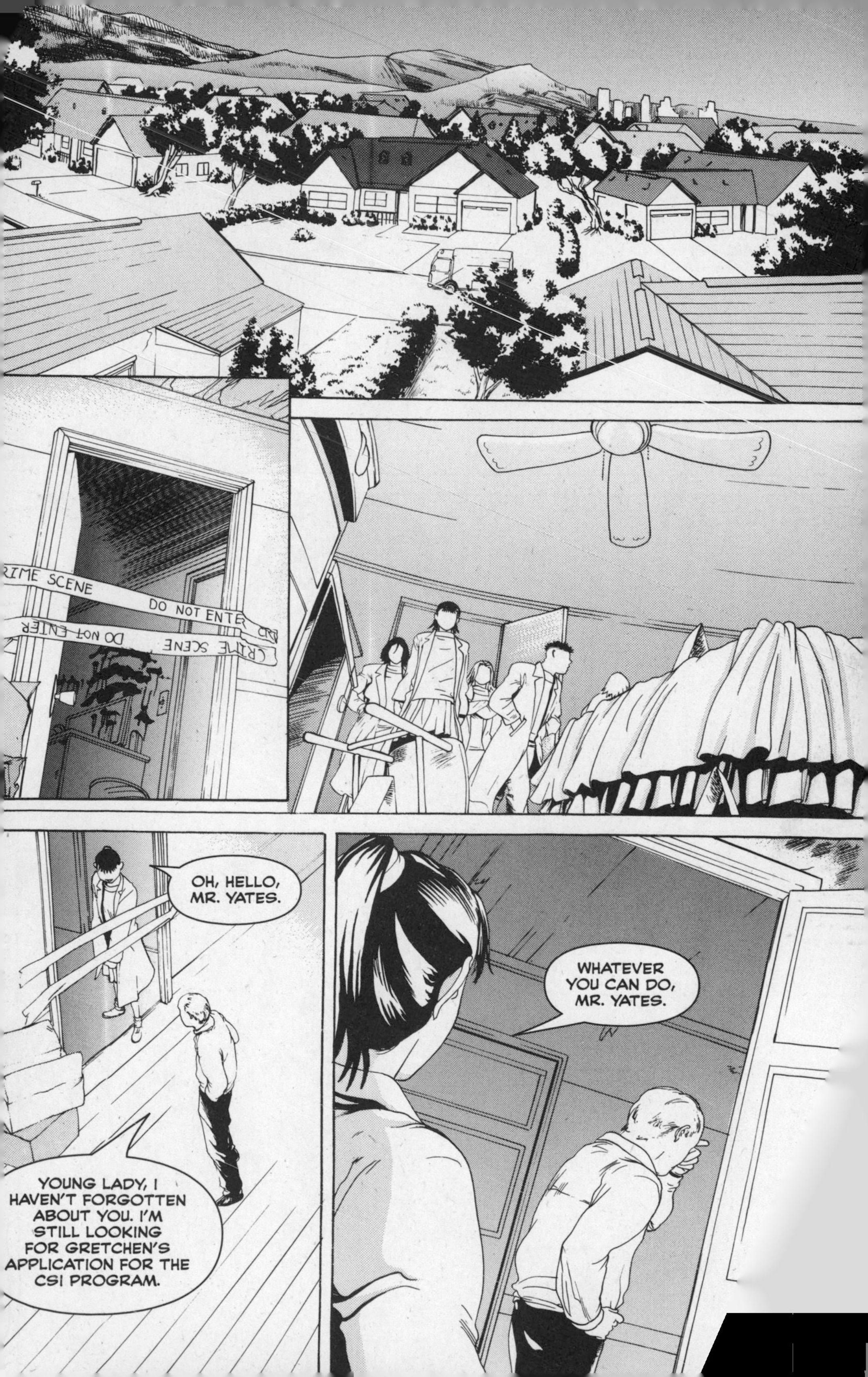

CRIME SCENE
DO NOT ENTER
OH, HELLO, MR. YATES.
YOUNG LADY, I HAVEN'T FORGOTTEN ABOUT YOU. I'M STILL LOOKING FOR GRETCHEN'S APPLICATION FOR THE CSI PROGRAM.
WHATEVER YOU CAN DO, MR. YATES.

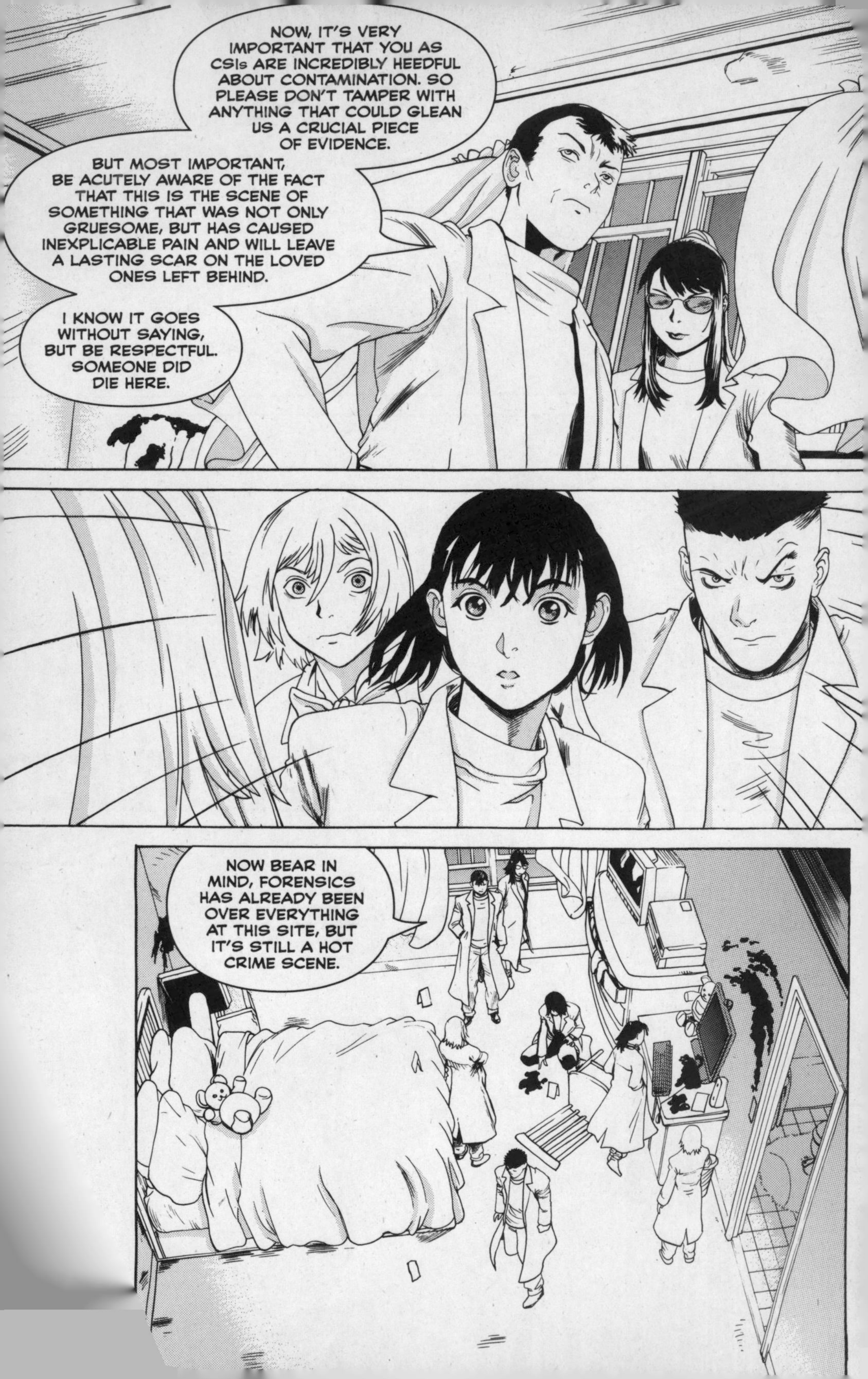
NOW, IT'S VERY IMPORTANT THAT YOU AS CSIs ARE INCREDIBLY HEEDFUL ABOUT CONTAMINATION. SO PLEASE DON'T TAMPER WITH ANYTHING THAT COULD GLEAN US A CRUCIAL PIECE OF EVIDENCE.
BUT MOST IMPORTANT, BE ACUTELY AWARE OF THE FACT THAT THIS IS THE SCENE OF SOMETHING THAT WAS NOT ONLY GRUESOME, BUT HAS CAUSED INEXPLICABLE PAIN AND WILL LEAVE A LASTING SCAR ON THE LOVED ONES LEFT BEHIND.
I KNOW IT GOES WITHOUT SAYING, BUT BE RESPECTFUL. SOMEONE DID DIE HERE.
NOW BEAR IN MIND, FORENSICS HAS ALREADY BEEN OVER EVERYTHING AT THIS SITE, BUT IT'S STILL A HOT CRIME SCENE.

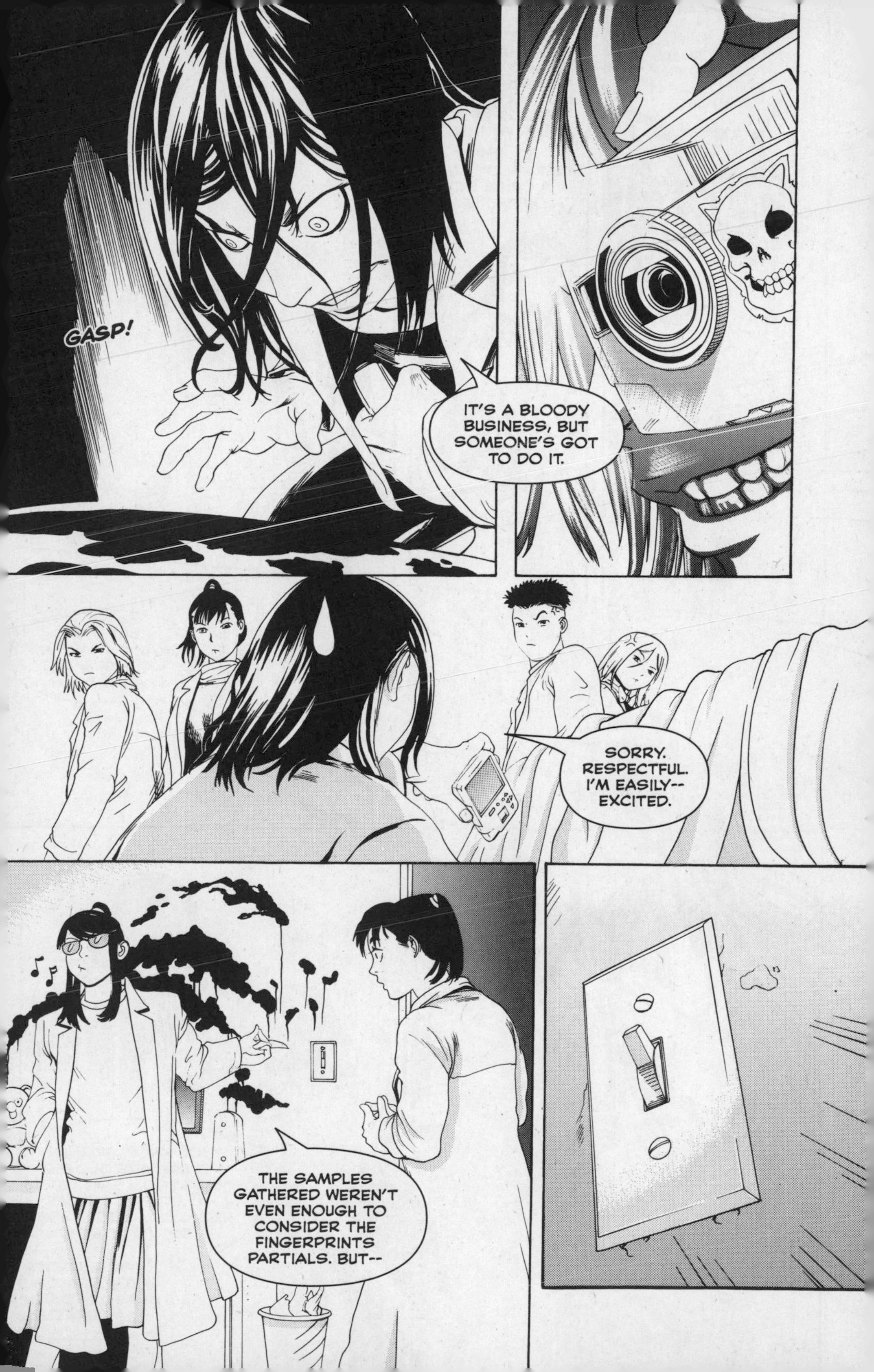
GASP!
IT'S A BLOODY BUSINESS, BUT SOMEONE'S GOT TO DO IT.
SORRY. RESPECTFUL. I'M EASILY-- EXCITED.
THE SAMPLES GATHERED WEREN'T EVEN ENOUGH TO CONSIDER THE FINGERPRINTS PARTIALS. BUT--

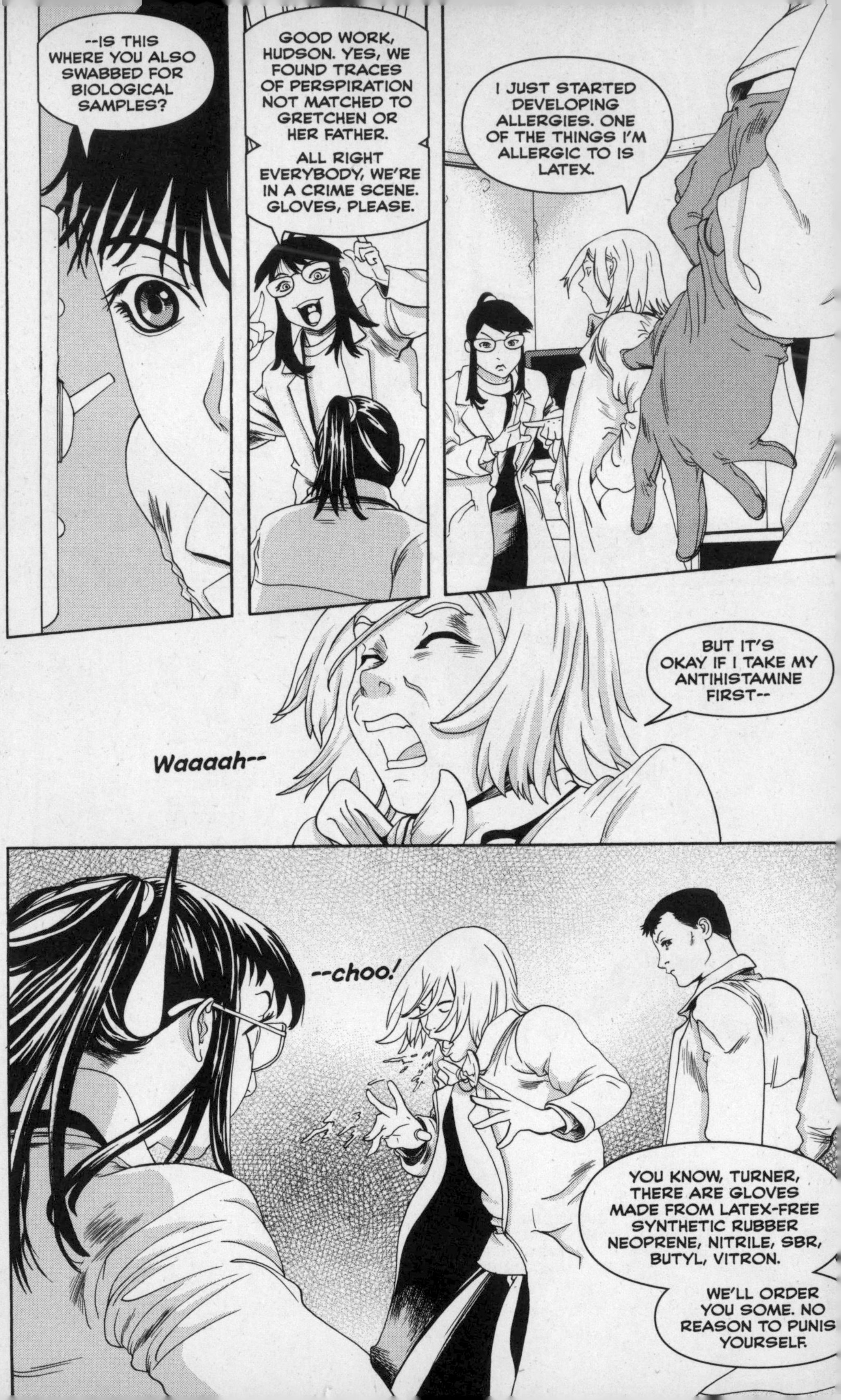
--IS THIS WHERE YOU ALSO SWABBED FOR BIOLOGICAL SAMPLES?
GOOD WORK, HUDSON. YES, WE FOUND TRACES OF PERSPIRATION NOT MATCHED TO GRETCHEN OR HER FATHER.
ALL RIGHT EVERYBODY, WE'RE IN A CRIME SCENE. GLOVES, PLEASE.
I JUST STARTED DEVELOPING ALLERGIES. ONE OF THE THINGS I'M ALLERGIC TO IS LATEX.
BUT IT'S OKAY IF I TAKE MY ANTIHISTAMINE FIRST--
Waaaah--
--choo!
YOU KNOW, TURNER, THERE ARE GLOVES MADE FROM LATEX-FREE SYNTHETIC RUBBER NEOPRENE, NITRILE, SBR, BUTYL, VITRON.
WE'LL ORDER YOU SOME. NO REASON TO PUNIS YOURSELF.

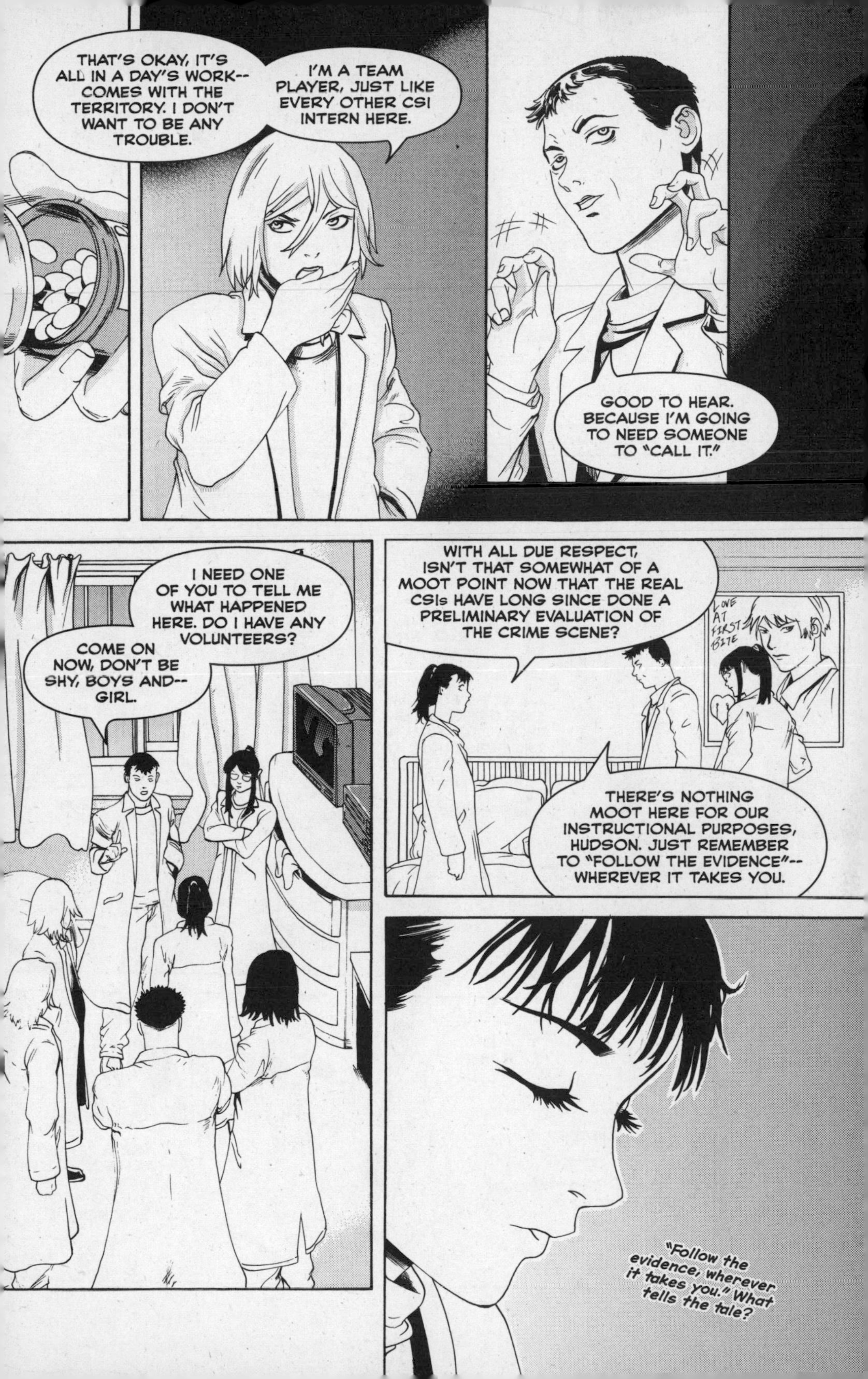
THAT'S OKAY, IT'S ALL IN A DAY'S WORK--COMES WITH THE TERRITORY. I DON'T WANT TO BE ANY TROUBLE.
I'M A TEAM PLAYER, JUST LIKE EVERY OTHER CSI INTERN HERE.
GOOD TO HEAR. BECAUSE I'M GOING TO NEED SOMEONE TO "CALL IT."
I NEED ONE OF YOU TO TELL ME WHAT HAPPENED HERE. DO I HAVE ANY VOLUNTEERS?
COME ON NOW, DON'T BE SHY, BOYS AND--GIRL.
WITH ALL DUE RESPECT, ISN'T THAT SOMEWHAT OF A MOOT POINT NOW THAT THE REAL CSIs HAVE LONG SINCE DONE A PRELIMINARY EVALUATION OF THE CRIME SCENE?
LOVE AT FIRST BITE
THERE'S NOTHING MOOT HERE FOR OUR INSTRUCTIONAL PURPOSES, HUDSON. JUST REMEMBER TO "FOLLOW THE EVIDENCE"--WHEREVER IT TAKES YOU.
"Follow the evidence, wherever it takes you." What tells the tale?

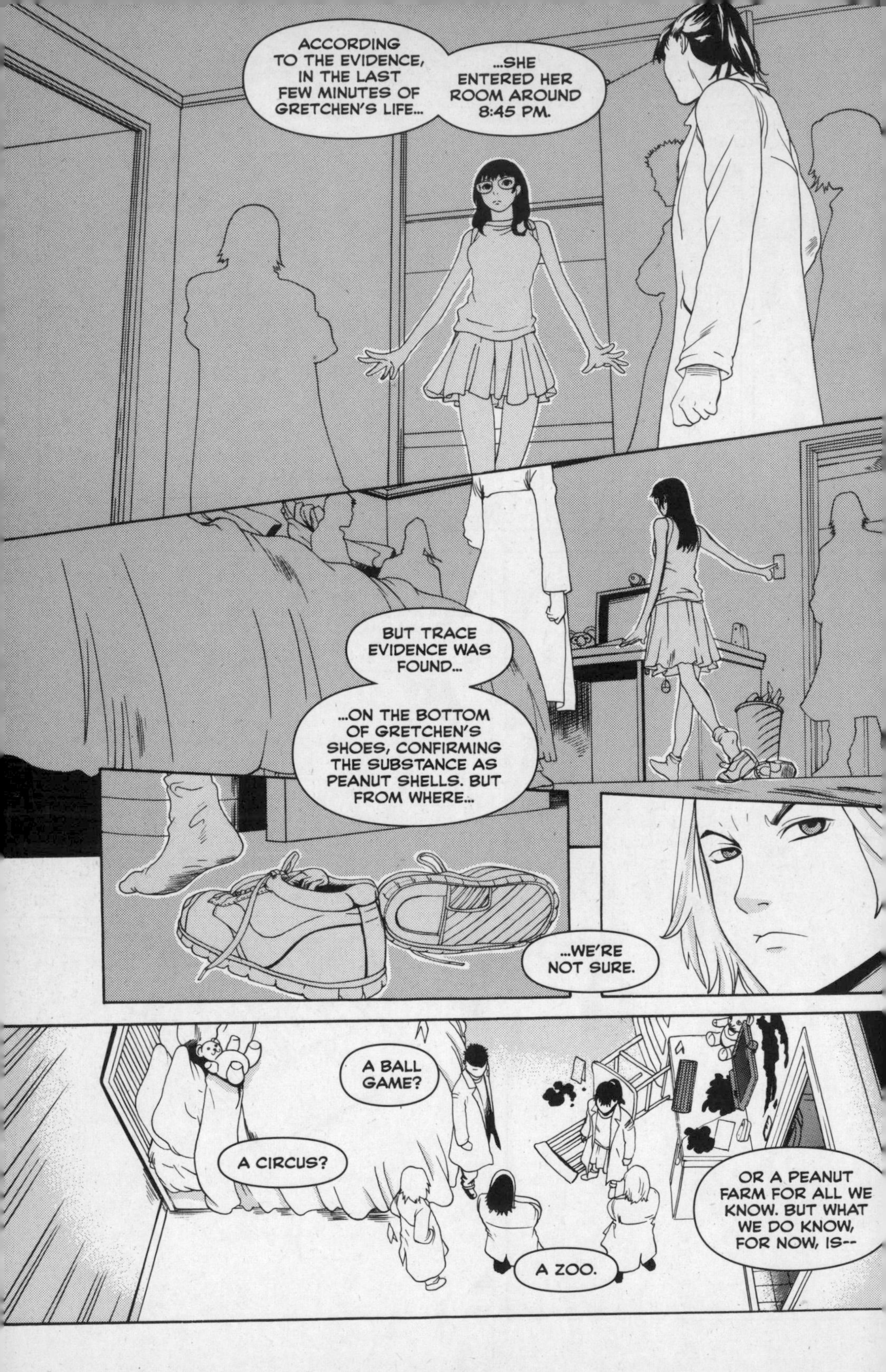
ACCORDING TO THE EVIDENCE, IN THE LAST FEW MINUTES OF GRETCHEN'S LIFE...
...SHE ENTERED HER ROOM AROUND 8:45 PM.
BUT TRACE EVIDENCE WAS FOUND...
...ON THE BOTTOM OF GRETCHEN'S SHOES, CONFIRMING THE SUBSTANCE AS PEANUT SHELLS. BUT FROM WHERE...
...WE'RE NOT SURE.
A BALL GAME?
A CIRCUS?
A ZOO.
OR A PEANUT FARM FOR ALL WE KNOW. BUT WHAT WE DO KNOW, FOR NOW, IS--

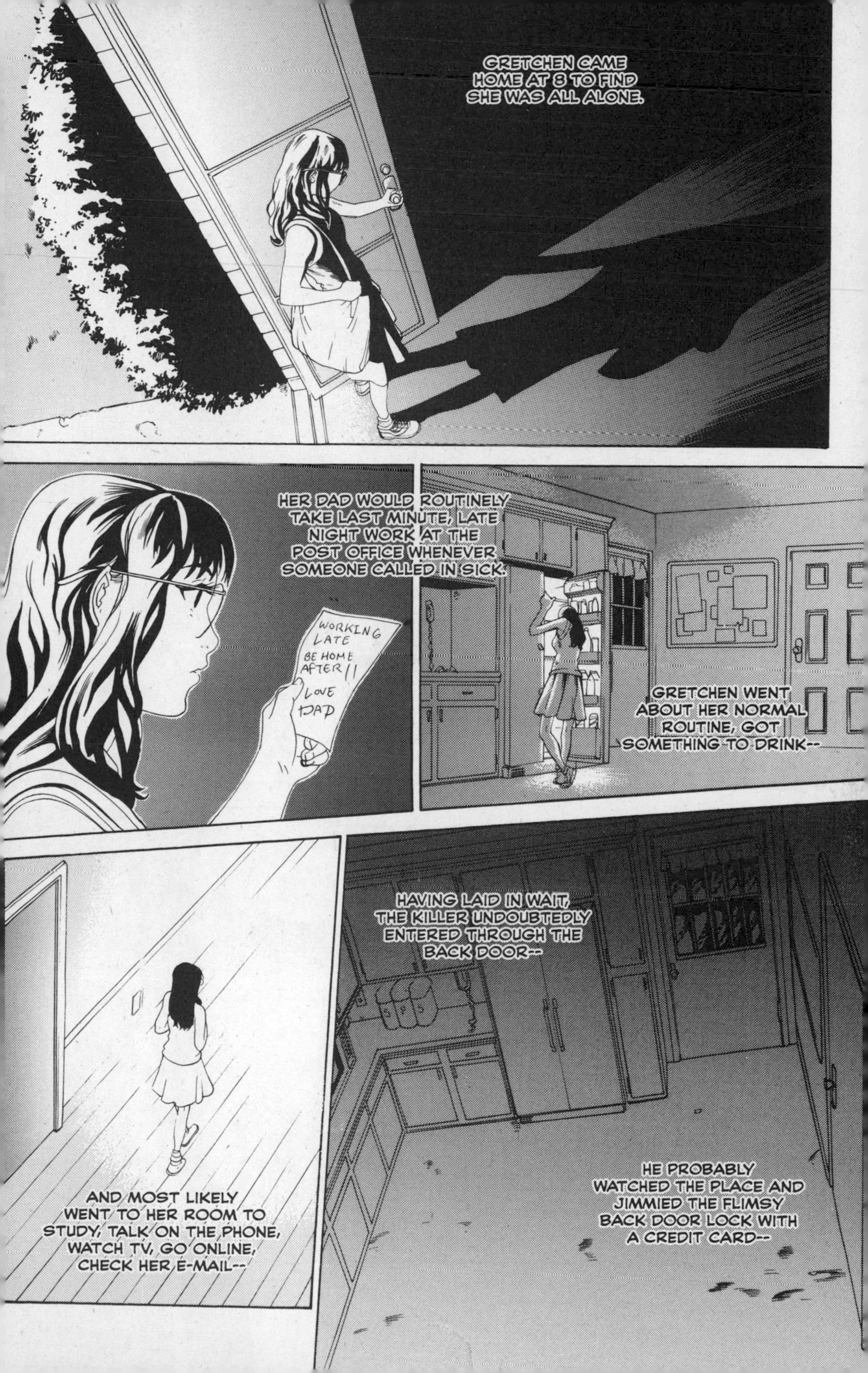
GRETCHEN CAME HOME AT 8 TO FIND SHE WAS ALL ALONE.
HER DAD WOULD ROUTINELY TAKE LAST MINUTE, LATE NIGHT WORK AT THE POST OFFICE WHENEVER SOMEONE CALLED IN SICK.
WORKING LATE BE HOME AFTER 11 LOVE DAD
GRETCHEN WENT ABOUT HER NORMAL ROUTINE, GOT SOMETHING TO DRINK--
AND MOST LIKELY WENT TO HER ROOM TO STUDY, TALK ON THE PHONE, WATCH TV, GO ONLINE, CHECK HER E-MAIL--
HAVING LAID IN WAIT, THE KILLER UNDOUBTEDLY ENTERED THROUGH THE BACK DOOR--
HE PROBABLY WATCHED THE PLACE AND JIMMIED THE FLIMSY BACK DOOR LOCK WITH A CREDIT CARD--

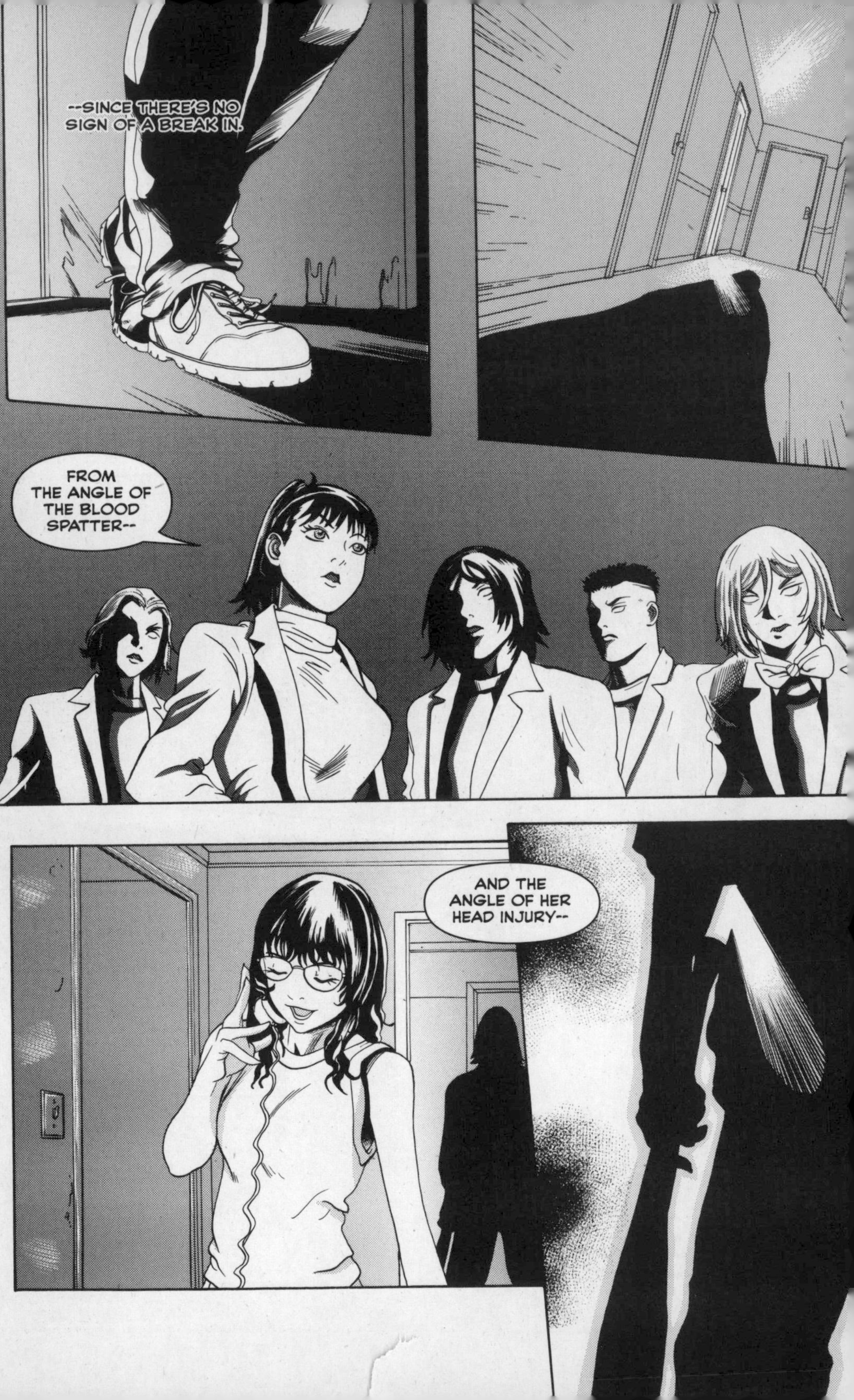
--SINCE THERE'S NO SIGN OF A BREAK IN.
FROM THE ANGLE OF THE BLOOD SPATTER--
AND THE ANGLE OF HER HEAD INJURY--

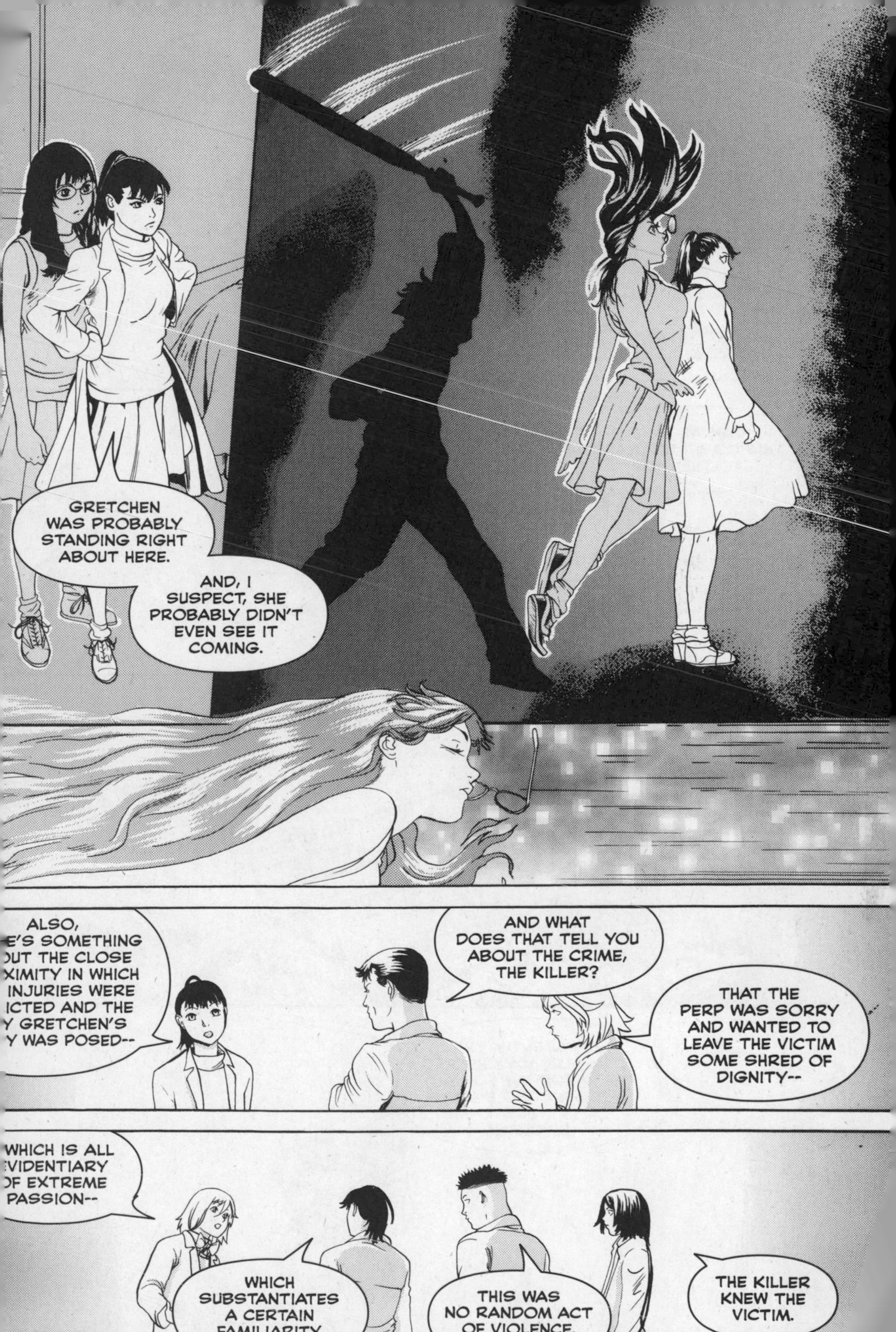
GRETCHEN WAS PROBABLY STANDING RIGHT ABOUT HERE.
AND, I SUSPECT, SHE PROBABLY DIDN'T EVEN SEE IT COMING.
ALSO, E'S SOMETHING OUT THE CLOSE XIMITY IN WHICH INJURIES WERE ICTED AND THE Y GRETCHEN'S Y WAS POSED--
AND WHAT DOES THAT TELL YOU ABOUT THE CRIME, THE KILLER?
THAT THE PERP WAS SORRY AND WANTED TO LEAVE THE VICTIM SOME SHRED OF DIGNITY--
WHICH IS ALL VIDENTIARY F EXTREME PASSION--
WHICH SUBSTANTIATES A CERTAIN FAMILIARITY.
THIS WAS NO RANDOM ACT OF VIOLENCE.
THE KILLER KNEW THE VICTIM.

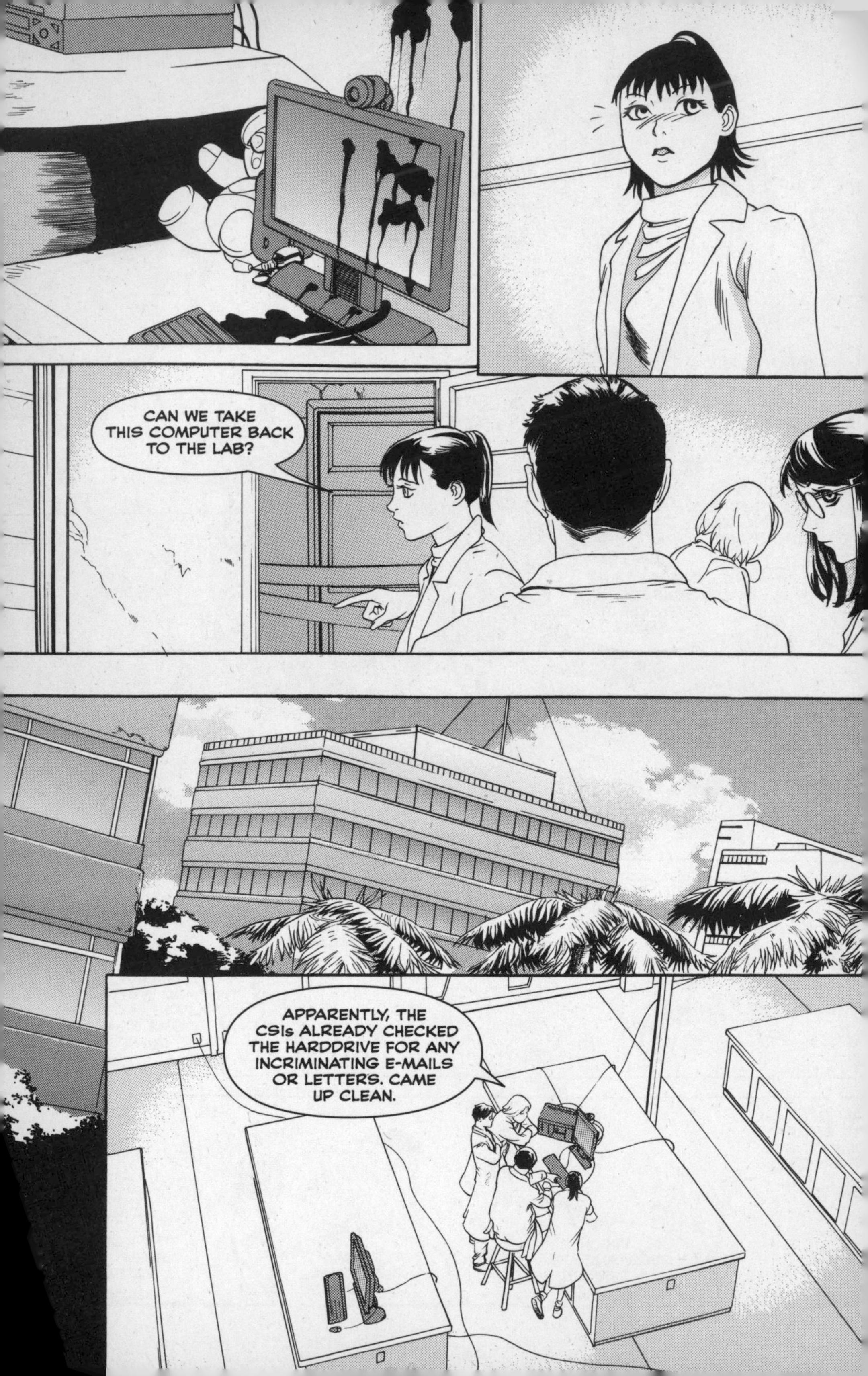
CAN WE TAKE THIS COMPUTER BACK TO THE LAB?
APPARENTLY, THE CSIs ALREADY CHECKED THE HARDDRIVE FOR ANY INCRIMINATING E-MAILS OR LETTERS. CAME UP CLEAN.

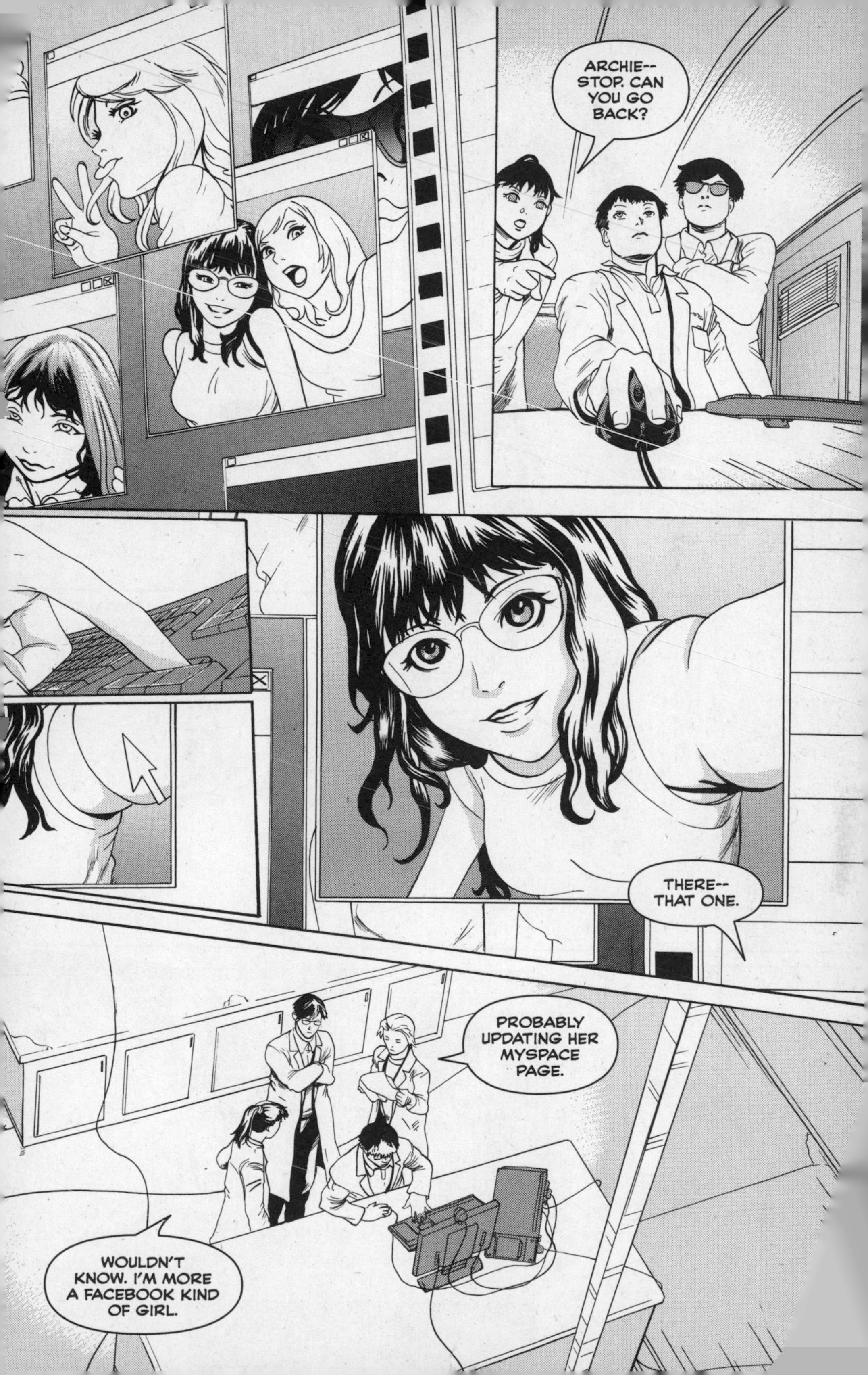
ARCHIE--
STOP. CAN
YOU GO
BACK?
THERE--
THAT ONE.
PROBABLY
UPDATING HER
MYSPACE
PAGE.
WOULDN'T
KNOW. I'M MORE
A FACEBOOK KIND
OF GIRL.

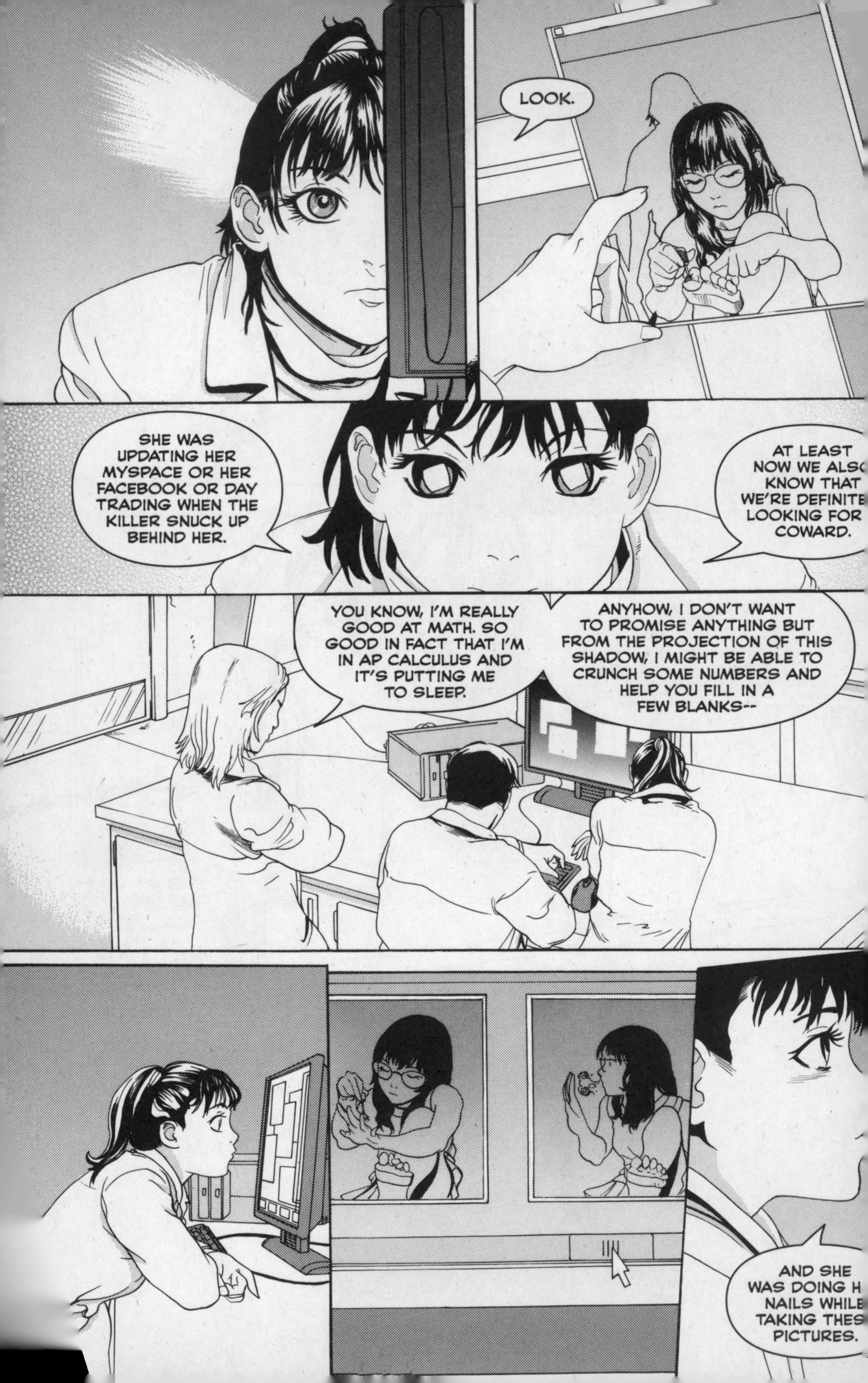
LOOK.
SHE WAS UPDATING HER MYSPACE OR HER FACEBOOK OR DAY TRADING WHEN THE KILLER SNUCK UP BEHIND HER.
AT LEAST NOW WE ALS KNOW THAT WE'RE DEFINITE LOOKING FOR COWARD.
YOU KNOW, I'M REALLY GOOD AT MATH. SO GOOD IN FACT THAT I'M IN AP CALCULUS AND IT'S PUTTING ME TO SLEEP.
ANYHOW, I DON'T WANT TO PROMISE ANYTHING BUT FROM THE PROJECTION OF THIS SHADOW, I MIGHT BE ABLE TO CRUNCH SOME NUMBERS AND HELP YOU FILL IN A FEW BLANKS--
AND SHE WAS DOING H NAILS WHILE TAKING THES PICTURES.

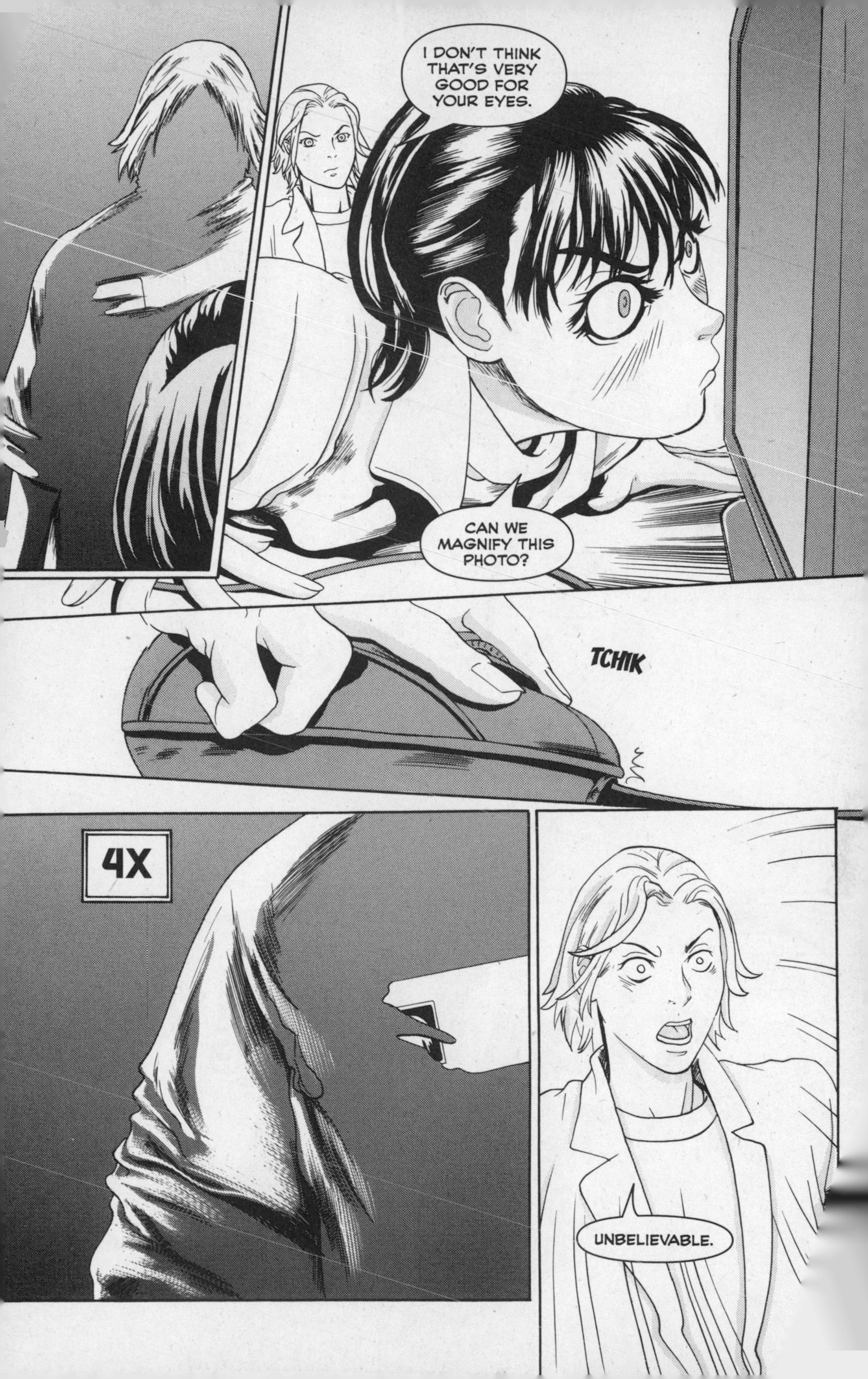
I DON'T THINK THAT'S VERY GOOD FOR YOUR EYES.
CAN WE MAGNIFY THIS PHOTO?
TCHIK
4X
UNBELIEVABLE.

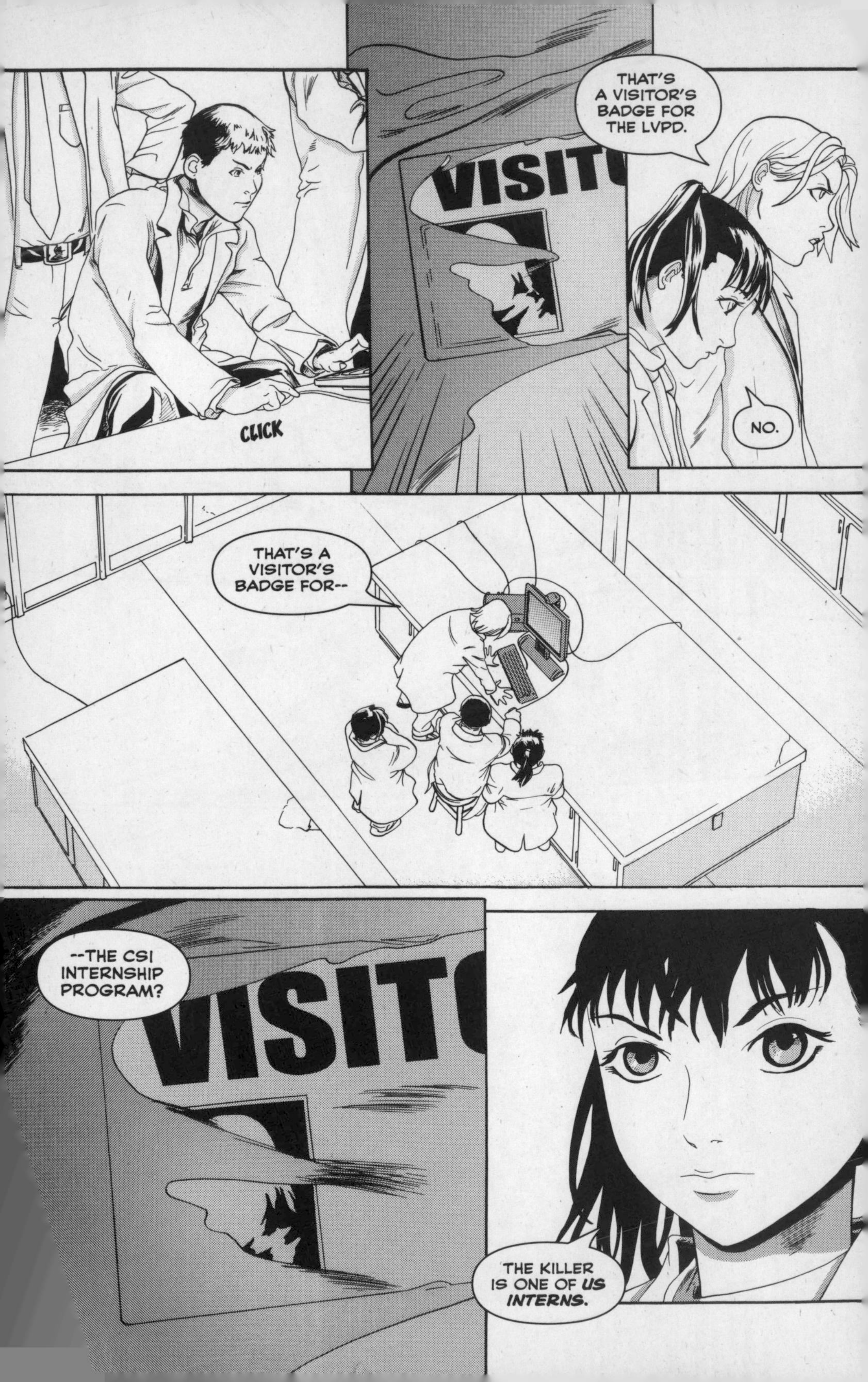
CLICK
THAT'S A VISITOR'S BADGE FOR THE LVPD.
NO.
THAT'S A VISITOR'S BADGE FOR--
--THE CSI INTERNSHIP PROGRAM?
VISITO
THE KILLER IS ONE OF *US INTERNS.*

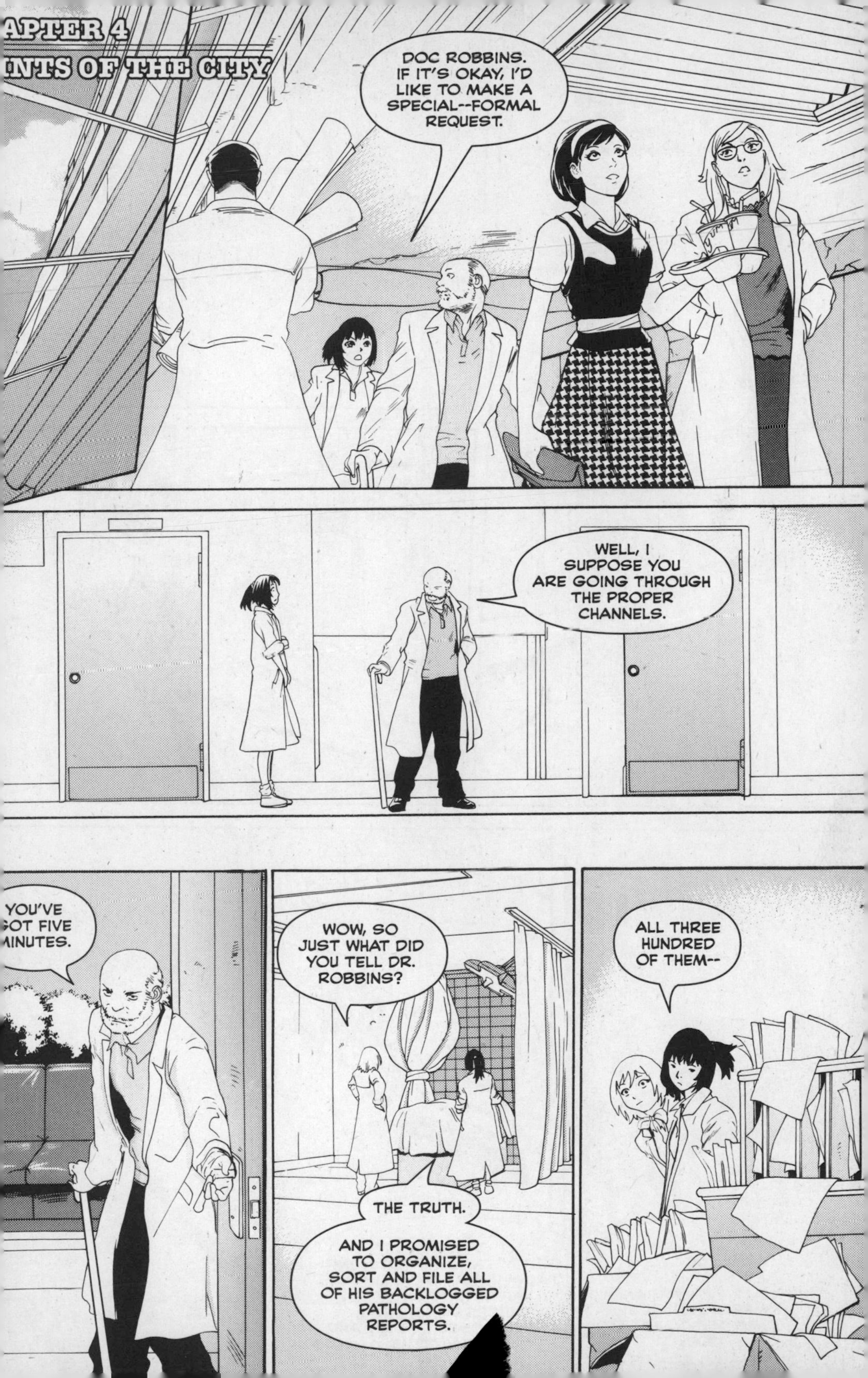
APTER 4
INTS OF THE CITY
DOC ROBBINS. IF IT'S OKAY, I'D LIKE TO MAKE A SPECIAL--FORMAL REQUEST.
WELL, I SUPPOSE YOU ARE GOING THROUGH THE PROPER CHANNELS.
YOU'VE GOT FIVE MINUTES.
WOW, SO JUST WHAT DID YOU TELL DR. ROBBINS?
THE TRUTH.
AND I PROMISED TO ORGANIZE, SORT AND FILE ALL OF HIS BACKLOGGED PATHOLOGY REPORTS.
ALL THREE HUNDRED OF THEM--

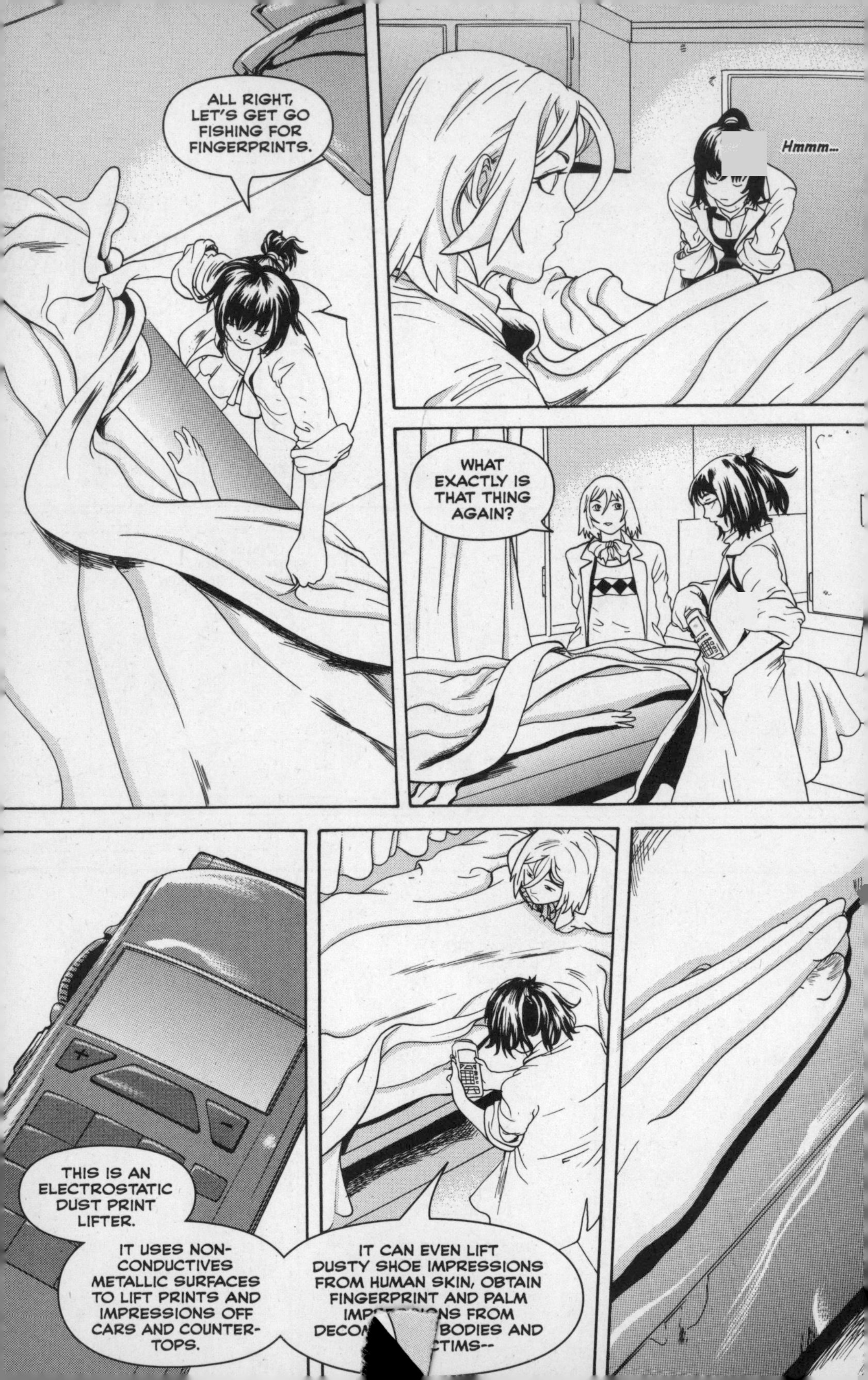
ALL RIGHT, LET'S GET GO FISHING FOR FINGERPRINTS.
Hmmm...
WHAT EXACTLY IS THAT THING AGAIN?
THIS IS AN ELECTROSTATIC DUST PRINT LIFTER.
IT USES NON-CONDUCTIVES METALLIC SURFACES TO LIFT PRINTS AND IMPRESSIONS OFF CARS AND COUNTER-TOPS.
IT CAN EVEN LIFT DUSTY SHOE IMPRESSIONS FROM HUMAN SKIN, OBTAIN FINGERPRINT AND PALM IMPR IONS FROM DECOM BODIES AND CTIMS--

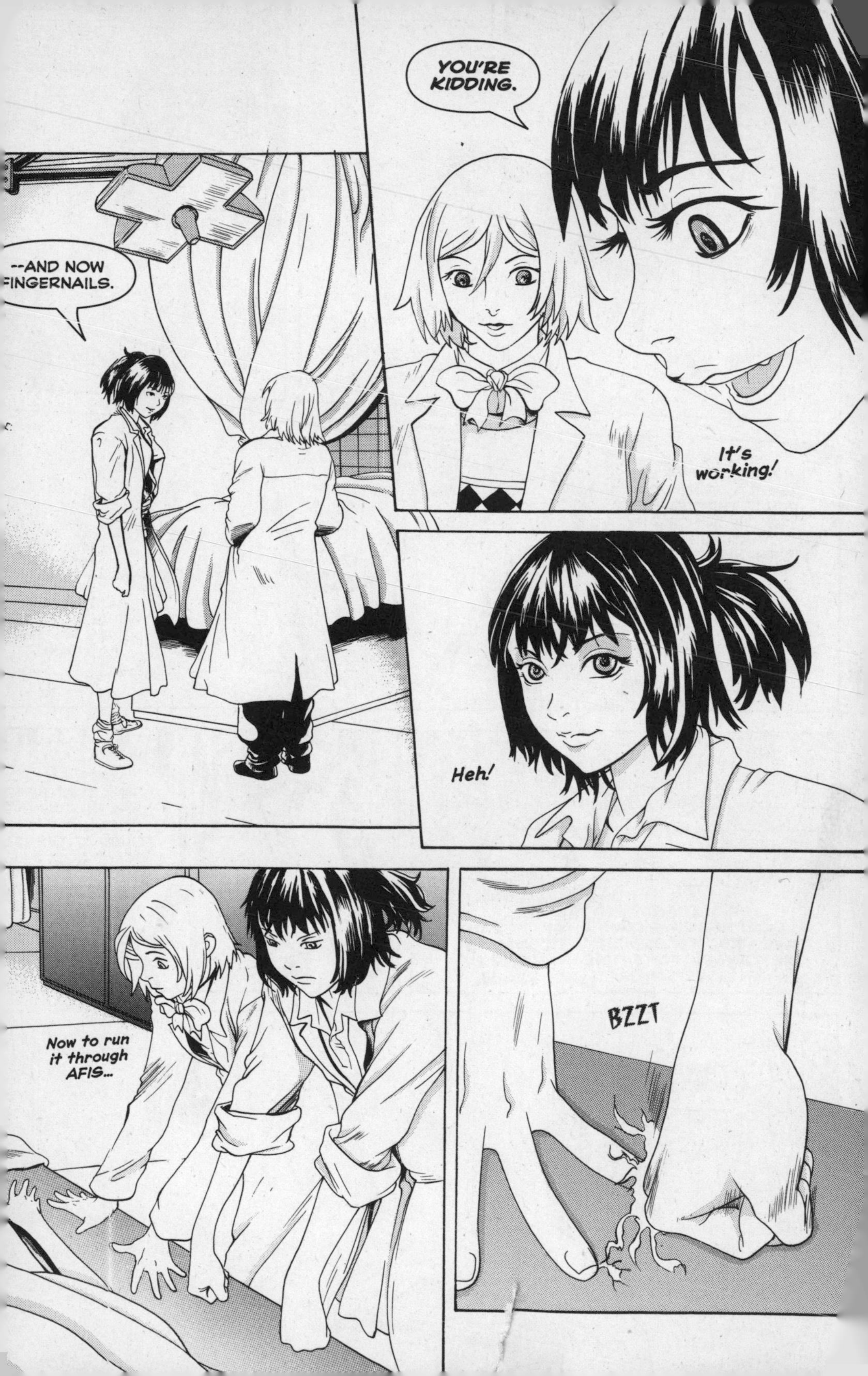
--AND NOW FINGERNAILS.
YOU'RE KIDDING.
It's working!
Heh!
Now to run it through AFIS...
BZZT

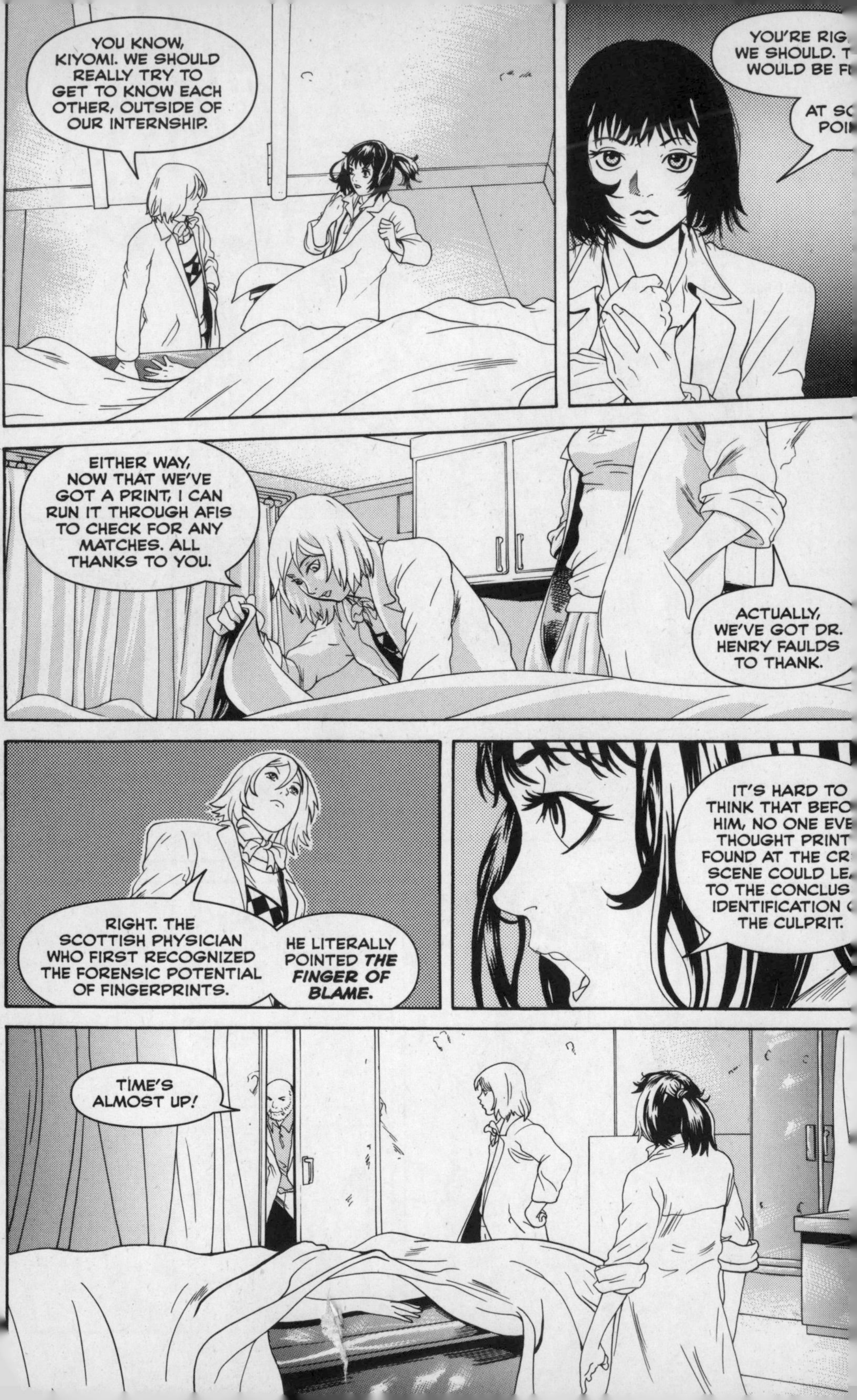

YOU KNOW, KIYOMI. WE SHOULD REALLY TRY TO GET TO KNOW EACH OTHER, OUTSIDE OF OUR INTERNSHIP.
YOU'RE RIG WE SHOULD. T WOULD BE F
AT SC POI
EITHER WAY, NOW THAT WE'VE GOT A PRINT, I CAN RUN IT THROUGH AFIS TO CHECK FOR ANY MATCHES. ALL THANKS TO YOU.
ACTUALLY, WE'VE GOT DR. HENRY FAULDS TO THANK.
RIGHT. THE SCOTTISH PHYSICIAN WHO FIRST RECOGNIZED THE FORENSIC POTENTIAL OF FINGERPRINTS.
HE LITERALLY POINTED THE FINGER OF BLAME.
IT'S HARD TO THINK THAT BEFO HIM, NO ONE EVE THOUGHT PRINT FOUND AT THE CR SCENE COULD LE TO THE CONCLUS IDENTIFICATION THE CULPRIT.
TIME'S ALMOST UP!

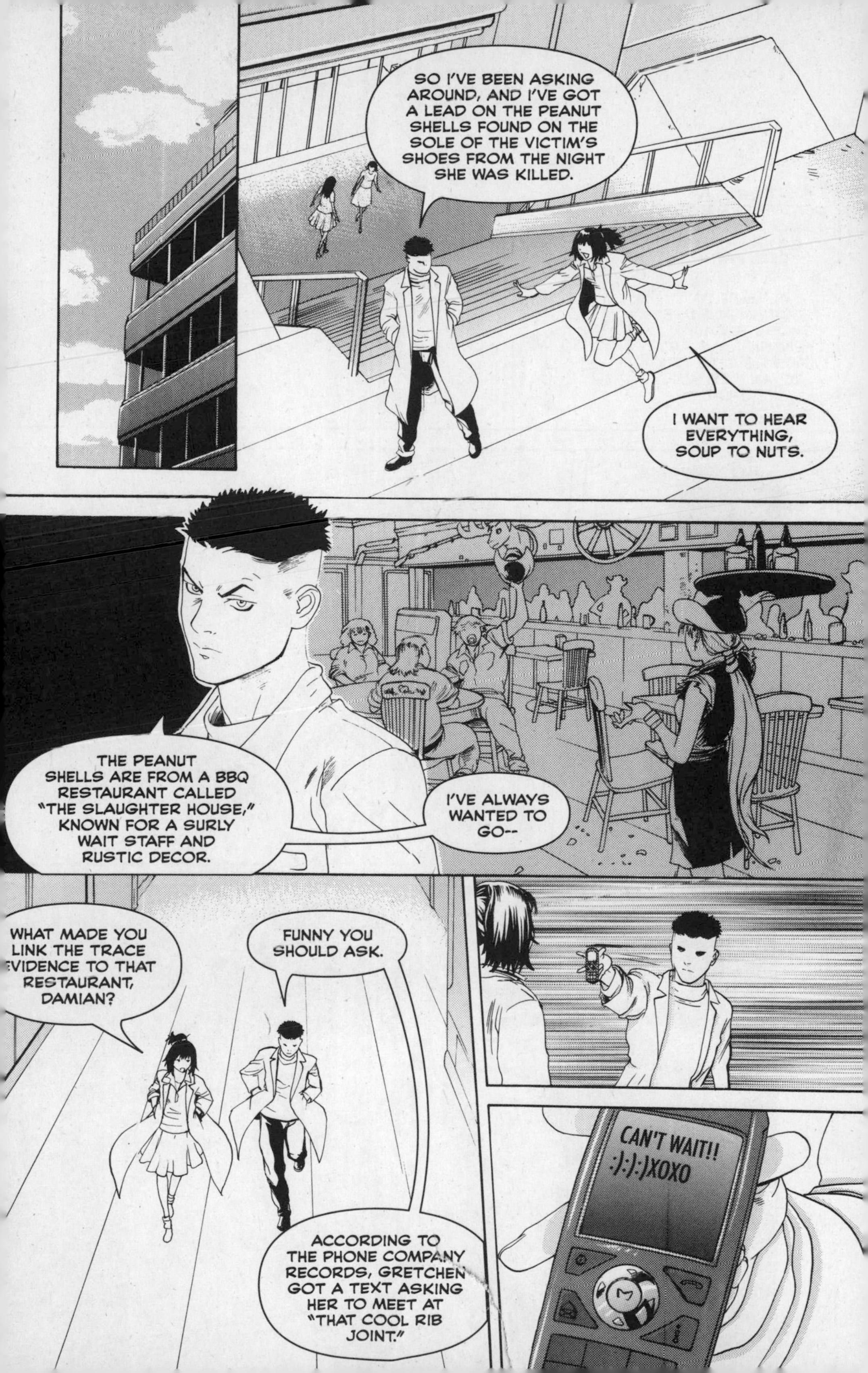

SO I'VE BEEN ASKING AROUND, AND I'VE GOT A LEAD ON THE PEANUT SHELLS FOUND ON THE SOLE OF THE VICTIM'S SHOES FROM THE NIGHT SHE WAS KILLED.
I WANT TO HEAR EVERYTHING, SOUP TO NUTS.
THE PEANUT SHELLS ARE FROM A BBQ RESTAURANT CALLED "THE SLAUGHTER HOUSE," KNOWN FOR A SURLY WAIT STAFF AND RUSTIC DECOR.
I'VE ALWAYS WANTED TO GO--
WHAT MADE YOU LINK THE TRACE EVIDENCE TO THAT RESTAURANT, DAMIAN?
FUNNY YOU SHOULD ASK.
ACCORDING TO THE PHONE COMPANY RECORDS, GRETCHEN GOT A TEXT ASKING HER TO MEET AT "THAT COOL RIB JOINT."
CAN'T WAIT!! :):):)XOXO

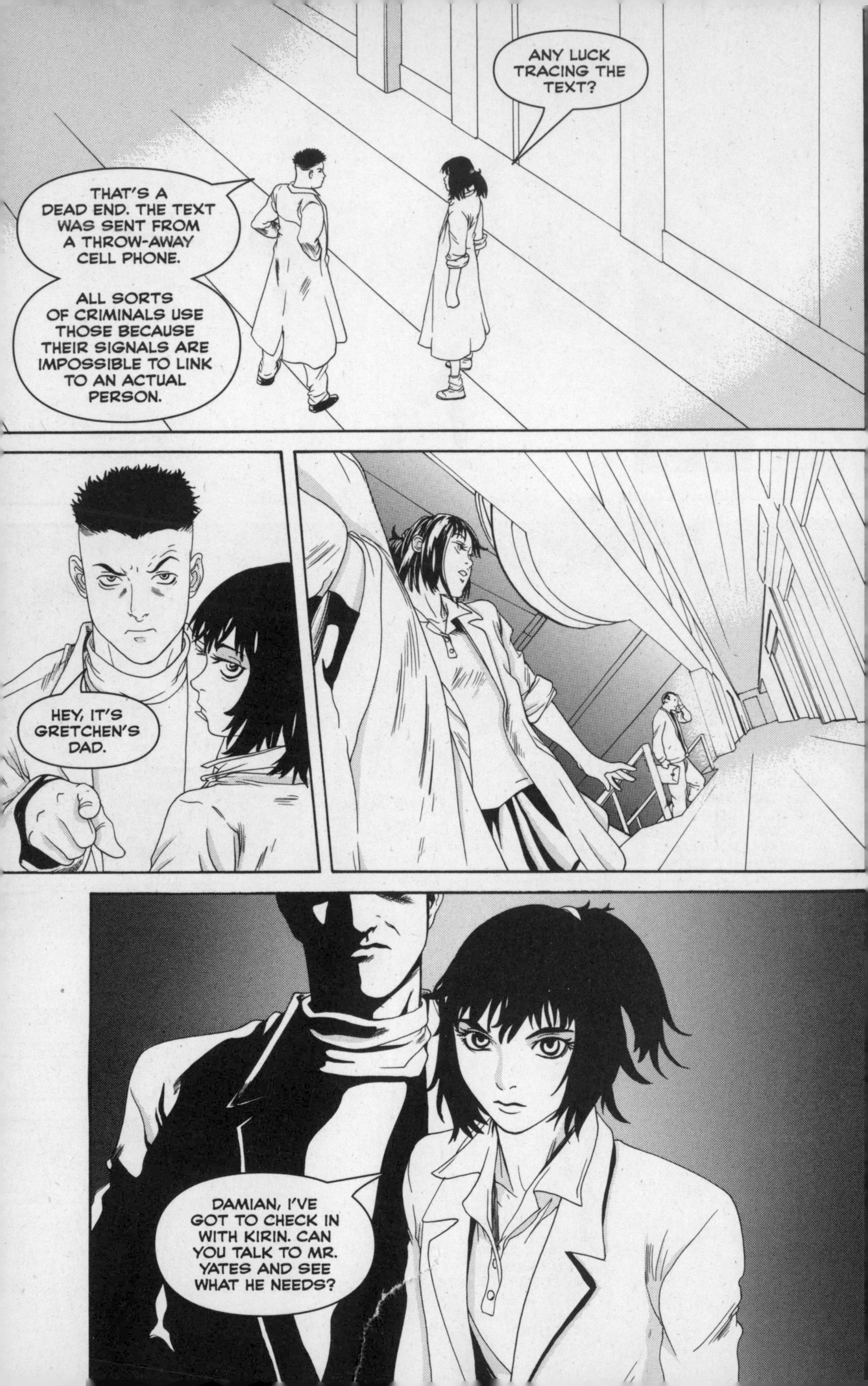
ANY LUCK TRACING THE TEXT?
THAT'S A DEAD END. THE TEXT WAS SENT FROM A THROW-AWAY CELL PHONE.
ALL SORTS OF CRIMINALS USE THOSE BECAUSE THEIR SIGNALS ARE IMPOSSIBLE TO LINK TO AN ACTUAL PERSON.
HEY, IT'S GRETCHEN'S DAD.
DAMIAN, I'VE GOT TO CHECK IN WITH KIRIN. CAN YOU TALK TO MR. YATES AND SEE WHAT HE NEEDS?

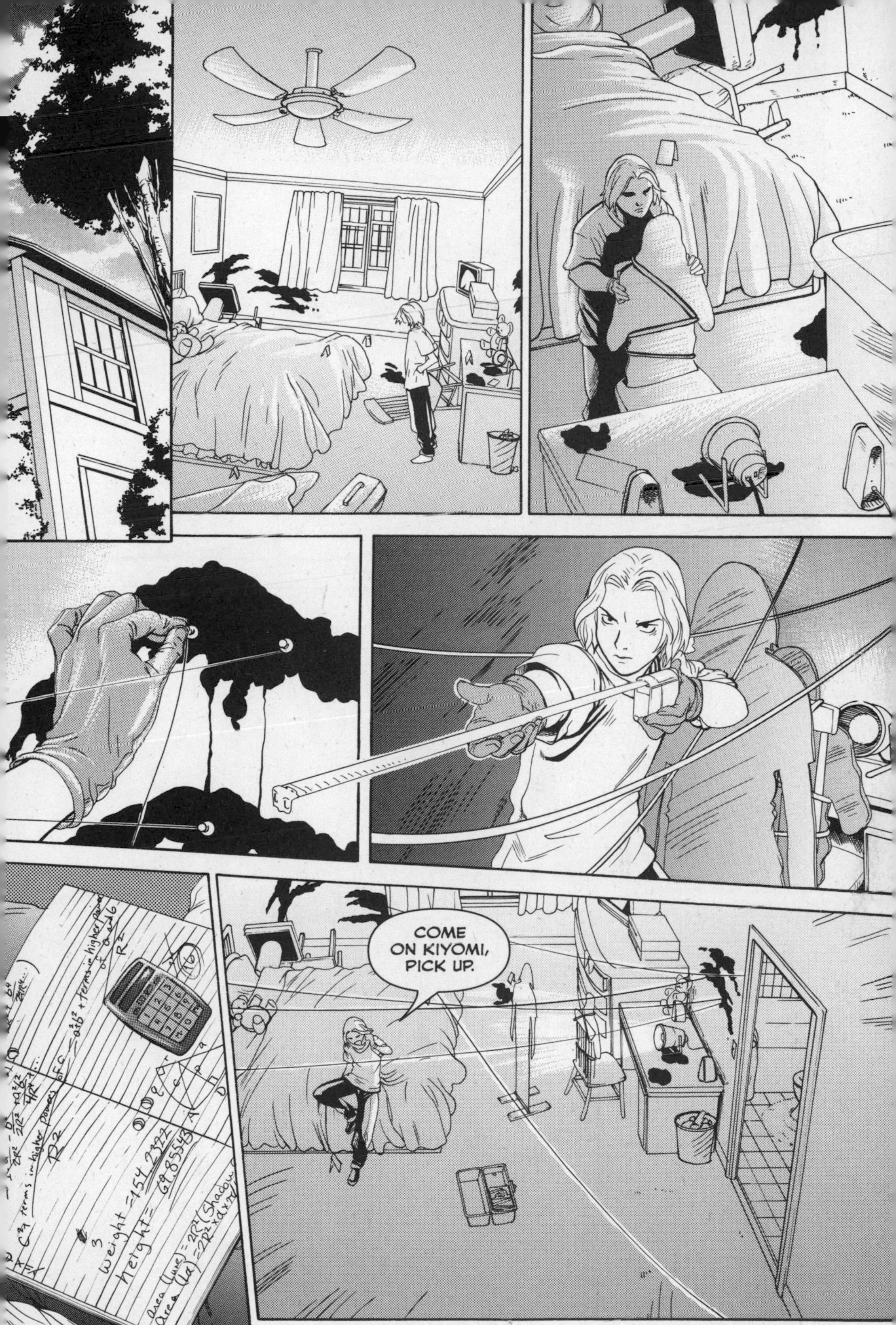
COME ON KIYOMI, PICK UP.
weight = 154.2322
height = 69.85543

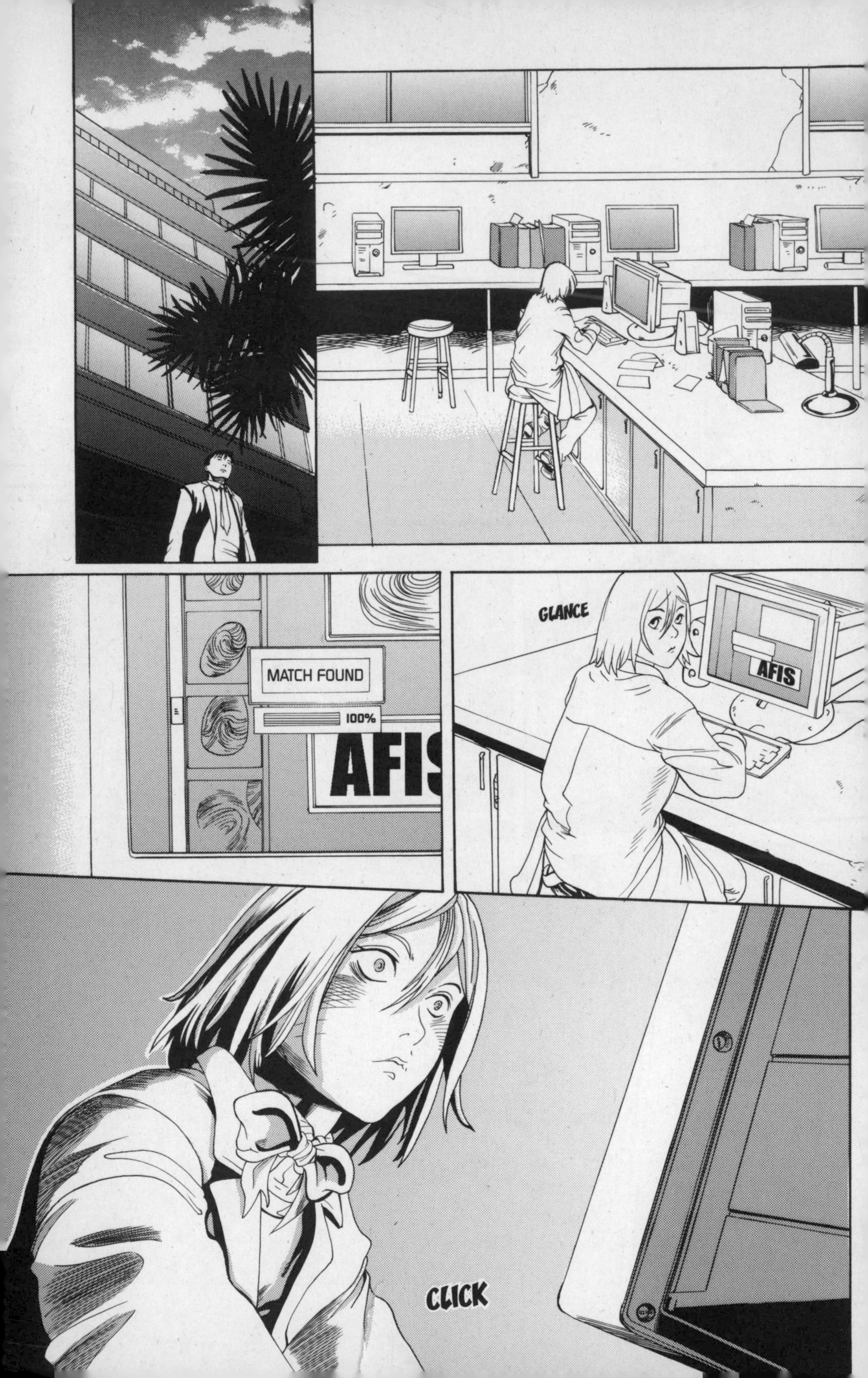
MATCH FOUND
100%
AFIS
GLANCE
AFIS
CLICK

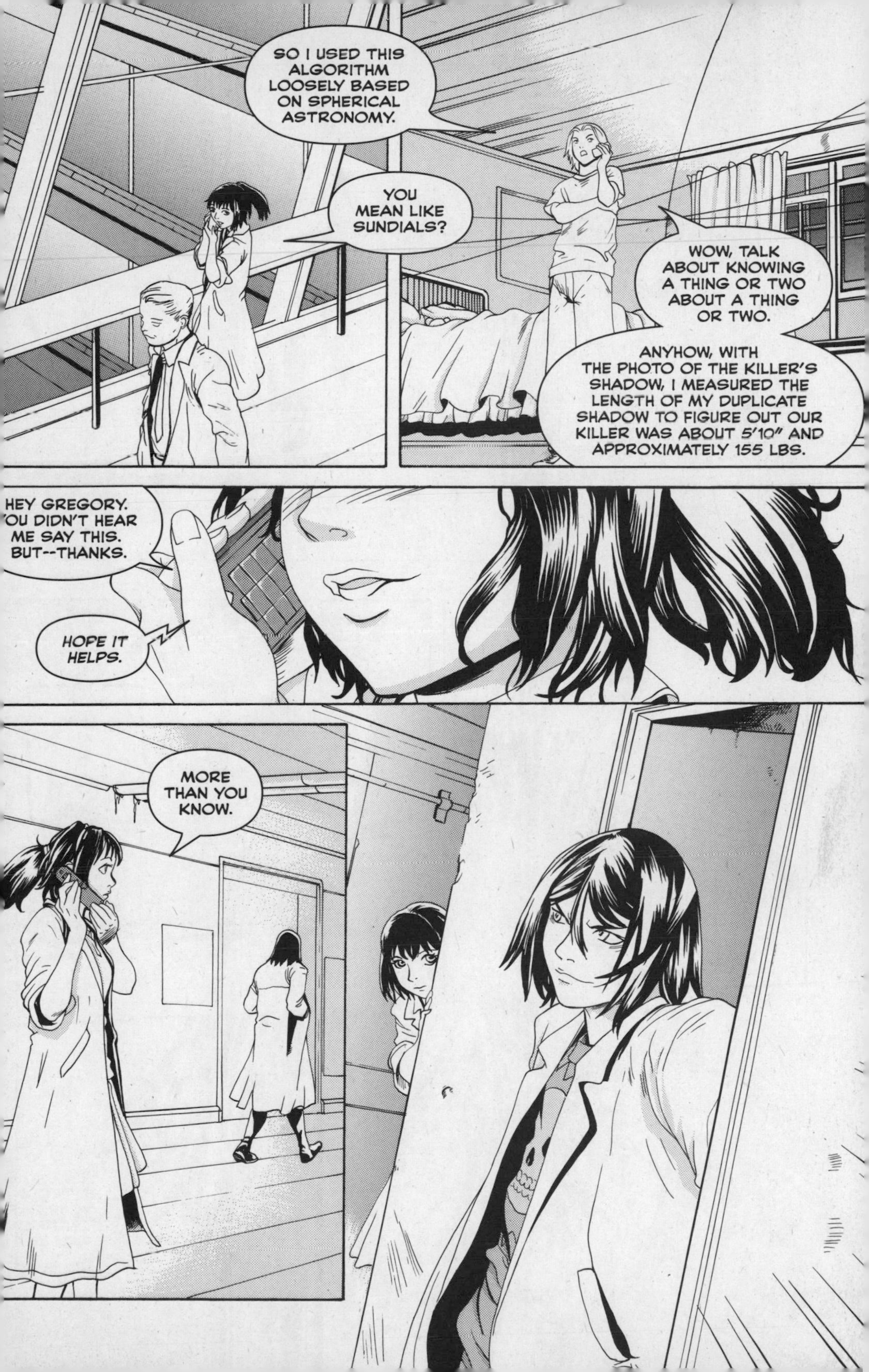
SO I USED THIS ALGORITHM LOOSELY BASED ON SPHERICAL ASTRONOMY.
YOU MEAN LIKE SUNDIALS?
WOW, TALK ABOUT KNOWING A THING OR TWO ABOUT A THING OR TWO.
ANYHOW, WITH THE PHOTO OF THE KILLER'S SHADOW, I MEASURED THE LENGTH OF MY DUPLICATE SHADOW TO FIGURE OUT OUR KILLER WAS ABOUT 5'10" AND APPROXIMATELY 155 LBS.
HEY GREGORY. YOU DIDN'T HEAR ME SAY THIS. BUT--THANKS.
HOPE IT HELPS.
MORE THAN YOU KNOW.

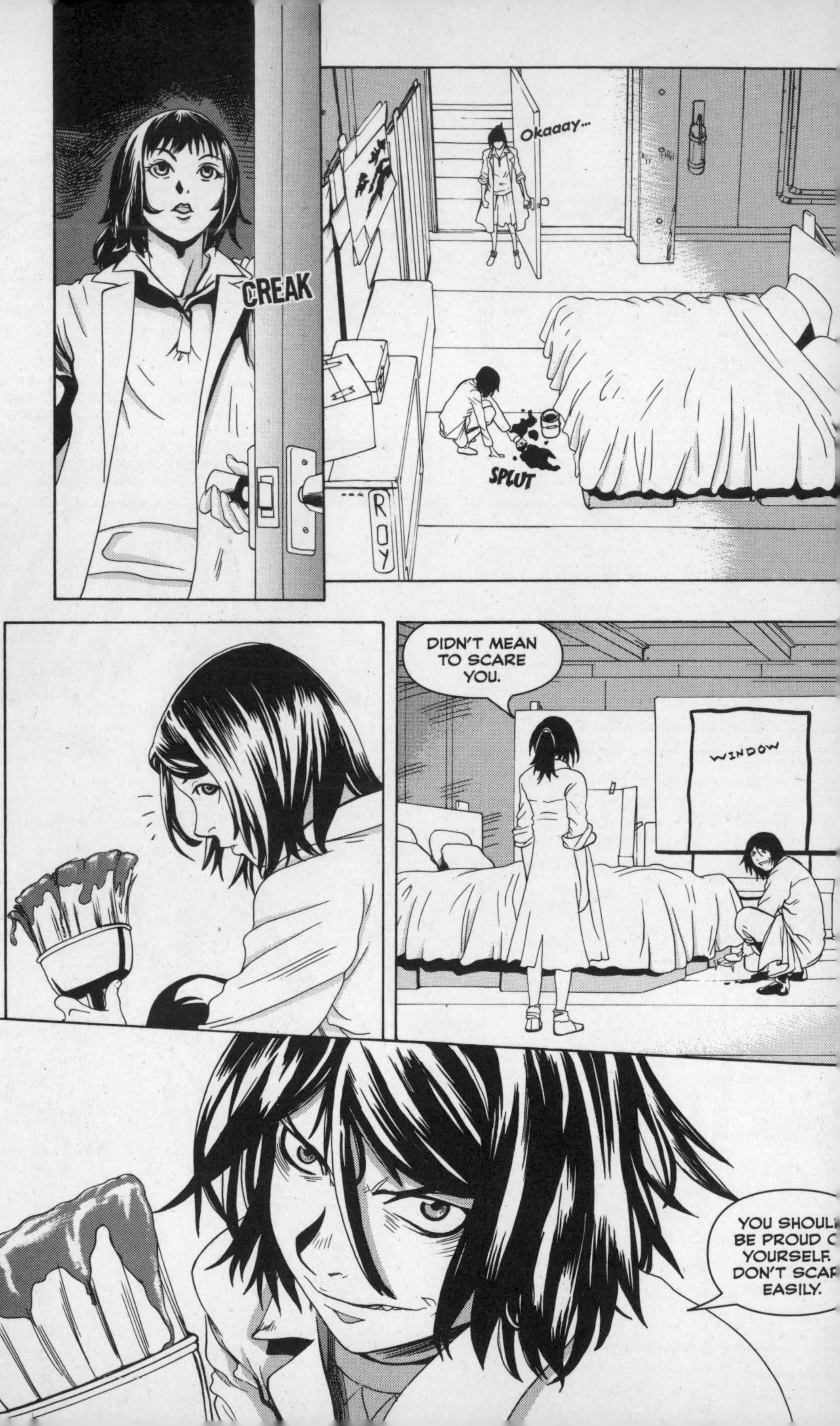
CREAK
Okaaay...
SPLUT
DIDN'T MEAN TO SCARE YOU.
WINDOW
YOU SHOUL
BE PROUD O
YOURSELF.
DON'T SCAR
EASILY.

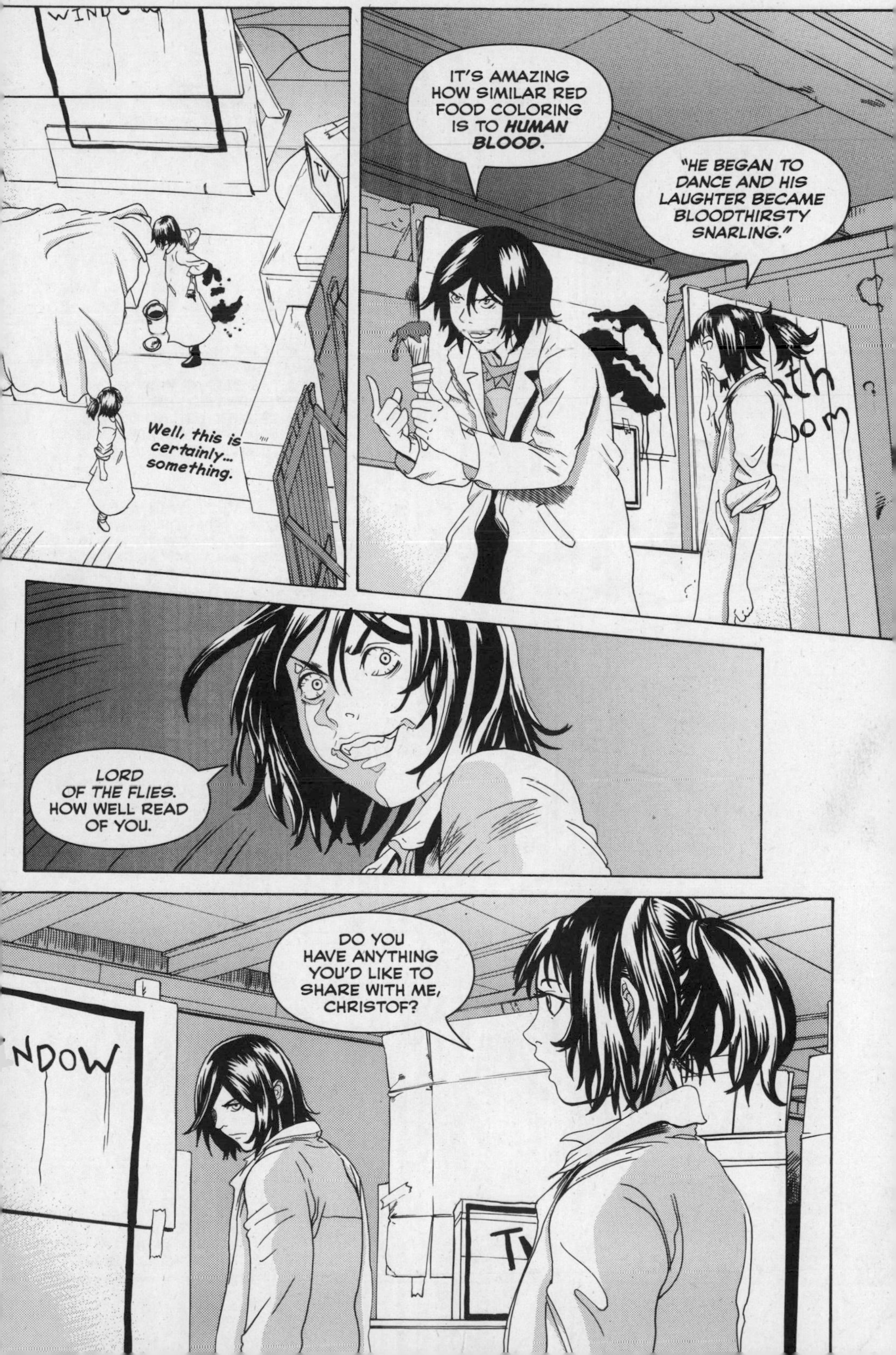

WINDOW
TV
Well, this is certainly... something.
IT'S AMAZING HOW SIMILAR RED FOOD COLORING IS TO *HUMAN BLOOD*.
"HE BEGAN TO DANCE AND HIS LAUGHTER BECAME BLOODTHIRSTY SNARLING."
LORD OF THE FLIES. HOW WELL READ OF YOU.
DO YOU HAVE ANYTHING YOU'D LIKE TO SHARE WITH ME, CHRISTOF?
NDOW
TV

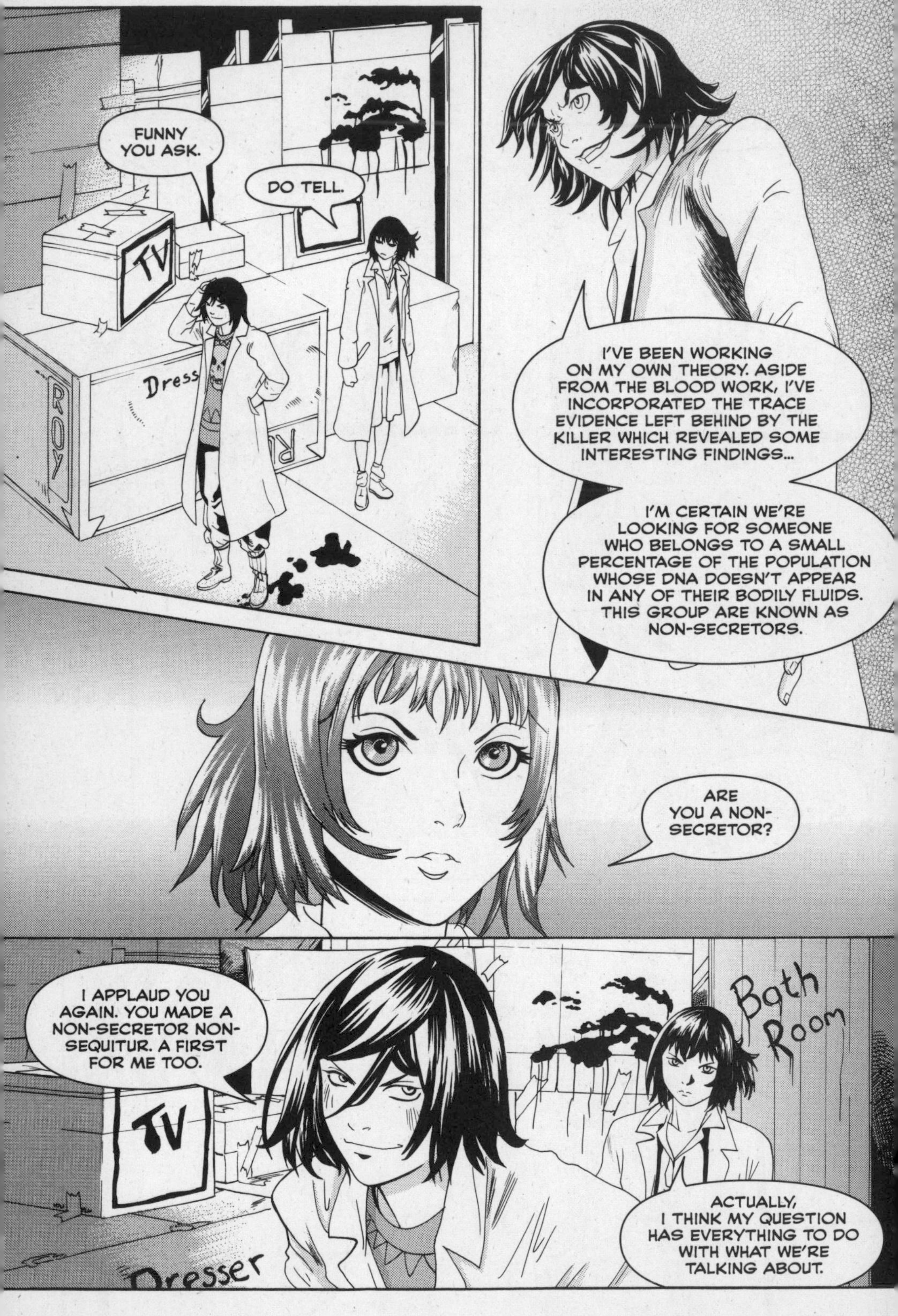
FUNNY YOU ASK.
DO TELL.
TV
Dress
ROY
I'VE BEEN WORKING ON MY OWN THEORY. ASIDE FROM THE BLOOD WORK, I'VE INCORPORATED THE TRACE EVIDENCE LEFT BEHIND BY THE KILLER WHICH REVEALED SOME INTERESTING FINDINGS...
I'M CERTAIN WE'RE LOOKING FOR SOMEONE WHO BELONGS TO A SMALL PERCENTAGE OF THE POPULATION WHOSE DNA DOESN'T APPEAR IN ANY OF THEIR BODILY FLUIDS. THIS GROUP ARE KNOWN AS NON-SECRETORS.
ARE YOU A NON-SECRETOR?
I APPLAUD YOU AGAIN. YOU MADE A NON-SECRETOR NON-SEQUITUR. A FIRST FOR ME TOO.
TV
Bath Room
ACTUALLY, I THINK MY QUESTION HAS EVERYTHING TO DO WITH WHAT WE'RE TALKING ABOUT.
Dresser

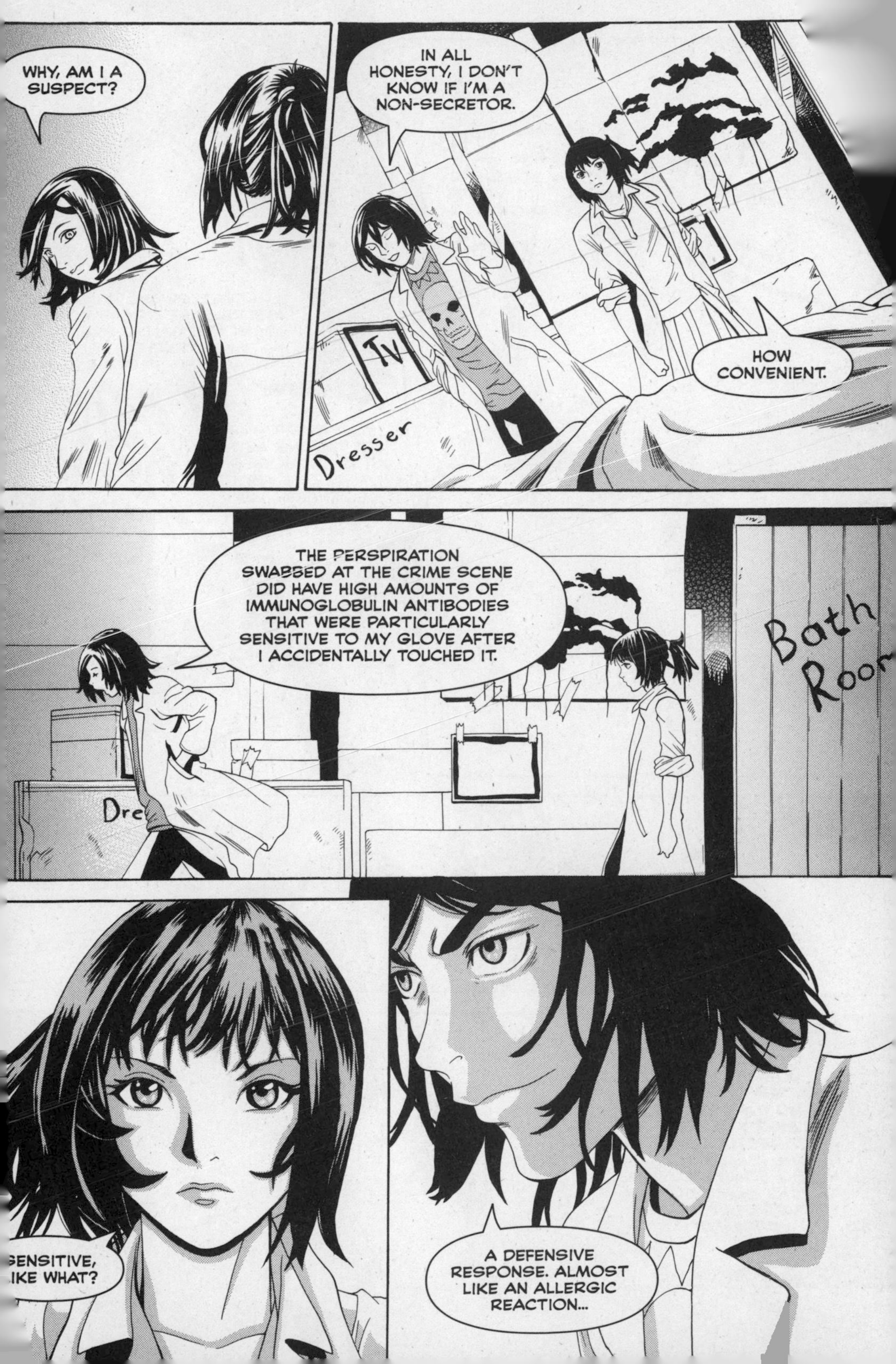
WHY, AM I A SUSPECT?
IN ALL HONESTY, I DON'T KNOW IF I'M A NON-SECRETOR.
TV
Dresser
HOW CONVENIENT.
THE PERSPIRATION SWABBED AT THE CRIME SCENE DID HAVE HIGH AMOUNTS OF IMMUNOGLOBULIN ANTIBODIES THAT WERE PARTICULARLY SENSITIVE TO MY GLOVE AFTER I ACCIDENTALLY TOUCHED IT.
Bath Roo
Dre
SENSITIVE, LIKE WHAT?
A DEFENSIVE RESPONSE. ALMOST LIKE AN ALLERGIC REACTION...

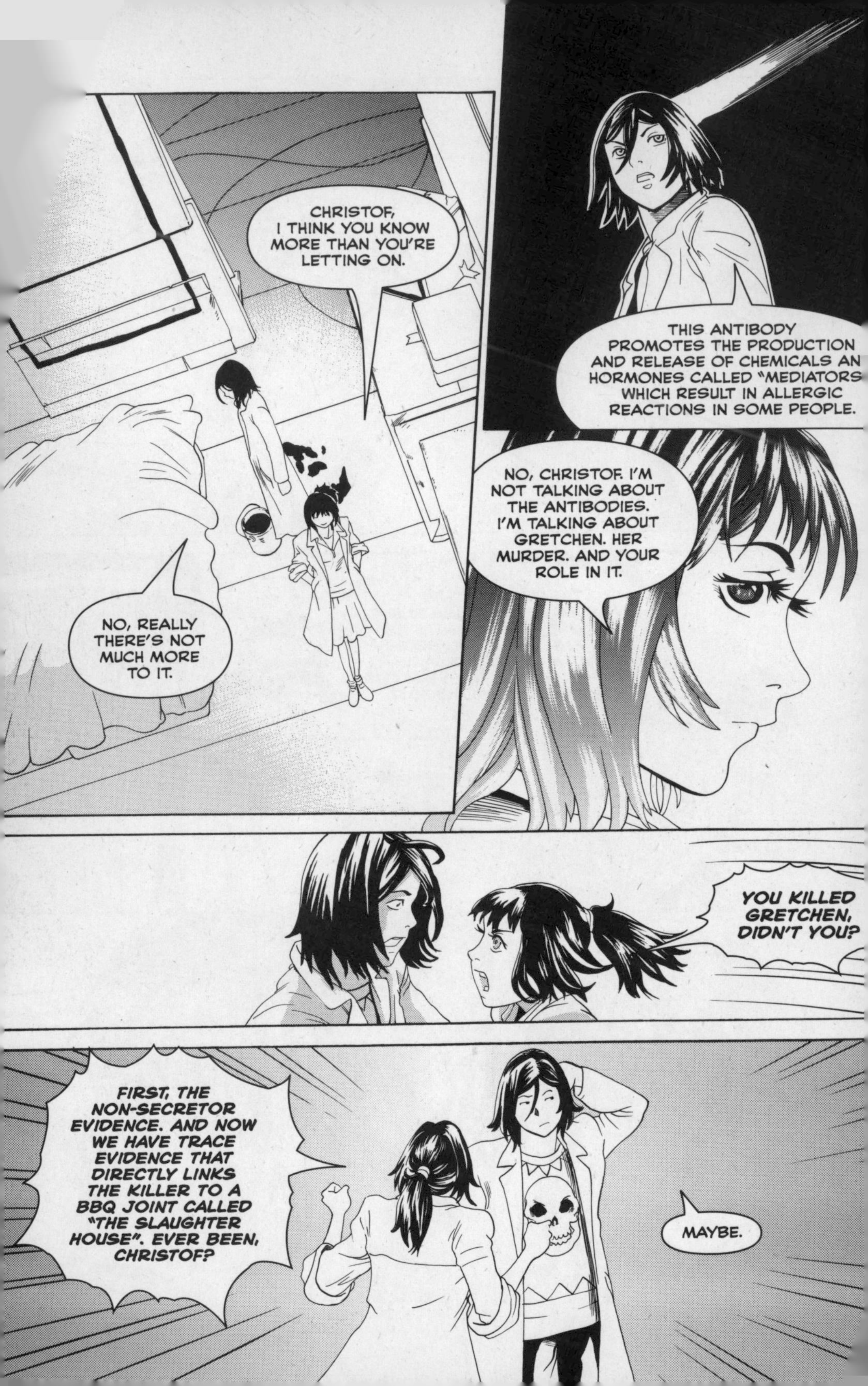
CHRISTOF, I THINK YOU KNOW MORE THAN YOU'RE LETTING ON.
NO, REALLY THERE'S NOT MUCH MORE TO IT.
THIS ANTIBODY PROMOTES THE PRODUCTION AND RELEASE OF CHEMICALS AN HORMONES CALLED "MEDIATORS WHICH RESULT IN ALLERGIC REACTIONS IN SOME PEOPLE.
NO, CHRISTOF. I'M NOT TALKING ABOUT THE ANTIBODIES. I'M TALKING ABOUT GRETCHEN. HER MURDER. AND YOUR ROLE IN IT.
YOU KILLED GRETCHEN, DIDN'T YOU?
FIRST, THE NON-SECRETOR EVIDENCE. AND NOW WE HAVE TRACE EVIDENCE THAT DIRECTLY LINKS THE KILLER TO A BBQ JOINT CALLED "THE SLAUGHTER HOUSE". EVER BEEN, CHRISTOF?
MAYBE.

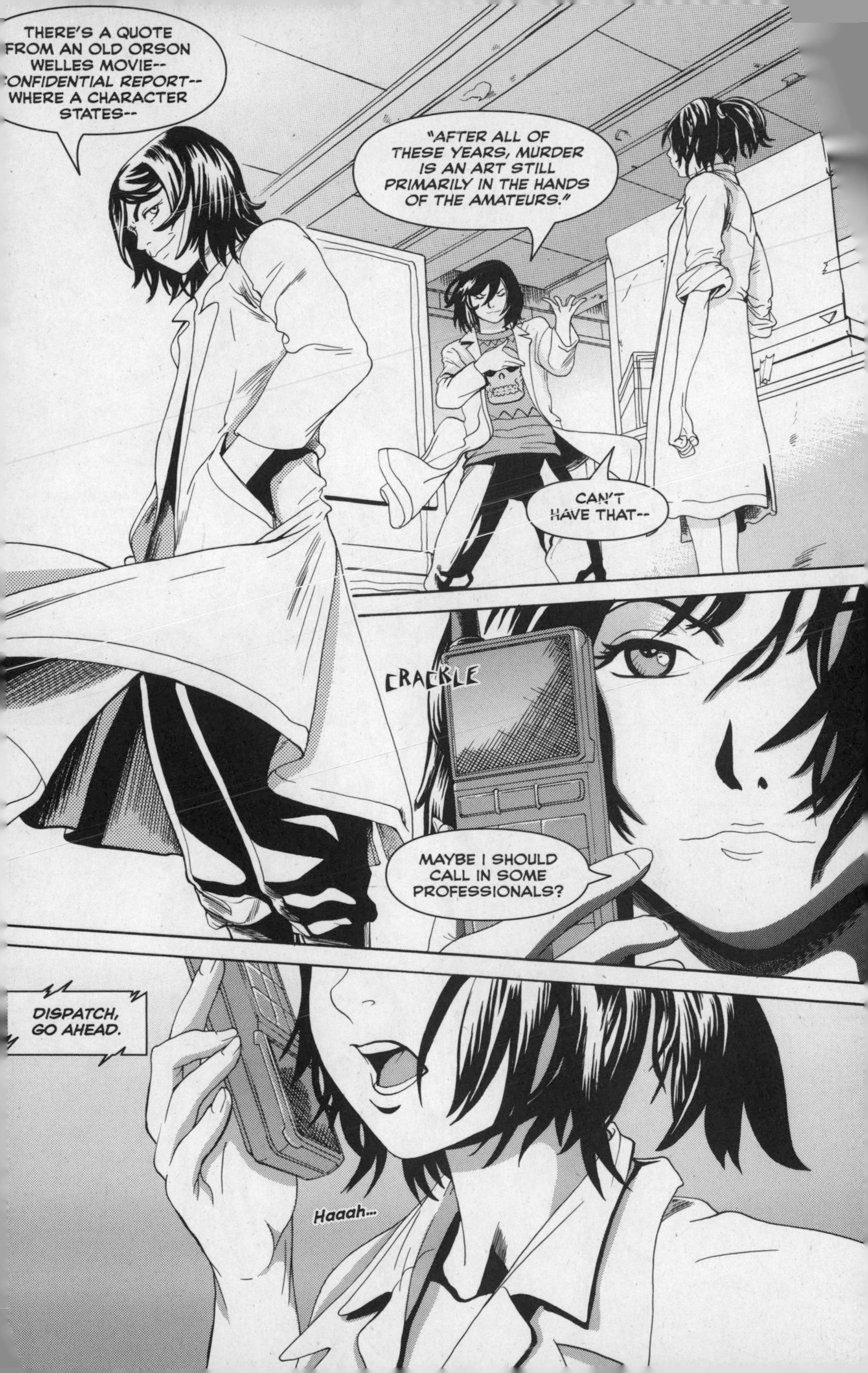
THERE'S A QUOTE FROM AN OLD ORSON WELLES MOVIE-- CONFIDENTIAL REPORT-- WHERE A CHARACTER STATES--
"AFTER ALL OF THESE YEARS, MURDER IS AN ART STILL PRIMARILY IN THE HANDS OF THE AMATEURS."
CAN'T HAVE THAT--
CRACKLE
MAYBE I SHOULD CALL IN SOME PROFESSIONALS?
DISPATCH, GO AHEAD.
Haaah...

CHAPTER 5
FINGER OF BLAME

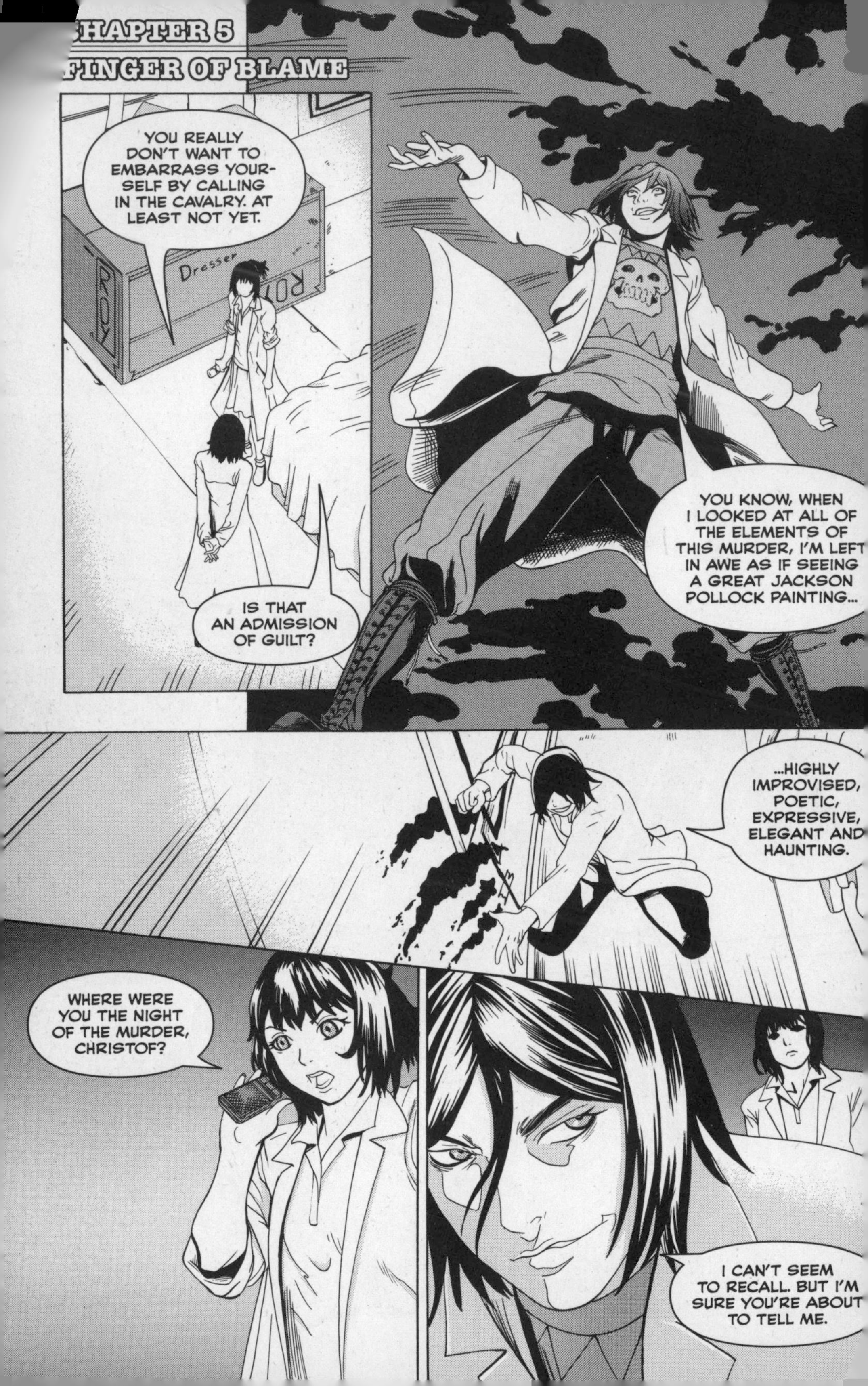

Dresser
ROY
YOU REALLY DON'T WANT TO EMBARRASS YOURSELF BY CALLING IN THE CAVALRY. AT LEAST NOT YET.
IS THAT AN ADMISSION OF GUILT?
YOU KNOW, WHEN I LOOKED AT ALL OF THE ELEMENTS OF THIS MURDER, I'M LEFT IN AWE AS IF SEEING A GREAT JACKSON POLLOCK PAINTING...
...HIGHLY IMPROVISED, POETIC, EXPRESSIVE, ELEGANT AND HAUNTING.
WHERE WERE YOU THE NIGHT OF THE MURDER, CHRISTOF?
I CAN'T SEEM TO RECALL. BUT I'M SURE YOU'RE ABOUT TO TELL ME.

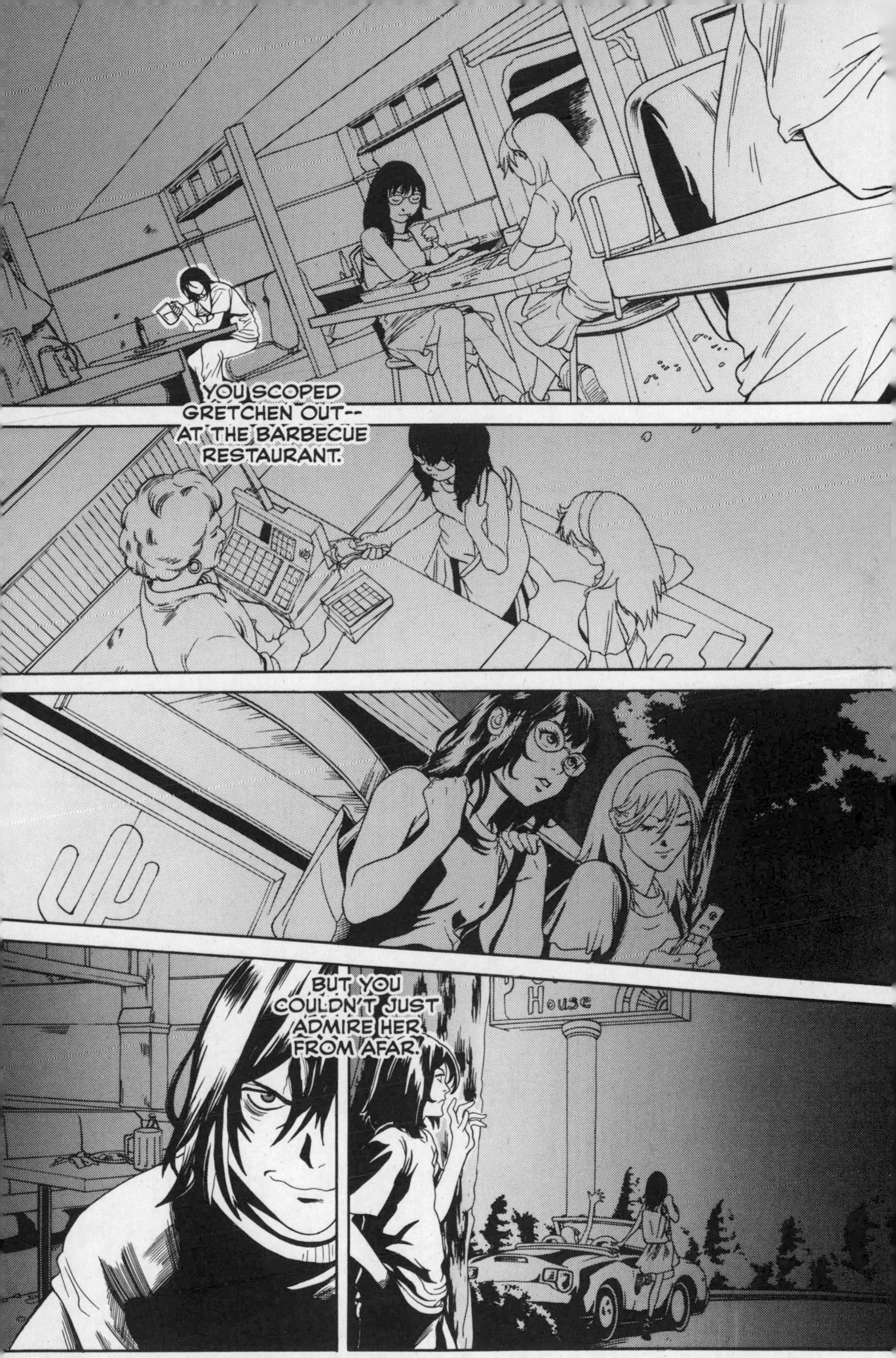
YOU SCOPED GRETCHEN OUT-- AT THE BARBECUE RESTAURANT.
House
BUT YOU COULDN'T JUST ADMIRE HER FROM AFAR.

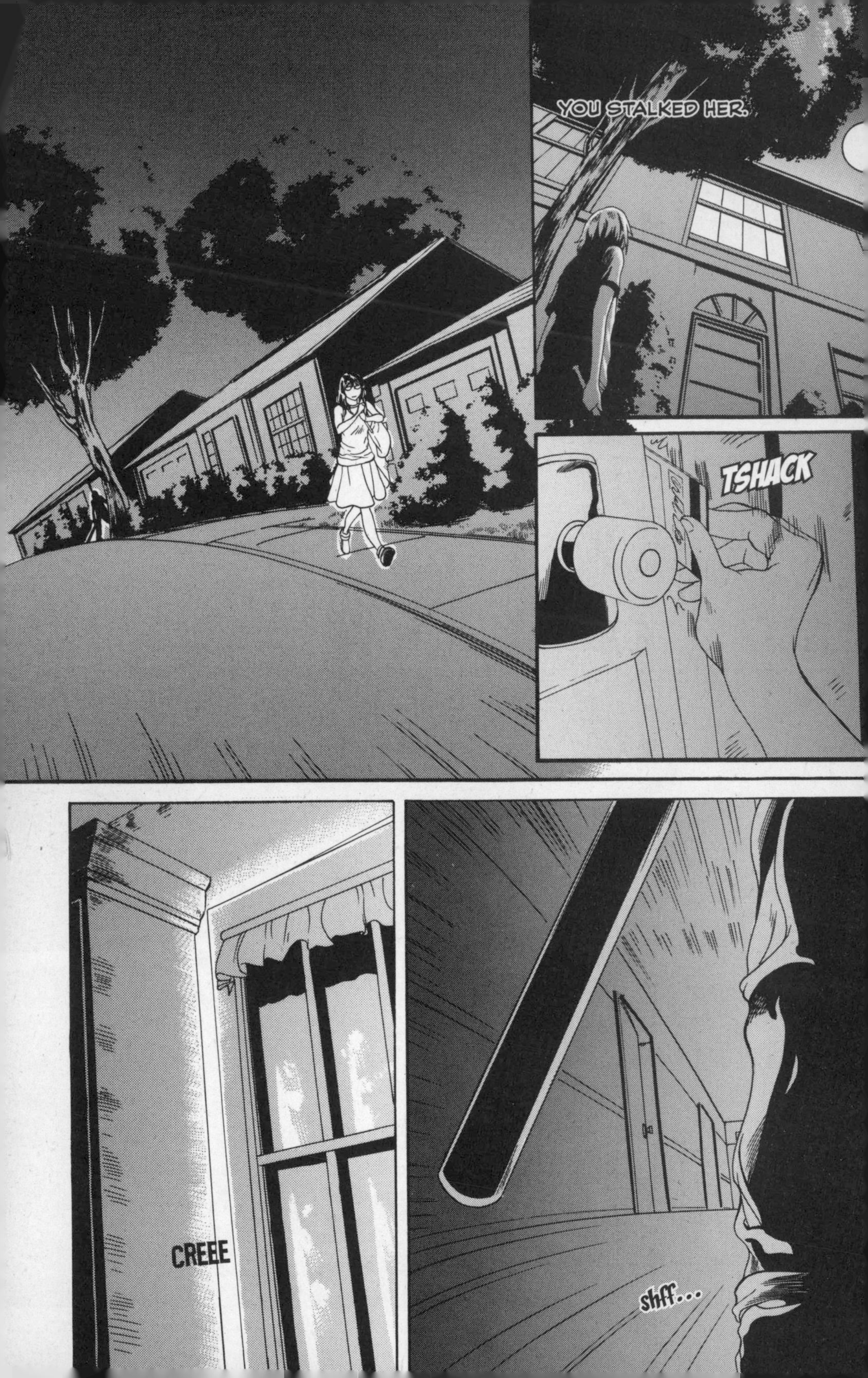
YOU STALKED HER.
TSHACK
CREEE
shff...

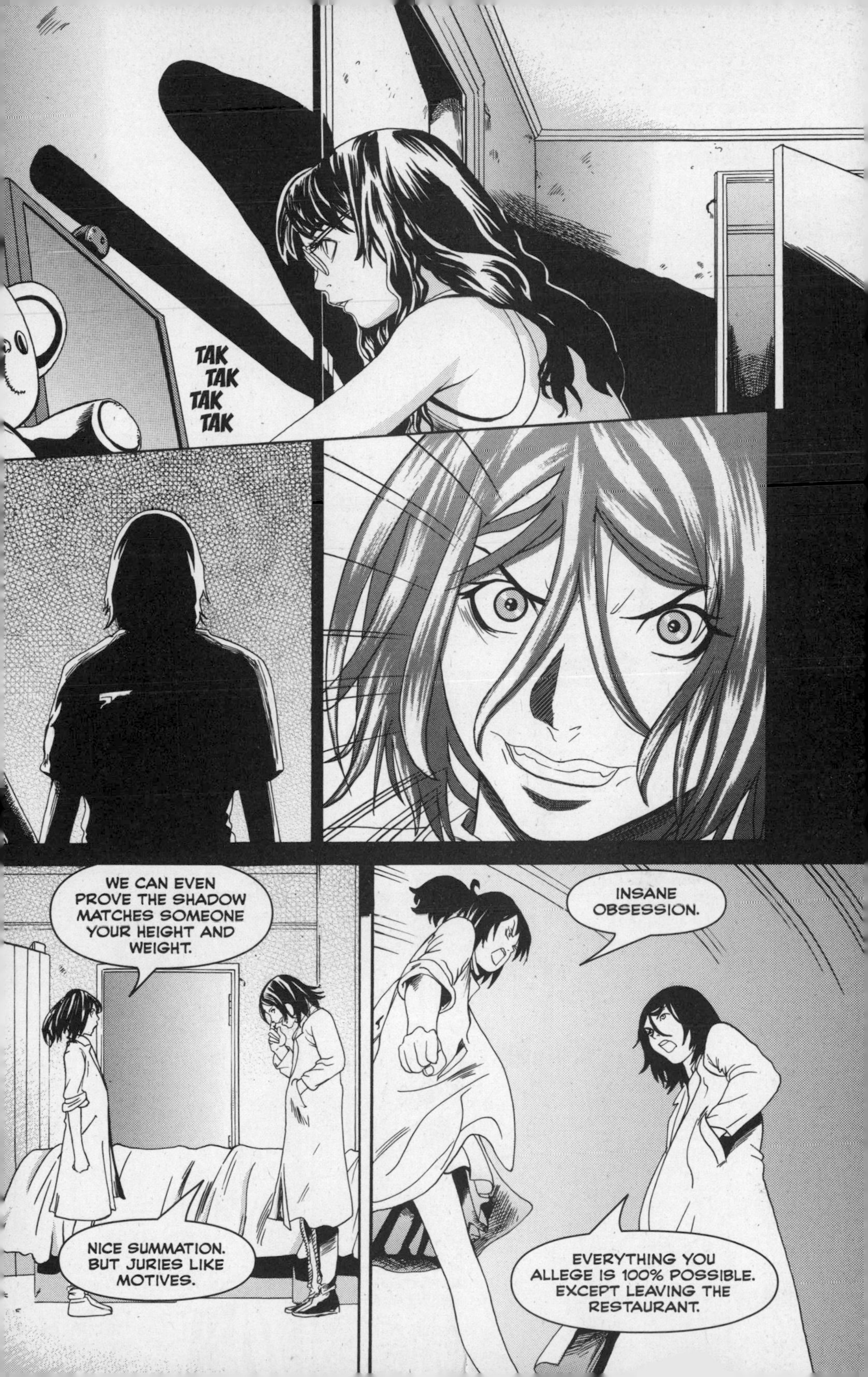
TAK TAK TAK TAK
WE CAN EVEN PROVE THE SHADOW MATCHES SOMEONE YOUR HEIGHT AND WEIGHT.
NICE SUMMATION. BUT JURIES LIKE MOTIVES.
INSANE OBSESSION.
EVERYTHING YOU ALLEGE IS 100% POSSIBLE. EXCEPT LEAVING THE RESTAURANT.

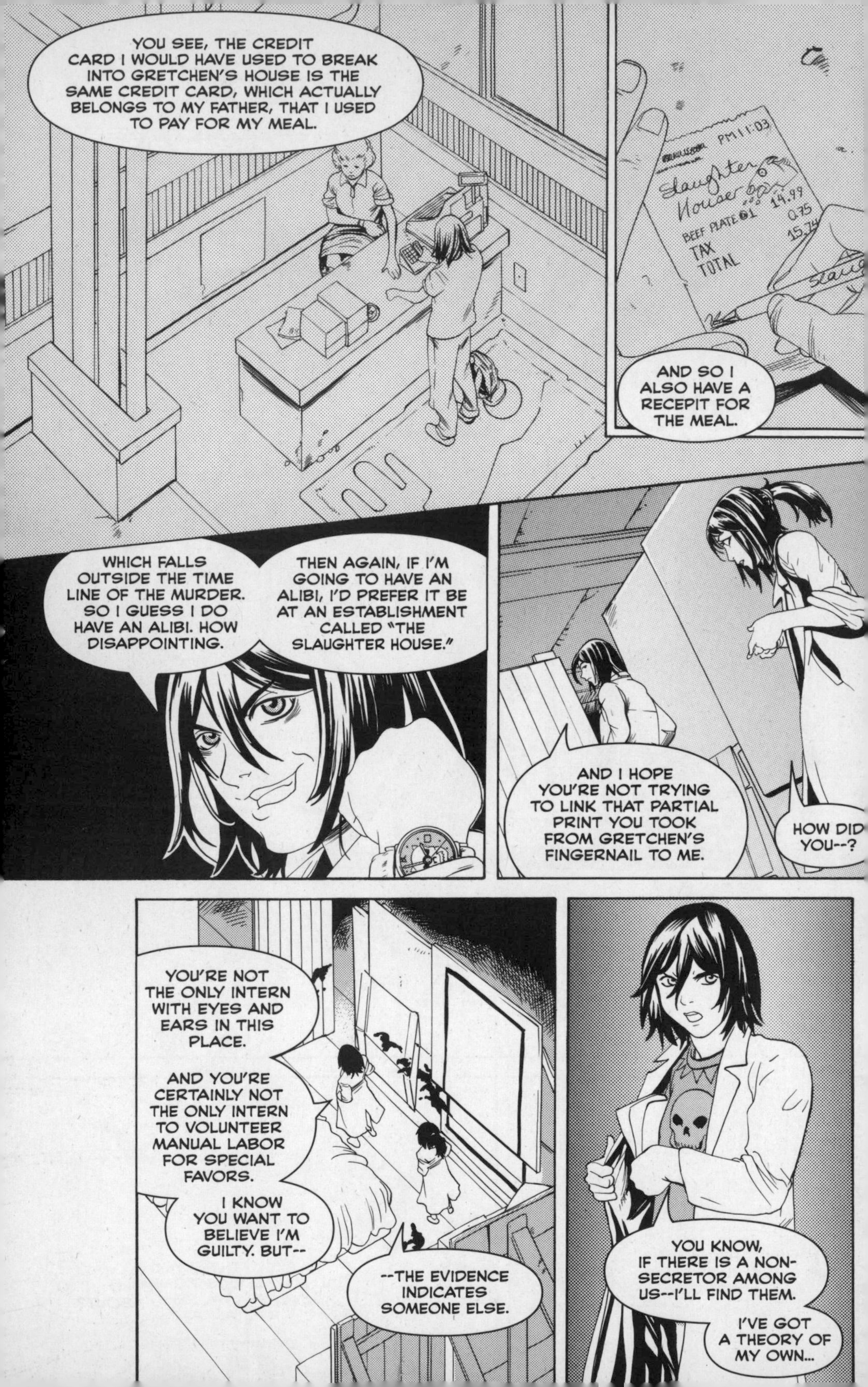
YOU SEE, THE CREDIT CARD I WOULD HAVE USED TO BREAK INTO GRETCHEN'S HOUSE IS THE SAME CREDIT CARD, WHICH ACTUALLY BELONGS TO MY FATHER, THAT I USED TO PAY FOR MY MEAL.
PM11:03
Slaughter House
BEEF PLATE 1 14.99
TAX 0.75
TOTAL 15.74
AND SO I ALSO HAVE A RECEPIT FOR THE MEAL.
WHICH FALLS OUTSIDE THE TIME LINE OF THE MURDER. SO I GUESS I DO HAVE AN ALIBI. HOW DISAPPOINTING.
THEN AGAIN, IF I'M GOING TO HAVE AN ALIBI, I'D PREFER IT BE AT AN ESTABLISHMENT CALLED "THE SLAUGHTER HOUSE."
AND I HOPE YOU'RE NOT TRYING TO LINK THAT PARTIAL PRINT YOU TOOK FROM GRETCHEN'S FINGERNAIL TO ME.
HOW DID YOU--?
YOU'RE NOT THE ONLY INTERN WITH EYES AND EARS IN THIS PLACE.
AND YOU'RE CERTAINLY NOT THE ONLY INTERN TO VOLUNTEER MANUAL LABOR FOR SPECIAL FAVORS.
I KNOW YOU WANT TO BELIEVE I'M GUILTY. BUT--
--THE EVIDENCE INDICATES SOMEONE ELSE.
YOU KNOW, IF THERE IS A NON-SECRETOR AMONG US--I'LL FIND THEM.
I'VE GOT A THEORY OF MY OWN...

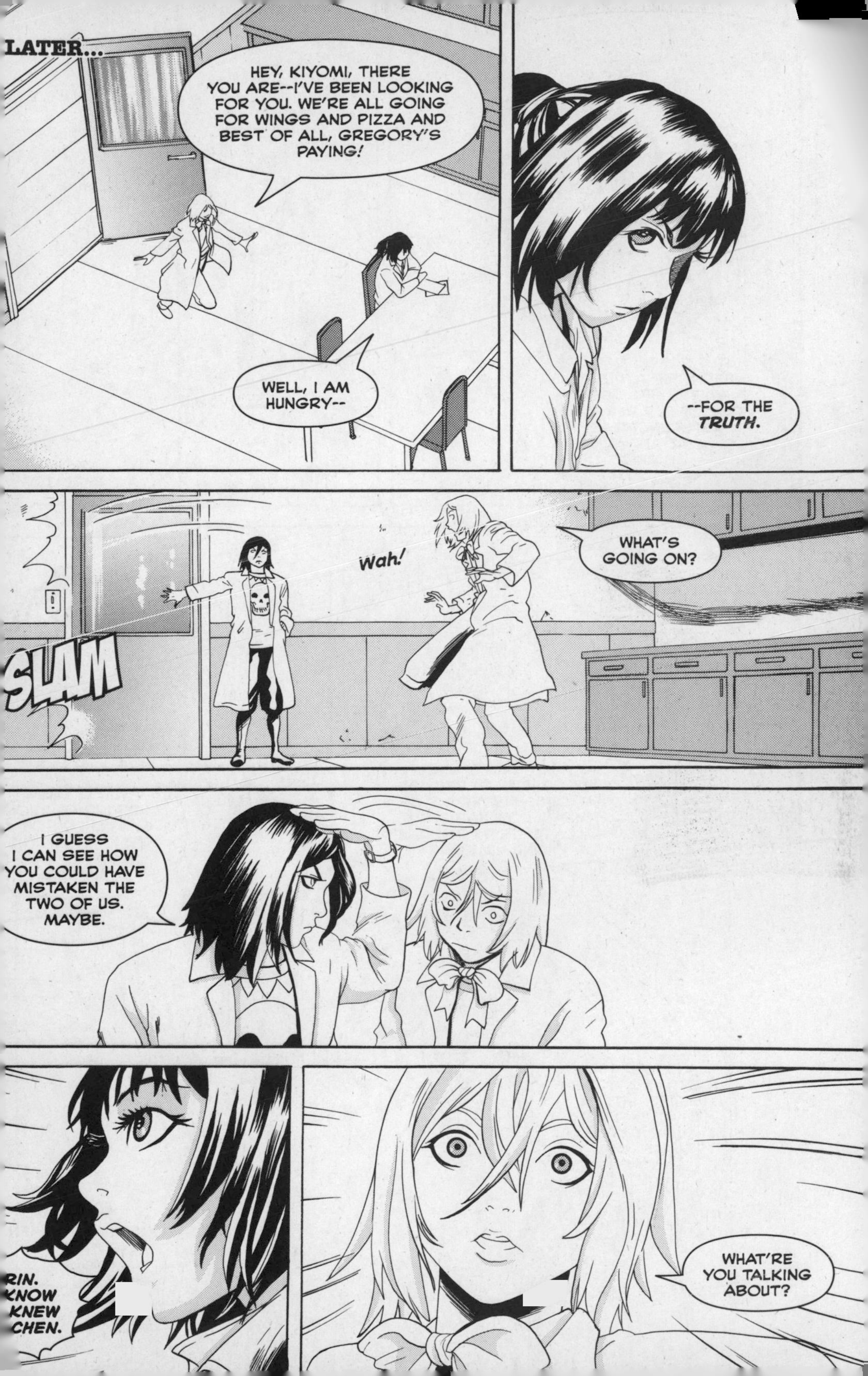
LATER...
HEY, KIYOMI, THERE YOU ARE--I'VE BEEN LOOKING FOR YOU. WE'RE ALL GOING FOR WINGS AND PIZZA AND BEST OF ALL, GREGORY'S PAYING!
WELL, I AM HUNGRY--
--FOR THE *TRUTH*.
SLAM
Wah!
WHAT'S GOING ON?
I GUESS I CAN SEE HOW YOU COULD HAVE MISTAKEN THE TWO OF US. MAYBE.
RIN.
KNOW
KNEW
CHEN.
WHAT'RE YOU TALKING ABOUT?

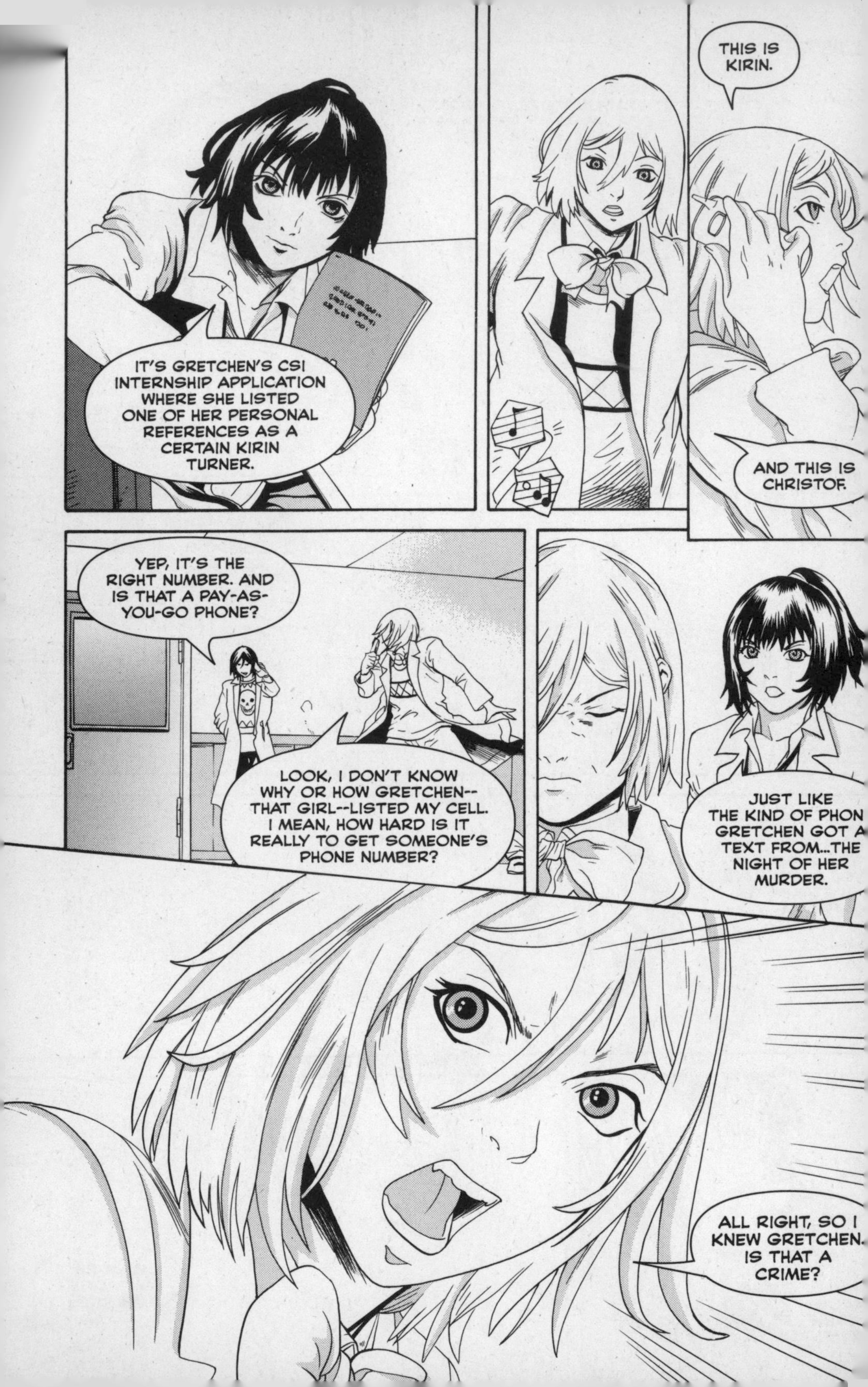
IT'S GRETCHEN'S CSI INTERNSHIP APPLICATION WHERE SHE LISTED ONE OF HER PERSONAL REFERENCES AS A CERTAIN KIRIN TURNER.
THIS IS KIRIN.
AND THIS IS CHRISTOF.
YEP, IT'S THE RIGHT NUMBER. AND IS THAT A PAY-AS-YOU-GO PHONE?
LOOK, I DON'T KNOW WHY OR HOW GRETCHEN--THAT GIRL--LISTED MY CELL. I MEAN, HOW HARD IS IT REALLY TO GET SOMEONE'S PHONE NUMBER?
JUST LIKE THE KIND OF PHON GRETCHEN GOT A TEXT FROM...THE NIGHT OF HER MURDER.
ALL RIGHT, SO I KNEW GRETCHEN. IS THAT A CRIME?

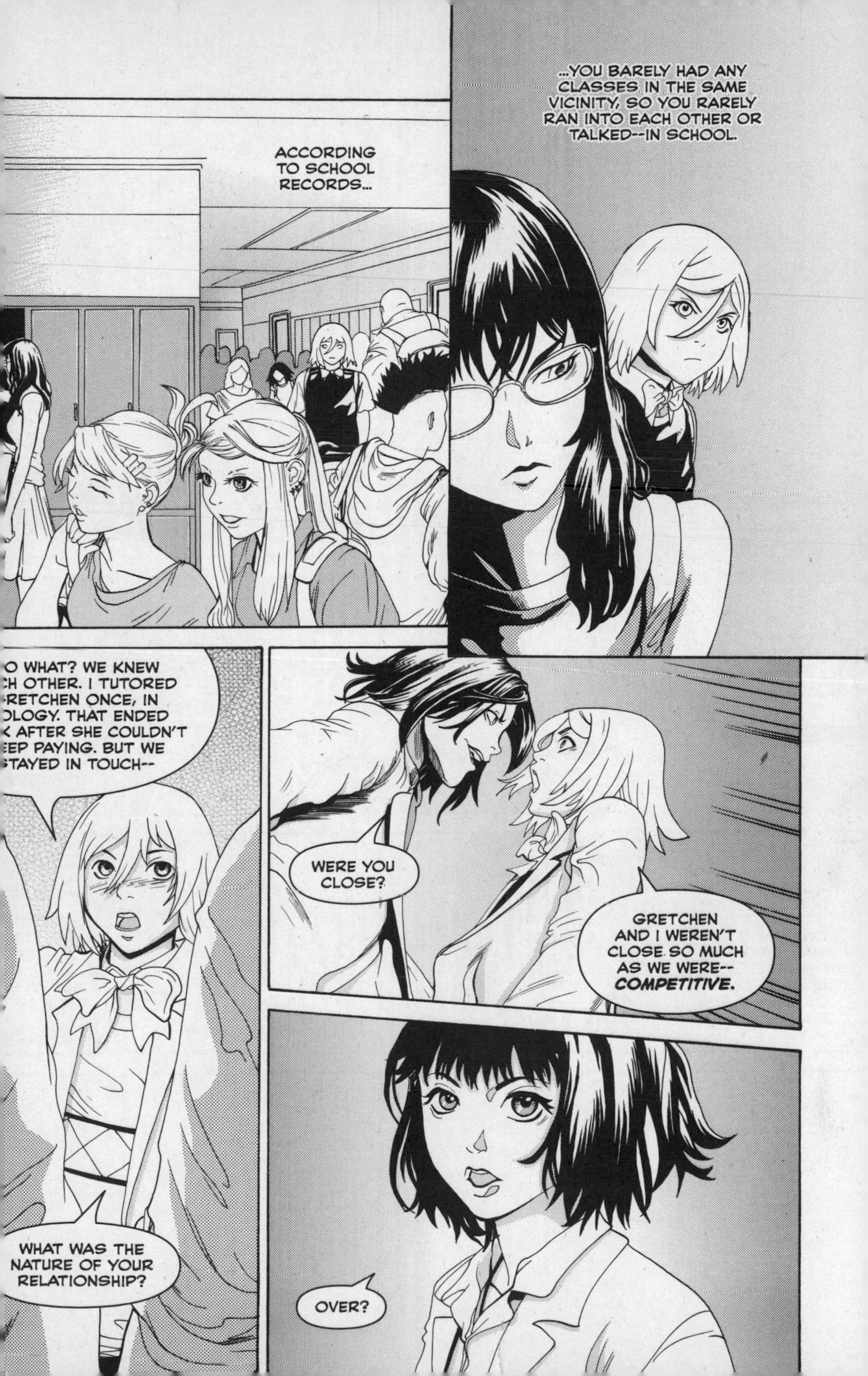
ACCORDING TO SCHOOL RECORDS...
...YOU BARELY HAD ANY CLASSES IN THE SAME VICINITY, SO YOU RARELY RAN INTO EACH OTHER OR TALKED--IN SCHOOL.
WERE YOU CLOSE?
GRETCHEN AND I WEREN'T CLOSE SO MUCH AS WE WERE-- COMPETITIVE.
O WHAT? WE KNEW CH OTHER. I TUTORED RETCHEN ONCE, IN OLOGY. THAT ENDED K AFTER SHE COULDN'T EEP PAYING. BUT WE STAYED IN TOUCH--
WHAT WAS THE NATURE OF YOUR RELATIONSHIP?
OVER?

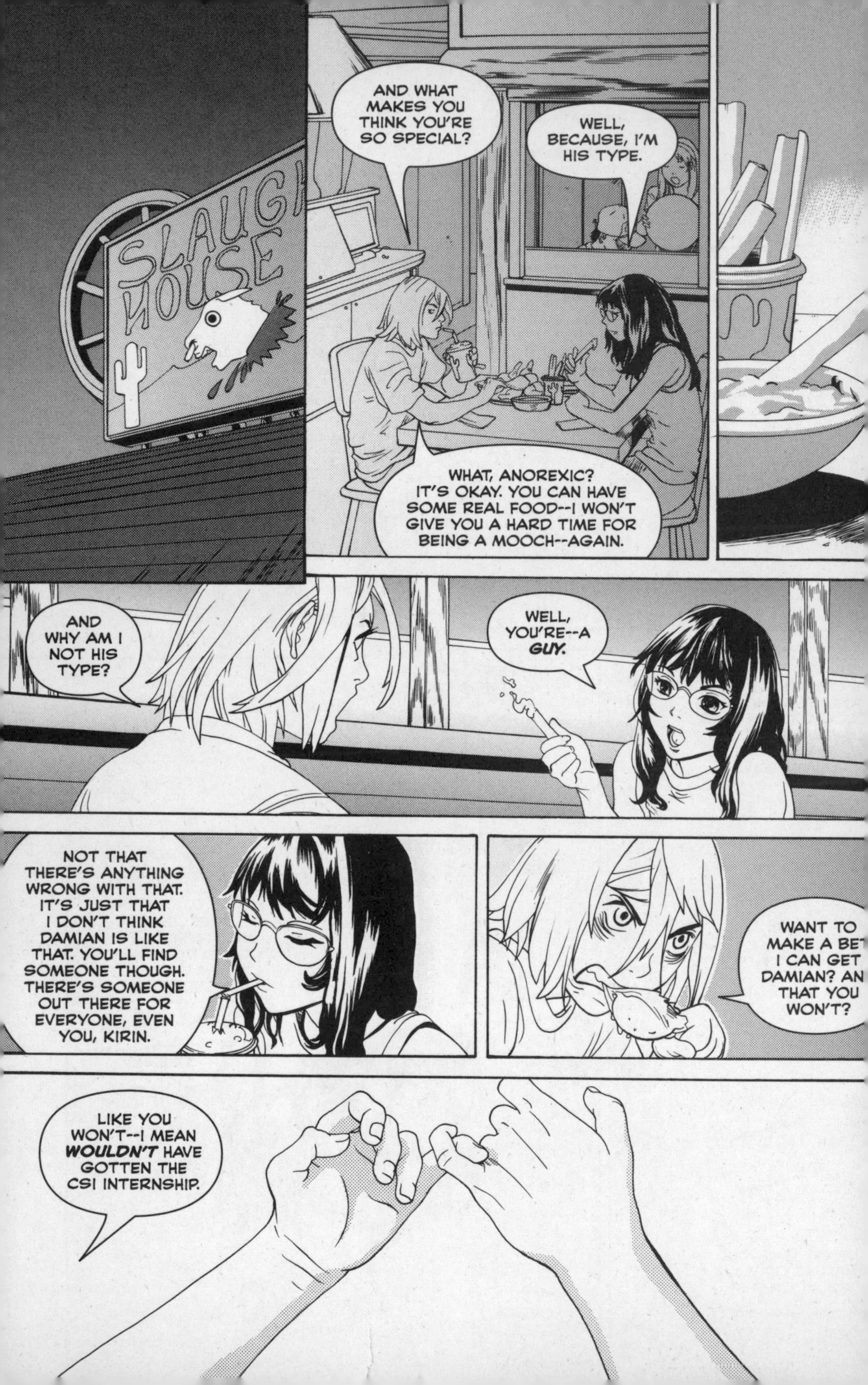
SLAUGH HOUSE
AND WHAT MAKES YOU THINK YOU'RE SO SPECIAL?
WELL, BECAUSE, I'M HIS TYPE.
WHAT, ANOREXIC? IT'S OKAY. YOU CAN HAVE SOME REAL FOOD--I WON'T GIVE YOU A HARD TIME FOR BEING A MOOCH--AGAIN.
AND WHY AM I NOT HIS TYPE?
WELL, YOU'RE--A ***GUY.***
NOT THAT THERE'S ANYTHING WRONG WITH THAT. IT'S JUST THAT I DON'T THINK DAMIAN IS LIKE THAT. YOU'LL FIND SOMEONE THOUGH. THERE'S SOMEONE OUT THERE FOR EVERYONE, EVEN YOU, KIRIN.
WANT TO MAKE A BET I CAN GET DAMIAN? AN THAT YOU WON'T?
LIKE YOU WON'T--I MEAN ***WOULDN'T*** HAVE GOTTEN THE CSI INTERNSHIP.

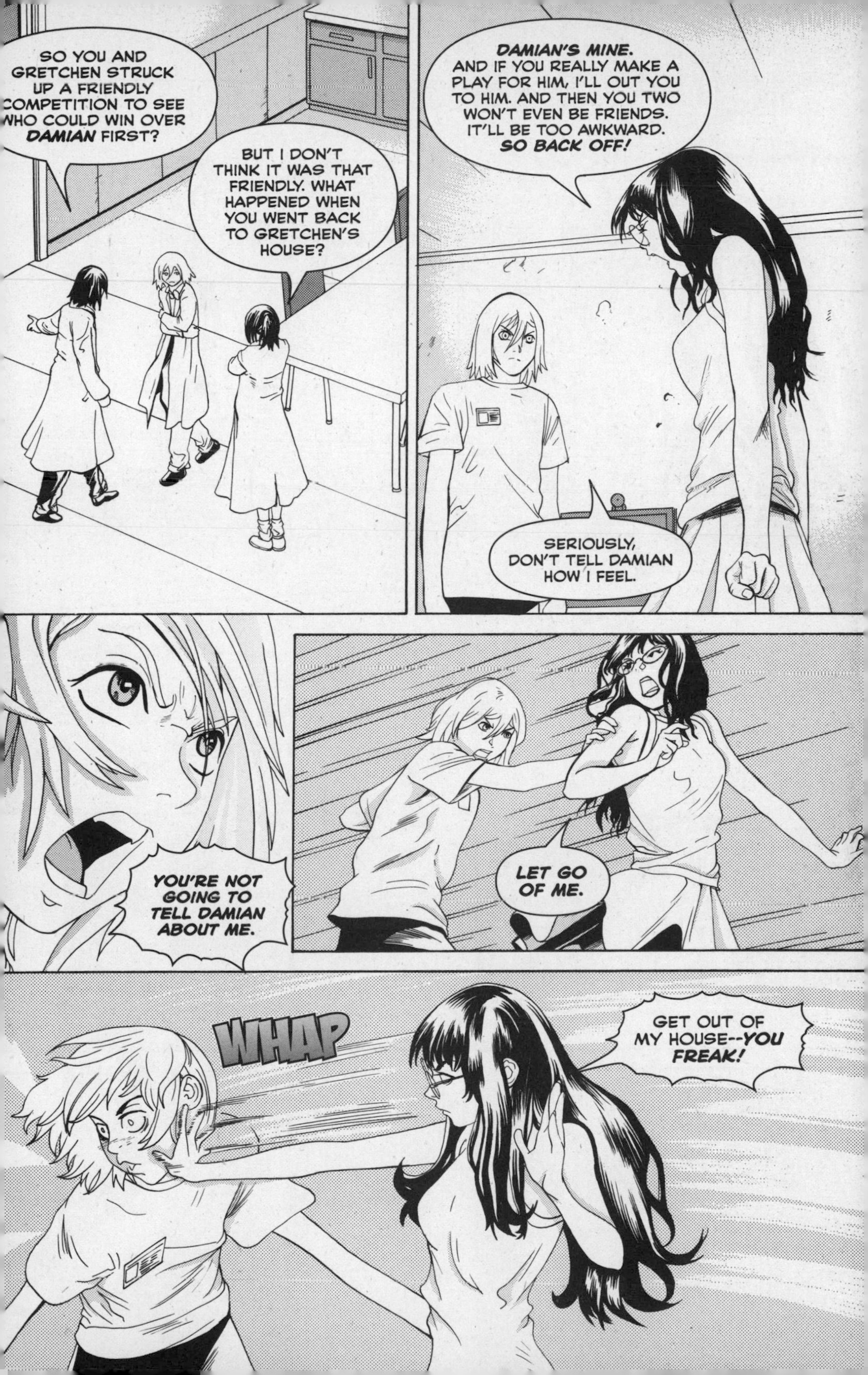
SO YOU AND GRETCHEN STRUCK UP A FRIENDLY COMPETITION TO SEE WHO COULD WIN OVER *DAMIAN* FIRST?
BUT I DON'T THINK IT WAS THAT FRIENDLY. WHAT HAPPENED WHEN YOU WENT BACK TO GRETCHEN'S HOUSE?
DAMIAN'S MINE. AND IF YOU REALLY MAKE A PLAY FOR HIM, I'LL OUT YOU TO HIM. AND THEN YOU TWO WON'T EVEN BE FRIENDS. IT'LL BE TOO AWKWARD. *SO BACK OFF!*
SERIOUSLY, DON'T TELL DAMIAN HOW I FEEL.
YOU'RE NOT GOING TO TELL DAMIAN ABOUT ME.
LET GO OF ME.
WHAP
GET OUT OF MY HOUSE--*YOU FREAK!*

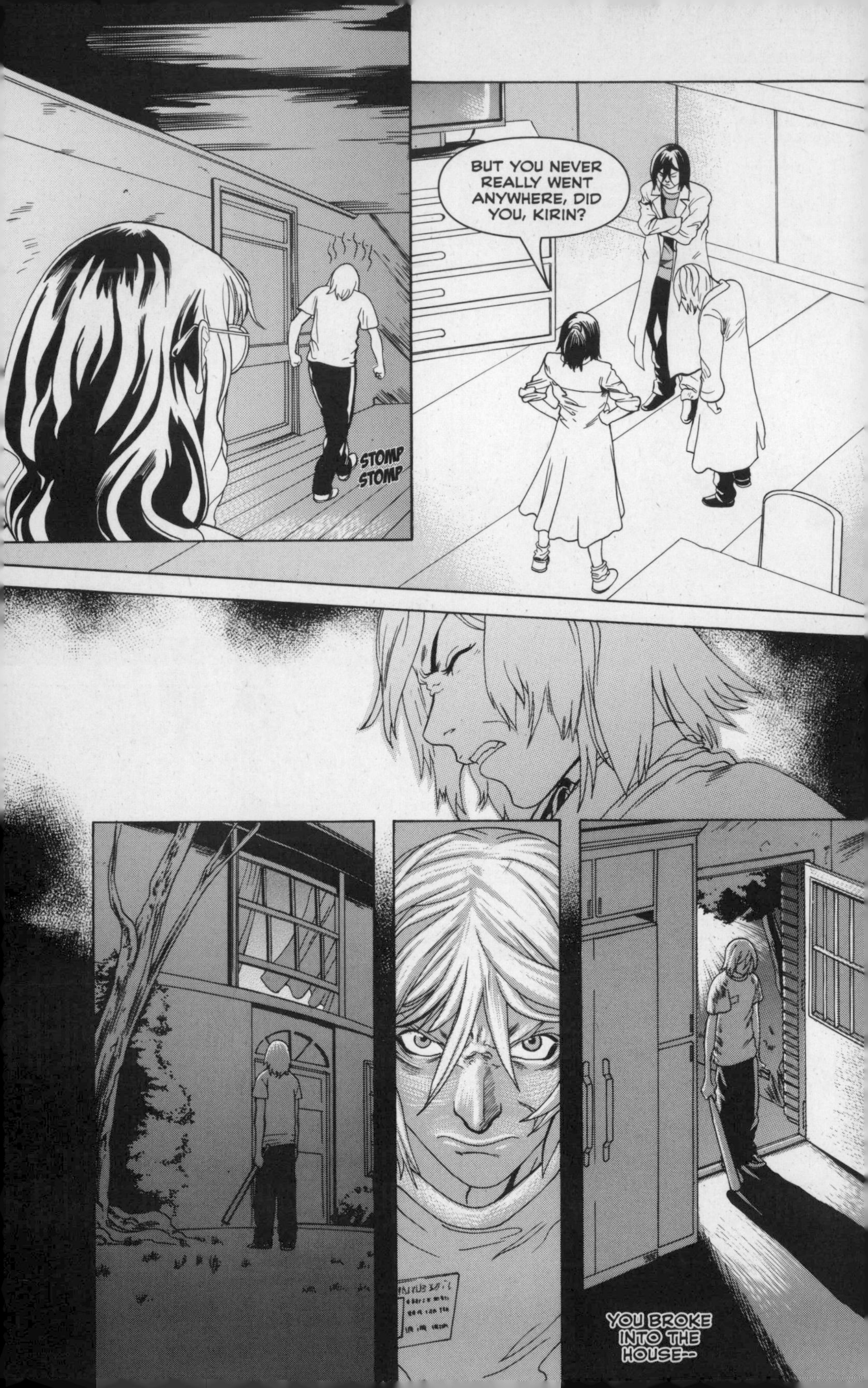
STOMP
STOMP
BUT YOU NEVER REALLY WENT ANYWHERE, DID YOU, KIRIN?
YOU BROKE INTO THE HOUSE--

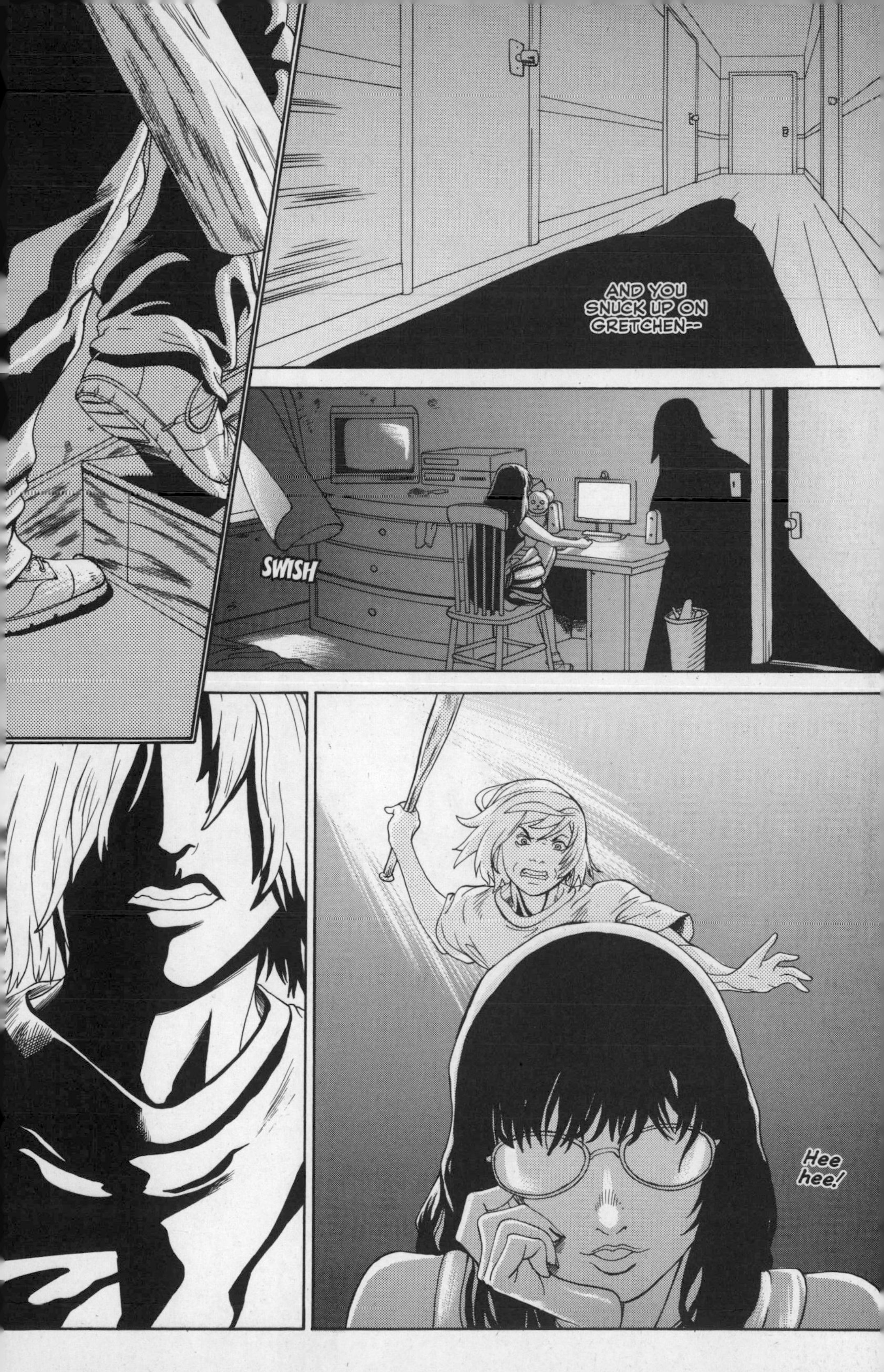
AND YOU SNUCK UP ON GRETCHEN--
SWISH
Hee hee!

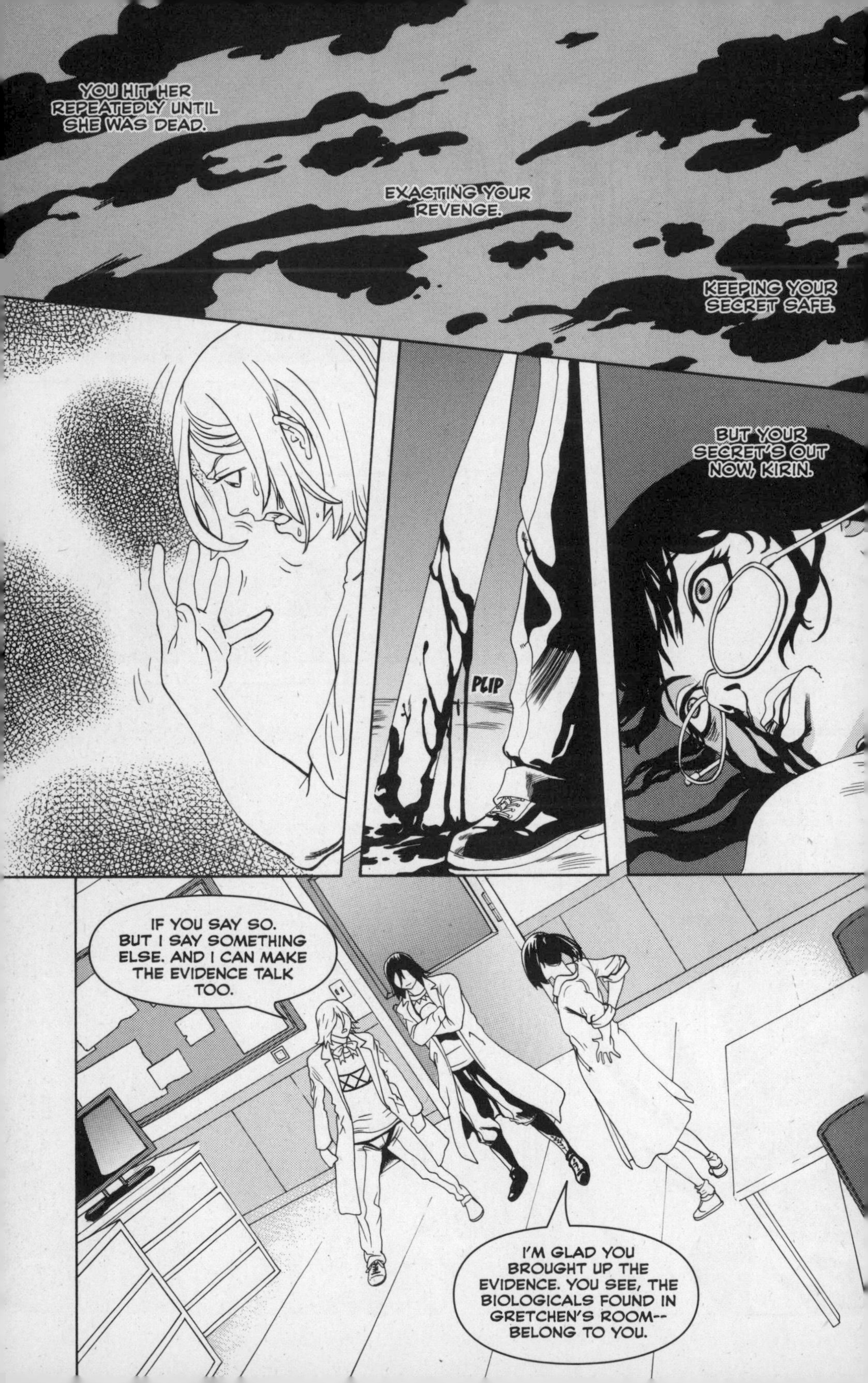
YOU HIT HER REPEATEDLY UNTIL SHE WAS DEAD.
EXACTING YOUR REVENGE.
KEEPING YOUR SECRET SAFE.
BUT YOUR SECRET'S OUT NOW, KIRIN.
PLIP
IF YOU SAY SO. BUT I SAY SOMETHING ELSE. AND I CAN MAKE THE EVIDENCE TALK TOO.
I'M GLAD YOU BROUGHT UP THE EVIDENCE. YOU SEE, THE BIOLOGICALS FOUND IN GRETCHEN'S ROOM-- BELONG TO YOU.

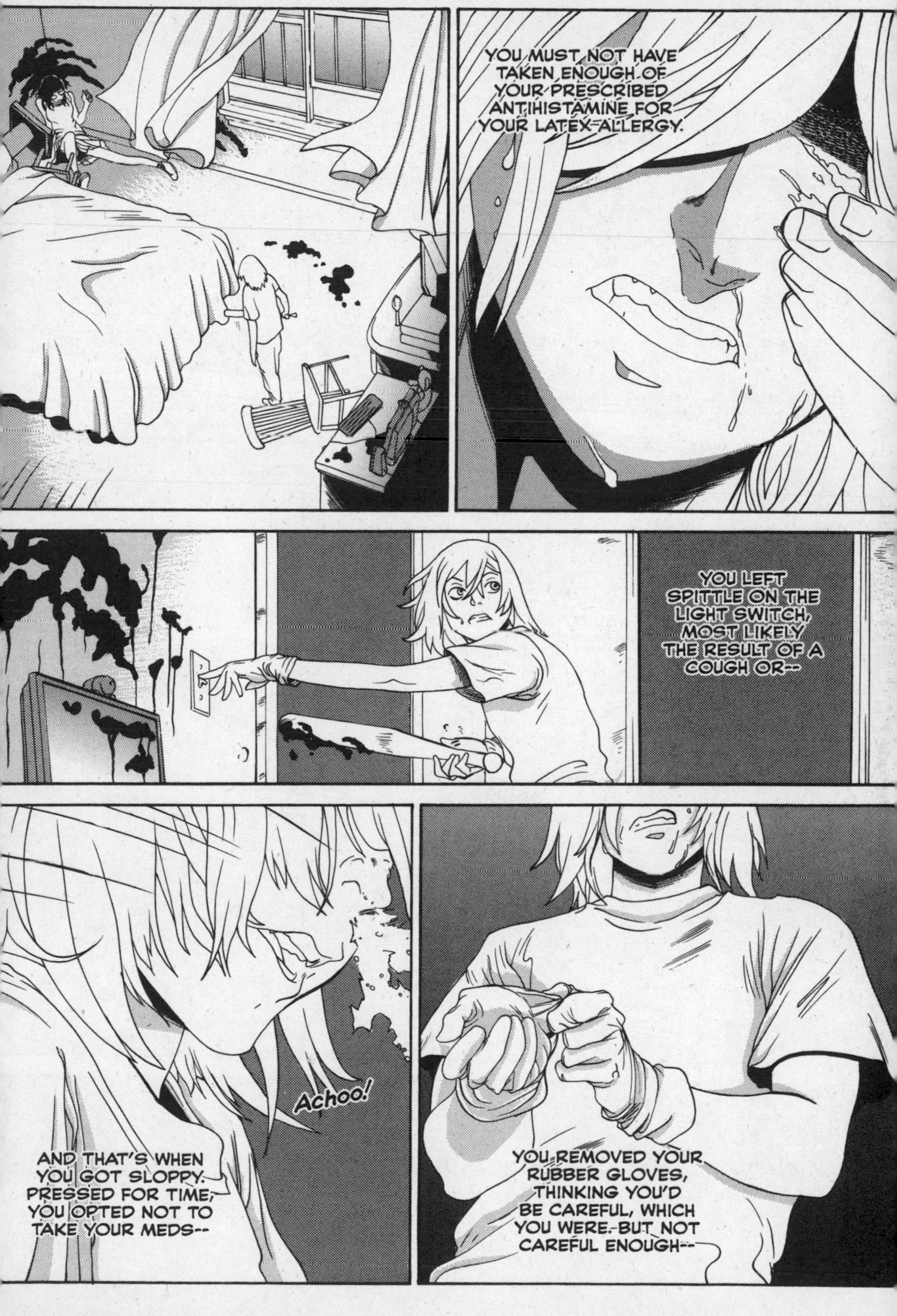
YOU MUST NOT HAVE TAKEN ENOUGH OF YOUR PRESCRIBED ANTIHISTAMINE FOR YOUR LATEX ALLERGY.
YOU LEFT SPITTLE ON THE LIGHT SWITCH, MOST LIKELY THE RESULT OF A COUGH OR--
AND THAT'S WHEN YOU GOT SLOPPY. PRESSED FOR TIME, YOU OPTED NOT TO TAKE YOUR MEDS--
Achoo!
YOU REMOVED YOUR RUBBER GLOVES, THINKING YOU'D BE CAREFUL, WHICH YOU WERE. BUT NOT CAREFUL ENOUGH--

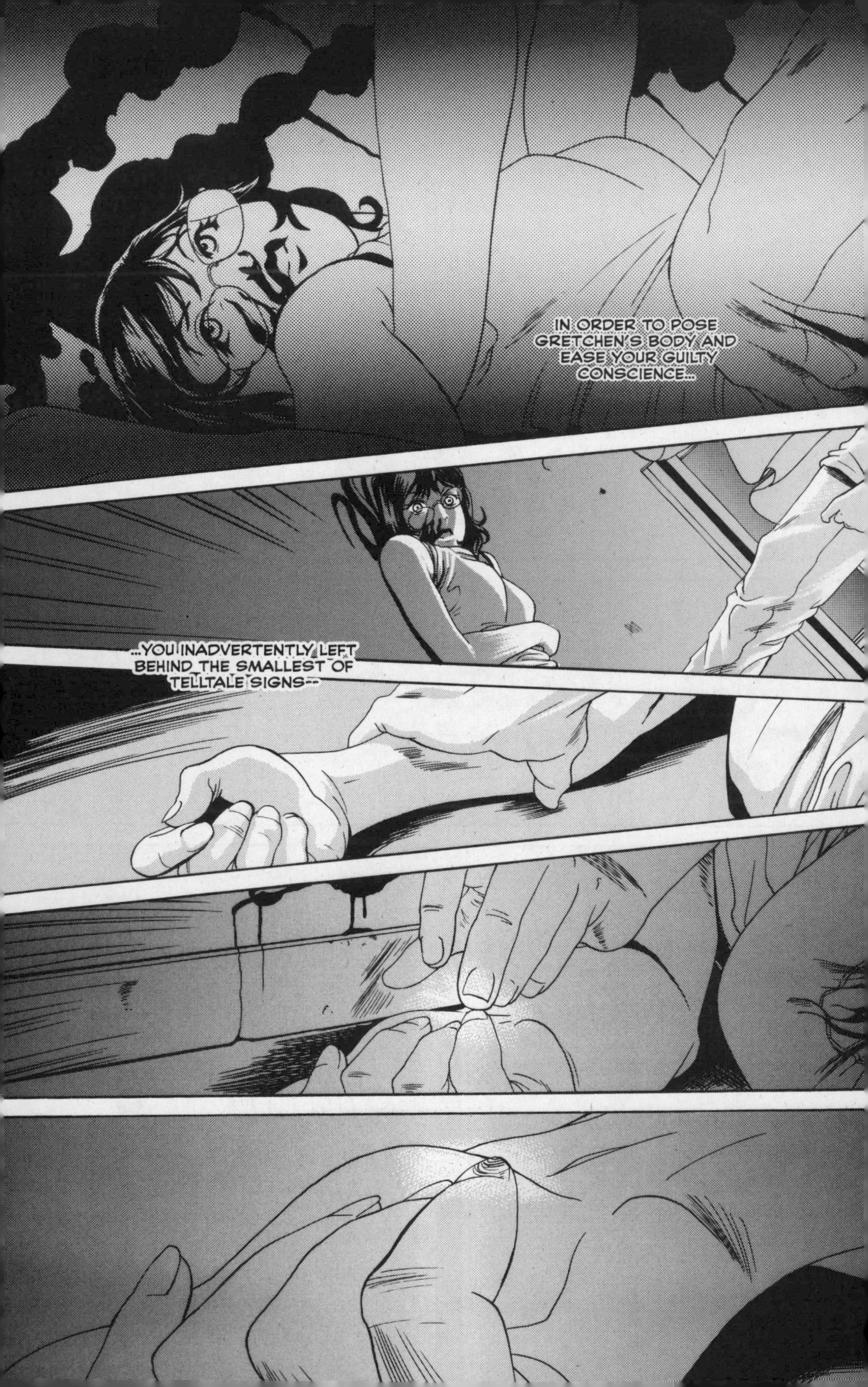
IN ORDER TO POSE GRETCHEN'S BODY AND EASE YOUR GUILTY CONSCIENCE...
...YOU INADVERTENTLY LEFT BEHIND THE SMALLEST OF TELLTALE SIGNS--

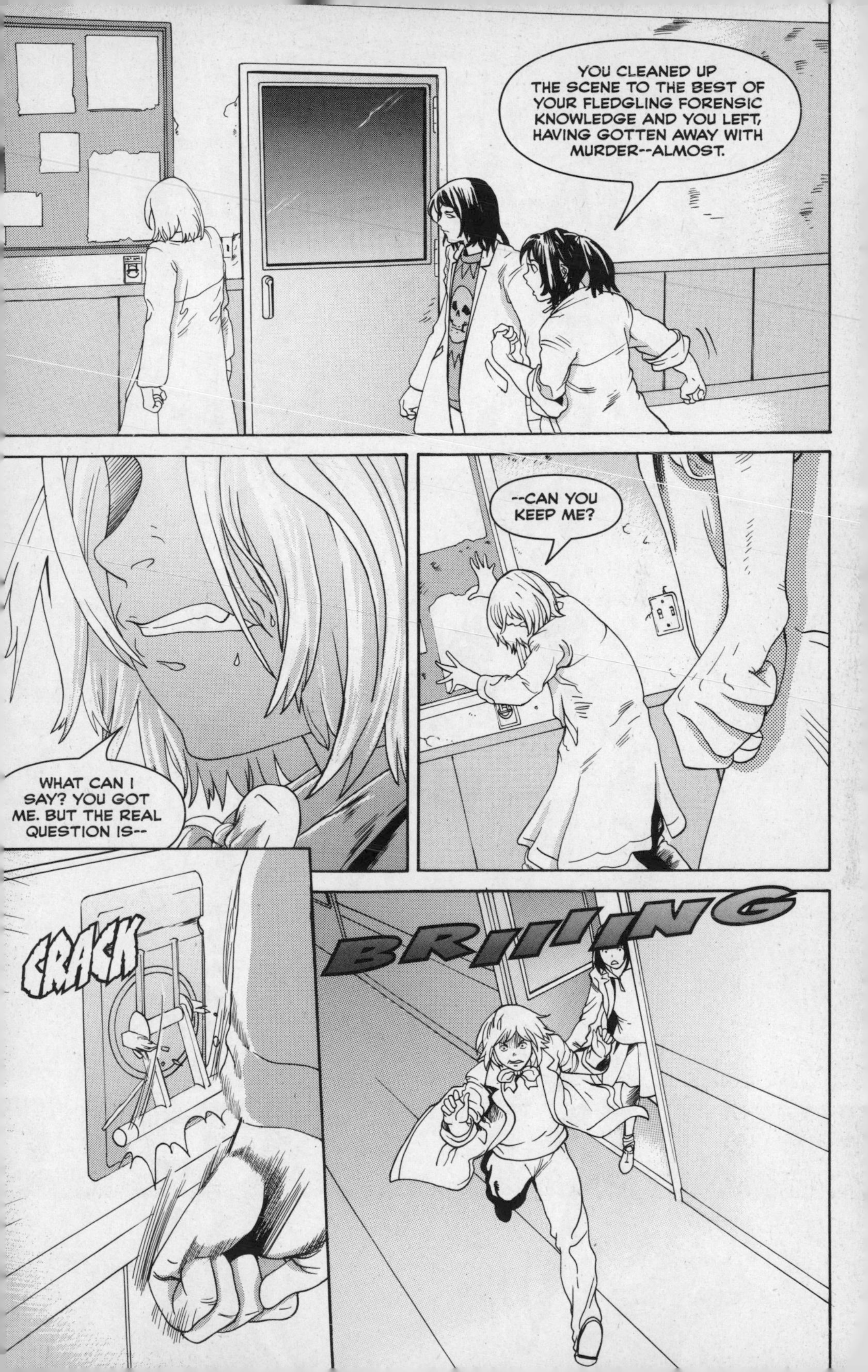
YOU CLEANED UP THE SCENE TO THE BEST OF YOUR FLEDGLING FORENSIC KNOWLEDGE AND YOU LEFT, HAVING GOTTEN AWAY WITH MURDER--ALMOST.
WHAT CAN I SAY? YOU GOT ME. BUT THE REAL QUESTION IS--
--CAN YOU KEEP ME?
CRACK
BRIIIING

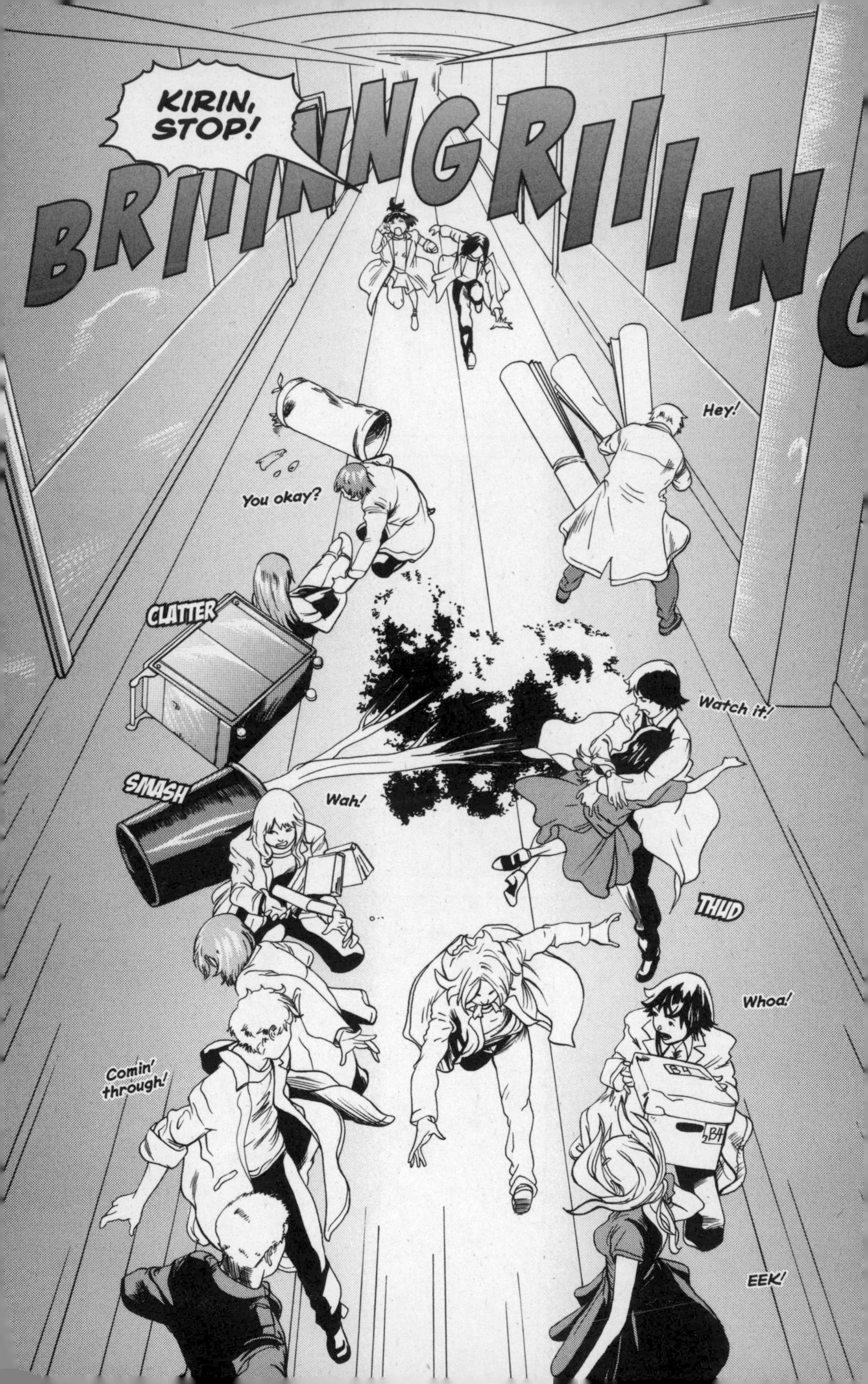
KIRIN, STOP!
BRIIIINGRIIIIING
Hey!
You okay?
CLATTER
Watch it!
SMASH
Wah!
...
THUD
Whoa!
Comin' through!
EEK!

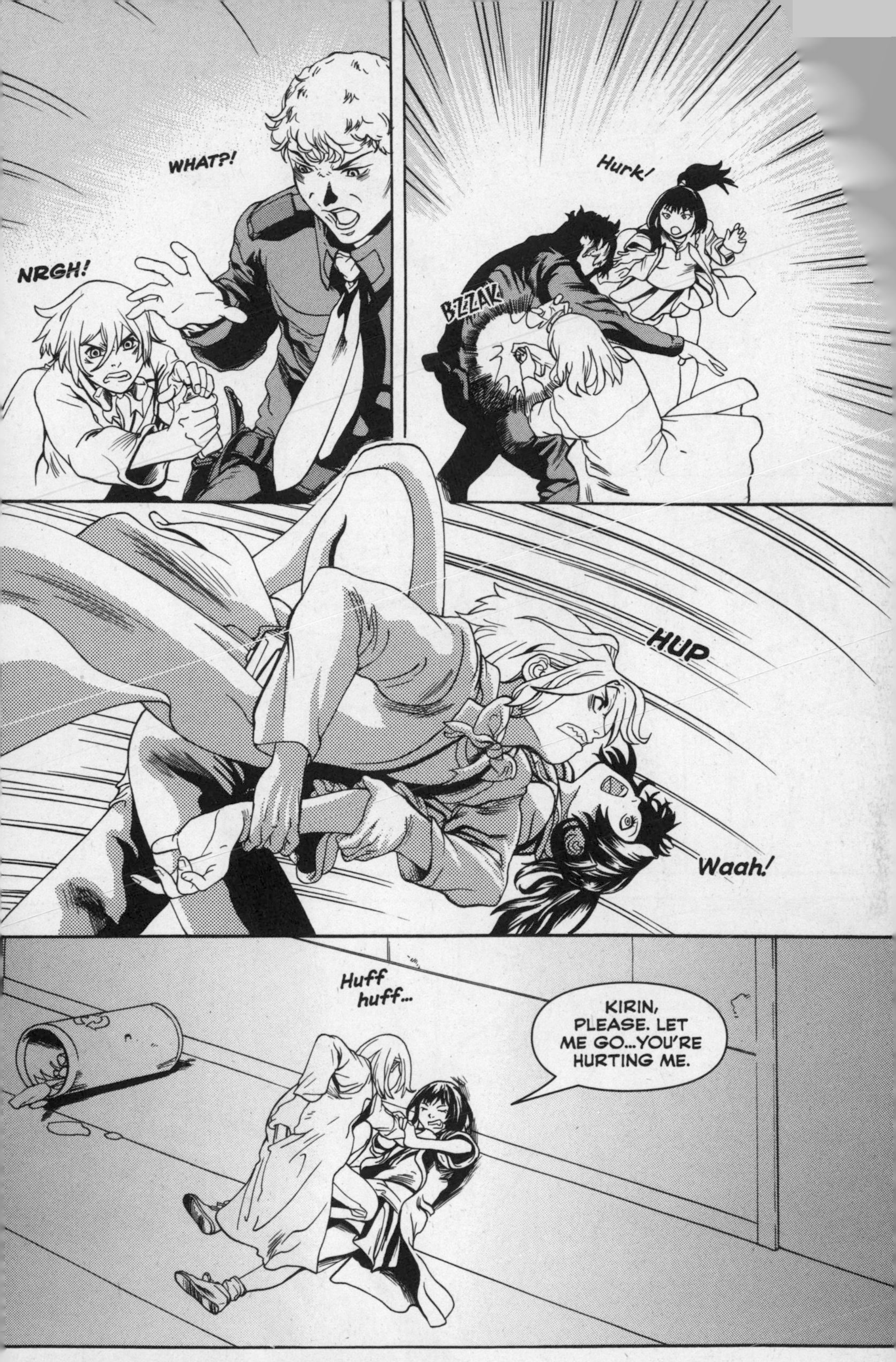
WHAT?!
NRGH!
Hurk!
BZZAK
HUP
Waah!
Huff huff...
KIRIN, PLEASE. LET ME GO...YOU'RE HURTING ME.

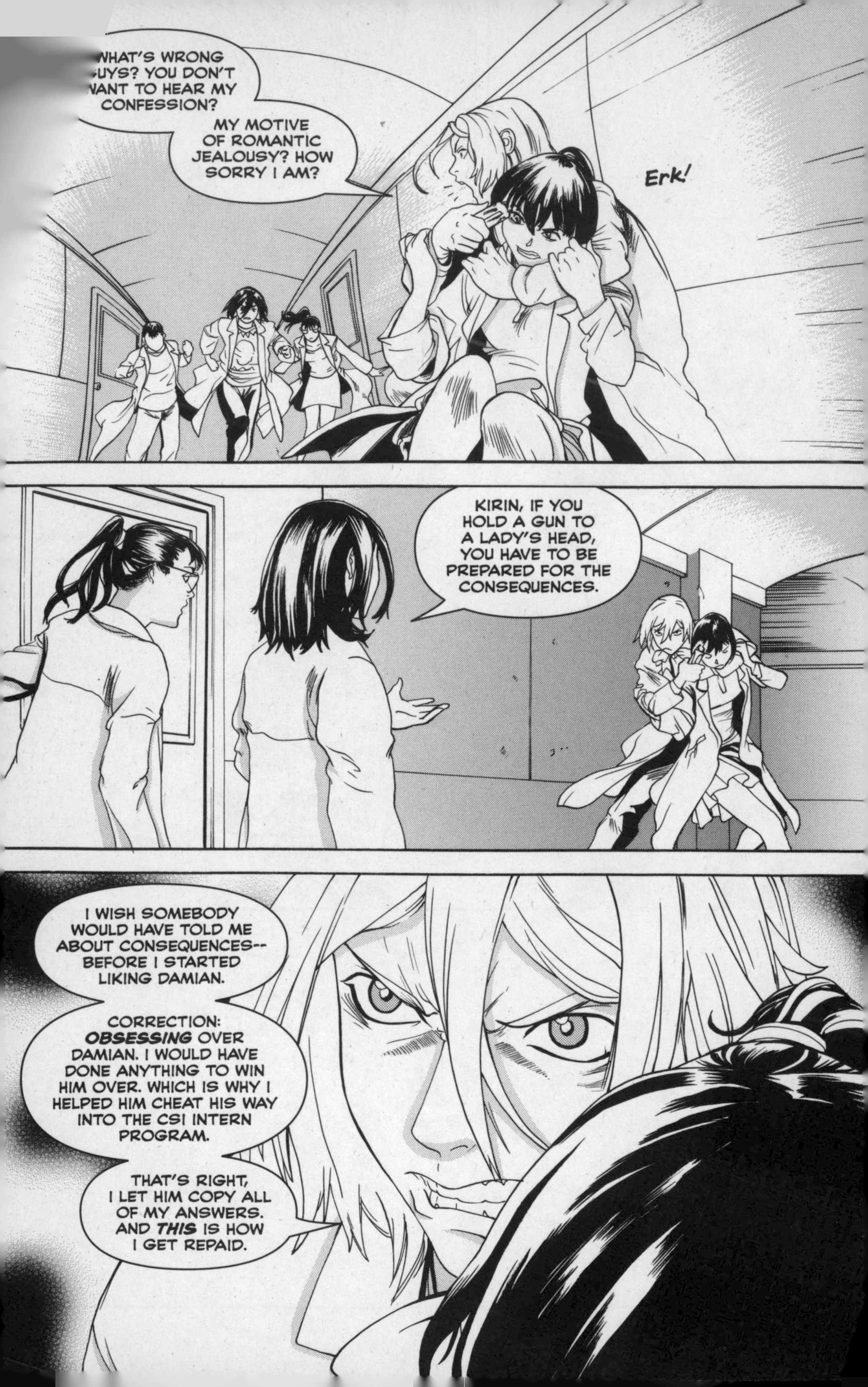
WHAT'S WRONG GUYS? YOU DON'T WANT TO HEAR MY CONFESSION?
MY MOTIVE OF ROMANTIC JEALOUSY? HOW SORRY I AM?
Erk!
KIRIN, IF YOU HOLD A GUN TO A LADY'S HEAD, YOU HAVE TO BE PREPARED FOR THE CONSEQUENCES.
I WISH SOMEBODY WOULD HAVE TOLD ME ABOUT CONSEQUENCES-- BEFORE I STARTED LIKING DAMIAN.
CORRECTION: OBSESSING OVER DAMIAN. I WOULD HAVE DONE ANYTHING TO WIN HIM OVER. WHICH IS WHY I HELPED HIM CHEAT HIS WAY INTO THE CSI INTERN PROGRAM.
THAT'S RIGHT, I LET HIM COPY ALL OF MY ANSWERS. AND THIS IS HOW I GET REPAID.

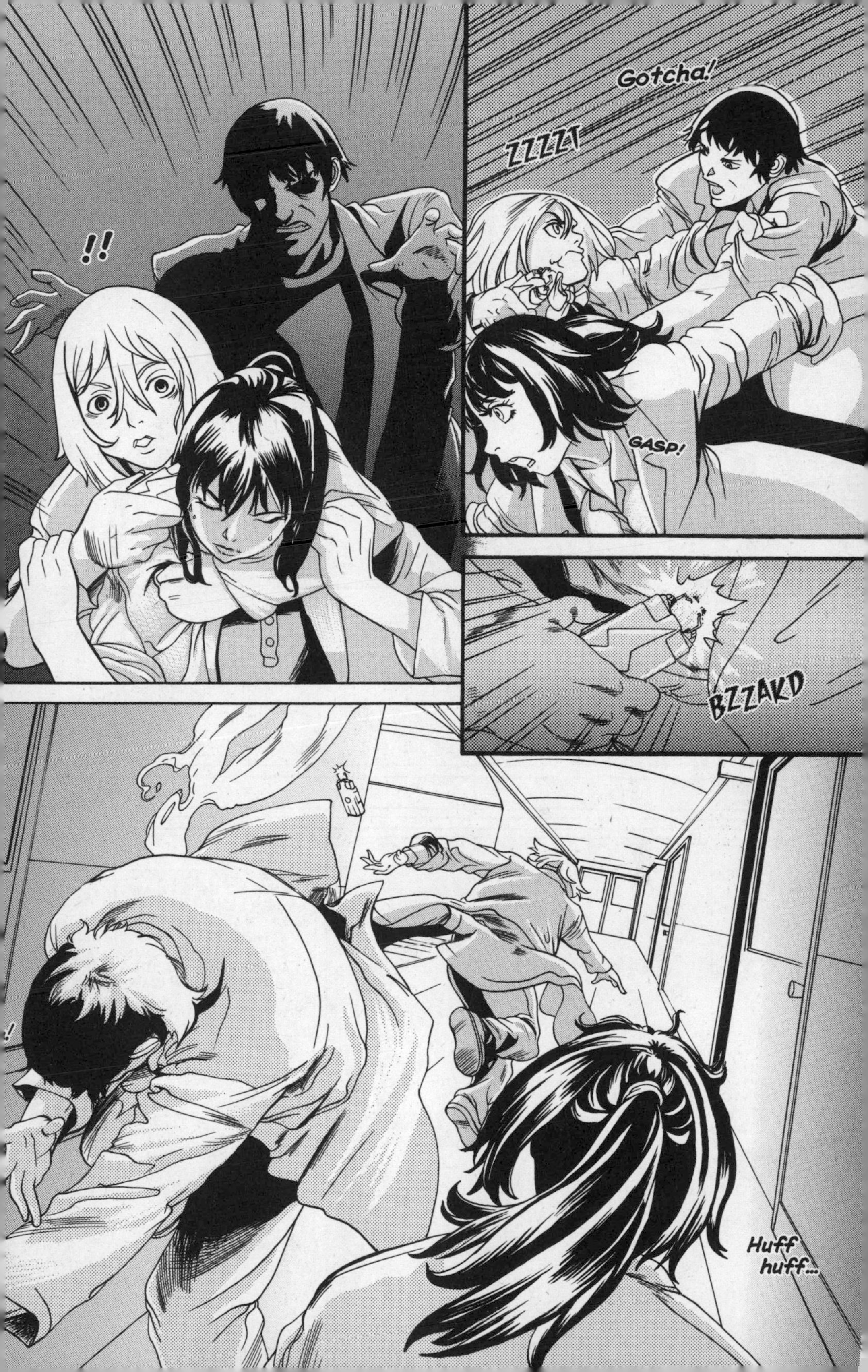
Gotcha!
ZZZZT
GASP!
!!
BZZAKD
Huff huff...

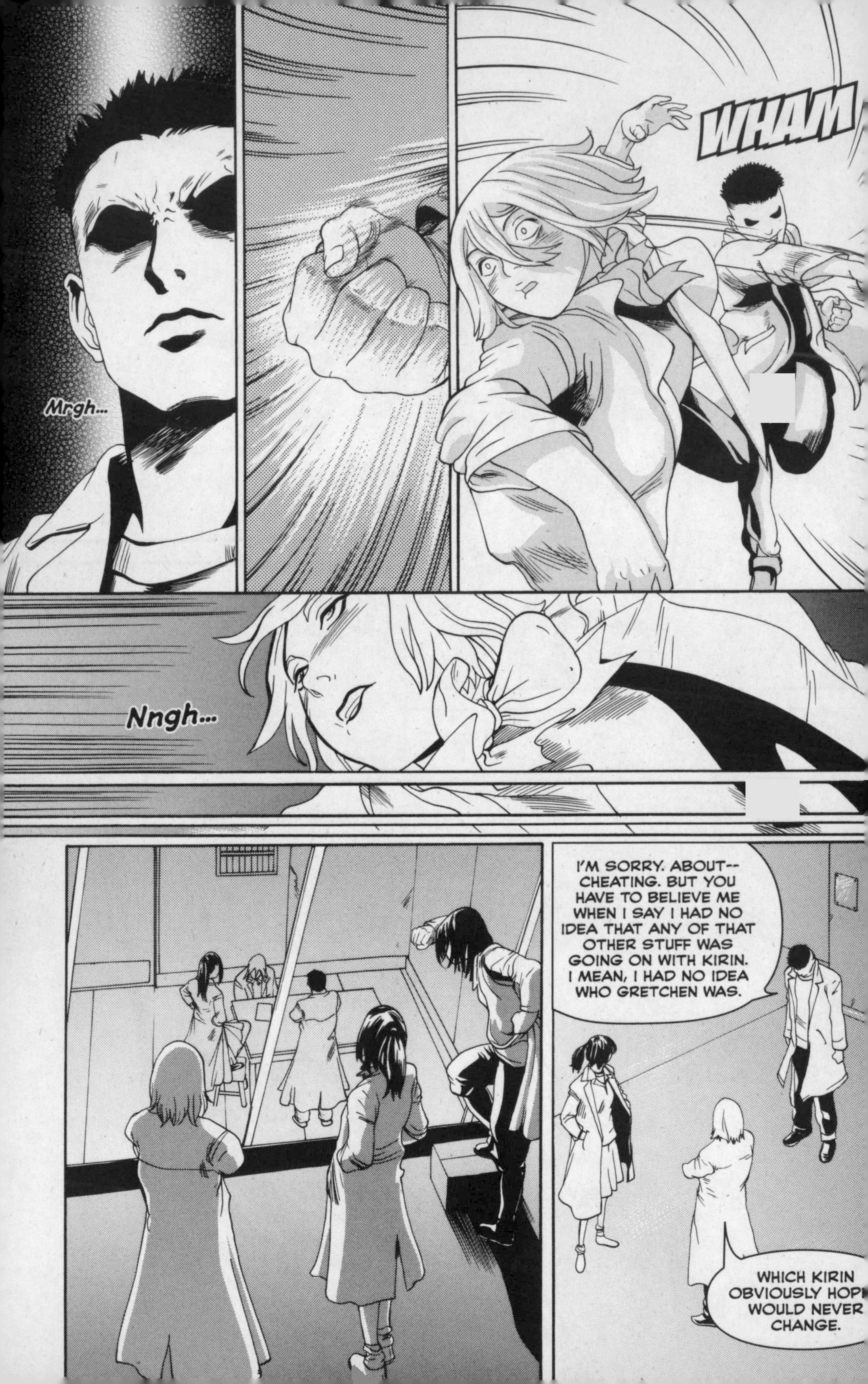
Mrgh...
WHAM
Nngh...
I'M SORRY. ABOUT-- CHEATING. BUT YOU HAVE TO BELIEVE ME WHEN I SAY I HAD NO IDEA THAT ANY OF THAT OTHER STUFF WAS GOING ON WITH KIRIN. I MEAN, I HAD NO IDEA WHO GRETCHEN WAS.
WHICH KIRIN OBVIOUSLY HOP WOULD NEVER CHANGE.

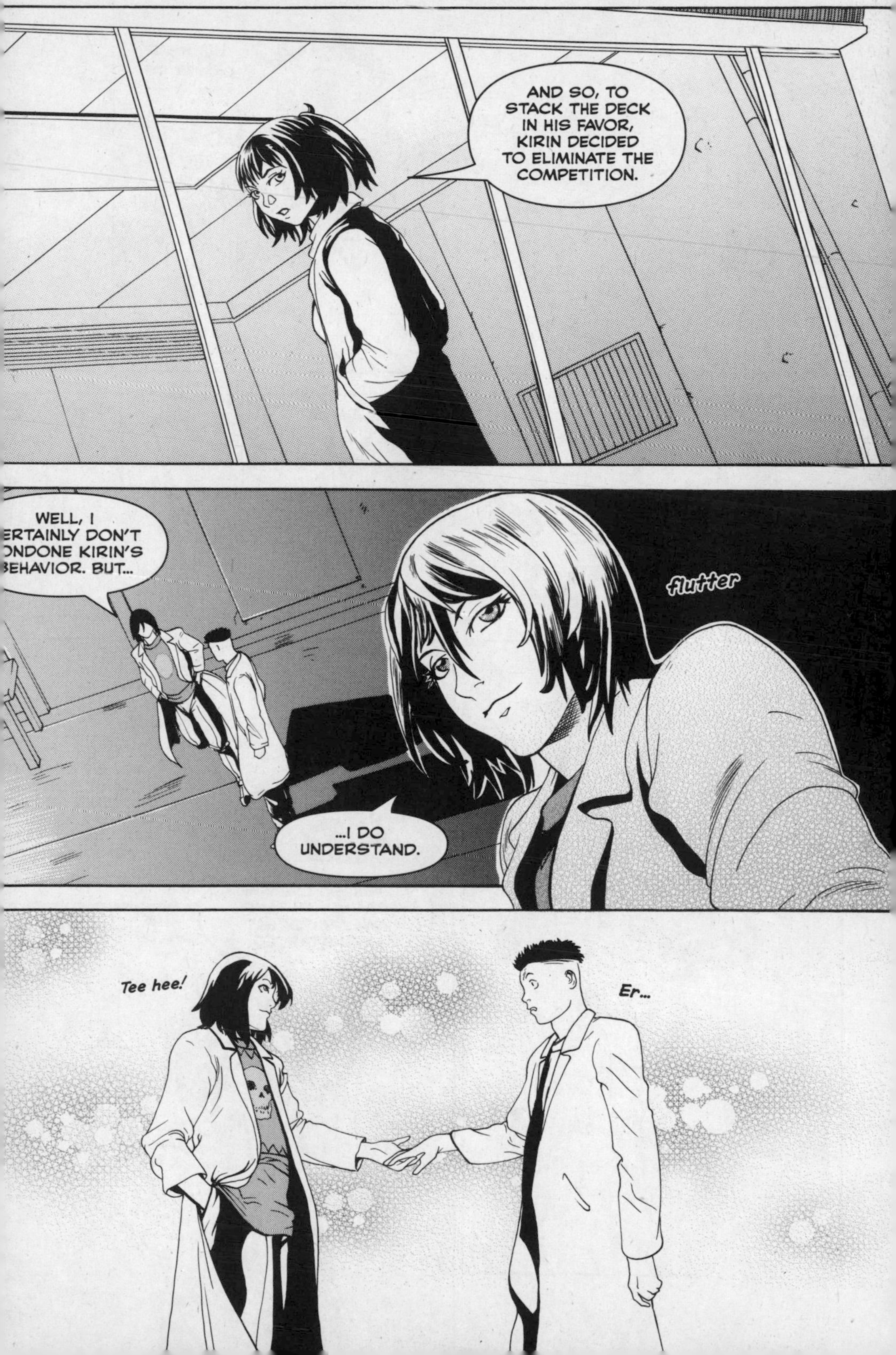
AND SO, TO STACK THE DECK IN HIS FAVOR, KIRIN DECIDED TO ELIMINATE THE COMPETITION.
WELL, I
ERTAINLY DON'T
ONDONE KIRIN'S
BEHAVIOR. BUT...
flutter
...I DO UNDERSTAND.
Tee hee!
Er...

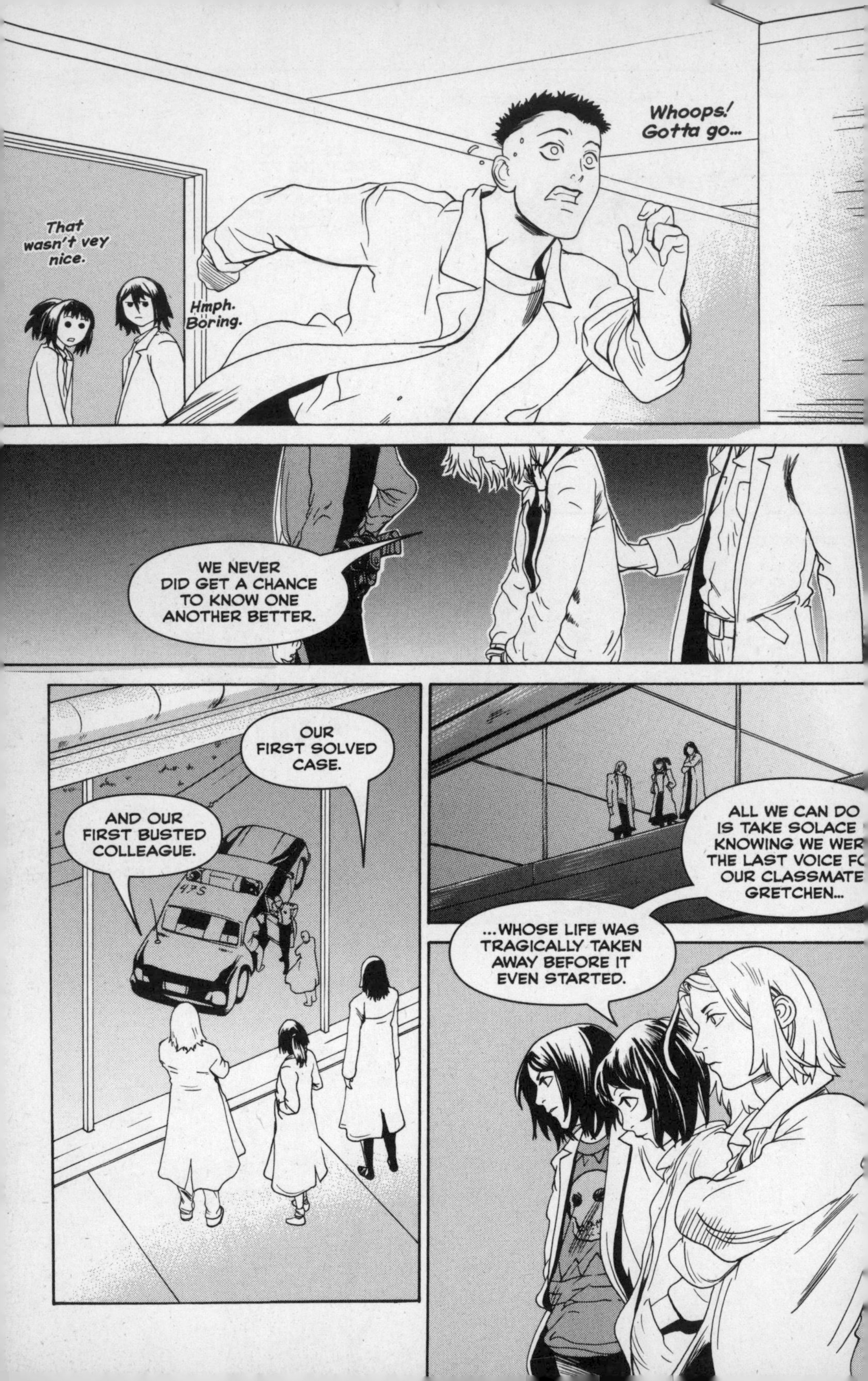
Whoops! Gotta go...
That wasn't vey nice.
Hmph. Boring.
WE NEVER DID GET A CHANCE TO KNOW ONE ANOTHER BETTER.
OUR FIRST SOLVED CASE.
AND OUR FIRST BUSTED COLLEAGUE.
ALL WE CAN DO IS TAKE SOLACE KNOWING WE WER THE LAST VOICE FO OUR CLASSMATE GRETCHEN...
...WHOSE LIFE WAS TRAGICALLY TAKEN AWAY BEFORE IT EVEN STARTED.

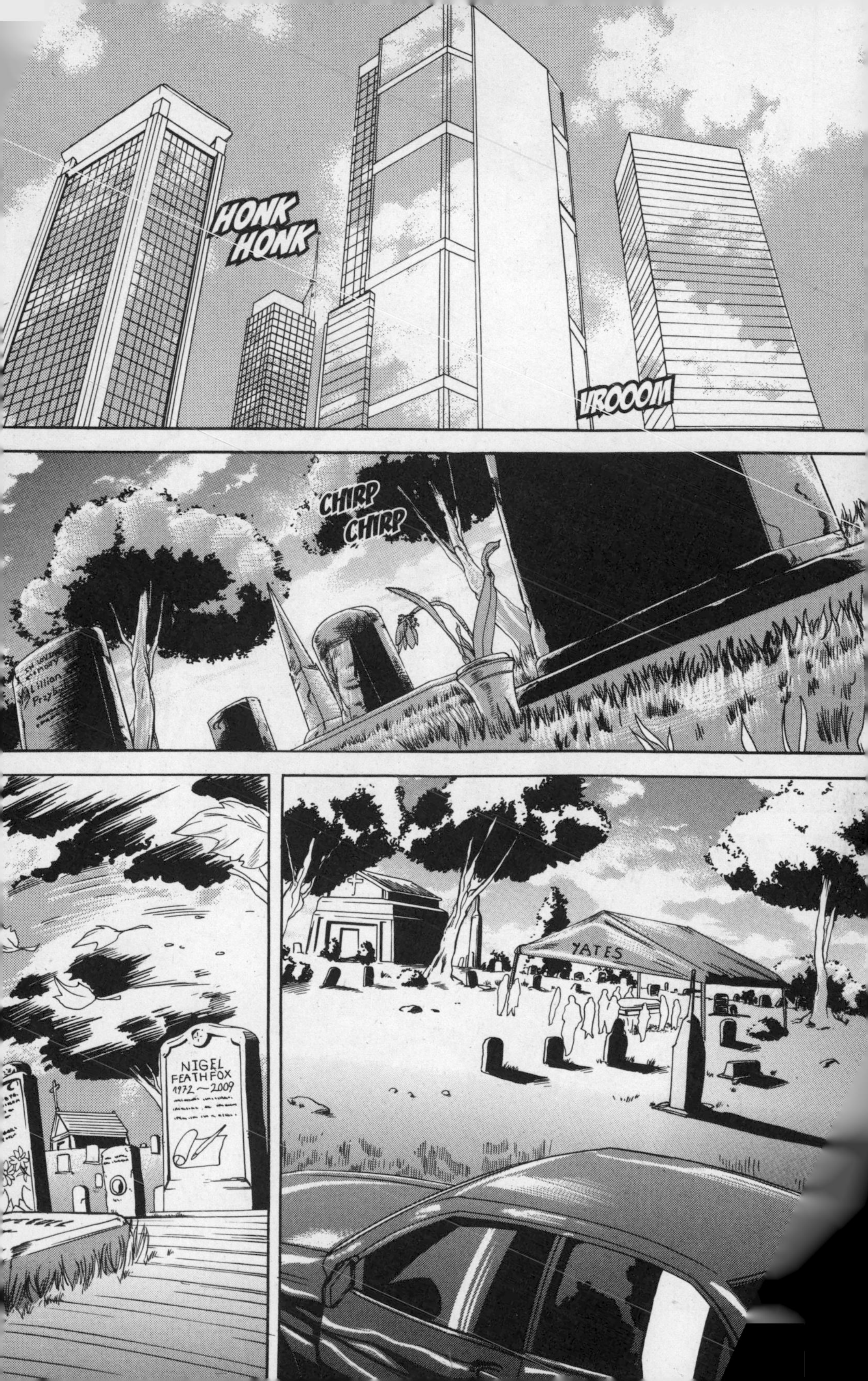
HONK
HONK
VROOOM
CHIRP
CHIRP
NIGEL
FEATHFOX
1972 ~ 2009
YATES

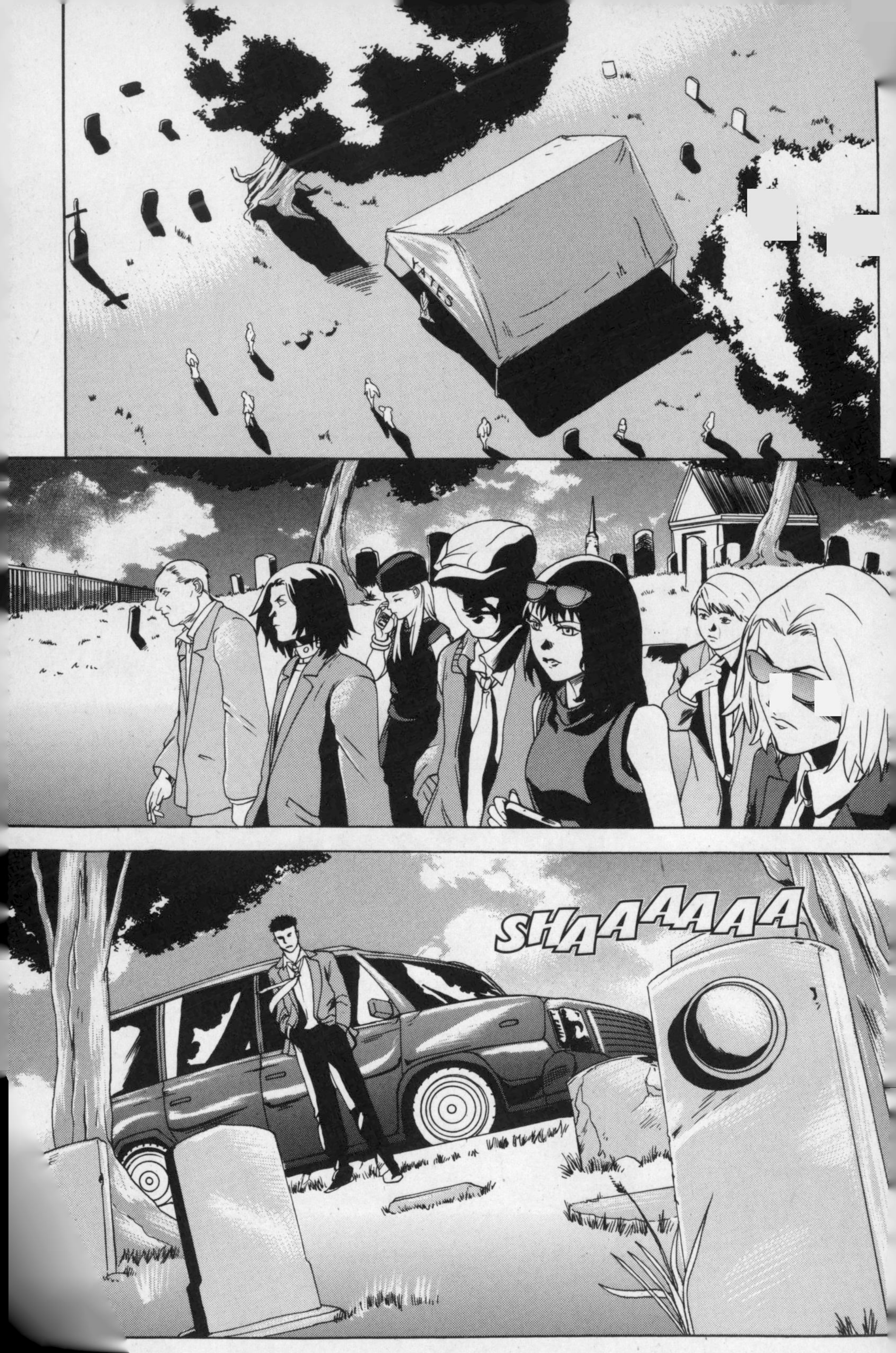
YATES
SHAAAAAAA

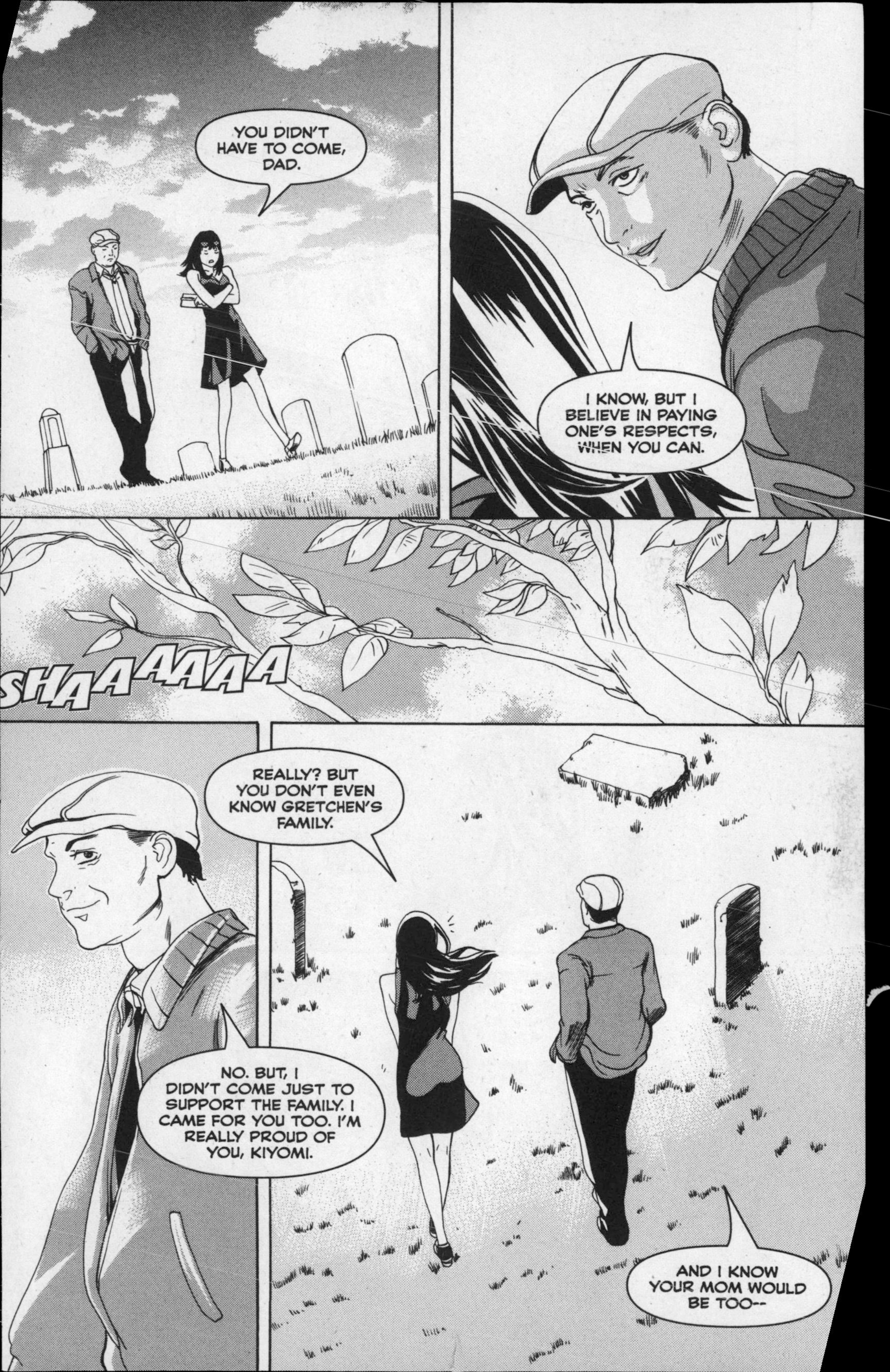
YOU DIDN'T HAVE TO COME, DAD.
I KNOW, BUT I BELIEVE IN PAYING ONE'S RESPECTS, WHEN YOU CAN.
SHAAAAAA
REALLY? BUT YOU DON'T EVEN KNOW GRETCHEN'S FAMILY.
NO. BUT, I DIDN'T COME JUST TO SUPPORT THE FAMILY. I CAME FOR YOU TOO. I'M REALLY PROUD OF YOU, KIYOMI.
AND I KNOW YOUR MOM WOULD BE TOO--

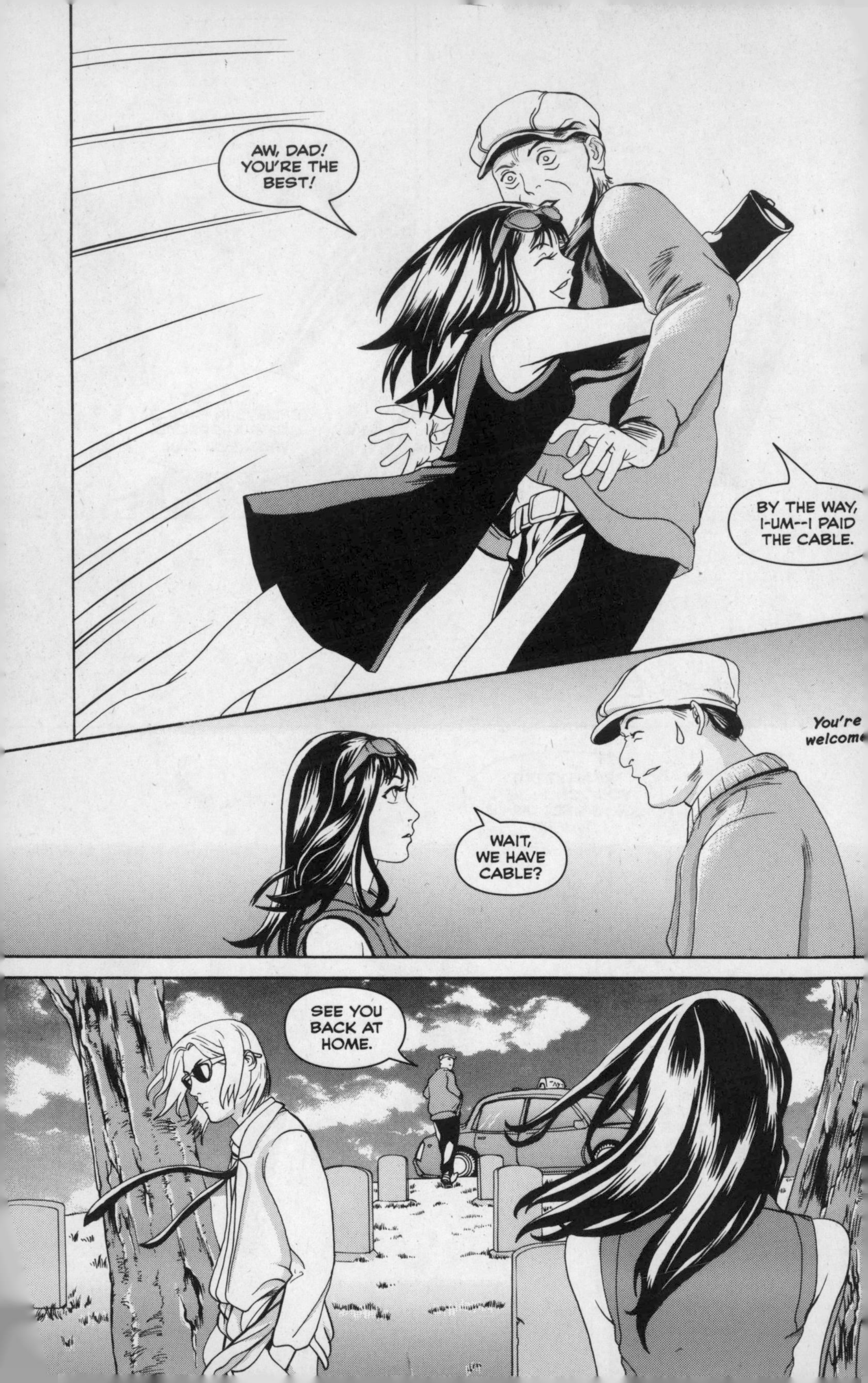
AW, DAD! YOU'RE THE BEST!
BY THE WAY, I-UM--I PAID THE CABLE.
You're welcom
WAIT, WE HAVE CABLE?
SEE YOU BACK AT HOME.

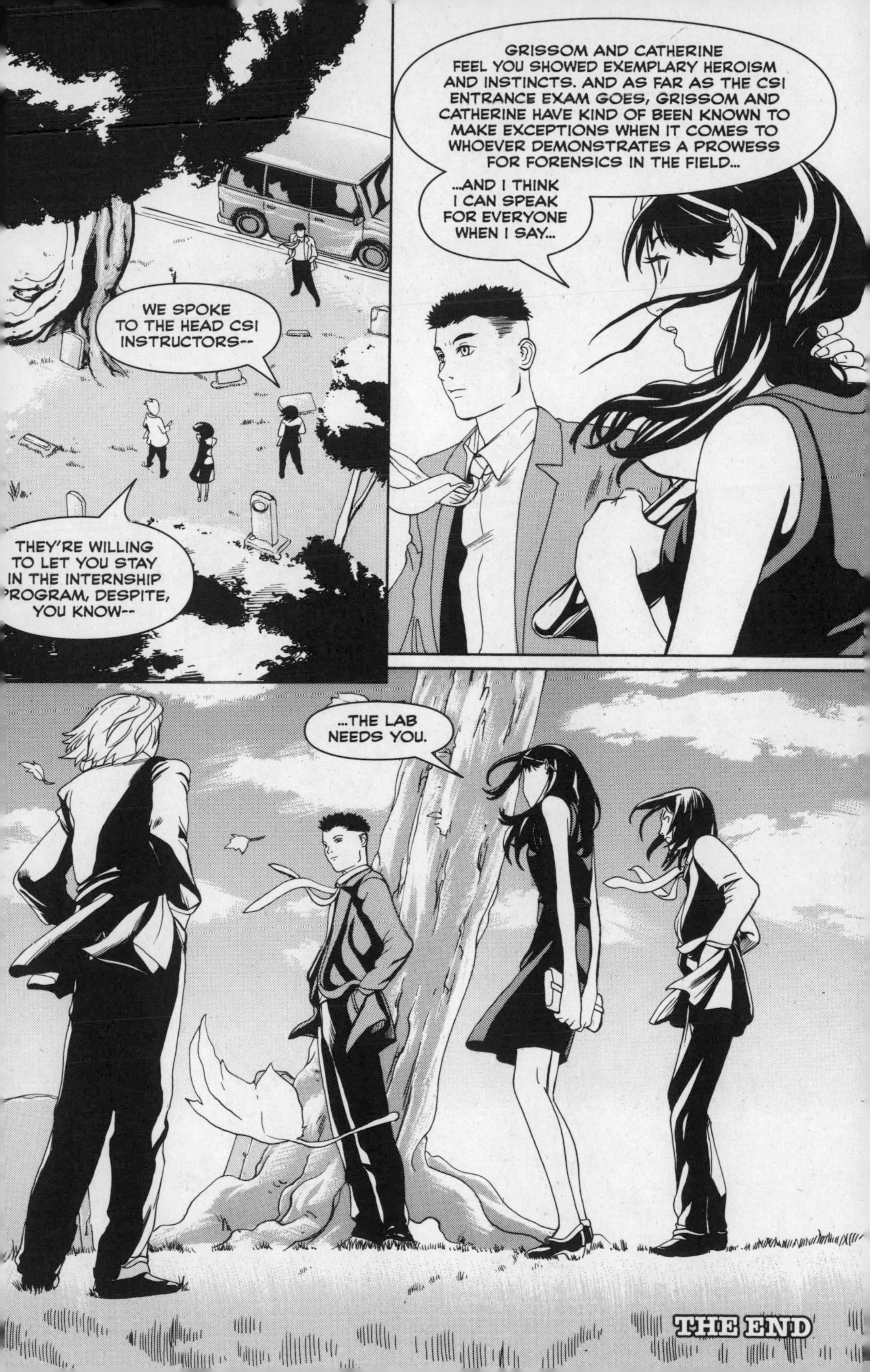
WE SPOKE TO THE HEAD CSI INSTRUCTORS--
THEY'RE WILLING TO LET YOU STAY IN THE INTERNSHIP PROGRAM, DESPITE, YOU KNOW--
GRISSOM AND CATHERINE FEEL YOU SHOWED EXEMPLARY HEROISM AND INSTINCTS. AND AS FAR AS THE CSI ENTRANCE EXAM GOES, GRISSOM AND CATHERINE HAVE KIND OF BEEN KNOWN TO MAKE EXCEPTIONS WHEN IT COMES TO WHOEVER DEMONSTRATES A PROWESS FOR FORENSICS IN THE FIELD...
...AND I THINK I CAN SPEAK FOR EVERYONE WHEN I SAY...
...THE LAB NEEDS YOU.
THE END

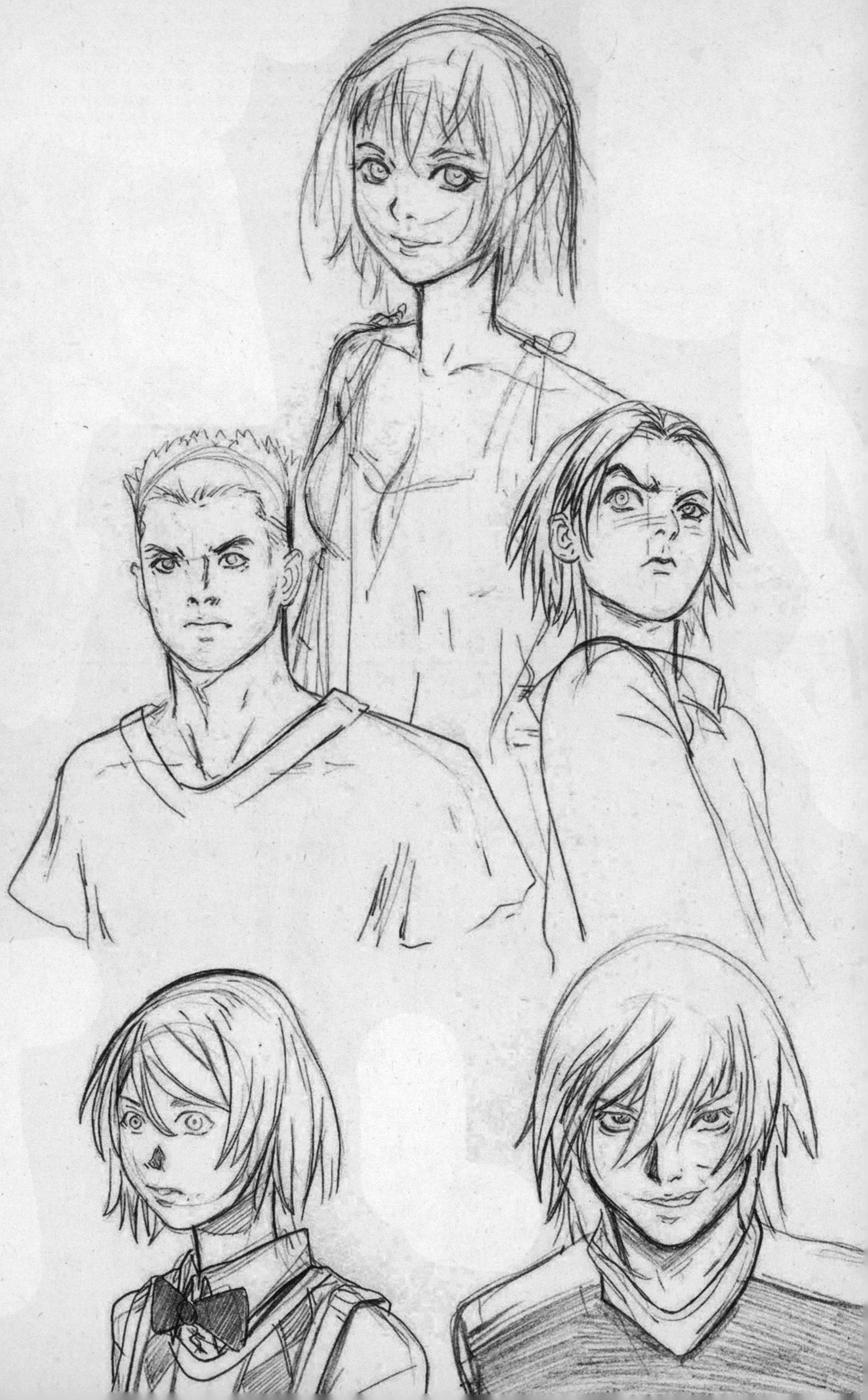

THE BULLETPROOF WINDOW was his first clue.

It shouldn't have been, but Brent McCurdy was beat. He had driven most of the way from Denver, snatching a couple of quick naps while his wife Charlene took her turn behind the wheel. They only had a week's vacation, and they wanted to spend that week in Las Vegas, playing slots and craps, watching shows and having fun . . . not staring at the highway between Vegas and Des Moines. So they powered through, Des Moines to Denver in one stretch and there to Vegas in the next, and by the time they reached the Rancho Center Motel at eight-forty that Friday night, Brent was stick-a-fork-in-it done.

A VACANCY sign burned in pink neon, like the legs of a flamingo set afire from within, but the motel office was dark, the door locked. Brent pressed his hands to the glass and stared inside. The place had a threadbare carpet with so many cigarette burns they looked like part of the pattern, and a scarred Formica counter with a big analog clock on the wall behind it. Had there been anyone inside, that person would have looked out and seen a man who was barely describable, of average height and average weight, with the slightest paunch swelling his dark blue polo shirt. His hair was brown, not long but not exceedingly short. His eyes were brown and unremarkable. In the eleventh grade, Brent's history teacher had recommended that he consider a career in the FBI, because he was a person who could blend in. He had decided against it, and now he managed a chain sporting goods store back in Iowa, and sometimes—but only rarely—regretted that decision.

Brent noticed a window built into the wall, almost like a drive-up window in a fast food joint, that could be accessed from behind the counter. He left the door and walked over to that window, finding thick, bulletproof plastic, scratched and fogged with age, with a little slot at the bottom to shove money or a credit card under and a small metal grate to speak through. A faint light glowed through the window, coming from a hallway he could barely make out. Looking through the Plexiglas was like trying to see through a blizzard. He'd had that experience a few times, which was why he had scheduled his vacation days for summertime. Driving in whiteout conditions didn't make for a relaxing beginning or end of a trip.

Finding the window tipped him off to the various signals that hadn't registered at first. Those had been, in fact, broken liquor bottles crunching under his feet as he walked from his parking place. Those had been used condoms and an empty syringe mixed in with greasy burger wrappers and lipstick-stained cigarette butts up against the curb. And those women he had barely noticed, coming out of a room at the end of the building? Well, back home he didn't see a lot of women in sparkly, low-cut spandex tops and skirts so short they could almost have qualified as belts, swaying with practiced near steadiness on four-inch heels, but that didn't mean he had never seen hookers before. Once in a while on the streets of Des Moines, but on TV, mostly. He had pay cable, after all. He should have known at a glance what they were.

He looked back toward his Ford Escape, a vehicle that had never before seemed so aptly named. Charlene and the kids were still inside, waiting, every bit as tired as he was, if not more so. They just wanted to get checked in and put their heads down on comfortable pillows. Brent had yet to inspect the pillows so he couldn't have testified to their comfort, but there was a young guy emerging into the hot July night from a room five doors down from that bullet-proof window, and he wore an expression of such rapturous bliss that Brent guessed he was either high or he had just gone through a profound religious experience.

The Rancho Center Motel didn't seem to lend itself to the latter.

He should have done more thorough online research. The location had been convenient to both the Strip and Fremont Street, and the price was definitely right. But this joint was no family motel.

The pool, surrounded by a chain-link fence out in the middle of the parking lot, didn't even have water in it.

He could tell by a shadow on an inside wall that someone was coming down the interior hallway, toward the bulletproof window. Brent didn't want to have a face-to-face conversation with anyone who worked here. He didn't even care about getting his deposit back. He could call and cancel the reservation later, and he would only lose one night's rent. All he wanted was to flee this dump and find another room somewhere in the city—a room at a place in which he wouldn't feel that his life and the lives of his family members were in danger at every moment.

He turned away from the oncoming shadow and hurried to the Escape. When he opened the door, the dome light came on and Charlene blinked at him and raised a hand to her cheek. "Is everything okay, honey?"

"Nothing's okay," he said. "We're going somewhere else."

"Somewhere else? You mean a different motel? Why?"

"Because this place is awful," he said. Brent Junior and Carnie were sitting up in back, sleepy-eyed but awake, so he didn't want to go into a lot of detail. There was no sense terrifying the kids on their first night in Las Vegas.

"But I wanna go to bed!" Carnie cried. She was only four and hadn't been looking forward to the trip anyway, except for the promise of a swimming pool at the motel. She shook a stuffed lion at him with animal ferocity. "I'm tired!"

"We're all tired, Carnie." Brent closed his door and clicked his seat belt into place. "We'll find a better place. It won't take long."

"But we have reservations here," Charlene said. "What if there's a convention in town or something and we can't find another place?"

"There's always a convention in Las Vegas, Charlene, but there are something like a million hotel rooms in the city. I read that somewhere." He was probably exaggerating, but there were a lot of them. He had read the precise number, but if he was any good with numbers he probably wouldn't be making his living with bats and balls and racquets and shoes. "We'll drive around all night if we have to, but we're not staying here."

"Aren't most of them more expensive than this one? That's what you said, right? This one was a bargain?"

He put the vehicle in reverse and backed out of the space. "So we'll skip the shows, or cut back on meals. I don't care. This place—"

Brent Junior had been about to register an objection of his own, his six-year-old whine already gathering steam, when a loud bang sounded from behind them and silenced the boy. Brent thought it was the sound of a door being slammed. He shoved the SUV into drive and stepped on the gas. The engine's growl nearly drowned out screams from the motel. But then he heard shouting and a sharp report, louder than the first bang, and saw a bright spark near the pool that must have been a muzzle flash.

"Somebody's shooting!" he shouted. "Call nine-one-one!"

Charlene was already pawing her phone from her purse as the vehicle surged from the parking lot, cutting the angle wrong and bouncing off the curb with two wheels. Brent didn't care.

He just wanted to get gone, while he still could.

"Catherine's in charge."

Those had been Gil Grissom's last words before leaving the lab for the airport. He was flying off to Washington, D.C., where he would be a featured speaker at a symposium on forensic entomology, after which he would testify before a congressional committee about the necessity of public financing for small city crime labs. As it was, most rural, small town, and small city police forces sent their case-loads to the big city labs, which were already backed up with their own big city crime. The additional workload slowed everything down, a vicious circle that left felonies unsolved and criminals on the streets. Gil would be more comfortable talking about the insects that frequented dead bodies, but his testimony before Congress would be sincere and convincing, and Catherine Willows couldn't help feeling a tickle of associational pride at the knowledge that her boss was helping to make a difference on a national level.

She also didn't mind being in charge. She had kind of enjoyed it, in fact, when she had temporarily been swing shift supervisor. If she rather than Gil had been the actual supervisor, the lab would be a different place, but primarily in small, cosmetic ways. Gil ran it well and she had few real complaints about his leadership. Still, she was an ambitious woman with ideas of her own and the drive to want to put them into action. But if Gil hadn't been out of town, she might not have had to go to the Rancho Center Motel, which was just the kind of hole that made her want to burn her clothes and scrub her skin down with steel wool when she was finished. On this hot night, with the overloaded window air conditioners dripping onto the sidewalk, the building itself seemed to be sweating. The parking lot held a peculiar reek all its own. And she hadn't even reached the DB yet.

That was still waiting for her inside Room 119. The door from the parking lot was open. Catherine and Nick Stokes had to pass under yellow crime scene tape and sign a log sheet to get to it . . . a far cry from the more exclusive spots around town, where the crowd control ropes were crushed velvet and the bouncers didn't wear uniforms and badges.

"Take a deep breath, Nicky," she said outside the door. "Bad as it is out here, it'll be much worse in there."

Nick raised an eyebrow and twitched his lips, the closest thing to a smile he could muster at the moment. He knew the score. Catherine didn't think the reminder would offend him, but she had to watch herself. She was nobody's mom but Lindsey's, and Lindsey didn't work at the Las Vegas Police Department's crime lab.

The motel room looked pretty much as she had

expected it to. She had been here before—this wasn't the joint's first homicide—and this wasn't the kind of place that spent a lot of money on regular remodels. A bed sat in the middle of the room, with a nightstand made of some woodlike substance next to it. A small dresser stood against the opposite wall, near the smashed-in door. Lying in the rubble, just inside, was the small black handheld battering ram, like the kind police used for hard entries, that had almost certainly done the smashing. There was a TV chained to a rack in one corner, six feet off the floor, and its remote was chained to the nightstand. The carpeting was of a mixture of colors chosen primarily for its ability to disguise vomit stains, and in the event of a fire would probably immediately turn into a poisonous gas. The walls were painted white, but on top of the paint was what looked like a year's worth of dust, giving it a flat gray appearance.

The foulest motel room's many sins faded in significance, however, when there was a body inside, and this one was no exception.

Assistant coroner David Phillips had already arrived. When Catherine entered the room, he looked up from the body, blinking behind his glasses. "Victim's been dead less than thirty minutes," he said by way of greeting. "Obviously there's no rigor present yet. He took two bullets. First one through the left trapezius muscle; the second entered through the lower lip and exited through the top of the skull." He tilted his head toward the ceiling, and Catherine saw the knot of blood, brains, and hair pasted there.

"Hello to you, too," Catherine said.

"Oh, yeah, hi, Catherine. Nick."

"Hey," Nick said.

"So I'm guessing that's our COD?" Catherine asked. "The head shot, anyway?"

"That's my initial determination," David said. "Vic is a thirty-six-year-old male. Wallet in his back jeans pocket, with a Nevada DL identifying him as—"

"Deke Freeson," Catherine said. She had walked around the body far enough to see his face. What was left of it, anyway. In life it had been reasonably handsome—not as square-jawed as Nick Stokes, maybe, but with a good firm chin, full lips, a nose that jutted forward like it meant business but not so far it rounded the corner before the rest of him. Deke's eyes were his best feature, a brilliant blue that people remembered and remarked on long after even the most cursory meeting with him. She found herself oddly pleased that the bullet had missed them. His hair was sandy and spiked. She had, on more than one occasion, seen him out on the town with some showgirl or other. Had he ever asked, she might have dated him herself.

"Yeah, that's Deke," Nick said.

"You both know him?" David asked. He seemed surprised.

"Everybody in Vegas knows Deke," Nick said.

"I don't."

"You run with the wrong crowd," Catherine said. "Or maybe it's the right one, I don't know. He was a private detective. Strictly low budget, but he's a decent guy and a good investigator."

"He was on the job, years ago," Nick added. "Ex-military, too. I think he was a Gulf War vet."

"Well, there's a photocopied PI license in the wallet too, which I was about to tell you. I guess that comes as no surprise, though."

"Not at all," Catherine said. She hadn't known Deke Freeson well, but like Nick had said, everybody in Las Vegas knew him. Every cop, at least. Every dead body was sad, but the sorrow sliced with a sharper edge when the victim was someone you knew.

"There's a gun here," David said. "Close to his right hand. I think he was holding it when he fell."

"Desert Eagle?" Nick asked. "Fifty caliber? Brushed chrome?"

"That's right."

"Deke did love his firepower," Catherine said. "You found a license for that too, right?"

"Yeah. Maybe it would be easier if you tell me what you don't know about this guy, and then I can try to fill in the blanks."

"That should be obvious," Catherine said.

"Obvious how?"

"What we don't know," she said, "is who killed him."

AFTER THE PHOTOGRAPHS were taken and David Phillips had completed his preliminary examination, what was left of Deke Freeson was taken away. Catherine and Nick were not so lucky.

Their task was to process the room, which naturally required them to remain inside it. The smell was horrific, blood and urine and sweat competing for dominance with less immediately identifiable stenches. The room contained more fluids than Catherine cared to think about. Her first pass through, she focused on semen; the blood was more or less apparent, and by locating and identifying semen, she would be less likely to stand or sit in it or to accidentally place a hand in it. Her hands were gloved in multiple layers of latex, so she could peel off any that became contaminated. But still . . . she had her limits of tolerance, and the Rancho Center Motel room seemed determined to test them all.

She started with a handheld UV light, under

which semen would often fluoresce. Holding the light, she moved in a careful pattern, sweeping the room to find each incidence. As expected, she found multiple specimens, none of them particularly fresh (and several, to her dismay, apparently having survived multiple launderings of the sheets and bedspread). Each spot had to be swabbed, and the swabs treated with alpha-naphthyl phosphate and Brentamine Fast Blue. More often than not, the swabs turned purple almost immediately, indicating positive results. All the spots were dry, which made collecting and bagging them easier, but given the sheer number of them in the room, it was still a long process. Each would have to be analyzed back at the lab, where DNA analysis would help determine who had been in the room. Given the age of the stains, she suspected they wouldn't factor into the investigation, but until she knew for certain when Deke Freeson had arrived at the room, and what he was doing there, she couldn't afford to discount any potential leads.

Nick, meanwhile, had been taking a more global approach. After collecting bullets from the ceiling and headboard, he rummaged through drawers and the closet and the single suitcase and purse found in the room. "The purse belongs to Antoinette O'Brady of Las Vegas," he announced. "There's a wallet and cell phone still inside. Plenty of cash. She's fifty-six years old." He showed Catherine the driver's license picture. Antoinette O'Brady looked young for her age and wore her long blond hair and makeup in ways that made her look like she was trying to come across as younger still.

"If she lives in town, what's she doing staying in a dump like this?" Catherine asked.

"And where is she now? Maybe she's the shooter, not a motel guest. The room was registered to Freeson. He checked in yesterday."

"Which doesn't necessarily mean that one or both of them weren't here before that, either staying with someone else or registered under a different name. I doubt this place is too picky about checking ID. We'll have to look for any connections between them," Catherine said. "What about that suitcase?"

"I'm pretty sure it's not Deke's," Nick said. "Clothing and toiletries are consistent with the woman's height and weight, based on her license."

"How old is the license?"

"Less than a year old."

"Most people shave a few pounds off when they get a new license," Catherine said. "But if it's that recent, chances are it's in the ballpark. And I've never heard of anyone bringing a suitcase on a hit."

"Even if they did, they wouldn't unpack their toiletries in the bathroom," Nick observed. "It looks like she expected to stay for a while. Few days, anyway."

"A few days in this room might be enough to make me start shooting people too," Catherine said. She had finished with fluids, and used tweezers to lift a hair from the carpet and drop it into a small plastic envelope. Like the semen and blood, it would go to the lab for analysis. Chances were good it would have nothing to do with Deke Freeson or

Antoinette O'Brady, but it had to be done. "What else do we have?"

"Well, blood," Nick said.

"Obviously there's no shortage of that."

"That's for sure." He pointed at the bed. "High-velocity spatter here and on the headboard. More on the ceiling. Consistent with the two shots David described. I think the shooter came in the door—"

"Using the battering ram," Catherine interrupted.

"—right. Smashed in the door, dropped the ram, and fired the first shot. It hit Freeson just below the collarbone. Freeson was standing in front of the bed—there's backspatter on the floor in front of his position—when the shooter came in and fired. Blood sprayed his feet and the floor there. Someone—presumably the shooter, since the transfer pattern doesn't match the shoes Freeson was wearing—stepped in it. The print is a sneaker print. Converse. And there's a void in the blood spatter on the bed."

"I noticed that too. So Deke was trying to shield someone—maybe Antoinette O'Brady—who was on the bed when he got shot. She was hit by blood spatter."

"Do you think Deke got off a shot?"

"Either that or just the sight of that big Desert Eagle made the shooter hesitate," Nick said. "The difference in the angle between the two shots indicates a delay of at least a second or two—first shot from a bit of a distance, the second closer, and at an upward angle."

"But if he did fire, where's his round? And a witness said someone fired from near the pool. What's up with that?"

"That's right. I'll have a look around out there."

"I'll be here," Catherine said. "Probably still collecting hairs."

Nick walked out to the pool area, stopping every few feet to look back toward the open door of the room. As long as there were no tall vehicles parked in front of the room, someone could have fired from around the pool. But why would they? And if there was someone else in the doorway, would they take the shot, knowing they might hit their partner or accomplice? He supposed the first shot could have been fired from there . . . but it didn't make sense to shoot at a closed door, and they hadn't found any sign of a bullet or bullet hole in the wreckage of the door. And no one would ram in the door and then run to the pool to shoot.

The pool smelled almost as bad as the room. Nick let himself in through an unlocked gate in the tall chain-link fence and walked around the concrete basin. At least a foot of trash coated the bottom, maybe more. He wondered if the motel had quit paying their Dumpster fees and intended to just use the pool instead.

He swept his flashlight's beam around but didn't spot any shell casings on the concrete surrounding the pool, or any other sign that someone had fired a weapon. He hoped he wouldn't have to go wading in the collected trash. But as he let his eye drift over the scene, taking in the fence and the view back toward the motel building, he saw that one corner of the fence, where it connected to an upright and a top rail on the side nearest the building, had been broken loose.

He circled back around the pool to take a closer look. The fence was broken so cleanly that it might have been clipped. But there was a crease in the top rail, the steel slightly blackened.

Nick stood in front of it and looked toward the room. Right on line.

He was starting to think the witness had been wrong. *The guy didn't see a muzzle flash*, he realized with sudden certainty, *he saw a spark*. Nick could confirm his hunch with laser beams, since the distance was too great for trajectory rods, but it looked like a bullet fired at a slight upward angle from near the bed in Room 119 would gain just enough elevation to hit the top rail right where the fence was broken. The witness reported that he was already trying to leave, that the first loud noise—no doubt the battering ram taking down the door—had frightened him. Looking through a rearview as he was trying to get the hell out of there, in the dark, even a small spark might have seemed like a bright flash.

If the round had glanced off the rail, then it had to have gone somewhere.

Unfortunately, the most likely place was down in the pool. The bullet would have been slowed, redirected by the rail, and fallen in. He shone a flashlight along the wall and spotted what looked like a fresh chip in the pool wall, but the momentum had been slowed enough that the bullet hadn't become embedded there.

Nick would have to go wading after all. And in something far worse than stagnant pool water.

EVERY TEXT COULD BE YOUR LAST

FUTURE DIARY™

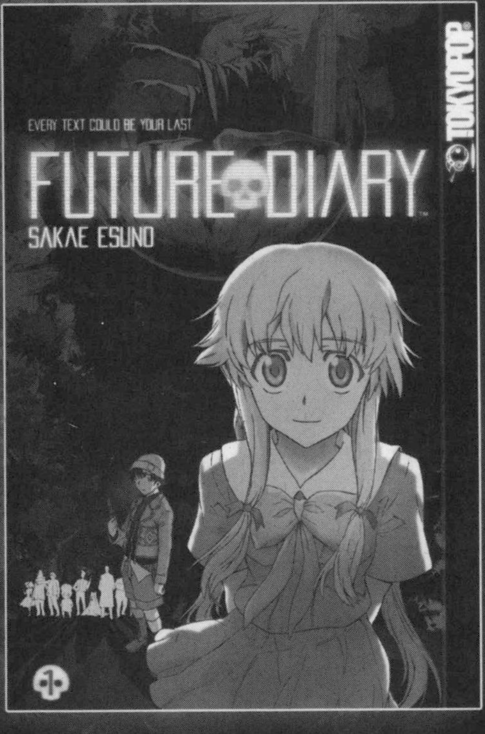
EVERY TEXT COULD BE YOUR LAST
FUTURE DIARY
SAKAE ESUNO
TOKYOPOP

Yukiteru has a secret that nobody knows about—his cellphone can tell the future! Now he's entered a vicious game of survival among twelve future diary holders—with the winner crowned god of a new world!

"ESUNO'S ART IS SPRIGHTLY, SWEET AND DECEPTIVELY INNOCENT."
—Publishers Weekly

BE SURE TO VISIT WWW.TOKYOPOP.COM/SHOP FOR EVERYTHING YOU COULD EVER WANT!

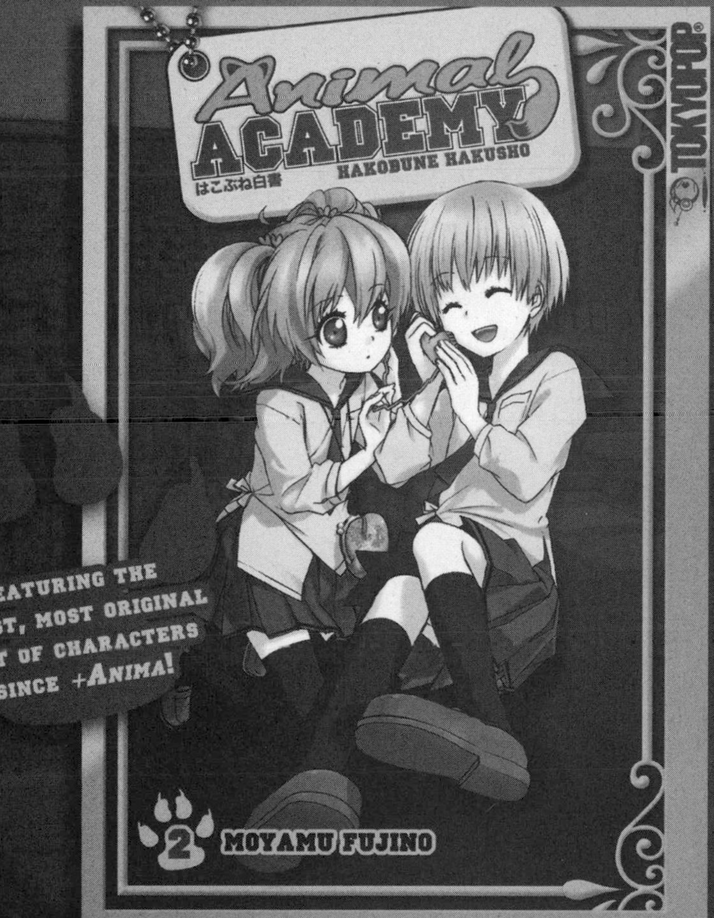
Animal ACADEMY
HAKOBUNE HAKUSHO
はこぶね白書
TOKYOPOP
FEATURING THE CUTEST, MOST ORIGINAL CAST OF CHARACTERS SINCE +ANIMA!
2
MOYAMU FUJINO

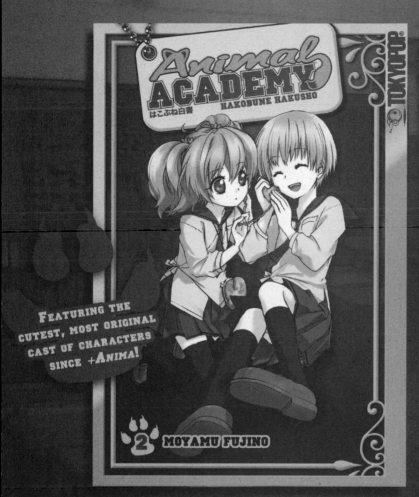

TOKYOPOP MANGA SUPPLEMENT

D•N•ANGEL

D•N•Angel Returns!

Forbidden love + suave alter egos + romantic adventure = D•N•Angel volume 12

In order to rescue Risa, Daisuke teams up with his longtime rival, Satoshi Hiwatari. Will they be up to the challenge against Argentine's devious plot?!

D•N•ANGEL
VOLUME 12 • YUKIRU SUGISAKI

FANTASY

T
TEEN AGE 13+

BE SURE TO VISIT WWW.TOKYOPOP.COM/SHOP FOR EVERYTHING YOU COULD EVER WANT!

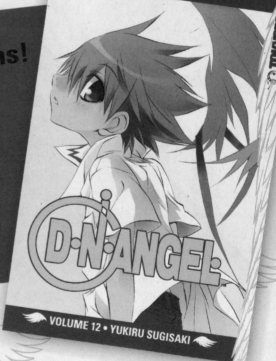

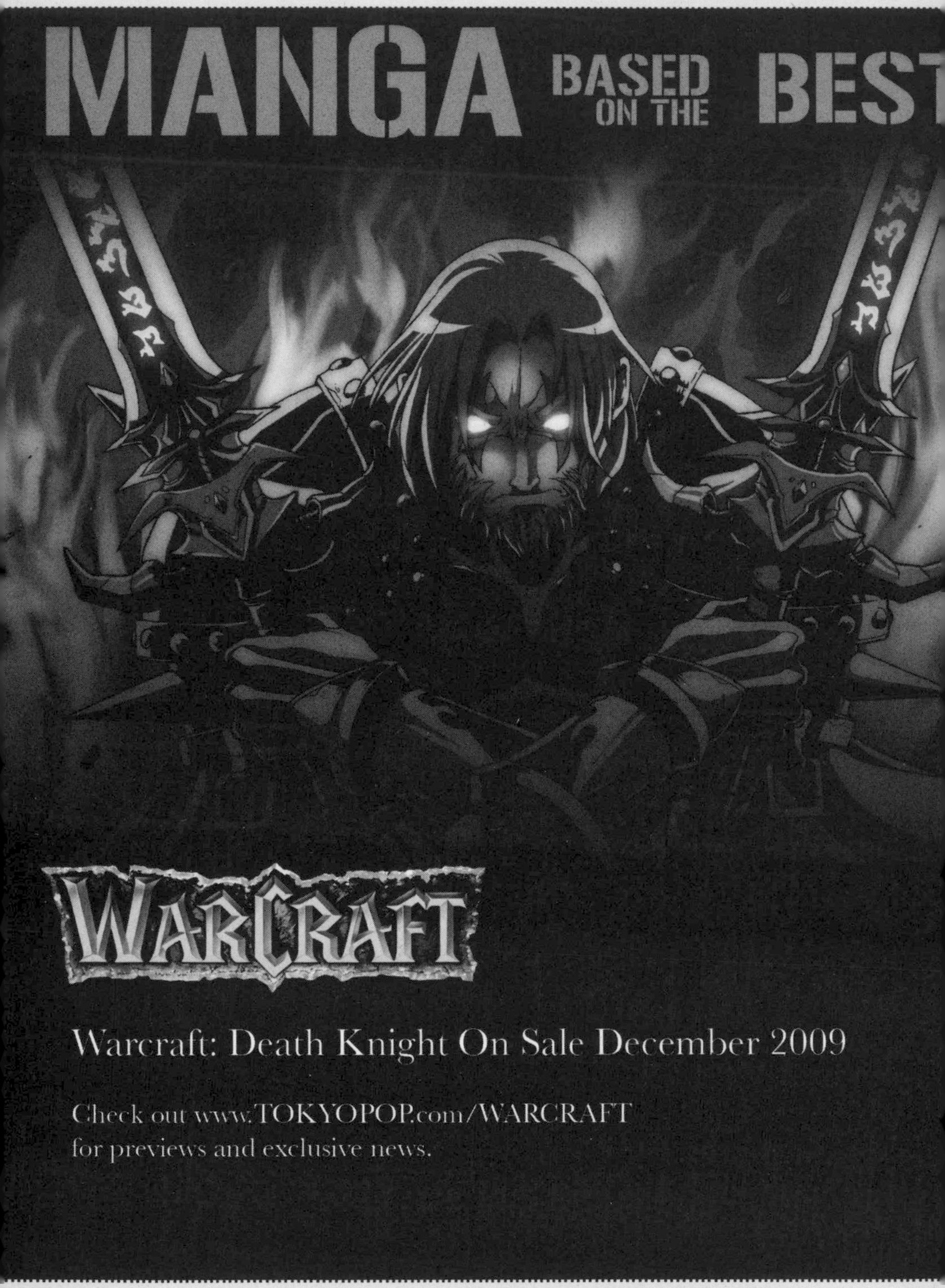
MANGA BASED ON THE BEST
WARCRAFT
Warcraft: Death Knight On Sale December 2009
Check out www.TOKYOPOP.com/WARCRAFT
for previews and exclusive news.

SELLING VIDEO GAMES

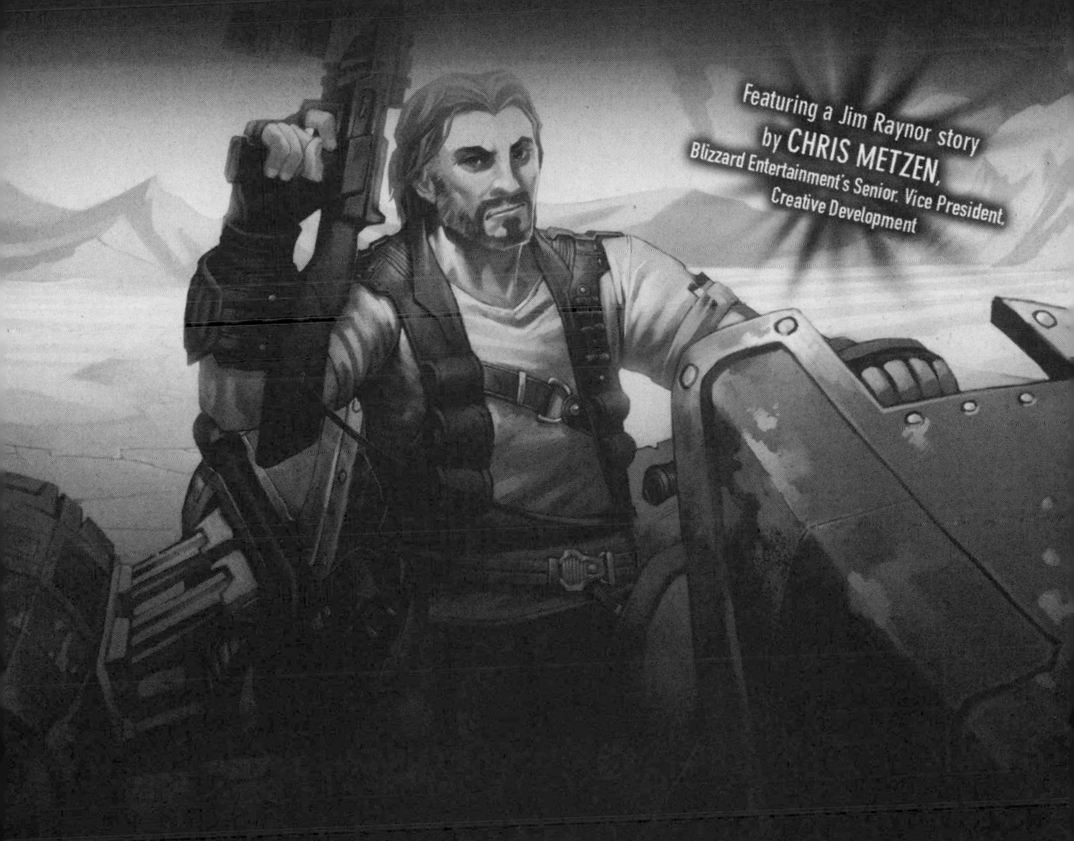
Featuring a Jim Raynor story
by CHRIS METZEN,
Blizzard Entertainment's Senior. Vice President,
Creative Development

STARCRAFT

StarCraft: Frontline Volume 4 On Sale October 2009

Check out www.TOKYOPOP.com/STARCRAFT
for previews and exclusive news.

AVAILABLE IN BOOKSTORES EVERYWHERE!

T TEEN AGE 13+

BLIZZARD ENTERTAINMENT

TOKYOPOP MANGA SUPPLEMENT

Is the World's #1 Shojo Manga

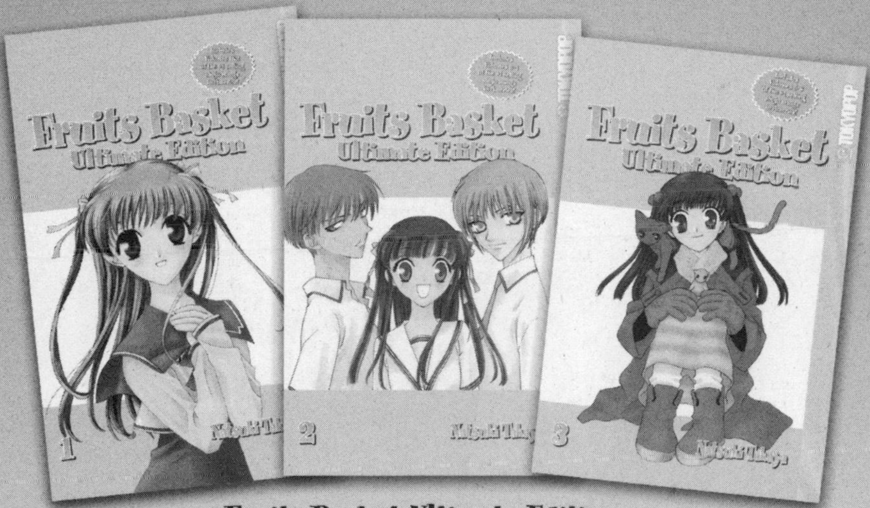
Fruits Basket
Ultimate Edition
1
Fruits Basket
Ultimate Edition
2
Fruits Basket
Ultimate Edition
3

**Fruits Basket Ultimate Editions
Volumes 1-3**

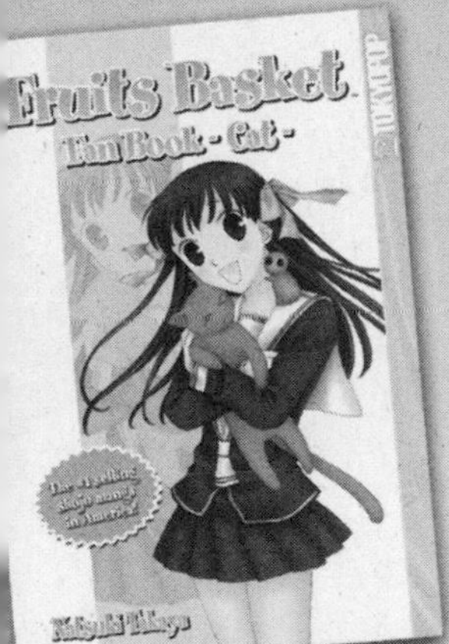
Fruits Basket
Fan Book - Cat -

**Fruits Basket
Fan Book -Cat-**

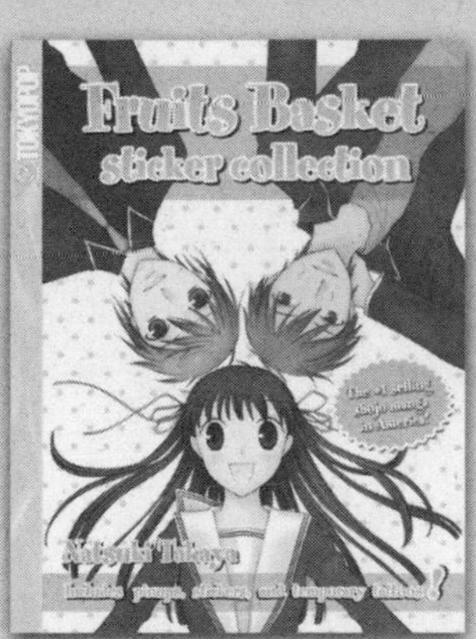
Fruits Basket
sticker collection

**Fruits Basket
Sticker Collection**

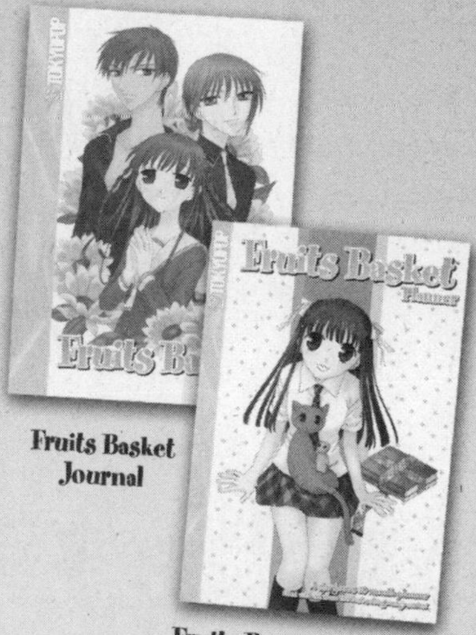
Fruits Basket
Planner

**Fruits Basket
Journal**

**Fruits Basket 18-month
Planner**

FOR MORE INFORMATION VISIT: WWW.TOKYOPOP.COM

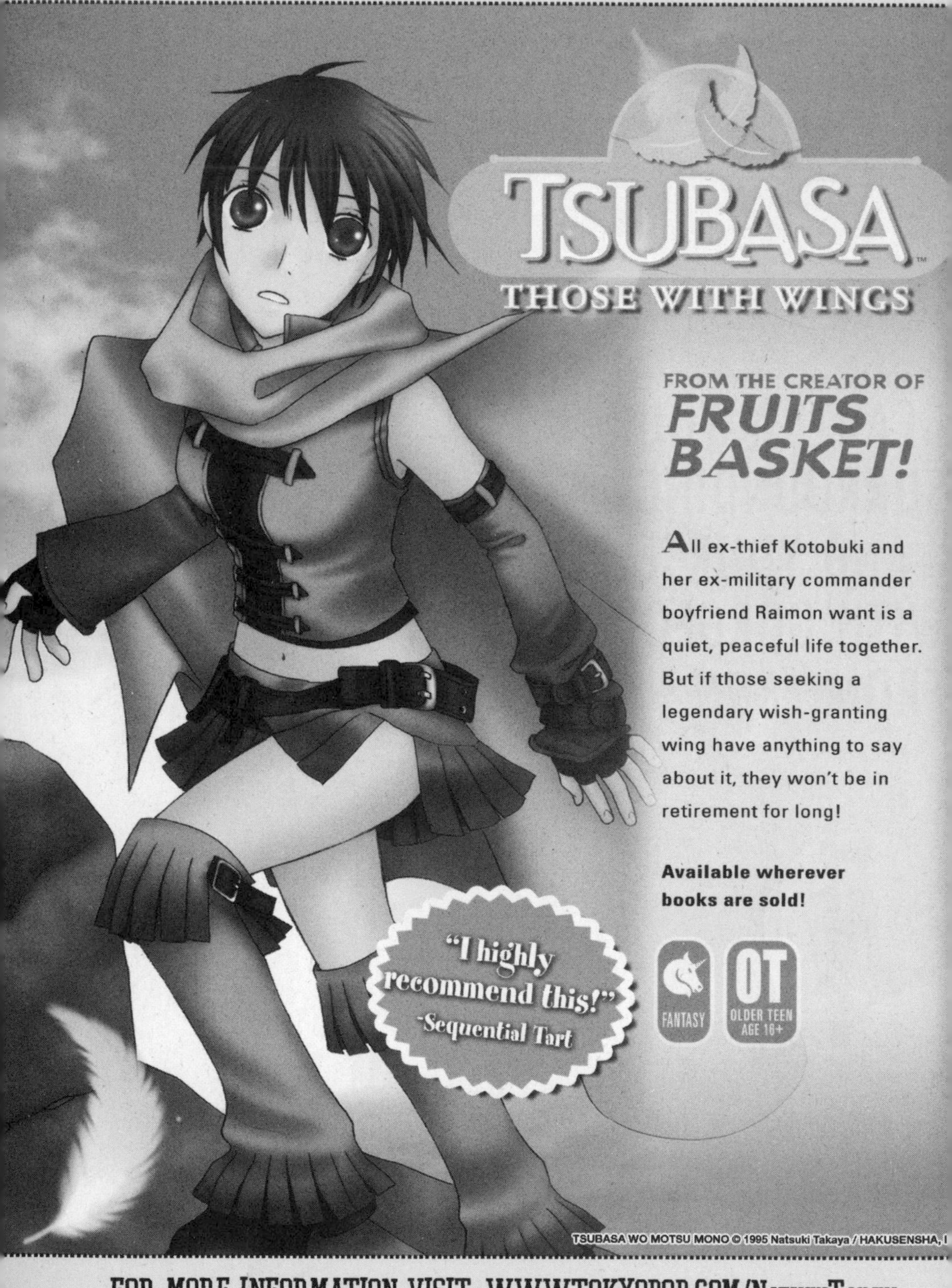
TSUBASA™
THOSE WITH WINGS
FROM THE CREATOR OF
FRUITS BASKET!
All ex-thief Kotobuki and her ex-military commander boyfriend Raimon want is a quiet, peaceful life together. But if those seeking a legendary wish-granting wing have anything to say about it, they won't be in retirement for long!
Available wherever books are sold!
"I highly recommend this!" -Sequential Tart
FANTASY
OT OLDER TEEN AGE 16+
TSUBASA WO MOTSU MONO © 1995 Natsuki Takaya / HAKUSENSHA, I